FALSEWORK, SMALLTALK

SOME BELOVED
productions

FALSEWORK, SMALLTALK

First electronic edition January 2021
First paperback edition February 2021

ISBN 978-1-7365290-0-3 (ePDF)
ISBN 978-1-7365290-1-0 (paperback)

Library of Congress Control Number: 2021931219

Subjects: Politics—United States, Global, Comparative, Institutions, Ideologies | Aesthetics—Art, Activism | Education—Community, University | Pandemic | Internationalism

Book design by Asma Abbas and Adnan Mir

This is a Common Tern Work
First published by Some Beloved, Inc. (Richmond, Massachusetts) and Folio Books (Lahore, Pakistan)
www.commontern.net | works@commontern.net

This book is published under the Common Tern Works imprint shared by members of Common Tern, an international cooperative of cultural workers. Produced by all-volunteer labors of love engaged in an extensive autonomous and participatory process across continents, this work has been published concurrently by founding members of the co-op. The digital version of this book is free to download and share. Please consider subscribing to Common Tern Works to support and access all works under this imprint. You may also wish to participate in the community being built in solidarity with cultural workers rethinking and remaking the world.

FALSE
WORK
SMALL
TALK

political education,
aesthetic archives,
recitations of a future in common

CURATED BY HIC ROSA COLLECTIVE,
WITH EDITORIAL TEAM LED BY ASMA ABBAS & COLIN EUBANK,
THIS IS A COMMON TERN WORK.

2,290,488
as of 6 February 2021
and countless beloveds who died of the pandemic, but not of
the virus...
and joined the hundreds of millions lost to the unnatural
causes of capitalism, colonialism,
and their various mutant strains that land on our bodies,
and live in, off, and with us.
there may be no justice. but we might come close one day.

Let me write a song for this day!

This day and the anguish of this day
For this wilderness of yellowing leaves— which is my homeland
For this carnival of suffering— which is my homeland

Let me write of the little lives of office workers
Of the railmen
And of the tonga-wallahs
And of the postmen
Let me write of the poor innocents they call workers

Lord of all the world
Promised heir to all that is to come

Let me write of the farmer
This Lord whose fief was a few animals—stolen
Who knows when
This heir who once had a daughter—carried off
Who knows when
The chief whose turban is a tattered rag
Beneath the feet of the mighty

Let me write of the Mothers
Whose children sob in the night

And, cradled in tired, toiling arms
Will not tell their woes

Let me write of the little houses
The narrow lanes and the courtyards
Where the earth is so unclean

Where the Shadows are so deep
That all life ebbs away like a sob, unheeded
The carmine of her garment
The tinkling of her bangles
The perfume of her tresses

Let me write of the students
Those seekers of the truth
Who came seeking the truth at the doorstep
Of the great and the mighty
These innocents who, with their dim flickering lamps
Came seeking light
Where they sell naught but the darkness of long endless nights

Let me write of the prisoners
In whose hearts, all our yesterdays
Dawned like sparkling gems
And burning, burning through the dark winds of prison nights
Are now but distant stars

Now let me write of the Heralds of the coming Dawn.

— Faiz Ahmed Faiz, "Intisaab," translated by Shoaib Hashmi

Contents

Prologue   xii
    Matter and Method   xiii
    Conversations and Conversions   xvi
    Dis/Assembly   xvii
    Convocations and Gratitude   xviii

Collaborators   xx

    Reading Key   xxiii

    Process Fragments   xxiv

Prelude | "...for today is also the future of something..."   1
    Eyes at a Distance of Six Feet | Hasan Mujtaba   3
    Susurrus: July 4, 2020 | Kenji C. Liu   6
    Punctuations | Eric Aldieri   7
    A Roaming Aesthetic I | Sadia Salim   8

First Dialogue | Politics Contra Crisis   9
    Companion Texts   10
    Pandemic Hospitalities   11
    What Does Crisis Name?   14
    Historical Instances of Crises and their Labors   17
    The Crisis at Hand   20
    On the *Muqaddimah* with Safi Alsebai   24
    On The Present Crisis   28
    Postscript to the Present Crisis   31
    Notes   35

First Interlude | Calls from the Impasse   39
    The End of the (End of the) World | Silvana Carotenuto   41
    March 15th, Plague Dreams | Colin Eubank   46
    Quarantine Meditations | Christopher Carrico   49
    Saraab (Delusion/Mirage) | Shahana Rajani & Omer Wasim   51
    March 2020 | Lillian Goldberg   52
    The I Notebook | Sumana Roy   53
    A Roaming Aesthetic II | Sadia Salim   70

Second Dialogue | Calls to Politics & The Ends of Political Action   71
    Companion Texts   72
    Ejeris Dixon on the Interregnum   94
    Notes   95

Second Interlude | In Our Bones   99
    The Love for Ruins | Silvana Carotenuto   101
    It's Up to Us to Stop Them | Ejeris Dixon   104
    Cráneos Rotos | Edgar Flores Noriega   110
    Who Cares About Care If Care Is The Alibi,
       Fragment I | Bonaventure Soh Bejeng Ndikung   111
    Toward a Political Education of Mutual Feeling |
       Zara Anwarzai & Colin Eubank   116
    A Roaming Aesthetic III | Sadia Salim   122

Third Dialogue | To Know and To Judge, Politically   123
    Companion Texts   124
    Introductions (in)to Political Knowledge   126
    Counterinsurgency, Judgment, Accountability, Inheritance   134
    Capacity, Affect, Imagination   137
    Communication, Common Sense, and the Political Work of Materialism   140
    Notes   147

Third Interlude | Aesthetic Archives, Political Possibility   151
    The Call for Future Oeuvres | Silvana Carotenuto   153
    Trump Threatens To Defund Education If Schools Refuse To Open
       Amidst Global Pandemic | Ashna Ali   158
    No Mammies on Saturn | Sy Klipsch-Abudu   159
    Letter to a Colleague on Struggling with COVID-19 | Lewis R. Gordon   160
    Morbid States, Struggling Bodies | Dresda Emma Mendez   169
    Spring Summer Writings and Bench, 2020 | Zohaib Zuby   171
    Defense Strategies | Heidi Andrea Restrepo Rhodes   174
    A Roaming Aesthetic IV | Sadia Salim   178

Fourth Dialogue | (Which) Society Must Be Defended?   179
    Companion Texts   180
    Part One   181
    Anna Poplawski on *Women Talking* as Abolitionist Method   188
    Part Two   190
    Notes   201

Fourth Interlude | Species/Being/False/Work   203
   Who Cares About Care If Care Is The Alibi,
      Fragment 2 | Bonaventure Soh Bejeng Ndikung   205
   Nature who never lies | Miri Davidson   210
   (untitled) | Hannah Walker   211
   The Convivial Animal | Bindu Menon Mannil   212
   A Roaming Aesthetic V | Sadia Salim   220

Fifth Dialogue | Just Institutions—What, Where, and How to Build?   221
   Companion Texts   222
   From Sociality to Institutionality (and Back)   223
   Misreading "Strategic Essentialism"   232
   On Electoral Punctuations and Constituting Mo(ve)ments,
      with Brianna Pope   237
   The Pedagogies of Movements and/as Institutions   241
   On the Political Theology of Falseworker as Neighbor   244
   The Pedagogies of Movements and/as Institutions (cont'd.)   248
   Notes   255

Fifth Interlude | Still Life in Motion   257
   Resting Places | Rei Terada   259
   Choreography of the Body's Collapse | Heidi Andrea Restrepo Rhodes   264
   Artist/Worker | An Exchange with Renata Summo O'Connell   267
   On a Roaming Aesthetic | Sadia Salim   269
   Identity/Crisis | Sanya Hussain   270
   Mushtarka Khushi | Hajra Haider Karrar   273
   A Roaming Aesthetic VI | Sadia Salim   292

Sixth Dialogue | Actors Between Historicity and Politics   293
   Companion Texts   294
   Bread and Roses   297
   If Agency is...then...   300
   Notes   308

Sixth Interlude | Windows/Breath   311
   Dispatches from Within the Knot of Pandemic Fascism   313
      Lebanon, Hudson Valley | Nathaniel Madison   314
      Turkey, Little Rock | Safi Alsebai   315
      Hong Kong, New Jersey | Ezra Lee   316
      San Diego, San Diego | Isabella Lee   317

Brazil, Oaxaca | Colin Eubank   318
Mexico, Oaxaca | Colin Eubank   319
Karachi, Karachi | Zahabia Khuzema   320
Italy, Italy | Renata Summo-O'Connell   322
South Asian Peninsula, Karachi | Sami Chohan   324
Karachi, Karachi (Tracing Feeling) | Yashfeen Talpur   327
Guyana, Baltimore | Christopher Carrico   329
Chile, Oaxaca | Colin Eubank   331
Who Cares About Care If Care Is The Alibi,
        Fragment 3 | Bonaventure Soh Bejeng Ndikung   333
"what would the world be without accomplices?" | Vianny Ruiz   337
Cazuela | Sean Brannock   338
A Roaming Aesthetic VII | Sadia Salim   340

Episode Seven | Falsework Futures   341
    Companion Texts   342
    The Limits of Some Present Maps   346
    Our Future with Political Institutions & the Internationalist Imagination   352
    Bringing Forth: An Education in Politics or a Political Education?   358
    Falsework on Halfway Homes: Communing at the Party Contra Party   364
    Notes   365
    Garden Sketch | Zohaib Zuby   367

About the Contributors   368

Bibliography   482

    Diasporic Deluge | Colin Eubank   397

Hic Rosa   398

    Eid Card | Valerie Fanarjian   400

Prologue

Falsework, Smalltalk: Political Education, Aesthetic Archives, and Recitations of a Future in Common is an experimental and collaborative archive of autonomous and internationalist political education and communication for this historical moment. It addresses key questions about intersubjective sustenance in the subjunctive tense, community building and institutional maintenance, social action and communication, and collaborative learning and knowledge production, that have been raised anew by the "twin crises" of the global pandemic and insurgent neoliberal fascism. This subject matter is addressed by a cohort of scholars, artists, curators, activists, writers, educators, organizers, and students who hail from various parts of the world and enjoy respect and renown in their respective, yet beautifully overlapping, lifeworlds that give us glimpses of a community and a world to come.

This relational, curatorial, and editorial expedition is moved by a commitment to politics as a living and not a dead labor. It is rooted in a relationship to knowing (and to institutions) in the name of something that has long been forgotten. And, it does not find any pleasure in the reactionary force to order. The project of education instantiated here is one that goes beyond educating people in known scripts, of political action and revolution, so that the production of knowledge is actually radical and reorients the relationship between education and knowledge. One piece of this is challenging the separation of pedagogy and knowledge production in the academy writ large. Another is being honest about our own struggles with the university, the artworld, and neoliberal political institutions—as objects of desire, as sources of approval, and places of refuge.

Centring, thus, a normative understanding of "politics as a living labor," the volume elaborates a method and performs certain practices that emerge from, and work toward, that normativity and its aesthetic and materialist imperatives. It is curated, crafted, written, and assembled by a transnational effort of artists, educators, organizers, and academics—in other words, cultural workers—addressing and summoning each other through modes of writing, reading, speaking, and thinking together, formulated in response to, and from within, the imposed distances and isolations of the multiple historical and contemporary global crises of our time, by no means limited to the pandemic. In this way, it is also written to and for a global audience of artists, educators, activists, organizers, academics, and cultural workers who would be well-served by new ways of being together, trustworthy solidarities, and timely models of internationalist political education that emerge from a materialist, anticapitalist, and anticolonial politics and aesthetics.

To this end, *Falsework, Smalltalk* consciously intervenes in the modes of legitimacy and value provided by the artworld, academia, and the world of nonprofit community organizing, in working across these boundaries and divisions of labor, challenging the institutionalities and publicities preserved in these modes. It is a multidimensional work spoken by and for the figure and labor of the cultural worker as a way to provincialize the neoliberal formations of the academic, the artist, and the political organizer. It does so in order to propose a wider self-determined aesthetics and politics that opts for new, mutually-constituted, and consensual grammars intimately and intuitively known by those hemming, and yet looking away from, the currently available institutional realms. This also requires looking toward a different tomorrow, and a different sense of location and place—a promise that the academic, the artist, and the neoliberal political expert guiding us to a victory nowhere in sight, in their current institutional formations and locations, do not seem to to have the capacity to fulfill.

Matter and Method

Falsework, Smalltalk began as the "Assembling the Future/Tense" Studio, a series of conversations organized by Hic Rosa Collective in response to the pandemic lockdown, to engage what then seemed to be the "twin crises" of the moment (the electoral defeats of progressive forces and vindication of neoliberal fascism on the one hand, and the global pandemic on the other)—cascading into the summer of abolitionist Black Lives Matter uprisings. We hosted call-in conversations on nine consecutive Saturday afternoons in March, April, and May 2020.

We built a community of study and discussion around the possibilities of political and social movements toward new forms of existence, and the impossibilities of history, political consciousness, and health and economic crises that confront the conduct of life and social existence "as usual." The goal was to find a language beyond "the world cannot be the same" that allows us to think about futurity, in a different key or urgency than what is eager to produce a new discipline through the crisis. Is that even a fair concern to have? Are autonomous forms of thinking passé or needed? Who are we relying on to lead us in the world-making that really matters if we are to save those we love?

These studio sessions, attended by about sixty individuals over the course of the sessions, about thirty of whom were regular attendees throughout many sessions of the series, were designed to allow us to work through some dimensions of the present in order to think with pressing questions of politics, and to wonder together about the aspirations and agendas that might yet walk with us into "the future." While the topics and dialogues were outlined earlier in our planning, the task of selecting the readings and hosting the weekly conversations fell on different members of the Hic Rosal Collective. These members crafted a layout for the forthcoming conversation on the basis of the preceding discussion, and prepared forays and interventions attending to the readings, giving context for their inclusion in the week's map. These readings were placed online two days in advance, but reading them was not a condition of participation.

For some weeks of the Studio, we reached out to friends who would help us think through certain matters, or prepare some observations and dispatches for us from their locations, gesturing to the shared texts where possible, to help us finesse our questions in common. In the very act of engaging with each other and formulating questions—certainly some of us had more of a history of doing that with each other—we were committed to producing a space that was anchored as much as possible in that moment's configuration of virtual bodies, and their degree of familiarity with the texts, or the history of earlier weeks. The aim was to foster not a taxing space of dissemination and reception of ideas with unspoken conditions of entry, but a learning crafted with the concrete availabilities of the session, hospitable to what we had the capacity for, dealing with everything else in the world. Instead of establishing abstract finalities or delusional certainties, we were sketching out contingent answers to the concrete question of what political knowledge, thinking, community, and conversation are needed in the moment, and must preface any thinking of what's to come. In other words, it mattered what we felt we could do together that given week, day, hour—and this shaped our accountability to each other and to the texts, serving as companions and occasions to host, not as tyrants or demanding guests. And it was fine. (At least we think so.)

Whether setting up the conversations, or this archive, we have not sought to console ourselves with premature kinds of certainties, commitments, or resolution—but have taken to heart the fact that the tasks of theory and the enactment of politics are irreducible to each other. With our bodies required to comport the requisite translations in every action, quickly subsuming one into the other, or finding legitimacy for one in the other, is not the way to go. We are impelled toward, and would like to think that we substantiate in our work, a method that comes from a number of thinkers, including but not only Karl Marx, that prioritizes relations within the totalities of inquiry and practice that confront and reshape us, understanding that the construction of that object of study, inquiry, love, or desire, is sometimes, maybe more than sometimes, in our hands and that we owe something to it which commands us to show up, and that we don't let it die in our hands or on our doorstep.

It is not for your sake, O House of Israel, that I am about to act, but for the sake of my holy name. — Ezekiel, 36:22

The will and torment to prevent the collapse of empire in one moment, and then to cause the fall in others. The forcibly imposed fate to hold positions not called tyrannical. The chronicle of resentment, desperation, beating the backhand, aimed to prove how one can survive—endlessly disappointed in shallowness and hoping for depth. You can survive even when everyone turns away, or is dead. How hard it is to manage a place that will always have the best in the past. A "negative" ideology that desires to transform the positive. A place that does not want to give up, obviously, to the rink of history. [...] You mentioned grammar, and I don't want to make too much of grammar as grammar, but might call attention to how we are talking about building connections *and* protecting "barriers of incomprehensibility." The forms of address "to whom" and "for whom are where we locate ourselves politically, always. — Sara

Continuing in our tradition of regarding forms of reading and writing as modes of being with each other, the task of political education has never felt more urgent, and also has never felt more in need of being charged with the tense of the future: in what key must we speak, to whom, and with whom? What definitive answers are needed? What is the relation between theory and practice in the way that does not reinscribe modalities of self-policing and a political discipline that everybody around us seems to value without ever coming clean about which bodies it falls on? How are subjects of political education to be understood under a regime of thought relating to action where the body itself becomes both transparent and doesn't exist, except as always already enlisted in the redemption of that which is already known and thought, ostensibly outside the body? The autonomy of thought notwithstanding, we have been working on thinking about what exactly is the modality of speech and reading that accompanies something particular, but yet unformed, that we wish for.

As has been our Hic Rosa/Falsework ritual for the past five years of working in local and international contexts of political education and counter-institutional thought and practice, we put together certain texts not as a final syllabus to lead us through every question, but as occasions for entry into what we saw as dimensions of the present assemblage of politics. The goal was to use those texts as occasions to together disassemble the inherited complexes shaping our reflexes in the moment, and also, hopefully to add liberatory dimensions to each of those. The different topics under consideration that shaped every set of readings and the conversation to follow themselves constituted an arc very familiar to our prior work together: interrogating a particular moment by unfolding its dimensions and then reassembling them back together by way of questions and commitments that reveal and clarify themselves through acts of collective determination and preservation and remembering—what should be left aside, and what should be non-negotiably placed on the table.

This, this, this! To birds. To stillness/stasis as flight. This counter-reading, metaphor, and quantum framing of the in/visible archives of what it is that we are doing. We are in murmuration, secret flight, fugitive planning.— Heidi

Conversations and Conversions

We abided by a certain code of conduct: these conversations were not aimed at reclaiming or finalizing an answer, nor coming at a resolution together, but reclaiming a space to think and be. Even text was a premise for us to refer to each other and to return to each other when we felt lost. Sometimes we didn't need that; other days it is what saved us and helped us re-arrive at some point together. We wanted our impulse toward each other to be generative and kind. We tried to lure ourselves away from the mode of interrogation and policing each other. We made conscious attempts not to fall into the trap of using our positions and stances as armors or weapons or instruments of shame, but to repurpose them as openings and vulnerabilities, as invitations to care and guide, not to prescribe or direct where crises and urgencies can make us cruel. We were opting for these urgencies to ask more and not less of us, to challenge our reflexes and to approach the political outside of the fake power of policing each other and resolving our discomfort on another's body. We know well that, even if so many people know or are able to figure out how messed up the world is—especially as the pandemic has hit—they have still relied on the world to continue to give us some of those comforts. While the differential kind of costs and experiences within the moment have been really something to behold, and the I-told-you-so's have been very tempting, we tried to not rely on them to start or end the conversation.

> This counters the absolute sense of impossibility—the unquantifiable space of power, or the impossibility of ultimate victory over it—by creating a new engagement with possibility that works from the wreckage, and doesn't seem to need to worry about those absolutes. This is where I think we get to decide what's possible rather than that be decided or prescribed for us. — Bella.

> But it is not an antechamber! an endeavour to make the inaudible heard, to induce writing and reading and reading where there is no writing. The disruption of the concept of the author, who is inscribed in the body, like a citation, a way of calling forth a relative authority with words that escape the wreckage that arrives, where by definition there is no property. Can we think of it as a restitution of a space and speech/discourse without hierarchy and causality, with meaning and unity? Can the words resurge in its amplitude as address, as beckoning, and appeal? — Zibby

The conversations evolved into this multifaceted collaborative writing project. Between transcribing, commenting, annotating, editing, and the invited contributions, the project materialized as a multi-layered text: the primary texts, our voices (prepared and unprepared), discussion, transcription, annotation, authorship. As many people were involved in the conversations, transcription, annotative, and editorial work, as there were solicited authorial contributions beyond these conversations. The first full assembly of the collaborative writing endeavor took about three months after our last conversation, and from then on, another three months. The magnitude of this project was unprecedented, and we were encouraged by friends to convert this into an archive of this time, with key lessons for the modes of political education that everyone on the left seems to be struggling with. Much of the experimental writing and curating work happened in defiance of time and space itself. Maybe that was the only possible response to the pandemic moment.

We bring this work into the world for the benefit of educators and students, of artists and scholars, of political activists and social workers, of healers and disruptors alike, who have only found hyphenations either within the academy or in neoliberal organizations (and hence on their terms), or whose modes of address and reception have been hurt by the suspicion of thought and conversation arising from the ways in which we have been betrayed by thinkers and by activists alike. Such relations to one's work, and to each other, find institutional manifestation in certain kinds of organized togethernesses and charitable, self-redeeming, behaviour (in place of mutuality and availability) that simply just doesn't work for most of us involved in the production of this space. Our ways of engaging and reading are our spurs to imagining and reimagining the social.

On feeling lost

Text, theory, thought, are counter-maps against our estrangements. — Heidi

I say... again, the "ungraspable" "discontinuous" with the materiality of solidarity and creativity. You say...solidarity seems more possible when thought about coupled with creativity, the two emerging in coevolution. We will see... Song, chanting, dancing. Let's take the "call to politics" seriously. It gives us one of the rarest moments in the grind of our daily existence. This call stops us and strikes us in the hearts and brings us to tears. Yes, pity, terror, song, togetherness remains precious. They need to be reanimated in the hearts of our time. — Zibby

Dis/Assembly

Assembling this multi-layered and multivocal text has been performative of the notion of assembling a futurity out of the dis-assembled complex of our current crises. In the experience of this making, from the initial idea, to the conversations as their own ends, and then the transformation of conversations into text and archive, all the participants collectively constructed seven dialogues in political aesthetic education. The practice of political education then became inseparable from a collective archival practice. The outcome, we hope, integrates pedagogical ethos, political affect and desire, habits of speaking, reading, listening, transcribing, annotating, storytelling, and riffing as forms of urgent political relations and hospitality not to be sacrificed to the crises and their attendant calls to order that traumatize into submission, and promise premature homecomings via their certainties, even as they seek to deliver us. It is true that our hospitalities might often be deemed as too lacking in instrumentalizability, or too politically inefficacious or nonproprietary, and our lack of submission or surrender (even self-eviction in order to not evacuate politics) sometimes seen ironically as a form of control. But, many of us are used to this charge, of being threatening or irreverent or authoritative in our own lack of claims and names, and in our attempt to reshape modes of authority and address in the name of something not drenched in the trendy authorizations and legitimations of the moment. On any given day, we'd rather be counted with those who quietly or loudly uttered, *not this, not here, not now. We can hold the pieces.*

The dialogues build on the studio sessions, and revolve around these themes: Politics and Crisis, Calls to Politics, Political Knowledge and Judgment, Which Society Must be Defended?, Just Institutions, Between Historicity and Politics, and Falsework Futures. Our work together, in its many divergences tethered to each other in this project, emphasizes the inseparability of political education, the need to rethink socialities and institutionalities signalled in our ordinary desires for life and living, and a commitment to liberatory anti-capitalist, anti-racist, anticolonial, abolitionist, and internationalist political desire in many forms, some yet to be known and discovered.

Interspersed between the dialogues are personal, creative, and scholarly reflections on the invited contributors' own situations during this pandemic, or which they felt were continuous with the moment. We requested from them a small souvenir of "politics as living labor" in these times, as a living example of continuing political education, encounter, desire, preservation, and opening in times of struggle and crisis which are, for some of us, times of annihilation. In assembling these, we conjured the falsework that we set out to approach to begin with, a protective exoskeleton for moments of actually sharing space of thought, care, and hope with each other. These works mediate the conversations, holding the structure in place, and inward from the world we summon in our smalltalk.

Convocations and Gratitude

The team that worked to actually integrate and finalize the manuscript was made up of 28 individuals, ranging from actors to artists, political theorists to graduate students, activists to economists. The final editorial push was carried out by seven of us—Asma, Colin, Safi, Sara, Nathaniel, Ezra, and Dan. Sanya Hussain was part of our journey as Hic Rosa Intern until we had our first full draft, from June through August 2020. We had an elaborate net of labor and investment, spanning editors, anchors, contributors, reviewers, scribes, and conversants, all the way to the first full draft, which Sanya handled gracefully.

Alfiya Halai guided and enabled our design autonomy and confidence. Adnan Mir courageously committed our vision to paper. Bard College at Simon's Rock—home or host to many of us at some point in our lives—supported the production with a faculty development grant awarded to Asma. Discord became known to us intimately through these times. Google Docs allowed us all the editorial interactions we needed. We held large editorial meetings on Zoom. Everyone was a volunteer, including two reviewers who helped us hear ourselves better, and improve this work.

Our friendly and supportive exchanges with Eileen Joy and Vincent van Gerven Oei at Punctum Books were a key spur to this project and our decision to give it this form. Bonaventure Ndikung at SAVVY Contemporary, Bilal Zahoor at Folio Books, and Hajra Haider Karrar, offered great advice and confidence along the way, as this project gradually showed us the way to manifesting Common Tern, an international co-operative of cultural workers. Fittingly, it is the inaugural project of this co-op's mutually-held site of cultural production—Common Tern Works—as a way to realize form-bending, politically educative, aesthetically dissensual, and radical internationalist, collaboration centring the Global South.

Shoaib Hashmi's translation of Faiz Ahmed Faiz's "Intisaab" as epigraph was used with kind permission of the Faiz Foundation, facilitated by Prof. Salima Hashmi.

All images in this book have been provided by the contributors whose work they accompany. (In the case of Sadia Salim's Roaming Aesthetic IV and V, the photographer was Humayun M.)

Yes, indeed, it is the case that the phenomenology of pandemic fascism—we called it that and are sticking to it—does entwine love and ressentiment (and grief, and anger, and helplessness, and guilt, and care, and sympathy, and abundance, and exhaustion, and dreamscapes, and phantasmagoria). This collective work, we'd like to think, made room for both the love and the ressentiment, and its size allows us an opportunity to tell the two apart.

Finally, we are just grateful that, despite all the gashes we each have to show for these pandemic times, and the relentless work of mourning that has suffused this falsework just as it does all falsework, those of us who started out together in March are still all here. As onerous and uppity as this project seemed on certain days we encountered it broken by the ordinary demands of these times, we are thankful for this literally life-affirming excuse to reach out and touch each other. It has been an honor to breathe and linger, without inhibition, within the thoughts, words, sounds, voices, and images of our friends in this world.

Come, sit near.

Collaborators

Editors and Project Leads
Asma Abbas
Colin Eubank

Associate Editors
Safi Alsebai
Ezra Lee
Nathaniel Madison
Sara Mugridge
Daniel Neilson

Editorial Anchors and Annotators of Dialogues
Safi Alsebai
Colin Eubank
Avonlea Fisher
Elizabeth (Zibby) Glass
Sanya Hussain
Isabella Lee
Jody Leonard
Nathaniel Madison
Sara Mugridge
Daniel Neilson
Heidi Andrea Restrepo Rhodes
Gabriel Salgado
Yashfeen Talpur
Hannah Walker
Milo Ward
Philip Zorba

Hic Rosa Project Intern, Summer 2020
Sanya Hussain

Audio Recording
Stephen Hager

Scribes
transcribed the studio sessions from audio recordings
Safi Alsebai
Colin Eubank
Valerie Fanarjian
Avonlea Fisher
Sanya Hussain
Ezra Lee
Jody Leonard
Nathaniel Madison
Coco Marcil
Daniel Neilson
Yashfeen Talpur
Hannah Walker
Charlie Yates
Philip Zorba

Speakers
who participated in a studio session recording and permitted attributed use of their words in the manuscript
Asma Abbas
Ethan Ackelsberg
Safi Alsebai
Isaac Brosilow
Christopher Carrico
Starling Carter
Colin Eubank
Valerie Fanarjian
Ciarán Finlayson
Ari Fogelson
Elizabeth (Zibby) Glass
Marvin González
Zahabia Khuzema
Ezra Lee
Isabella Lee
Jody Leonard
Nathaniel Madison
Daniel Neilson
Lucy Peterson

Brianna Pope
Heidi Andrea Restrepo Rhodes
Gabriel Salgado
Renata Summo-O'Connell
Yashfeen Talpur
Hannah Walker
Milo Ward
Philip Zorba

Contributors

whose invited work appears in the interludes of the book and who were not participants in the studio sessions

Eric Aldieri
Ashna Ali
Zara Anwarzai
Sean Brannock
Silvana Carotenuto
Sami Chohan
Miri Davidson
Ejeris Dixon
Edgar Flores Noriega
Lillian Goldberg
Lewis Gordon
Hajra Haider Karrar
Sy Klipsch-Abudu
Kenji C. Liu
Dresda Emma Mendez de la Brena
Bindu Menon Mannil
Hasan Mujtaba
Bonaventure Soh Bejeng Ndikung
Anna Poplawski
Shahana Rajani
Sumana Roy
Vianny Ruiz
Sadia Salim
Renata Summo-O'Connell
Rei Terada
Omer Wasim
Zohaib Zuby

Reading Key

house font for this volume, and used for all transcribed dialogue

block quotes from companion texts

annotations by scribes and dialogue editors

authorial contributions to interludes between dialogues

On invitations, recitations, and beginnings

COLIN: I was reading this section and thinking about the repetitions and differences of the introductions in each transcript of our live conversations... and I was kind of thinking about this in relation to how we interact with each other and the maintenance of (or aspirations to) a certain kind of ethos of being together. Rather than being didactic, the introduction seems to function as a kind of a recitation (a prayer). I think about who its audience is intended to be, who it is meant to address, what part of each of us (newer and veteran members of these conversations) it activates, and what its utterance/reference as a beginning to many of our sessions might induce. I think, more than anything, it demonstrates a desire for a kind of mutuality or shared sensibility that we also recognize to be constantly liable for sabotage—even by each other, or those that we call our friends. I think about the trust it requires to engage in sociality, or sharing & being shared. This (re)citation, this prayer, is one of those things that attempts to address problems of spatial and temporal conjugation, or the simultaneity of beginning and continuation. That said, I wonder when, and under what conditions, the utterance or the repetition of such a ritual becomes another way of making something invisible (I often think back to the acknowledgements about a university's occupation of indigenous land which opened each session of the Critical Ethnic Studies Association conference in Vancouver in 2018). To what extent does talking about something become nothing more than a deferral of its enactment rather than a welcome foot- or hand-hold for us to steady ourselves in the continuation of this journey? And how does recitation become a way that we can do something other than critique to facilitate a mode of being together which still can effectively refuse the domination of oppressive structures that work on the level of the individual which often thwart collectivity.

I don't think these thoughts necessarily belong in this session, but this particular moment reminded me of these questions.

ZIBBY: I think the questions you pose about this repetition are crucial. In some ways, history is built on this feminine capacity to always reproduce, and so we have become increasingly comfortable in saying that the archivable object becomes itself through disappearance, as it becomes the trace of something that remains once its action has disappeared. This logic with an emphasis on loss—a loss which the archive can regulate, maintain, institutionalize—while forgetting that it can be a loss that the archive produces... the importance of scripting the material of the enactment not just as disappearing but disavowing recurrence... .revolution also a result of repetition, a repetition that does not contradict "newness" but produces it.... the disruption of repetition as a cycle....

BELLA: I also think there's something interesting in how the recitation/prayer changes subtly in each session, it evolves over time, some things disappear from it too, some things are added, its affect changes.

On transcription

HANNAH: In the early stages of the transcription process, I was acutely aware of how I heard the text in my head as I read and annotated it. As the project had multiple scribes, I often found that I would hear other parts of the script in the voice of those other scribes rather than the voices of those who actually spoke the words.

This difference in voices was also due to the significant syntactical differences in our sections of the transcript. Each section was an interpretation of sorts, boasting diverse decisions in how to present filler words, how to interpret unclear sentences, where to denote pauses. When the three of us scribes spoke on the phone for the first time about the transcript, one said that he was convinced that sentences do not exist in spoken English. Therefore, before any annotations were added, any sections highlighted, and discussion of what other layers would look like, the transcript was already a multilayered text because it brought forth two voices simultaneously, already in conversation with one another.

As scribes, we were not merely stenographers, we were writing an understanding of our friends' speech and voices. Now, weeks later, the document having gone through a meticulous editing process and many drafts, I do not hear the voices the same way. They've been shifted, (re) moved, joined, and smoothed so that our voices have been replaced once again with the original speakers in my head. As I read these chapters I am reading a text, but here and there a word or turn of phrase jumps out at me and I hear the vocal inflections, the warmth and character of the voices of the people who first spoke these words aloud so many months ago. The joy and kinship that their words brought me during the first few months of lockdown reverberates again as I read. As scribes, editors, and annotators, we were given immense trust over the keeping and representation of others' words—a responsibility that we took pains to honor.

VALERIE: The Saturday Studio Sessions felt like a sacred space, where people were doing their best to maintain a level of attentiveness to each other, trying to discern together what each were saying and what directions those conversations could lead. I put the Saturday Session on bluetooth and played it outside and would either sit and work on my plants or my art, and sometimes people would come by and they would sit for a while and listen. But when I would see people and they would ask, "Oh, well, what did you do this week?" I'd try to explain to them our time together and I just couldn't. I tried to explain that it wasn't just being with people that I loved or whose lives I had been in for so long, and it wasn't just that they were sort of reading and discussing all sorts of political theory, but it was more like feeling a comfort of being in the company that were really working on thinking together.I found such sanctuary in this space, so much so that I was sad when the sessions were over.

I'm sure people struggle—struggle to get the right words, struggle to get their points across— all the time. But to the extent that those struggles are so deeply shared in such a kind way was so very special to me. I am so moved by that use of and care towards language.

So, when I started transcribing the sessions, one of the things I thought about was these Buddhists that I'd met while I was running a sawmill. I was curious about how they made their money, to which they told me that everything that was on the internet (or a lot of what was on there, because this must've been the '80s) is stuff that a collection of Buddhists had manually transferred from books into searchable text for the web search engines. This work was something the Buddhists excelled at because they had the time and the patience to do this repetitive work. Anyways, I found myself kind of doing the same thing: entering these words into text one letter at a time for future learning and experiencing. And because I wanted to get it right, I would read what I'd written over and over and over again. I would read it, type it, read it, type it, all while listening to the repetition of peoples voices, their words, like a type of prayer. In this meditative pattern I really was able to focus on language at the level of the sentence and see the art of words being strung together.

The whole point of witnessing is to keep a space, or a way of being together, alive in the world. That was the point of art I made during the sessions, and scribing the recordings—to translate experiences (whether in words or in images) in order to keep that feeling.

Once again, out of nowhere, you have gifted me with such a beautiful experience after I thought surprises like this were over. Thank you

prelude

FOR TODAY IS ALSO THE FUTURE OF SOMETHING

Eyes at a Distance of Six Feet

Hasan Mujtaba
translated by Asma Abbas & Sanya Hussain

He stood six feet away from me
Gloves, mask, and helmet-like hat on his head
Only his eyes were open
Glaring, peeking, surveying, gazing, smiling, crying,
Eyes that recall a little, eyes that forget so much
Eyes seen one last time before someone is captured
At home, going to work, teaching children at school, strolling in a park, going shopping,
Eyes seen being covered with a hood
In the wrinkles of the faces of the mothers of the disappeared protesting in front of press clubs
Eyes that rain all seasons, the monsoon, winter
Inquiring
(Or so I felt)
Do you recognize me?
I, too, attempting to breathe through my mask, say some words
Ask something
The Irani restaurant?
Or outside the bar?
Asking for a light
Those eyes saying thank you.
With the breeze came a strange thought
These couldn't be Sajid Baloch's, could they?
Who chose to escape to Sweden, rather than be disappeared from Lyari
Alas, now he's already done being found, disappeared, and killed where he ran to safety
"It's been a few days since the State found its pastime
To kill children as they come of age."

Could they be the eyes of those dozens of boys I met
Without name
These eyes
Trapped in the reverberating strings of Faqeer Imamuddin Dakhan's ektara
"Who, who, am I? No one knows me"

Present but unseen, unrecognized
"Next five"
Calls out the Sikh elder guarding the door to the shop
Still six foot apart
Those eyes move a little
See, you fool!
Your heart be a mirror
Into which you crash like a bird
Unprovoked, this morning
My sweet-scented shaving brush, drenched in Old Spice, lathering the sides of my face
Said to me
Hey, you, don't try so hard to be a Krishan Chander
I replied
"What are you talking about, you spicy old man, old fashion,
Long past Krishan Chander's time
It's the era of Umera Ahmed and Tik Tok"
Said the brush patting my cheek,
But those eyes...
Staring from six feet away, saying sweet nothings
Who, what, are they?
Oh, wait! What did you say?
Nazir Abbassi's eyes that now grace the face of his daughter Zarqa?
Smiling, laughing, dreamy eyes
Do tell the Brigadier
That he was not able to kill those
That he cannot wash away his sins.

Are these the eyes of my beloved?
Lover's eyes in a cat's dream
The cat can also be the beloved
(As can the dog)
Now cats have stopped lurking under the butcher's block.
Playing chess at the Lebanese tea and shisha shop on Astoria Boulevard
Those distant eyes, inviting,
"Come along, let me show you the Bazaars of Egypt"
Those eyes that taught me some Nizaar Qabbani
Neither Syria remains nor he
Did you recognize me?
I am Khayat Tatheer

I return in every era
Born in the Nablus lockdown
Raised by the lockdown
Orphaned in the lockdown
Do tell, what did you make of the lockdown in New York?
You must have heard me in the symphonic Psalms of Muhammad Fairouz
Six feet away, I was startled!
Symphony of Psalms indeed
The heaven and hell of sounds
Those C-130 engines, igniting, taking off, landing
Bring our murdered prime ministers back to their villages
Where their pauper's funerals take place
What does it matter now?
There's a pauper's funeral for princes and paupers

In America now, lunch is free without any reason
Keep the ventilators, keep the PPEs,
But give free lunch.
Across a big "thank you,"
I saw Elmhurst Hospital
Turn into the eyes of the doctor
Who commits suicide.
And recognized
Indeed, I recognized
From six feet away
I recognized,
Six thousand miles removed
In a Kabul hospital
I saw the eyes of those little angels
Open into this world
Only to be morphed into streams of blood.
Children killed in Haifa bombings
To be buried six feet under.

Six feet away, safe, a Chinese boy, coughing,
And his mother,
Walk by me.

New York, May 2020

Susurrus: July 4, 2020

Kenji C. Liu

Sharp reverberations bristle across Los Ángeles. Braids of fire bursting into hair. Beheaded statues purr from hollow necks, release throats of smoke. Explosions roosting over and over. An akimbo scene. Eyes climb into the sky to surveil, rain down their lasers. They read the book of faces. Such dapper thieves. The city disappears into each of us, the aftertaste xerox and cherry-scented, this is how protection works. A procession of small fingers tracking inward, beyond talking. And we, tiny holes torn in the regime, we almost became real citizens of this place. What's coming isn't hidden. A country declines slowly on television. A national nervous system stretched on tacks. Each day ghosts poke us like old peaches. Crow, eucalyptus, clouds—we are calling to report a crime larger than language. How to repair things except together, we unprofitable beasts.

"Punctuations"

Eric Aldieri

Asleep, I find myself at a yard sale. I purchase an iron loon. Intrigued by my choice, the woman tending the tables invites me into the basement to have a look at some other items—wooden mallets, rusted lawn chairs, an old baseball mitt. They belong to my grandfather. Having evaded memory's appetite, they remain perfectly preserved in the physical space of a dream.

Two days later, eight picnickers enjoy a summer night in Grant Park, Chicago. Sitting no more than thirty yards away from a statue of a very sad man, they take pleasure and delight in the uninhibited display of police terror, nodding in approval as we are beaten, gassed, and demoralized. One can easily imagine a pair of mitts on their blanket, surrounded by the same teal-colored chairs and a wooden croquet set—each object uniquely implicated in the ongoing spectacle of law-preserving violence. They, too, remind us: "There is nothing innocuous left."[1]

When quarantine's empty duration is punctuated by missed funerals and tear gas, psychosis functions as ethical response. Oscillating between familial dreamscapes and clumsy baton blows, I wonder: to what realm have we now been delivered? Still, in the very abyss of time's "bad eternity,"[2] a hint of the divine enveloped. Now in a glance, again for a stranger, rinsing our eyes out.

Notes

1. Theodor Adorno, *Minima Moralia*: *Reflections from Damaged Life*, trans. E.F.N. *Jephcott* (New York: Verso, 2005), A5.

2. Adorno, 165.

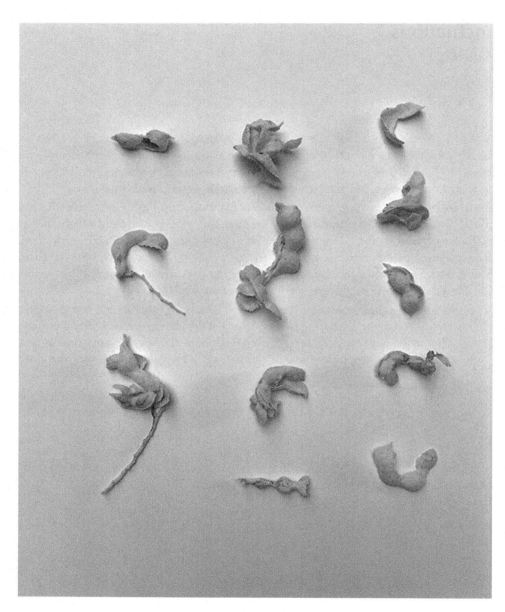

Sadia Salim, *A Roaming Aesthetic I*

first dialogue

POLITICS
CONTRA
CRISIS

21 March 2020

Companion Texts for Studio Session

Benanav, Aaron and John Clegg. "*Crisis and Immiseration: Critical Theory Today.*" in *The SAGE Handbook of Frankfurt School Critical Theory*. SAGE Publications Ltd., June 2018.

Chuang. "Social Contagion: Macrobiological Class War in China." http://chuangcn.org. Published in February 2020.

Dols, Michael. "The Comparative Communal Responses to the Black Death in Muslim and Christian Societies." in *Viator* Volume 5. Brepols Publishers, 1974. 269-287.

Federici, Silvia. *Caliban and the Witch: Women, the Body, and Primitive Accumulation.* New York: Autonomedia; London: Pluto Press, 2004. 44-47.

García Márquez, Gabriel. *One Hundred Years of Solitude.* Taiwan: Harper Collins, [1967]2003.

Khaldun, Ibn. *The Muqaddimah: An Introduction to History—Abridged Edition.* Translated by Franz Rosenthal. Edited by N.J. Dawood. Princeton University Press, 2020.

Lowell, James R.. "*The Present Crisis.*" In *English Poetry III: From Tennyson to Whitman (Harvard Classics, 1909-14)*. P.F. Collier & Sons, [1845]1910.

Mamdani, Mahmood. "Reading Ibn Khaldun in Kampala." In *Journal of Historical Sociology*. Issue 30. Wiley & Sons, Ltd., 2017. 7-26.

Marx, Karl. *The Eighteenth Brumaire of Louis Bonaparte, 1852. Translated by Saul K. Padover.* CreateSpace Independent Publishing Platform. [1852]2015.

Neurath, Otto. "Utopia as a Social Engineer's Construction." 1919.

Osborne, Peter. "A Sudden Topicality Marx, Nietzsche, and the Politics of Crisis." *Radical Philosophy*, 160. Published in March/April 2010. 19-26.

Wallace, Rob. *Big Farms Make Big Flu: Dispatches on Infectious Disease, Agribusiness, and the Nature of Science.* New York: NYU Press, 2016.

Wallace, Rob. "Notes on a Novel Coronavirus." *Monthly Review Online.* Published on January 29, 2020. https://mronline.org/2020/01/29/notes-on-a-novel-coronavirus/.

Hosts | Asma Abbas, Ciarán Finlayson

Speakers | Asma Abbas, Ciarán Finlayson, Gabriel Salgado, Colin Eubank, Dan Neilson, Philip Zorba, Jody Leonard

Scribes & Annotators | Asma Abbas, Safi Alsebai, Ezra Lee, Milo Ward, Ari Fogelson, Jody Leonard

Pandemic Hospitalities

ASMA

Good afternoon, everyone. It's 3:02 somewhere in the world. 3:02 pm in Richmond, Massachusetts, where I am. I wanted to welcome you all and set up a bit of a background for today and introduce our intentions. Alongside all the unfoldings of new and old forms of fascism (a word that we, at least within the Hic Rosa Collective, like to use to refer to the things that are happening across the world, including the US, which confirm for us that fascism, colonialism, and capitalism have never been separate from each other and have always been kept in place by the continuing life of liberalism) the past few weeks and months have somehow managed a return of a sense of futurity. This has had a lot to do, for many of us, with the Bernie Sanders campaign in the US as an occasion to remember past struggles and the futures they imagined.

Here we are, just a few weeks into the aftermath of the return of an invitation to build something. After years of putting the question of futurity on hold and trying to at least defend and preserve the spaces in which it was possible to be, for many of us the insistent domestication of a possible global transnational or internationalist thinking has also been part of the tragedy and casualty of US imperialism and a corollary of creeping fascism. Within this, Donald Trump appeared hardly as an exception or shock.

So, the question is: how can a particular moment of thinking and looking forward—even in the belly of the empire, about the possibility of some different kinds of accountability and conversations even among ourselves—get so swiftly undercut or distracted by this plague? So many of us are caught standing on one foot, and then the other, and the only gesture we can make is to try to hold each other up, even if grounding completely with both feet on our ground is not possible right now.

The impulse here is to go back to the place that has held many of us: the space of study, reading, and understanding something together, as something more than the conveying of knowledge, the claiming of expertise, or a particular policing of thought and action. This studying, this working and thinking, is where we have sought to escape to, from certain boundaries, and to build alongside other structures. Literally, "falsework," a word that was suggested by a dear friend a number of years ago when we were setting up the Hic Rosa Collective. This "building alongside" that which is decaying, that which has failed us or which must be destroyed; or, a rehearsal of that which doesn't exist yet. That's been our animation, for five years now.

Together, many of us started to do this because we wanted to sustain and retain something of a space of thinking, being, loving, imagining, and desiring together—rooted in ways of reading understood as accountability and as reconstruction. Something that is not just for ourselves. This has also made us question the boundary of the classroom, and then the university, and to ask ourselves over many years: to whom and to what are we beholden?

This question of to what and to whom we are beholden is crucial to what I think we are doing today. We are trying not just to identify and clarify the object of knowledge, or the object of political action or survival in the moment, but seeking to be beholden to something and to find other ways of being in the moment. To move and comport ourselves and our thinking differently, and in ways that support each other. To materialize the forms of mutual aid, mutuality, and reciprocity that emerge from a sense of self and other that has been bludgeoned by neoliberalism.

In politics, we have to build in many different ways. That's what is behind our effort to just talk to each other, to listen to each other, and to receive each other differently. To try to hold together the world inside our homes that might be unbearable for many. To still make furtive gestures to the world outside as still something to be desired, loved, and made better (with the hope to re-enter it one day and find others who stayed). To remember each other and make connections that don't seem merely intellectual, merely scholastic, merely a deadening will-to-knowledge. To also remember that what we're facing has everything to do with histories of capital and colony unfolding in their own way everywhere, into and outward from our bodies, physical and social.

Today, we hope to map some coordinates of our lives together in this time, alongside people who have thought a little bit about this, identifying the axes and dimensions of political life that need to be dealt with. All the instructions we receive about the right time, the right sequence, the correct order of political action, increasingly sound and feel completely arbitrary—not to mention the fact that their truth hasn't quite been borne out in reality. We are at this point *not despite*, but *because*, many of those proclamations, made especially in times of crises, and we now once again confront what else comes with them—what's waiting at the door. Speaking about crisis, as we wish to do here, has to include addressing its attendant politics of order. Perhaps we might hear and respond to those calls differently, for the sake of someone else who will live on past this crisis, and live differently, because many of us won't, or our lives will never be the same.

As far as we want to think about a future, we should also know that today what we are confronting is also the future of something. What is that, and are there names for it? We know they are systems. We call them capitalism, colonialism, fascism, neoliberalism. But it isn't enough to speak about what these systems do, without speaking what they do to us, and to our capacities to be with each other and build together again, and against them. It is really crucial that in thinking of Palestine, Kashmir, American Slavery, Brexit, and femicide in South America, we keep in mind that they are not independent or exclusive realities. The presence of the Sanders campaign has allowed some of us to feel that, somehow, all these things that we were hiding under our pillows for years, like all the love notes to different places that were never acknowledged in anybody's mourning of our lives, are finally going to have a space not because he would read them on a list or place them on a ticker on his livestreams, but because we were part of something. With much to lament, perhaps ours is not an impulse springing from a moment lost, but one pulling us toward a moment that is yet to be found.

This series of conversations, which we will be calling the Saturday Studio Sessions, will speak to what it means to recover or re-assemble a "future tense," with requisite play on all those words. In order to do that, we have, the best we could, dis-assembled the current moment into its various dimensions that call for a political inquiry. I now want to introduce Ciarán Finlayson, who will start us off on this search today. It is an honor to have known Ciarán for many years now. Currently, Ciarán is Assistant Editor at Art Forum and has obliged by free-writing to our provocation, and offering some texts for reading in common, and letting us be beholden to something as we inaugurate this set of conversations. I would request that we set ourselves to a task, not of interrogation and investigation of each other, but of being beholden to how people read and are trying to be and do in this moment, and what they must do in order to have it make sense. So, yes, political judgment is required, but it should not be confused with merely taking exception.

The texts that we have put together in consultation with each other are there for reference along the way. We might turn to them in our conversation, but the goal is to use them as occasions for other voices, to see what people are thinking, and how we can establish joint points of departure and be clear about them at least to each other, many of whom are meeting for the first time today.

What Does "Crisis" Name?

CIARÁN

Thinking through the theme of politics contra crisis, the immediate things I've been sitting with this week are the limits of political action today. The limits of political action today may be in relation to what seems to be the non-ideological fulfillment of a lot of our social democratic demands—when you think about the healthcare system being nationalized in Spain, all of a sudden. We're in a history that seems to be speeding up. Add to this the general situation of what seem like political transformations taking place, that is also a situation of social distancing where we can't leave our houses. So, I was trying to look for texts that do some kind of summary of the history of leftist thinking about crisis.

The main text that I was interested in is Peter Osborne's "A Sudden Topicality,"[1] which traces a number of things. It says that each crisis features its own revival of Marx's theory of crises. A first moment of this return to Marxist theory of crisis happens after the First World War. You have Rosa Luxemburg and Henryk Grossman holding to theories of economic breakdown. Then you have these dissident Marxisms of the middle of the century, the Frankfurt School, operaismo situations, etc. There is less an interest in the supposed economism or determinism of the crisis theory Marxism. Another recursion happens in the '70s, and then again after the 2008 financial crisis. Osborne says, basically, that if one were to distill a general theory of crisis from Marx's writings on economic cycles, there's a disjunction between two senses of crisis. One is a general, historical character of crisis, where crisis is what leads us into a new mode of production. Then there's the kind of conjunctural or the narrow political economic idea of crisis, which is that capitalist crises are cyclical.

In other words: on the one hand, crises are the modes of appearance of structural contradictions. And, on the other hand, crises give way to temporary solutions, and then every solution renews the terms of those contradictions, heightening the barrier to overcome them. Most of the available literature is focused on trying to determine whether there is such a thing as an inevitable breakdown. This is the idea of an economism or determinism.

Osborne's main insight is that Marx is not a theorist of crisis in that way. Most of the "crisis theory Marxists" tend to emphasize the "economy" part of the political economy, where there are no permanent crises. Every crisis is an opportunity for a decision; it's a decision point where something actually could change. Thus, conventional crisis theory is somewhat inadequate to the political meaning of crisis, which is conjunctural.

Osborne opens this up in a way I find useful, and he does it without prophesying a final crisis. He opposes the notion of crisis as an event with the notion of it as a process that has a duration of decades or perhaps even centuries. This keeps what Marx calls "social revolution" from being reduced to a merely political revolution.

We are in a situation today of what looks to be a broad economic collapse. It is unclear whether it's a recession that will turn into a depression or any of these types of things. But it is clear that there's a total absence of an organized left that could respond at the level of the globe to what seems to be a global crisis.

Adequate attention to existing crises would have to address three temporalities. First, there's the longue durée of the transitions between modes of production. Then, there is a second sense of crisis as part of the cycles of the political economy of capitalism. Third, it would also need to attend to all the concrete conjunctures. For example, when Osborne was writing in 2010, it was the global financial crisis. In what follows, I work through some of the other texts in the mix for today in conversation with these temporalities—suggesting how they can be brought to bear on existing crises in our discussion.

One text for this week is an excerpt from Sylvia Federici's *Caliban and the Witch*.[2] She's doing the longue durée style. She talks about the black plague creating a crisis of the supply of labor in Europe, which, in many ways, was instrumental to the transition from feudalism to capitalism.

Another text I included this week presents an example of the second of Osborne's theorised temporalities—cyclical crises of capitalism. It is "Crisis and Immiseration: Critical Theory Today" by Aaron Benanev and John Clegg.[3] It tries to do some type of assessment of the cyclical crises, especially since the industrialization, the 1970s, and with the disappearance of the worker as the revolutionary category. Then they get into stuff that's relevant today in terms of how we are looking at who the frontline workers are today—being that they are mostly people in the reproductive and service work.

Then, I included a *Monthly Review* article by Rob Wallace, "Notes on a Novel Coronavirus."[4] That's more of an example of a concrete conjuncture of today. There's one of these viruses every year, often coronaviruses. Starting with SARS to several others that didn't spread or didn't become mediaitized moments in the same way, Wallace asks, what are the conditions that lead to these "natural" crises, these viruses? He does a pretty close examination of the wet markets in China and the real subsumption of what seemed to be smallholders (people who forage for exotic animals), the industrialization of this process, the deeper trawling into the forest, the disruption of the mechanisms by which the forests have broken down transmission cycles. This is in terms of understanding how we will continue to see more and more of these viruses and outbreaks as a result of the transformations in the food supply chains. Those are the texts I have constellated for today.

The "concrete conjuncture" could be useful to think about as a bridge between historical crises and theorizing present and future crises. The conditions are often determined based on the grouping of crisis in a given temporality which may miss other narratives or make objects in history out of subjects (or leave subjects behind). — Ezra

The claim about today's limits of political action emerging from "the non-ideological fulfillment of a lot of our social democratic demands," has haunted me a lot. I don't think it was true at the time vis a vis Spain; in the sense that they actually have a somewhat socialist government which pushed the nationalization of healthcare. But maybe the hope was that Spain would show the way for others who, in the end, have bought capacity from the private sector or didn't have a public health system which could be bolstered or nationalized. It might be useful to ask ourselves whether this is basically the introduction of a "state of exception"-type of thinking all over again. Instead of gaining new insights, as always, we see the amplification of existing ideologies. This relates to how we are thinking about liberalism alongside fascism, and to revolutionary thinking in an American context: any inquiry about the distinctions between social democratic party politics and that of liberal parties, or how institutions like the state become meaningfully different in the contexts of Ireland, America, and Pakistan do not emerge as complicating forces worthy of study (even in a call for the study of purportedly concrete conjunctures of crisis). — Ari

ASMA

Thanks, Ciarán, for providing such a solid foray into the crisis of crisis. The question of duration and continuity of crises takes me to an article by Chuang that I read this morning, "Social Contagion: Microbiological War in China."[5] It puts together the geography of mass movements with the geography of crises, making apparent a diachronic relation over even just the twentieth century, as we went headlong into understanding and codifying politics as a particular kind of profession in the face of crises that we were complicit in producing, and did so at the high point of mass movements. At least, obviously initiated in the United States, there is a siphoning off of collective energy into corporate forms of tamed and managed togetherness in these social movement "organizations" and the corporate subsumption of the union. All of these things that were supposed to be redemptions are now confronting us like strangers, even enemies.

Further, the article discusses the geography of capital in relation with the geography of pandemics and disasters as one might understand them to be, even when they're natural. It really helped me think more multi-dimensionally about the idea and potentiality of the frontline worker who is, as Ciarán mentioned, engaged in reproductive and service work through the pandemic—and what ways, given these parallel and intersecting histories, we might be able to return afresh, that is, not saddled with the weight of having to defend pre-existing forms because god knows we have had to defend them so much. The question of human possibility together with each other and organizing alongside these questions of crises (and the accompanying crises they encode outside of them) is, I think, a really important one. I want to pin it to my brain for the rest of the weeks to come.

> One thread in the "Social Contagion" piece by Chuang is the movement which characterizes crisis. Crisis can be seen moving in our peripheral vision constantly and becomes more translucent as its temporality is marked. By narrating crisis in terms of response, especially state response or state-adjudicated event, it becomes difficult to see the cultivation of conditions as a fundamentalism of human-life-as-conflict. Crisis and, specifically, the stoppages and shutdowns during the proliferation of SARS-CoV2 offer the chance to see what objects and forces such as the concept of wilderness—from the scale of microbiology to the flashes of the new world waiting to be fertilised and peopled—have been kept alive for expansion of state sovereignty, capitalist accumulation, and reckless geographical annexation. — Ezra

Historical Instances of Crises and their Labors

GABE

Thank you, Asma and Ciarán, for opening this up, for your remarks, and for going through the readings. I wanted to mention one thing mostly related to the Sylvia Federici piece on the plague. It had to do with this question, Asma, that you brought up, about how crises get lumped in with calls to order. I had trouble thinking about how to situate myself or think in relation to Federici, because her work starts with the plague killing off thirty to forty percent of the European population. She sees it as an exciting and even hopeful moment for what peasants would be able to do. Our excerpt ends at a moment of great upheaval, with peasants looking to seriously take on the structures of feudalism. We know what the order was that came after that feudal order, and how the reconstitution of European society, not just through capitalism, but very soon afterwards the colonization of the Americas, went.

What are we to make of that hopefulness in relation to the reminder about what these calls to order are or can be that follow these moments? Ciarán, thank you for pointing out the different temporalities of crisis. Combining Federici with that, perhaps it might be helpful, I am now thinking, to distinguish between crises under capitalism, and the tendency toward crisis within capitalism. Liberal mainstream accounts that treat the COVID-19 pandemic as an exceptional moment often invite the response, including by the Bernie folks, "Well, no, we obviously need to understand how this is embedded within all these other structures of capitalism." This is something the Wallace article does very nicely as well. However, I am wondering, following Osborne and Federici, if the conjunctural moment we are in right now also potentially exceeds even that framing, if we are to accept that there is some element of longue durée temporality to this crisis as well. Those are my thoughts for now.

ASMA

I wonder if part of what can be brought into Federici's analysis is another thing that follows this moment: the colonization of the Americas. The Chuang essay also nudges us to track what happens in the path of these plagues—the modality and force of these disasters that spread outward and downward from the metropole, and summon the body that first receives, and then signifies, disaster, efficiently eliding the origins and sources of that disaster. Anyhow, there's a paragraph I'd like to pick up in the Chuang article that compellingly enframes a series of capitalist plagues.

> Three different pandemics occurred in eighteenth-century England, spanning 1709-1720, 1742 1760, and 1768-1786. The origin of each was imported cattle from Europe, infected by the normal pre-capitalist pandemics that followed bouts of warfare. But in England, cattle had begun to be concentrated in new ways, and the introduction of the infected stock would therefore rip through the population much more aggressively than it had in Europe. It's not coincidental, then, that the outbreaks were centered on the large London dairies, which provided ideal environments for the intensification of the virus.[6]

The text moves on and talks about how the outbreaks were managed. The next paragraph makes me think about the motion of violence outward from the metropole. The Bengal famine is a perfect example of this produced disaster. No shock that this was contemporaneous with the very idea of disease, and "diseased populations," that was flourishing with the Nazis, whom the mass murdering Churchills of the world were ostensibly fighting. This paragraph says,

> But this example from capitalism's homeland must also be paired with an explanation of the effects that capitalist agricultural practices had on its periphery. While the cattle pandemics of early capitalist England were contained, the results elsewhere were far more devastating. The example with the largest historical impact is probably that of the rinderpest outbreak in Africa that took place in the 1890s. The date itself is no coincidence: rinderpest had plagued Europe with an intensity that closely followed the growth of large-scale agriculture, only held in check by the advance of modern science. But the late 19th century saw the height of European imperialism, epitomized by the colonization of Africa. Rinderpest was brought from Europe into East Africa with the Italians, who were seeking to catch up with other imperial powers by colonizing the Horn of Africa through a series of military campaigns. These campaigns mostly ended in failure, but the disease then spread through the indigenous cattle population and ultimately found its way into South Africa, where it devastated the early capitalist agricultural economy of the colony, even killing the herd on the estate of the infamous self-professed white supremacist

Cecil Rhodes. The larger historical effect was undeniable: killing as many as 80-90% of all cattle, the plague resulted in an unprecedented famine across the predominantly pastoralist societies of Sub-Saharan Africa. This depopulation was then followed by the invasive colonization of the savannah by thornbush, which created a habitat for the tsetse fly which both carries sleeping sickness and prevents the grazing of livestock. This ensured that the repopulation of the region after the famine would be limited, and enabled the further spread of European colonial powers across the continent."[7]

So goes the production of these vulnerabilities that are going to be then sent out to the colony, presaging fascist violence as well as the global post-colony as a particular breeding ground for fascist, racist violence that learns from these particular forms of "natural" destruction.

Marx's *Eighteenth Brumaire* and I have never been much far apart since we first met, so it's no surprise that I would turn to that in this context too, reading it next to the US Civil War. Of course, we can talk about that later, but it's also important that it allows us to think of the reconstitution of the peasant, especially because the peasant becomes such an untrustable subject. There's something in the psyche of the mid-nineteenth century mobilizations that clearly Marx isn't trusting: there's a way that the political subjectivity of the farmer combines with ways of thinking about the spread of destruction, disease, and violence, in response to which capitalist, liberal restitutions seem appealing.

COLIN

I appreciate this gesture to how these iterations, these eugenicist innovations that come out of certain crises, are then applied in other places. When that experimentation happens, many do not necessarily see or realize it. And then, later, it just appears as if it's a natural progression.

There is a really remarkable series of collective actions that are happening right now in the US. It is depressing that these small things, like calling for a rent freeze in the community and actually getting it, feels so remarkable, or is such a welcome break in the narrative. What accompanies these actions is a really profound kind of presentism necessary for this collective action to even be conceivable at all. It seems to me that this presentism ensures that collective, coordinated, action proceeds only on the grounds of some sort of liberal humanitarian consensus, rather than on any other set of political premises and ideological or programmatic assumptions,or invoking other frameworks of human relations.

So, everything is conceivable right now, in this moment, but only for as long as this pandemic moment will last because, when the dust settles, we won't be able to talk about universal basic income or healthcare or things like that. I was thinking about that with respect to the Coronavirus and talking to friends and family. The presentism that underpins a generally liberal democratic orientation to elections is so familiar to us, even without the pandemic brand of crisis. It either masterfully thwarts any strategic concern or care about what comes next, or seeks to adapt election infrastructure into something that aids the struggle that lived before and beyond it.

What about those of us not actually invested in the election? Or, invested only to the extent that we actually want what comes after it? We want the friends that we make and the movement that it inspires, right? So, that's where my head's at. What you all had said before was helpful in clarifying or organizing some of the calls to order: the operations of the moment, or how certain movements and potentialities are already, preemptively, being hemmed in as these really awesome efforts of mutual aid are sprouting up quickly and effectively.

That term "eugenicist innovation," as opposed to maybe "genetic innovation," is really helpful for thinking about Federici's understanding of transition from feudalism to capitalism. It's not some kind of natural evolution between the two stages, even if there's a naturalized imagination of that transition. It's a reaction to the shift in the power dynamic between peasants and landlords that occurs as a result of the labor shortage that Gabe mentioned—a reaction against the anti-feudal peasant struggle that contains within it protests against rape, ius primae noctis, and the social-religious necessity of marriage, childbearing and childrearing. So, that way, we can think of nascent capitalism—along with the strict sexual division of labor into the productive and the reproductive—as a kind of counter-insurgent response from the lord and merchant classes, one that, like Colin and Asma mentioned, has a lot to do with the on-the-ground violence of management. — Safi

The Crisis at Hand

DAN

Much of my thinking of crisis comes from thinking about financial crises. That's not by any means all of what we see in front of us now, but it is an important piece of what's going on. One of the features of crisis is the synchronization of vastly different time scales. I think this is actually something people feel. (I feel it in our house right now.) We're in a critical moment, one where we know that the resonance of our decisions now is long. It's critical in the sense of being in the crisis and critical in the sense of being at the edge, a turning point. So, I appreciate the perspective of this conversation in the sense that we're very close to the future. We're also very close across far distances, though the irony, of course, is all that comes with us retreating into our homes.

ASMA

It's crucial to bring in the financial crisis, not only as a metaphor, but as a concrete reality, and also to ask: at what point do crises historically become separated from each other? When does the crisis secularize between the political and the financial? It is crucial to question "financial crisis" as a category itself in terms of what allows finance to be enclosed in this way as an independent realm. I think people have been saying how this shows that the removal of the C from the M–C–M transformation that Marx talks about is that which allowed us to think of finance as this self-regulating or self-reproducing force or space to begin with, which is now having to confront that absent and brutalized "C," the labor or the commodity in the middle. What better way to capture it than to think of this synchrony of times and temporalities that you're talking about, given that this is about that missing thing that allowed finance to become what it is, that missing body in the middle. The erasure, the shunning, and the secularization of biopolitics from the realm of the economy.

In this collapse of time and this rapidity that you mention, Dan, we will have to see exactly what it is about this crisis that is "vacuuming" up everything into the moment. There are people saying things like, "oh, please, everybody write your diaries and journals, so that this is all documented for those to come," and I keep thinking, "but what for," and then, "oh, wow." At some point somebody will be reading these to chronicle and to see that what was this seemingly very, very shrunken moment in time was actually not that way, because people were doing so much.

On that note, I just wonder whether Federici's hindsight is what allows her to see the longue durée, or if we create a longue durée from this moment of collapse. I think that that's part of reclaiming something. It requires jamming the quick re-assembly, but that's, again, in a hopeful, subjunctive mode. As for the relationship of militarization to production, all crises in the US are wars, even if what all its wars produce for others is crisis. Not only that it's the go-to metaphor, "this war against whatever," but also that the Defense Production Act literally is what binds war and production together. Not very non-corporatist, are we? There's a gearing of that national effort in this way and the fact that we are now talking about that here, which is also noteworthy.

GABE

I wanted to go back to a couple of things you've mentioned, Asma. First, how the epidemic keeps being discussed in militaristic terms like the phrase, "the war on the virus," and so on. I also wanted to bring up something that you also mentioned very early on in our discussion, which was the call to order being a humanitarian response. I feel like that's the other side of the same coin of terrible ways to think about the pandemic, or about crisis in general. I've been thinking and writing a lot about humanitarianism for the last couple of years, in the context of the Spanish colonization of the Americas. One thing that came to my mind last week was that there are all of these accounts from the early sixteenth century about how smallpox was introduced to the Americas by this black sailor on the conquistador Pánfilo de Narváez's ship.[8] This narrative becomes a way of shifting blame and scapegoating—that's the simplest way of putting it. The whole fault is this black sailor's. All the most obvious racial politics come in with identifying him as the person who definitively introduced smallpox to the Americas, as if no one else did it.

What I found very fascinating was that it's all done under the language of Spanish missionaries who are very "concerned." They see themselves in the frame of humanitarians, and they couch everything in terms of the care and love that they have for the indigenous people in the Americas who are being devastated by, not just smallpox, but all kinds of plagues. Being able to shift the blame onto another as needed becomes part of the job of the Spanish missionaries, as the actual humanitarian saviors of indigenous people. So thinking about how those moves to extend humanitarian care are in no way opposed to war and the logics of war, but rather can operate alongside it or do often just follow, right before or right after, the same kinds of invocations.

Thinking back to questions of solidarity and, and of having to build more than what we just overthrew—and what comes next—I've been watching way too much cable news in the last few days, and all of the threats of punishing China as a responsible party is something that keeps sticking with me. Hopefully, it's not a sign of what is to come, but at the same time, it's something that I can so easily imagine as couched in the very humanitarian language which naturalizes precursors in order to validate reactions. Phrases like, "Well, in order to protect the rest of the world," or "We've seen XYZ things…." I'm just very suspicious now of all those kinds of humanitarian moves that pretend to defend someone, but always come up with a lack of care for someone else.

ASMA

I think this makes it crucial to understand that thinking in terms of geography is not always reducible to thinking in terms of country. How might we avoid that particular trap? If we allow this to become a way to further fortify, of course, national boundaries, not only physically, but in a way that uses the state of emergency to "settle" the boundary questions and the question of boundaries in order to make countries into non-negotiable units of analysis and interlocutors in this crisis, then we are going to be reliving the origins and worst impulses of political science, with no fewer terrible effects than the first many times over. It's as if, just as we were trying to destroy political science, we become the agents of its restoration. So, I think the terms are so crucial: this moment could totally put us in a place where we unironically turn to characterizing regimes and governments in a certain way without thinking that their people are not, of course, sovereign in those places, even when these governments, so to speak, are sovereign. I think that that might be an interesting complication to bring into our lives, because it'll be very hard to remain in denial of this reality. Especially if, in the fall, near the election, when everyone's willing to forgive Donald Trump for everything. Given that he is, I think, fundamentally non-ideological, what if he can absorb so much of one's left agenda and produce actual corporate fascism which will make the last four years seem like a warm-up? So, I'm just thinking: what of the national turn, even in defense of people? I don't know what the way out is, but I think we have to start to think maybe in terms of racial, colonial/postcolonial, or transnational market geography, and in terms of the distribution of vulnerability across these boundaries rather than simply use countries as harmless shorthand without footnotes. It's a recovery of the nation, which we don't want to happen. I think it will be very tricky in the months to come, and we have to be aware of the temptations.

I had taken a look at the original Arabic of the portion of Ibn Khaldun's *Muqaddimah* that we read, and I ended up doing some re-translating.

The original text is not in verse, but it lacks punctuation—instead you read conjunctions and prepositions, usually a thread of never-ending "ands." It has an odious/ode-like quality that Arabic poetry has. And the passage itself isn't too prosaic either. So I tried to translate it into verse:

Intermezzo, from *Muqaddimah*

"And then came Al-Bakri afterwards, and he did similar things with regards to routes and estates—and with regard to little else, since the tribes and generations of that era had yet to find much motion or great transformation.

As for this era—that is the end of the eighth century [H.A., fourteenth century A.D.]—a great revolution and a total change in the conditions of the Maghreb have occurred, to which we ourselves have been spectators.

And the Berbers on foot were exiled, being replaced, in the fifth century [H.A., eleventh century A.D.], by the Arabs, who broke through them, and overpowered them, and took land-spoils, and split between each other what all was left of the Berber's estates.

That is, until what befell cities East and West in the middle of this eighth century: a vehement plague, which encroached on tribes and took with it whole generations.

And it finalized many of the fruits of civilizations and then erased them.

And the nations hence met the moments of their apexes, reached a telos, were cut down to their own shadowy limits, their authority thus weakened.

And each nation, it bid disintegration, and its funds decayed, and all construction was undone in the undoing of mankind, the undoing of what they produced and their means of production.

And note all the routes and postings, the empty manors and houses, the weakened nations and tribes.

All that rested here was transformed.

And it is as if what befell the East was similar to what had befallen the West [the Maghreb], but at its own rate and on its own scale.

And it is as if the voice of the cosmos called out in lethargy and gloom to the world, and the world responded: 'It is God who inherits the earth and all who inhabit it.'

And if you alter the totality of conditions, it is as if you have altered all of creation itself, and the world is transformed altogether—as if it were a new creation, a genesis reiterated, a world on the cutting edge.

So this this era needs scribes of the conditions of such creation and of such horizons and of such generations— and the accountabilities and associations that have changed in the hands of those who make their dwelling in them

Just as Al-Mas'udi set out to be such a scribe for his own era, so such a newness of method will be required of historians from now on."

— Safi

GABE

I had some thoughts about the García Márquez excerpt, and, actually, it's connected to the Ibn Khaldun reading as well. In *One Hundred Years of Solitude*, there's a plague of insomnia that sweeps through the town, and everyone is trying to hold on to the meaning of things.[9] Later, people start trying to label things, in order to hold onto their meanings, to keep their memories of what these objects are. But then they forget. They remember the names of the objects but they don't remember what they're for. So they start attaching longer and longer explanations to the objects. You end up with this absurd situation that García Márquez writes about, where people are doing things backwards, or they're trying to go through the motions, but it doesn't actually accord with what things were before. So, one of the characters who used to tell futures with tarot cards starts telling people their past with the cards instead. There's a severed connection to the depth of all of these actions that they're marginally able to repeat.

And, making a bit of a leap to Ibn Khaldun: I was really interested in the end of the excerpt, because he's concerned with the plague as well, and he has listed it in his introduction as one of the conditions that has reshaped the world that he's in now.[10] He says something to the effect of: "When there is a general change of conditions, it is as if the entire creation had changed and the whole world been altered, as if it were a new and repeated creation, a world brought into existence anew." He goes on to say there needs to be a new way of conceiving or writing history that accords to these new conditions. In thinking about plague and crisis through these two texts, one of the questions that comes to my mind is: what is the depth of these revolutions? Both texts give us a call for something completely new, an opportunity that I see in this moment too. Some of my concerns—and maybe some of the other concerns I hear echoed with the reminder that there's a call to order after these crises—pertain to the question of what can and must be brought forward, and what can and must be left behind. Let's not assume that these transformations are always so deep or so total; whatever is new, whatever inversions, new meanings, and forms of knowledge-production that follow them are just there to be done. But we'll still have to remain with the question of what is still being brought forward underneath the semblance of having to constitute a new order. So, what is that depth of the revolution or change, and what is it that still carries on underneath it, and how to be vigilant and attentive to that?

PHILIP

I want to think about history and collective fiction because the first time Gabe spoke, he called coronavirus an "exceptional moment." Colin talked about rent moratoriums and that for the first time they are suddenly realistic. I've been reading Mark Fisher's *Capitalist Realism*, where he says that, "...emancipatory politics must always destroy the appearance of a 'natural order', must reveal what is presented as necessary and inevitable to be a mere contingency, just as it must make what was previously deemed to be impossible seem attainable."[11] It also ties into something Chris Carrico said, when he talked about this moment of political education and the rethinking of what is realistic. We have to keep an eye out for accumulated fictions that have developed and that might hinder what we ask for and what we imagine is possible.

JODY

At the same time, Philip, I guess I'd point out how almost fictional this moment feels. It's as if it's part of a movie script or out of some sort of author's head. Everything from the distinctions between the Sanders campaign and the Biden campaign, to the immediate succumbing of the Sanders campaign, more or less, in that one debate—I don't know if anyone watched it, a sort of one-on-one debate, where real ideological rifts were on display in terms of whether you think about the now or you think about the future, whether you think about the little picture or you think about the big picture. And from both perspectives being explored in that debate, to the perspectives of this moment, whatever this virus is and what it will become, the identifications of these differences have exploded.

It's just stunning how much of the rotten contours of everything are being exposed. People were talking earlier about how it's hard to argue with liberals, and one calling card of liberals' deck has been how unemployment is down and at healthy levels. The retort there has been that a lot of those jobs are very precarious. And then, the counter-retort is something like, "we're giving people something at least." And now you have a situation where unemployment is skyrocketing, and I think I remember seeing it might go as high as 20% depending on how this unfolds. It's like every facet of what people have been idly and airily discussing for the past couple months across the Democratic Primary is now being folded into something that's more real and physical than it's ever been before (at least for some people). And even the solutions that we could maybe agree upon as being necessary can only be fulfilled by mechanisms that are disgusting, right? Like the thing where Andrew Cuomo had New York state prisoners mass produce hand sanitizer. I think we could say it's a useful thing to have the State doing, but he did it by prison labor and paying prisoners less than $1 an hour to produce it.

ASMA

I think a question could be: What is the plane of this motion, right? Are things moving? Is this something that grows and engulfs and then leaves other things aside? Or is the movement more archaeological? It's a really interesting challenge—to work at least on these two axes, of thinking of what isn't bargaining, or exactly what's left in our hands when, maybe, Trump takes on universal basic income or something—and then what do we do? What is the effect of that appropriation on something else? And connected to the way that Gabe is invoking the figure of depth in the reading of *One Hundred Years of Solitude*—it is really, really interesting—this issue of layers of time also, besides the movement forward and back.

I wonder if there is a way to think about how this task of remembering is to be held? Maybe it's just such a useless thought experiment, but if one thinks of the fact that we're not just in the movement of structures, that we are actually agents of these motions of time, then neoliberalism has done something to us that beholds us to these particular dangers in a real way. So, I'm just thinking about a reimagining and reallocation of life in a collective mode, or life in forms of mutuality, that are going to also have to repair the neoliberal subject.

SAFI

Taking this question back to Gabe's leap to Ibn Khaldun, as introductory as the passage from the *Muqaddimah* is, we glean from its understanding of history a kind of early historical materialism. The "vehement" plague and reactions to it are spoken of at the same register as the daily maintenance of the medieval states that it disintegrated. So, foreshadowing, even if in hushed tones, Rousseau's account of the Lisbon earthquake, for example, Ibn Khaldun's account of the plague is an account of political history as opposed to natural history. And it is the plague in his account—like Federici's in hindsight—and the responses to the plague, that precipitate in a moving forward of time on that longue durée scale, as well as, therefore, requiring, as Gabe brought up, a new way of reading and spectating upon and scribing and inscribing that history.

At the same time, I'm thinking about Michael Dols' comparison between medieval Christian and Islamic responses to the plague.[12] He explains that the Islamicate response seemingly void of the kind of racial-religious scapegoating present in Christendom—and that Gabe explained earlier played a vital role in the dual humanitarian-military logic of the Spanish colonization of the New World. Something else missing from (at least some) Muslim-world responses to the plague, which is an apocalypticism or a millenarianism. Maybe, then, that "newness" that Ibn Khaldun describes at length of the post-plague world—and he uses quite a few words to encapsulate all the kinds of "newness" that entails, to the point that it's important to strain one's ear and hear "cutting-edge" instead of "modern"—is at the same time not a total break in time. It requires a different sense—yes, what Gabe brought up—a depth of historical temporalities in crisis and revolution. Or, what Asma proposed, an understanding of the layering or sedimentation of time.

ASMA

Absolutely, thanks for that contribution. I think that might be the place where we're thinking of the lateral or oblique movements of history, in addition to the depth that Gabe is talking about. I mean the worst thing that can happen is if in the turn to the biopolitical we forget the subject that was produced. I think that that's maybe where the task of educating and the political consciousness that Emir and Chris have both referred to lies. But alongside that, this role of memory to unhinge us, this kind of clumping of time, I think, is really crucial. So I can't believe I'm saying, "Oh, we have to create a linearity by unpacking the coronavirus molecule," but I think that there's something to be said for what gets engulfed and appropriated in the congealing of movement. And, perhaps part of the Marxist method—for lack of a better term— is to disarticulate these things that seem to congeal and clump together in a moment of crisis and make us equally clumps or congealed feeling and labor and whatnot. I think this plagues us right now, and I think that, in a strange way the almost defeat of the Sanders campaign will entrench the defensiveness around certain ways of everyone feeling so wronged, when it is instead a chance to take some responsibility for what memory we are not factoring into the words that we have used and will use.

SAFI

Yes, and if early and medieval Islamic responses to the plague weren't millenarian or apocalyptic, and yet are able to, in Ibn Khaldun's case, offer new ways of, for example, approaching history, then they move against the lure of the logic of the virus' total annihilation, toward an approach that brings us into a new mode of sensibility and reading instead of a new mode of fatalism.

On the Present Crisis

ASMA

I had posted a link to James Russell Lowell's poem called "The Present Crisis" that was written in 1844-5, when slavery was considered a crisis—another war. (It also turns out to be the spur to Du Bois's naming of the NAACP journal in 1910). And that particular poem and the moment it describes is helpful to me in thinking about the crises of the US alongside European colonization and European revolutions—which thought about the movements of revolutionaries and the people who were doing things very differently—and a countermotion to the way European countries were establishing their own empires and closing their boundaries internally. I think that that's where the idea of crisis seems to do something other than call to order. And, I wonder if we can unhear that call, to hear something else instead.

[We play an audio recording of Lowell's "The Present Crisis."][13]

[...]

Through the walls of hut and palace shoots the instantaneous throe,
When the travail of the Ages wrings earth's systems to and fro;
At the birth of each new Era, with a recognizing start,
Nation wildly looks at nation, standing with mute lips apart,
And glad Truth's yet mightier man-child leaps beneath the Future's heart.

So the Evil's triumph sendeth, with a terror and a chill,
Under continent to continent, the sense of coming ill,
And the slave, where'er he cowers, feels his sympathies with God
In hot teardrops ebbing earthward, to be drunk up by the sod,
Till a corpse crawls round unburied, delving in the nobler clod.

[...]

Backward look across the ages and the beacon-moments see,
That, like peaks of some sunk continent, jut through Oblivion's sea;
Not an ear in court or market for the low, foreboding cry
Of those Crises, God's stern winnowers, from whose feet earth's chaff must fly;
Never shows the choice momentous till the judgment hath passed by.

New occasions teach new duties; Time makes ancient good uncouth;
They must upward still, and onward, who would keep abreast of Truth;
Lo, before us gleam her camp-fires! we ourselves must Pilgrims be,
Launch our Mayflower, and steer boldly through the desperate winter sea,
Nor attempt the Future's portal with the Past's blood-rusted key.

CIARÁN

How do you feel it speaks to our theme of politics contra crisis?

ASMA

The way it even framed the moral question: slavery does something to challenge that particular way of thinking about time that moral claims have to rely on. For its time—and it's three years before the *Communist Manifesto*—I am drawn to the fact that it is able to frame the question of slavery and abolition in terms of things that are cross-continental. Again, I don't need to see the mid-nineteenth century as somehow the age of ignorance by any means. But something has always struck me, that certain things that were happening in that moment—even in the US around abolition—that were far more forward-looking and far more "global" and sharply-framed than the modes in which gender and race conversations translate that legacy after the Civil War. And this is why, of course, the crisis is indexed in Du Bois: publishing *Crisis*, clearly invoking this poem. So for me, the fact that there is a way that something that is a moral question, and of sense of what it means for human beings to make certain kinds of decisions, is not relegated to a realm of a claim to humanity or to a form of secular morality—that is for me anti-political—seems like an amazing way to frame the crisis. Because it's so paltry when everything, then, gets, in contemporary times, whittled down to an ethical-moral issue. The poem doesn't sound like this, right? There's something humanitarianism does that disfigures what is present in this call to crisis—I feel that. So my sense of trying to, first, make politics into something that it isn't, in order for it to call on and encounter crisis through this act of disarticulating that which seems to be clumped and has no history, seems important and very anachronistic given what we are made to think of struggles in the US, I guess. And then that normalization of a form of national discourse around everything.

CIARÁN

Thank you.

ASMA

I mean, if we were to read this next to the spectre that's haunting Europe, I think that would be really interesting.

COLIN

Yeah, that would be cool.

Postscript to the Present Crisis

MILO

The conversations Hic Rosa hosted from March to May transpired during the crystallization of a set of connected world-historic crises. The leading crisis, the pandemic, was widely received by most on the left as a dimension of other interlocking crises: an an ecological crisis brought on by global capital markets and industrial farming; the crisis of the neoliberal state, particularly its barbarous delimiting of health capacity and political will to profit margins; the yawning economic precipice that appeared as labor markets skidded to a halt; the crisis of political direction and organization in the US left following the collapse of the Sanders campaign; the crisis of apprehension resulting from the flickering glimpses of the many faces of incipient or routine fascism well within the berms of liberal society; and then, the struggle in the streets of cities across the US, spilling into streets around the world, which might appropriately be seen as a crisis of the authority of the police order. The ballistics that lit up mass perception to old and new conditions, the snap and crack of conjunctions, provoked every party with an eschatology of crisis to race to distribute sewing patterns to darn the torn fabric of the day back together with some design of past and future. These, of course, only exacerbated the general crisis of epistemology that had already been the preferred response by liberals to the waning popularity of their own brand of politics and sensibilities since their unimaginable loss to Trump in 2016. Of course, the rebranding of truth and knowledge as a post-Trump imperative, does not encompass the epistemic spasms that have continued to agonize and organize both critical and neoliberal administrative discourse in academia for some time. Similarly, for much of the left in the US, the various crises of 2020 have only enhanced the condition of endless paroxysms of organizational and strategic acrimony, which rarely go beyond fretting over the absence of a coherent project or point of embarkment for action.

In *The Eighteenth Brumaire of Louis Bonaparte*, Marx comments on a similar series of events where various social and political struggles, seemingly caught circling the drain of inescapable crisis, suddenly break out of what Marx describes as a revolutionary ouroboros—or where present movements are tethered to the limits of past ones—as "conditions themselves cry out Hic Rhodus, hic salta! Here is the rose, dance here!"[15] We have read this not to mean that crisis manifests a political prescription that relieves the paralysis of revolution through the coronation of the object of political strategy, but where the crisis yields to the often otherwise unthinkable capacity and possibility to reach one another, together becoming responsible to something without succumbing to what Asma has described as the compulsion within liberalism to translate the exigencies of crisis into "tragic unfreedom" where markets of tough decisions are ruled by the logic of scarcity, and where victims of decision are reconciled through "abstract principle[s] of action."[16] So in this way, developments like the mutual aid efforts that sprung up around the world, appeared not as laboratories or experiments in finding ways out of the crises of the day, but as a refusal to become the managers of subcontracting the subjects of the revolution, and of making the revolution the way of reaching the subjects of the crisis.

Asma links the revolutionary episteme of politics that Marx articulates in the Brumaire with Lowell's description of the moment of abolitionist catharsis. Du Bois recognized this link when he reflected on what the actual stakes of having to take on the abolition of the institution of slavery, meant, connected to, in terms of other struggles, both nationally and internationally. He writes in *Black Reconstruction*:

> The true significance of slavery in the United States to the whole social development of America lay in the ultimate relation of slaves to democracy. What were to be the limits of democratic control in the United States? If all labor, black as well as white, became free—were given schools and the right to vote—what control could or should be set to the power and action of these laborers? Was the rule of the mass of Americans to be unlimited, and the right to rule extended to all men regardless of race and color, or if not, what power of dictatorship and control; and how would property and privilege be protected? This was the great and primary question which was in the minds of the men who wrote the Constitution of the United States and continued in the minds of thinkers down through the slavery controversy. It still remains with the world as the problem of democracy expands and touches all races and nations.[17]

In his framing of the question of democracy or rather the questionionable future of democracy as inextricably tied up with slavery in the US, Du Bois projects how this problem is inseparable from the fate of the rest of the working people of the world. The slave issue, he explains, is an issue of democracy, just as the issue of democracy cannot be recognized or resolved without treating it as an issue of colonialism, which is of course also one of capitalism. Simply, the moment of abolition that Lowell bores into, that Du Bois reads from the nineteenth into the twentieth century, sutures revolutionary cause to all that had been deceptively abstracted apart.

As insightful as the analytic defragging of this band of domination is, it is important how Du Bois gleans the events of abolition as not simply initiated through some broader theoretical tendency that culminates in the movement, but by the actions of the enslaved during the Civil War. Du Bois describes what slaves and freed people did during the Civil War as a general strike, and these were waged on two fronts: first, in spite of the total resistance to and lack of desire by the Union Army to free the slaves from Confederate territories that fell under Union control or to incorporate them into the general struggle of the war, these freed people refused to leave the army—despite often terrible conditions, receiving little to no aid, and often facing outright violence from the Union Army. The formerly-enslaved literally made encampments alongside the Union encampments, following, assisting, and aiding in the effort to liberate the rest of the country and their comrades in bondage. This strike, this occupation of the army, was the abolitionist pressure that forced the political powers in the north and the army itself to submit to the new reality that the war they were fighting was to be directed for the purposes of those below and not by Washington. The second, was the general slow down by the slaves on the plantations, putting a drag on the slave engine that fueled the slaveholders fight with the North. Particularly, the first revolutionary action, taken by freed slaves, for Du Bois, must be recognized for its revolutionary entanglements, for it is by refusing to fall into whatever new condition of dispossession and relegatory distribution the north would have left for them, these people redirected the meaning of the conflict and initiated a recognition of their social reality, which had to reconfigure what the democracy would do with that reality, which forced the government to begin, even before the war was over, to collaborate with them into building the social responses that became the first social welfare program in the US—the Freedmen's Bureau, which regardless of its devolution and the real issues of its implementation, must be recognized as preceding even Bismarck's mass welfare programs in Germany.

Setting aside matters of purely historical importance, identifying how something that Du Bois wants to call the general strike, which for him is to recuperate the real social action taken by those who have only been understood as victims or objects of abolitionist struggle, can be seen as in dialogue with what Marx apprehends in the Paris Commune. Marx writes in *Civil War in France*:

> All reactions and revolutions had only served to transfer that organized power—that organized force of the slavery of labor—from one hand to the other, from one fraction of the ruling class to the other. It had served the ruling classes as a means of subjugation and of self. It had sucked new forces from every new change. It had served as the instrument of breaking down every popular rise and served it to crush the working classes after they had fought and been ordered to secure its transfer from one part of its oppressors to the others. This was, therefore, a revolution not against this or that Legitimate, Constitutional, Republican, or Imperialist form of state power. It was a revolution against the state itself, this supernaturalist absorption of society, a resumption by the people for the people of its social life. It was not a revolution to transfer it from one fraction of the ruling classes to the other, but a revolution to break down this horrid machinery of class domination itself. It was not one of those dwarfish struggles between the executive and the parliamentary forms of class domination, but a revolt against both these forms, integrating each other, and of which the parliamentary form was only the deceitful by-work of the executive. The Second Empire was the final form of this state usurpation. The commune was its definite negation, and, therefore, the initiation of the social revolution of the nineteenth century....The Commune—the reabsorption of the state power by society as its own living forces instead of as forces controlling and subduing it, by the popular masses themselves, forming their own force instead of the organized force of their suppression—the political form of their social emancipation, instead of the artificial force (appropriated by their oppressors (their own force opposed to

and organized against them) of society wielded for their oppression by their enemies. The form was simple, like all great things..."[18]

Echoing Marx, Du Bois views the general strike as a departure from the normal play of political conflicts, which merely shuttle between different forms and authors of class domination. Common to the Commune and the general strike was a struggle that went beyond the object of whatever particular crisis in organization of the state had catalyzed the conflict of the day, to a more revolutionary self-recognition by a people that the pretexts for their own domination and fragmentation are illegitimate and on the basis of this self-aware sociality, they cannot accept yet another "reabsorption," to use Marx's word, into some new arrangement with the same outcomes. This social consciousness, or the social consciousness of these movements, is what separates Marxist social revolutionary ideas and radical abolitionist ones from the more common liberal interpretations of these struggles.

Whatever the direct antagonisms that provoke a revolutionary situation, when struggle becomes one for social life for itself, it poses a threat to the vast constellation of forms of authority that order the status quo. In such moments, those powers which enforce social reality as a disorienting kaleidoscope of irreconcilables are revealed for the more naked forms of coercion, which conservatives like Edmund Burke recognized as fundamentally interconnected and perpetually vulnerable—no concessions could be made to even the liberal revolutionaries of the past, just as today conservatives understand that bent knees during an anthem, if left unchecked, can lead to the collapse of any other kind of legitimacy of authority. Of course, the mysticism of defiance does not substitute for the necessity that material conditions are available to meaningfully challenge a status quo or respond to a crisis. For Du Bois, these freed people, just by refusing to disband at any cost, presented an unlimited threat to racial capital and settler democracy, because in that system there was nothing that could incorporate this force, and therefore, their social reality became one that not only directed the purposes of the war, but also put the entire system in jeopardy.

Notes

1.   Peter Osborne, "A Sudden Topicality." *Radical Philosophy*, 160 (March/April 2010), 19-26, accessed December 26, 2020, https://www.radicalphilosophy.com/article/a-sudden-topicality.

2.   Silvia Federici, *Caliban and the Witch: Women, the Body and Primitive Accumulation* (New York: London: Autonomedia; Pluto, 2004).

3.   Aaron Benanav and John Clegg, "Crisis and Immiseration: Critical Theory Today," in *The SAGE Handbook of Frankfurt School Critical Theory* (SAGE Publications Ltd, 2018).

4.   Rob Wallace, "Notes on a novel coronavirus," *Monthly Review* Online, published January 29, 2020, https://mronline.org/2020/01/29/notes-on-a-novel-coronavirus/.

5.   Chuang, "Social Contagion: Microbiological War in China," published February 2020. http://chuangcn.org/2020/02/social-contagion/.

6.   Chuang, "Social Contagion."

7.   Chuang. "Social Contagion."

8.   Geronimo De Mendieta, *Historia Eclesiástica Indiana: A Franciscan's View of the Spanish Conquest of Mexico.* (Lewiston: Edwin Mellen Press, 1997).

9.   Gabriel García Márquez, *One Hundred Years of Solitude* (New York: Harper, 2006), 417.

10.   Mark Fisher, *Capitalist Realism: Is There No Alternative?* (Winchester, UK: Washington, D.C.: Zero Books, 2009), 17.

11.   Ibn Khaldun. *Muqaddimat Ibn Khaldun.* (Beirut: Al-Matbaa' Al-Adabiyyah, 1900). See also: Ibn Khaldun. *The Muqaddimah: An Introduction to History: Abridged Edition.* Trans. Franz Rosenthal. Ed. N.J. Dawood. (Princeton: Princeton University Press, 2020).

12.   Michael Dols. "The Comparative Communal Responses to the Black Death in Muslim and Christian Societies." *In Viator*, vol. 5. 1974. pp. 269-287.

13.   James Russell Lowell, "The Present Crisis," 1844. https://poets.org/poem/present-crisis. Accessed December 26, 2020.

14.   *Gramsci 44*, directed by Emiliano Barbucci (2016; Italy: Ram Film, 2016), DVD.

15.   Karl Marx, *The Eighteenth Brumaire of Louis Bonaparte*, 1852. Trans. Saul K. Padover (CreateSpace Independent Publishing Platform, [1852]2015).

16.   Asma Abbas, *Liberalism and Human Suffering: Materialist Reflections on Politics, Ethics, Aesthetics* (New York: Palgrave Macmillan, 2010).

17.   W.E.B. Du Bois, *Black Reconstruction* (United Kingdom: Free Press, 2019), 13.

18.   Karl Marx, *The Civil War in France* (London, 1871).

On fascism and hunger

So, I saw a documentary, *Gramsci 44*.[14] Gramsci gets sentenced to exile on the island of Ustica with a bunch of other people for two years. Ends up being sent away from there to Turin after 44 days for getting into trouble with the local fascists. It's a really painful film, and I didn't expect it to be so, I don't know why I didn't. It has some reenactment but most of it is just narrative documentary. By the way, today is the 25th of April, the anniversary of the end of fascist regime and Nazi occupation, and Gramsci didn't live to see that day. The film keeps returning to one guy, who remembers fascists and hunger together every time, without fail. I have never seen something that does that so simply and beautifully convey hunger as a unit of the memory of fascism. Watching in a class on education, we had a moment of realising that "all of the living memories of that moment are the memories of people who were children then." So you have this act of remembering the interlude of time, mutuality, and possibility where Gramsci and other exiles create a school in this penal colony. (This same island didn't even have a high school until 1991.) Why is it that in this moment of people building alternative institutions to literally feed and sustain each other, fascism and its history are rendered irrelevant to the task at hand and besides the point, and the memory of fascism today seems exclusively wielded in relation to ideas of freedom or repression? Let's, for a moment, not sunder the memory of fascism from the memory of hunger. It might be necessary practice in thinking about institutions concretely: not erasing the memory of what it is that they are responding to. I think most of what flabbergasts me about being in the US is, and I know it sounds banal and repetitive to say, "what we don't remember." But I also think that the insistence on proceeding on certain terms seems to be an instance of the success of the university as an imperial institution and its convenient amnesia when it comes to fascism's internal relations to class, race, and colony—anything but liberalism and that, too, in a fake alarmist relation to individual freedom and such. We have to keep the memory of hunger attached to fascism, and keep a memory of the worker connected to, for instance, all the brutalizations and indignity suffered by the body within and beyond the frame of wage labor that are the past of today's present. I think Chris said this last week, that we need to be really thinking about our capacities and being honest about what these past decades have shaped us to be able to do, including showing up for each other in certain ways.—Asma

first interlude

CALLS
FROM
THE
IMPASSE

The End of the (End of the) World

Silvana Carotenuto

where danger threatens
grows also what saves
– Friedrich Hölderlin

Today, a "tone" speaks the generalized culture of the apocalypse in the world:

> ... Hegelian eschatology... the eschatology of Marxism... the end of history, the end of class struggle, the end of philosophy, the death of god, the end of religions, the end of the subject, the end of man, the end of the West, the end of Oedipus, the end of the earth. Apocalypse Now, I tell you, in the cataclysm, the fire, the blood, the fundamental earthquake, the napalm descending from the sky by helicopters... and also the end of literature, the end of painting, art as a thing of the past, the end of psychoanalysis, the end of the university, the end of phallocentrism and phallogocentrism... [1]

In "Of an Apocalyptic Tone Recently Adopted in Philosophy," Jacques Derrida is interested in understanding the "structure" of the "apocalyptic" discourse, which, as he greatly fears, might bear the extreme consequence of putting an end to all critical interpretation of the end of (the end of) the world. Aware of using the tone of/in his writing, the philosopher chooses two specific bibliographic references in order to analyze and deconstruct the complex question. First, it is the interpretation offered by Immanuel Kant in the pamphlet "Of an Overlordly Tone Recently Adopted in Philosophy" (1796), (whose title is "mimed," "parodied," "departed from," and "deformed by" the Derridean essay); it follows the retracing of its Biblical origin in the discourse devoted to the "Apocalypse" by the apostle John.

Kant vindicates the concept of Reason against the use of metaphors that the "mystagogues" of his time adopted to announce the end of the world. Derrida accepts Kant's appeal to vigil thinking, advocating, at the same time, the deconstruction of the binomy of "concept" and "metaphor" which is essential to the German philosopher's analysis, if the latter is necessarily co-implicated with its other, and if both need to be valued in the overcoming of any simplistically negative interpretation of the apocalyptic discourse. Derrida thinks of the "conceptual metaphor" in full expression in the Biblical Apocalypse, through the composition of the scene in which John reports what Jesus prescribes to him on the end of the world. The "structure" of the scene is exposed to deconstructive reading: Jesus does not present himself to John but dictates his vision through the "tone" of his voice; in its turn, John's task is to transcribe what Jesus's tone dictates. "Absence" frees the apocalyptic discourse from any identifiable address or destination, disseminating in the future-to-come of its reception. The proliferation and division of the tone advocates its difference from the presence of the subject; testimony is given as writing as writing appears as testimony; the whole scene inscribes the always-possible non-arrival of the letter. It is finally the injunction "Come"–*veni, veins*–that marks the spacing of the voice promising what, perhaps, one day, might save and protect from the–risk of the–end of the world. "Come" structurally says salvation from the apocalypse, in that–also explaining why Derrida adopts the apocalyptic "tone" in his writing– it refuses to be caught in any representative or categorical frame, materializing the "end" of the "end of the world":

> "Come," opening the scene, could not become an object, a theme, a representation, or even a citation in the current sense, and subsumable under a category, whether that of coming or event...[2]
>
> ... the catastrophe would perhaps be of the apocalypse itself, its fold and its end, a closure without end, an end without end).[3]

In the contemporary time exposed to global catastrophe, the deconstructive analysis of the "structure" of the discourse on "the end of (the end of) the world" incises its tone in the scroll "Apocalypse" presented by the Chinese artist Bingyi at the Museum of Modern Art, in Istanbul, in 2016 (its creation dates the period 2011-2014), during the collective exhibition on art and ecology entitled "Till it's gone."[4] The scroll consists of an immense silk-panel (2600 x 90 cm), painted in ink wash, which, in the artist's vigilance on the generalized rhetoric of the end of the world, is not meant to reproduce any apocalyptic event, but rather to pay attention to/take care of the anxiety and fears of the ones exposed to the threat of the end of the world. In determination or sensitiveness, the scroll inscribes the deconstructive structure on/of the Apocalypse in its full composition.

In order to create her work, Bingyi goes back to the originary tradition of the Song-dynasty, the period when, as she greatly appreciates, poetry and painting come together. Positioning her art in this historical aesthetic setting, what motivates her artistic engagement is not an individual will or the subjective decision to deal with the apocalypse, but the desire to respond to an "injunction." In 2008, while working on an installation in the area of Sichuan, Bingyi witnesses a terrible earthquake followed by massive flooding: "I did not anticipate it, nobody could; I was just working there ... I did not go to the earthquake site, the earthquake come to me."[5] The "coming" of the injunction resounds like the raising of Jesus's voice here translating "tone" into tonos: "... the tight ligament, cord, rope when it is woven or braided."[6] Bingyi responds to the injunction that comes from the catastrophe by bringing testimony thought her "writing," l'oeuvre that weaves, braids, ties together eight parts, movements, phases or poetic "sentences":

> 1. Shattered earth, crumbled heaven (it is the world wide open and the observation of the

coexistence of humans and nature);

2. An earthquake petrifies the world (like a fossil);

3. Lost souls and wandering ghosts (it is the earth that rumbles underneath the magnificent continent);

4. Knotted trees (the wood grows into a knotted forest);

5. A thousand mountains under water (in an instant, mountains and seas collapse);

6. Drifting wood (logs, chips and splinters in their drift);

7. A grave for the masses (in one pit lies the burial of the dead);

8. A secret garden (seven years later, the cells of the trees remake a garden). [7]

"Apocalypse" is the "compositional allegory"–because "visually-driven"–which writes on its silk scroll a series of explosions, homeless spirits, fairies, strange creatures and fantastic forms, human and superhuman shapes. Its intricate textile shows gigantic mountains, caves, ghosts and faces, inviting the viewer to ceremonies of burial where gigantic flowers transform into fireworks. The scroll is "apocalyptic" in that, by unfolding/opening from right to left, it discloses, uncovers, unveils, displays, and allows seeing (donne à voir) the terrible destruction, and, in the same coup, the event of its overcoming. Its unfolding reveals, in the end, which is a beginning, the act of nature which re-appropriates the site of the earthquake and the flood, seven years after their happening, by producing "a secret garden," as recites the last sentence of the poetic textile. Will this natural image provide the assurance of safety and protection from the catastrophic threat? Indeed, the "dissemination" of its "Festivity" (at the end of the artistic tour, the scroll, which has proved apt for agile transportation, shows, in the exposure to the usury of time, the finite materiality of its tatters and "ruins") unfolds its new vision to the eye and the mind:

> Is the earthquake the same for humans and for insects? Could it not be that, from the "point of view" of the bugs, it liberates from obstacles and difficulties so as to sign a Festivity? Should we not deconstruct the centrality of (the stance, the point of view of) the human so as to allow the "come" of the natural world? [8]

If, for the benefit of the scroll, "Come" rises from the natural world, it signs for Bingyi the arrival of the art of painting. The uncanny scroll unravels the unanticipated encounter of thinking and practice, given in singularity and concentration, resonance and fluidity, beyond all individual perspectives, as the emergence of their co-existence in the journey which, in its destinerrance, opens the apocalyptic "Come" to the secret of "happiness." Bingyi states her welcoming address to the art of painting in this long poetic passage:

> I could not imagine your arrival, neither its time nor its place.
>
> I could not imagine your fierceness, your speed, your quietude, your mystery, your nuance, your agility, your existence. I could not even imagine your form. Your appearance could not be

anticipated, just as we can never predict a flood. A flood eradicates all intelligent life, but it also creates the greatest opening for myriad things to flourish. A flood is nature's mutation.

My painting! ...

How far I traveled in life before our encounter! The solitude and insecurity of this experience, and the patience and attention it demands, only those who have gone through it can know. Because of your singularity, I realized that I could only sense your presence in complete concentration. Only when my world was void, only when I was in the deepest and most unforgiving state, could I feel your peace. You emptied yourself completely to give my contemplating mind the only possible space for resonance.

So you needed me to be quiet, pure, lucid. I could not be moved by anything else. In this way you became the only fluid form in my world. All time and space was still. You--like a flood, like a wild beast — consumed me whole.

... This is my message to painting: ... What painting needs is not a self-centered painter. What it needs is someone who knows how to live with it. To coexist with a flood and a wild beast is to transcend life. It is to embark on a journey to uncover an infinitude of beauty

and potential--a journey distant, uncertain, without destination, without structure, but one that ultimately gives us utmost happiness.[9]

Notes

1. Jacques Derrida, "Of an Apocalyptic Tone Adopted in Philosophy," *Oxford Literary Review*, vol. 6, n.2 (1984), 20-21.

2. Derrida, 33.

3. Derrida, 35.

4. See http://www.istanbulmodern.org/en/exhibitions/past-exhibitions/till-its-gone_1743.html; and https://www.artforum.com/uploads/guide.003/id18941/press_release.pdf. For Bingyi's career, see Ink Studio, "Bingyi - Overview," http://www.inkstudio.com.cn/artists/75-bingyi/overview/. For an overview of her poetics, see also A. Majid, "Seeing the Unseen World: The Art of Bingyi," in *Yishu Journal of Contemporary Chinese Art* (14:6), Nov/Dec 2015.

5. See "Apocalypse: An Interview with Bingyi!" accessed on December 27, 2020. http://www.inkstudio.com.cn/video/8/.

6. Derrida, "Of an Apocalyptic Tone Adopted in Philosophy," 8.

7. For the details of the work's eight sentences, cf. "Bingyi: Apocalypse," trans. Alan Yeung, accessed on December 27, 2020, http://www.inkstudio.com.cn/press/27/,

8. From the transcript of an interview with Bingyi, see "Apocalypse: An Interview with Bingyi," 2015, accessed on December 27, 2020, http://www.inkstudio.com.cn/video/8/.

9. Bingyi, "Painting is a Flood and a Wild Beast," 2017, accessed on December 27, 2020, https://www.inkstudio.com.cn/press/17-painting-is-a-flood-and-a-wild-beast/.

March 15th, Plague Dreams

Colin Eubank

Gabriel García Márquez tells the story of an insomnia plague that infects a remote town called Macondo.[1] While José Arcadio Buendía greets this plague as the neoliberal dream of infinite productivity—a town with workers that never sleep, who squeeze as much as they can out of life—it is the Indian who clarifies the devastating malady that comes with insomnia: forgetting. The loss of sleep becomes the loss of memories. Buendía swiftly organizes the community into a quarantine, devising a new normal wherein the townsfolk restore the rhythm of work, and a life without sleep becomes natural. The slow march of amnesia is met with a rigorous but futile combat to preserve the present. Although everything has its name written on it so as to preempt forgetting, the relentless loss of memory makes it possible (according to Buendía) that one day, sometime in the future, we might remember these things (forks and pigs and the like) without ever really being able to remember their proper use.

One Hundred Years of Solitude demonstrates the cycle of problem and solution that animates choreographies of crisis in global neoliberal capitalism today; it lays bare the eugenic efficiencies tested in the pronouncements of state emergency; it articulates a new normal born precisely of these predatory experiments while praising the supposed miracles of human resilience and pragmatism in the face of catastrophe; and it performs the relentless presentism required for awesome bouts of collective action premised on the parlays liberalism makes with enduring fascisms in the name of humanitarianism.

But the plague also brings to mind the necessary relationship between memory (or history) and dreams (or futurity)—a relationship that might be more instructive than the aforementioned lessons of the plague. The townsfolk lose their capacity to remember because they no longer have the capacity to dream. If our attentiveness to history is only made worthwhile by our dreams and desires for a future, the gift of futurity seems something too precious to sacrifice to the maintenance of a present that can, at best, guarantee a preservation of the past. Are dreams and desires today really so rare, so indulgent, that their defense in general is required? (This is not really a philosophical question. Look no further than the Democratic Primaries to find an answer.) Have we come to inhabit such an impoverished position so as not to be able to make a distinction between the kind of claims one can (and does!) make on behalf of a shared future?

For instance, José Arcadio Buendía's revelation about the possibility of forgetting the proper use of things, from the vantage point of the present, seems like a bad dream—one where we know bread is called bread, but we do not know that it is used for eating—about the cessation of life itself, the complete loss of traditions, a dream about the end of the world. But this is because it is the dream of a man who has already forgotten how to dream, a man who has no sense of future. It is a liberal who has forgotten what possibility beyond property might actually mean. If claimed another way, could not this possible future be the liberation some of us have long desired? A liberation from the constraints of present exploitative structures arbitrating proper use as a mask over the possible uses of things that could flourish when finally allowed to dance beyond their chains?

Let's counter Buendía and his bad dreams with another one, delivered to Mexico on International Women's Day, where a mobilization brought women to the streets all across Latin America in a show of force stronger than ever before. The following day, March 9, Mexico then witnessed their absence, as women and gender non-comforming persons across the country participated in a general strike and "disappeared" from the visual, cultural, economic, and emotional circuits of capitalist operation to protest the statistically high rate of femicidal violence in Mexico. Here in Oaxaca, many compare this awakening to a sense of profound possibility felt back in 2006, when the teachers unions brought the city to a halt, building a commune in the Zocalo, broadcasting messages across the state in occupied university radio stations, mobilizing convoys to occupy key locations in Mexico City, and openly resisting the austerity measures imposed by the municipal police and national guard in the streets.

While the mandatory curfews and neighborhood lockdowns of 2006 smothered a political movement, Oaxaca's calls for COVID-19 quarantine won't allow the public to evade the pressures of the political moment today. A week ago, on March 8 and 9, when many women refused to cast their lot in the service of this world, they began building another both in the street and in their homes. Now, as husbands are being sent home from work and children are turned away from schools, all have no choice but to return home. Those of us committed to politics today have already conscripted our homes in the service of another future—claiming it for other possible uses. In other words, we find ourselves in a situation where we know a home to be a home, but we are forgetting its proper use as the womb of machismo culture, the private domain where we beat and abuse each other, the space wherein the endless labors of care-taking are constantly presumed and always also repudiated. Feminist rebels, in virtual and physical networks, have cast the home as something otherwise: a site of sociality and solidarity, wherein indigenous and queer knowledges are transmitted and negotiated, where equality is educated differently and collective life is beginning anew. We know the words for what is found in the home, but now there is no alternative except an intense embrace of the new possible meanings that they might harbor. This is the dream of a world wherein a home is collectively made and maintained, wherein the constant labors of care-givers are recognized and actually substantively redistributed, wherein the home is understood not as an exception to public political life, but actually negotiated as a historically extant alternative threshold for thinking, contesting, and reworking our relations and collective desires.

Talking and dreaming of the home in this way is dangerous for the regime of proper use, attacking the cult of natural order which stabilizes racial capitalism in all its possible flavors and permutations. This threat is felt immediately. On March 9, newspapers report that Mexico City is barren, with record low ridership on the Metro and street traffic reduced to but a trickle of cars and empty buses. Local markets and big retail chains report a major loss in customers. Schools receive reports from students of locked classrooms and an almost entirely absent teaching staff.

Is transforming the home into a site for contestation against the habitual violence that spouses, family members, public officials, and society-at-large perpetrate against women (on the eve of what promises to be an extended global quarantine), enough to remind us that we've already been forced to live in a world spawned from the dreams of those who had long ago forgotten how to dream? In times of epidemic death and economic collapse, where a future cannot be made certain, do not be led astray. Let us at least remember: not all dreams are equal. Not all futures are worth defending. Only with those dreams which indulge the invention of possible uses—for things like bread, forks, pigs, and our homes—can we make another world.

Notes

1. Gabriel García Márquez, *One Hundred Years of Solitude* (New York: Harper, 2006), 417.

Quarantine Meditations

Christopher Carrico

Quarantine might have suited Pyrrho well. Some days, I doubt the existence of the world outside of my house. It's been a time for intense, focused reflection; but it often feels less like a hermeneutic circle, and more, like I'm a dog chasing my own tail.

Recent events have given us more than enough reasons to be plagued with doubt. People and places that gave us some kind of hope, crushed by imperial capital. The coup in Bolivia, the defeat of Corbynism, Bernie's campaign self-destructing. Guyana—in the midst of an electoral crisis that has gone on for more than a year and a half. Meanwhile, the radical right takes advantage of the Pyrrhonist moment: adding a dispute with the germ theory of disease to its ones with climate change and evolution. Unafraid to directly assault reality. Each morning, I start my day with news and social media looking at new atrocities and trying to gauge how far neofascism advanced while we were asleep. Unidentified police and military, and white supremacist militias intermingle, indistinguishable from each other. Even the opposition leader calls for the arrest of "anarchists." There's no telling where it will all end.

Is this moment cause or symptom of our radical skepticism? Pyrrhonism is the postmodern condition and the modern condition. But I don't believe that it is simply the human condition.

David Hume doubted whether there was a self, whether there was continuity between the objects which he saw today and the same objects seen yesterday, and whether or not there was cause and effect. Bertrand Russell said that Hume's problems were the human condition. To me, it sounds like Alzheimer's. Even a geocentric model of the universe would've been impossible in a state like this, let alone a Copernican Revolution. How could we know that the sun that rises today is the same as the sun that rose yesterday? The sun must touch bodies with sense organs, feelings, brains, and minds. But these bodies, hearts, and minds also need others. They need cultures and communities with histories and languages.

We face the same contradictions over and over again. Capitalist Mad Men work around the clock to multiply desire—nneeds and wants for an edless array of goods and services; while at the same time imperial capital bars the fulfillment of basic needs for large sectors of humanity and destroys the very conditions for the reproduction of life on a planetary scale. We are way past anything like a "legitimation crisis." A dominant ideology with any semblance of coherence doesn't exist. The dominant ideology is Nihilism.

And yet at this moment we stop short of demanding a real alternative. We're clear about what we don't want. We don't want to die of COVID or to be evicted from our homes. We don't want a boot on our necks. But we stop short of something bigger. We'd need a positive vision of an alternative for that. And the 20th century taught us that communism can't work. Maybe. But 21st century capitalism pushes society towards self-implosion, and perhaps even to species suicide. Capitalism's institutions are collapsing, but imperial capital also destroyed or deformed every institution that came before it. The remains are inadequate for giving us the tools to grasp present conditions. Our knowledge about the world consists of fragments of the distorted, contradictory, and self-defeating sciences of capitalism, and the memory that it didn't have to be this way.

We can try to end our suffering by turning away from the world, like Pyrrho. We're already social distancing. Turn off social media. Renounce desire. Maybe go on antidepressants. One kind of happiness is the absence of pain. Ataraxy. Epicurus at least thought we also needed friends, and food and wine. But he also said we need to stay away from politics. Epicurus retreated to his Garden as Alexander's Empire fell. Lucretius wrote his poem as the Roman Republic was dissolved and Julius Caesar declared himself Emperor. Apolitical ataraxy tempts many today as well. As does the Liberalism of Fear.

Saraab (Delusion/Mirage)

Shahana Rajani & Omer Wasim

We have been thinking a lot about community, queerness, and survival in the face of death, grief, and mourning in the past year. We have been planning to start a creative practice that can open up ways to share space in collective, intimate, and tender ways; to come together to navigate an increasingly hostile world that holds us apart; to draw on older, and form newer, rituals to mourn and simultaneously heal, to live, share and witness the erasure and violence aimed at our queer bodies and communities. We are calling our practice Saraab, nazar ka dhoka, a quiet, amorphous entity that can go undetected, while being unapologetically sensitive to its surroundings and political concerns. In such difficult times, our hope is for us to come together to form a tenderness kit, a queer collection of meditations, mediations, conjurings, and reflections on being together while apart.

As we learn and practice new rules of social distancing, we are experiencing isolation in unimaginable ways. Borders have hardened around us: not just of the nation-state, but borders that relegate us to home and family. This return to the home, has registered, and continues to register, for some of us as a return to the closet. A big part of identifying as queer has historically been aligned with finding family that is elsewhere, away from biological realities, constraints, and ideas of kinship; instead we rely on relationships and connections that are informed by love and shared experiences than those that we inherit and are born into.

We are confronted with a form of interiority, heightened by ongoing isolation and quarantine; and in these moments, we have found ourselves disconnecting from our bodies, and from the new realities that are our present. As the world moves online, distance seems to have immensely grown and expanded between us and the communities we inhabit. We simply do not have the vocabularies for existing and being together virtually. We have mostly shared lived spaces, and do not have the registers for making peace with virtual, intangible bodies.

How do we think of, grapple with, and arrive at community in this time of crisis? How do we build solidarity, to expand our community, and turn to those more vulnerable around us? How do we think beyond the impasse of immunology based on the family unit and the nation-state? To not detach and dissociate from ourselves, our bodies and each other, nor fall back on individualistic, engrained mechanisms of self-reliance, but turn to each other, to be vulnerable together, to seek intimacy.

— *Saraab*

March 2020

Lillian Goldberg

shuffle, sweaty, before the note: Thank You Loyal Customers
spring trees their pink opens to narrow sky and row house bricks are, too, split and hematic

the carless, they traffic in heartburnt time
my boss, he texts us on March 16th: Thank You Loyal Workers

three options: viral randomness, fascist fantasies of healthy bodies, or hopeful immuno-divination
what other than our pandemic sincerity could bite us this way?

in the fully empty city this makes invisibility feel like social rejection: Thank You Loyal Neighbors
this makes early notes on the doors break their promises, makes me leave notes of my own

on nearby doors, which never promise much of anything, not in this heat
studies show that your quarantine pod could be ten thousand strong: Thank You Loyal Rebels

long March makes auto-immunity finally lose coherence as a political metaphor or metaphor for
politics

THE] NOTEBOOK

SUMANA ROY

I and...

Sumana Roy

I do not sit straight. That is not my natural posture. I have the genes of a recliner—I hunt for a backrest. My "I" is like me—slightly bent forward while walking, leaning backwards when resting. I cannot draw a straight line. I wonder whether artists who draw straight lines sit up straight—I cannot imagine them sitting straight and drawing a straight line. "I" is a straight line. As I type this, I notice the difference between the "I" on the keyboard and the "I" of my drawings.

"Drawings." I say "drawing" with great hesitation. I am no artist. I never was, not even as a child. I might have been interested in light—like all schoolchildren, I learnt that it travelled in straight lines. To my nine-year-old eyes, that is what distinguished it from water and from air: these two elements were unruly, they were disobedient, they did not travel in straight lines. I discovered their character in my father's village. The urinals were far away from the tin-roofed building where my grandparents and uncles and aunts lived. I had to sit on my haunches and urinate—it was a moment of wonder for me, to watch the patterns of water move towards the drain. The floor was stained with older rust-like urine marks, but mine chose another path. Close to the toilet was the pond, and around it thin strips of bamboo on which clothes were hung to dry. I watched the clothes, particularly the legs of pants and pyjamas, fight the wind as if I were watching a game of football—the wind was like a footballer chasing the ball to the goalpost. It did not move in a straight line, and I imagined that was why the clothes dried unequally.

Adulthood, and an entry into the Anglophone, even Euro-America-centric, world meant that I was gradually using a vocabulary where the hegemony of the straight line, in thought and discourse, about everything—gender, art, race, class, nature, architecture, literature, everything—was unquestioningly dominant. As a provincial in a distant outpost, I felt annoyed by it—the straight line wasn't how I understood myself or my community. But all these thoughts were—as they usually are —pushed away to the back of my consciousness. Until the lockdown necessitated by Covid-19 started and I was compelled to reflect on the nature of "I." The situation in India was difficult to put in words: every day, on our phones, were images of workers walking back home to their hometowns from metropolitan cities. Even as we blamed the government, till our protests became nothing more than water for gargling, I couldn't help seeing this as a consequence of what I'd long suspected to be inevitable—the collapse of emotion structures because of the extremities of relentless individualism.

Struggling for words, I found myself turning to the most basic unit: the letters of the alphabet. There was just one letter for the individual: I. How had it come to exist? What was its relationship with the other letters of the alphabet? In asking these questions I was perhaps trying to investigate the relationship I had (temporarily lost) with my community. And so I began to draw—this is drawing as much as it is writing, for all I am working with are the letters of the alphabet. These amateur sketches are structured as dialogue—a dialogue between "I" and another letter of the alphabet. In them is a record of my thoughts at night: of my unease both with the straight line and "I," their breath and their breadth of power.

Sumana Roy, *The "I" Notenook*

Sumana Roy, *The "I" Notenook, A*

Sumana Roy, *The "I" Notenook, B*

Sumana Roy, *The "I" Notenook*, D

Sumana Roy, *The "I" Notenook, E*

Sumana Roy, *The "I" Notenook, H*

Sumana Roy, *The "I" Notebook, N*

Sumana Roy, *The "I" Notenook, O*

Sumana Roy, *The "I" Notenook, S*

Sumana Roy, *The "I" Notenook, U*

Sumana Roy, *The "I" Notenook, V*

Sumana Roy, *The "I" Notenook*, W

Sumana Roy, *The "I" Notenook, Y*

Sumana Roy, *The "I" Notenook, Z*

Sadia Salim, *A Roaming Aesthetic II*

second dialogue

CALLS TO POLITICS AND THE ENDS OF POLITICAL ACTION

28 March 2020

Companion Texts for Studio Session

Adorno, Theodor. "Marginalia to Theory and Praxis." in *Critical Models*. Translated by Henry W. Pickford. Columbia University, [1969]2005.

Beauvoir, Simone de. *The Ethics of Ambiguity*. United States: Citadel Press, 1970.

Benjamin, Walter. "The Work of Art in the Age of Mechanical Reproduction." in *Illuminations*. Edited by Hannah Arendt. Translated by Harry Zohn. New York: Schocken Books, [1935]1969.

Bilaval, Saib. "Dear Bernie." filmsforaction.org. *Films For Action*. Published on March 19, 2020. https://www.filmsforaction.org/articles/dear-bernie/.

"El pueblo unido, jamás será vencido!" ("The people united will never be defeated"). A Chilean orchestra. *Redfish*, October 28, 2019. https://www.facebook.com/watch/?v=474265866777193

Endicott, Katie. On a panel of striking teachers in West Virginia. WeAreManyMedia, 2018. 21:54-26:13.

Gogarty, Larne Abse and Hannah Proctor. "Communist Feelings." newsocialist.org. *New Socialist*. Published on March 13, 2019. https://newsocialist.org.uk/communist-feelings-lessing-gornick/

Gornick, Vivian. *The Romance of American Communism*. Basic Books, 1977.

Kanafani, Ghassan, interview by Carleton, Richard. Beirut, 1970. 2:21-4:07. https://www.youtube.com/watch?v=3h_drCmG2iM&feature=youtu.be&t=141

Kollontai, Alexandra. "Make way for Winged Eros: A Letter to Working Youth" Translated by Alix Holt. Molodoya Gvardiya, 1923. https://www.marxists.org/archive/kollonta/1923/winged-eros.htm

New Edition of the Babylonian Talmud. Translated by Michael L. Rodkinson. Boston: New Talmud Publishing Company, 1903.

Patten, Mary. *Revolution as an Eternal Dream: The Exemplary Failure of the Madame Binh Graphics Collective*. Chicago: Half letter Press, 2011.

Salaita, Steve. "Palestine in the Revolutionary Imagination." stevesalaita.com. Published on April 3, 2019.

Weber, Max. *Politics as a Vocation*. Translated by Hans-Heinrich Gerth and Charles Wright Mills. Fortress Press, 1965.

Hosts | Ethan Ackelsberg, Isaac Brosilow, Colin Eubank, Lucy Peterson

Speakers | Asma Abbas, Ethan Ackelsberg, Isaac Brosilow, Christopher Carrico, Colin Eubank, Ari Fogelson, Zibby Glass, Daniel Neilson, Lucy Peterson, Heidi Andrea Restrepo Rhodes, Gabe Salgado, Charlie Yates, Philip Zorba

Scribes & Annotators | Avonlea Fisher, Zibby Glass, Isabella Lee, Sara Mugridge

ASMA

Every week we unpack a dimension of our current moment, prying open those things that feel so inextricably tied that they feel continuous and too much of a whole that they might not actually be. What is the need to dis-assemble en route to assembling an ambiguous, yet not ambivalent, future? We follow a compulsion to a method inspired by people like Marx—but not only him—that prioritizes relations within the totality of what we inquire into or practice, and those that we shape and confront, that leaves open this ostensible object of engagement to perhaps live another day and hopefully not die in our hands. Our work together is inspired by a commitment to politics as living and not a dead labor. That is what we hope brings us together here; to maybe make those distinctions between the living and the dead labors of politics because we have the space and time to do that. This goal, then, is not tied to readings but to each other; we see texts as occasions to come together and to return to with each other when we feel a bit lost, and to leave them when we're lucky enough not to need them. As an excuse to be with each other, it is also a moment to savor and celebrate, and I have a feeling that today will be one of those days. In the same spirit, since these conversations are aimed at reclaiming a space together, our impulse to each other is generative and capacious. We still think character matters, even in the expediencies of politics, and we have no apologies for the imperative to behave kindly towards each other, not as interrogators or as police. We are here not to use our positions and stances as armors or as weapons but as openings and vulnerabilities, as invitations to care for each other and to guide, not to prescribe or direct. Where crises and urgencies can make us cruel, as we are seeing, they're also making us aware of our needs for each other, and here in the space we are opting very deliberately for these urgencies to ask more and not less of us; to challenge our reflexes and to approach the political outside of the fake power of policing each other and resolving our discomfort on another's body.

We understand that even if so many people knew intellectually and found themselves on the right side of critiquing systems, so many among us were still, practically, within the safety of the history they knew would unfold, ultimately in a way that would allow them to find a way back in after their adventures into being on the right side of philanthropic and guilt-ridden politics were done. Today, many of us find ourselves needing to be patient with those who thought something was working, especially if they could use it even to do some good. Where guilt and philanthropy came from attachment to systems that were bad, but could somehow be repurposed, we feel that that repurposing is greatly limited and perhaps has run its course. But, we will ask kindly into that brutality and allow what is being said to be an opening to saying something further—not in the spirit of "debate"—but of preparing the ground for more and better thought. We are here to think with, not against, each other and certainly not to deride thinking. Today we move on to speak about the various callings of politics beyond guilt and philanthropy, how we hear them, how we interpret them, and how we embody them.

COLIN

Last week, we shared our thoughts on the work of crisis as a kind of tool which calls to order a series of new innovations to maintain systems of domination and hegemony. We also spoke about political education beyond crisis, taking stock of the potentialities manifest today that could allow us to conceive of our present moment as well as our relationships to history and futurity differently than those tenses have been traditionally scripted for us. On Tuesday, a bunch of us watched *Cradle Will Rock*, a film about the events surrounding the 1937 musical with the same name by Mark Blitzstein, which discusses the role of art and power in the 1930s amidst the struggles of the labor movement.[1] We laughed, we joked, someone cried, and we began speaking about the presence of doubt, ambivalence, listening, and failure in political action. We began to think about the relationship between art and performance with respect to politics.

In that spirit, we'd like to enter into the conversation about political engagement both with respect to the self and the individual, as well as individuals and collectivities. So, in our own journeys to politics, how might our understanding of the place of performance in and as politics be shaped by feelings of surprise, desperation, triumph, failure, laughter, and the sheer duration of time itself? Who is it that determines the efficacy and ends of a political action? When, sometimes in the name of solidarity or expediency, do we determine this on behalf of others?

I often say that I came to politics because as a student I couldn't keep myself from listening to the conversations of others—in the dining hall or the classroom there's always people who are having arguments and discourses, asking questions and expressing desires that felt to me that they couldn't be left unengaged. I can't tell a story about politics, or political action, or even convey my thinking about politics to a loved one without turning to these moments and spaces. Of course this kind of awakening to the vocation of politics involves sit-downs and workshops and political mobilizations and votes of no confidence...but my mind always goes back to the moments with my peers and my teachers, where we began to build a grammar to learn about ourselves and each other.

LUCY

I want to use this opening to reflect a little bit on how calls to crisis may or may not inform our understanding of the means and ends of activism. I'm going to take a little time to diagnose problems with how the activism communities I'm a part of navigate times of crisis, and then pose questions I've been thinking about. Then, as promised, and prompted by Colin, I'll give an example from my own organizing. It's not too personal, don't worry. I think you'll be able to relate to it—some people, anyway. And then I'll reflect a little bit on why I chose the Alexandra Kollontai reading for this week's conversation.

The problem I want to raise comes from my experiences over the past three years after the election of Donald Trump and now, with the coronavirus pandemic. Both of these events have been framed and proclaimed as global-level crises by establishment Democrats, progressives, most of the professional academics around me, and liberals of all kinds. In my activist communities there's a certain resistance to jumping on that bandwagon, an attitude exemplified by the phrase "capitalism is the crisis." It's a little bit haughty—I think you know what I'm talking about—but there are reasons for it.

There's a worry that if we succumb to participating in "official" crises, the less "eventful" crises—struggles we have been waging in the names of anti-capitalism, racial justice, and anti-colonial liberation—will be silenced, at best, or appropriated well beyond our control, at worst. In an effort to maintain some semblance of control over the narrative and over our perspective, we have numbed ourselves to the temple of everyday politics and decided that we have heard everything we will ever need to hear from those who have succumbed to colluding with government forces, Bernie Sanders, AOC and really, all progressives included. That's kind of the attitude around me. (I'm a participant in it, I don't mean to say that I'm not.)

Afraid of the very powerful forces of appropriation, especially, but not only, in the context of crisis, the activist communities I'm a part of have anchored themselves in values like mutual aid ideals, like non-hierarchical organizing, and prefigurative and imaginative politics informed most centrally by anarchism. All of these strategies are how we hold one another accountable to each other and how we measure whether we are truly acting on behalf of the most vulnerable. They are also the bases for communicating with one another and for learning to trust those who join us, so that the material of how we relate to one another is not easily extracted from who we are.

I worry that we have become so afraid and suspicious of the reactionary forces of compromise, centrism, etc., that we have forgotten how to listen, how to learn, and how to build solidarity in a way that can usher in the kind of world we want to live in. In other words, we become so fixated on being representatives of our values that we have rendered our personal impact meaningless and consigned ourselves to the realm of impossibility. To put it in Weber's terms, "We are men of conviction, but have suppressed or excluded all the men of responsibility." And Adorno would no doubt put it more harshly, as a form of solidarity with the cause whose ineluctable failure is discernible and therefore nothing, other than some exquisite narcissistic pain.

I have two questions I want to pose in light of this: How do we hold the tensions between our convictions and our responsibilities? And, how can we come to recognize when our ideals are shackles and muzzles, and what do we do about that?

These tensions have manifested in various activist groups I work with around whether or not we should devote energy to Bernie Sanders's campaign, and whether or not he can be trusted, and if so, so what? The past few months have been tense and taxing in my communities. Some of us believe that to turn our backs on a candidate like Bernie Sanders would be irresponsible, and to me it epitomizes the failures of some of my fellow activists to think about what solidarity looks like when not built on conceptual or ideological community. Some of us who have given our energy to the Bernie Sanders campaign are effectively imperialist traitors, and though they will welcome us back when we come to our senses, there has been a serious breach of trust and understanding about what we thought we were doing when we said we were anti–imperialists and anti–capitalist. This rift continues to grow and at some point there will be a reckoning among all of us. That is what I'm trying to prepare for and maybe this call will help. Maybe some of you are in a similar situation.

To now turn to Alexandra Kollontai's "Make Way for Winged Eros." I recently taught this essay in a class on feminism and political theory. The students didn't like it as much as I did, but maybe you will. I like this essay because she is very attentive to the way that values change in the context of changing scenarios, and I feel like my own communities could be better at being responsive to our material conditions, especially as it relates to collectively imagining what it means to live up to our values. If nothing else, Kollontai provides a story in a totally different time and political place—Soviet Russia—when the revolution has been successful, bearing no resemblance to our own world (sadly and obviously). She writes,

> The new, communist society is being built on the principle of comradeship and solidarity. Solidarity is not only an awareness of common interests: it depends also on the intellectual and emotional ties linking the members of the collective. For a social system to be built on solidarity and co-operation it is essential that people should be capable of love and warm emotions. The proletarian ideology, therefore, attempts to educate and encourage every member of the working class to be capable of responding to the distress and needs of other members of the class, of a sensitive understanding of others and a penetrating consciousness of the individual's relationship to the collective. All these "warm emotions"—sensitivity, compassion, sympathy

and responsiveness—derive from one source: they are aspects of love, not in the narrow, sexual sense but in the broad meaning of the word. Love is an emotion that unites and is consequently of an organizing character. The bourgeoisie was well aware of this, and in the attempt to create a stable family bourgeois ideology erected "married love" as a moral virtue; to be a "good family man" was, in the eyes of the bourgeoisie, an important and valuable quality. The proletariat should also take into account the psychological and social role that love, both in the broad sense and in the sense of relationships between the sexes, can and must play, not in strengthening family-marriage ties, but in the development of collective solidarity.[2]

Kollontai models what it would look like to ask questions that are pressing for that specific time and place at the same time as she continues to speak using an intelligible Marxist vocabulary. So there's continuity and discontinuity. She isn't utopian or optimistic without warrant—one of the issues with Silvia Federici's rendering of how the plague shaped property conditions in Caliban and the Witch.[3] Kollontai is telling us that, if our conditions have changed, then we can't keep relying on the knowledge that used to inform how we made judgments. We have to take stock of our new conditions in order to better understand how we might relate to one another in the service of freedom. We need to understand the material foundations of hope and possibility if we want our activism to have the impact that we imagine it would.

ETHAN

When I think about my own politicization, the starting point for it always comes from when I was in high school. I grew up in Wisconsin and in my first year of high school Scott Walker came in as governor and tried gutting the unions right away. I went to Madison with my family to march with teachers in the streets, and it was quite literally when I learned what the word solidarity meant. But I also learned it in a much deeper sense, witnessing firsthand the power that people have when we can overcome the atomization of our society.

Looking back, it was a strange initial moment of politicization and awakening to the power that ordinary people have, because as everyone probably knows, it ended as quite a crushing defeat. Scott Walker won, there was a recall campaign, and he won by an even larger margin in the recall. The labor movement in the state of Wisconsin has been really devastated by the last decade. In some ways that prepared me well for being an activist on the left because most of our time as activists is being defeated and losing battles going up against capitalism. I think there's a bad habit that develops on the left of trying to spin every defeat as a victory.

I was looking back at a quote from an Austrian Jewish leftist named Erich Fried who wrote, "I am tired of defeats, and still more tired of friends who, after each defeat, explain that 'basically, it was a victory.'"[4] At the same time I think there was a piece of victory that I felt in Madison. Without the uprising in Madison it's hard to imagine some historical linkage between that and the victorious strike in Chicago that came in 2012, the Occupy Movement, and now the revival of the militant labor movement that's been led by educators, nurses, hospitality workers which started with the statewide teacher strike in West Virginia. We are thinking about how historical memory influences politics. A West Virginia teacher who participated in those strikes, Katie Endicott, says that in Mingo County the person who gave them the confidence to walk out and know that they could win was someone who had been in a previous round of strikes before the evisceration of the union movement there.[5] To some extent, I think I've always been stubborn about not wanting to follow rules that I consider irrational, and I think the entirety of capitalist society is irrational, so I have a certain stubbornness about that. But outrage isn't really enough to keep going. It can sustain you for a short period of time, but you need more. I think what's important in the long-term has been a transformative experience of catharsis and struggle. I think of "El Pueblo Unido, Jamás Será Vencido," a short video of an orchestra playing a public performance in the midst of the revolt in Chile. It's hard to express it in words; there is this wave of emotion that washes over you in the experience of watching or listening to it.

I've had experiences of a similar sort that really keep me going politically. By being in particular moments of struggle I've learned there's actually a possibility of a world based on human solidarity and human creativity. I've experienced it, however fleetingly, being on picket lines or in the streets where you can actually feel the power around you. The last time I saw Colin in person, we were both in DC to oppose the fascist mobilization on the anniversary of the murder of Heather Heyer. On that kind of occasion, you don't really expect any kind of positivity. There were fascists gathering, and I got up early in the morning to drive to DC to get them out of the city and make sure no one dies (that's the main concern). But so many people showed up to the mobilization that we actually outnumbered the fascists. By the end, we were standing in the streets just a couple blocks from the White House, a bunch of socialists singing, dancing, chanting with this feeling—very briefly of course—that we had taken over the city and won something. Those particular moments in struggle become symbols or metaphors that can continue to drive us forward. What is the relationship between these different struggles and issues as actual material things, and as metaphors or symbols for driving people into political action? It would be easy to say the material is more important—I think in most senses it is—but the material change can't happen without symbols or metaphors driving people into action.

ISAAC

I've been interested in exploring the pulp of the political moment which Colin so beautifully related to those conversations in the Simon's Rock dining hall, in which I definitely was a participant, instigator, sometimes a bad listener, sometimes not so bad a listener. But those were so important to me. Particularly the kind of heartbreak that we were discussing with those political movements certainly weighed on my mind, especially navigating being a person involved in the mundane grit of political struggle—the boringness, the tedium, the frustration, the setback. To have that kind of experience, both on this mundane level, and in our imagined solidarity, our projection that radiated out from it, and the distance between those two. It wasn't until I started to encounter art and novels that were made by people who experienced similar things that a real understanding, a path, was produced.

I'm now going to do what I've been doing for almost a year now, studying—primarily the *Talmud*.

We're going to go back to the third century, maybe the fourth or the fifth—it's unclear as to when this was actually written, but it was attributed to someone in the third century. There's a saying that is attributed to Rav, who was one of the first generation Jewish sages to have crossed over from ancient Palestine into Babylonia, today Iraq: "Even if all the seeds would be ink and the reeds that grow near swamps would be quills, and the heavens would be parchment upon which the words would be written, and all the people would be scribes, all of these are insufficient to write the unquantifiable space of governmental authority," meaning all the considerations with which the governmental authorities concern itself. Rava bar Mehassia said, "What is the verse that alludes to this?" They take a verse from *Proverbs*, "[T]he heavens on high and the land to the depth and the heart of kings are unsearchable."

So, what the hell? This translation takes a lot of liberties and it can be hard to get past the surface level of it to the inside text meaning what this says. When you look at the actual Aramaic it starts to get interesting: אֲלָלָה (chalela) is this word that means an opening or a valve of a heart. And when it says that it would not be possible to open chalela, it means to say it's not possible to write an opening into power or into authority. It's not possible to rupture power or authority, even if all the seeds were ink, all the reeds were quills, all the people in the world were scribes, and the sky was parchment, it wouldn't be possible to write an opening onto authority. Then it asks, how do we know this? Because the depths of the heart of kings is unsearchable. There might be a word play between this *chalela*, the valve of the heart, and the heart of the kings. It's quite literally saying that no matter how much you try, you can't criticize the power structure. We don't have the ability. It's an authoritarian sentiment to the highest degree. We feel that it's not possible for us to puncture the authority structure, to make a break into our authoritarian system, right? But, there are times when we think the failures build upon each other and that the invention of powerful systems will continue. I think the rabbinic tradition contains a subversive potential that's locked in this text that I instinctively want to be there. I think as leftists we also want it to be there.

And Rabbi Akiva, a giant in the rabbinical imagination, asks, "Is this the law?" He is sitting outside the house of study. They ask him, "why are you doing this? Is this the law? That you're supposed to sit outside a place where you study?" And he says, "the law is outside of what's contained in the heart of kings." In this magnificent sense, so is the law. And he says "the Torah is outside." And then he arose, and they say, "Akiva's outside. Make room for him." So what is happening?

He's saying, fine, the law is outside, the Torah's outside—let's go. I think this contains seeds of a radical potential.

I came to this kind of stuff much later than I did political theory and political art and novels. It reminded me of Vivian Gornick, who was a member of The Madame Binh Graphics collectives in the '70s in New York, and a host of different writers who understand both the pure limitations of the political moment, and at the same time really work their way through. I'll end with this little bit I wrote: "Grandiose political desires supercharge these moments of frustration and boredom which are the pulp of political life. What would I do without my comrades to brag when I come home, reeking of sheep, mud and solidarity? It would be a shame to let such moments, with their good, bad, and ugly go unexamined. There's a path cleared away from these dense forests of nostalgia and reality, packed away by novelists, filmmakers, and printmakers who have bound themselves to political causes and have been undone by them. I return to my apartment where I am waiting for the virus to pass, the world to both wake up and fall apart, in the morning after my exercise I say the morning prayers and in my prayer shawl and tefillin. Afterwards, I sip coffee and write in my journal, grateful to believe that such a path exists."

And that path is exactly what I'm really interested in exploring with everyone. I also think that it's something that the rabbinic tradition has alluded to, for as long as people have struggled against power and have articulated what power means, and endeavor to do so, and I hope to with you all.

Hey, Democrats, progressives, most of the professional academics around me, liberals of all kinds! We ask if these established and establishment positions make up the "who" that "determines political efficacy and ends of (our) political action." In choosing to answer (or not), we understand that specificity announces a politics.
By the way, can we inscribe "who determines political efficacy," on kings? — Zibby

Not the "right political act," not "shunning desire," not history "looming above us," but politics as account-giving. What possibilities are foreclosed when we reduce who or what we are fighting for—our political desires—to some articulable outcome, or a thing that can be named? What possibilities could be opened up by a refusal to objectify desire in this way? — Avonlea

COLIN

Maybe we can focus for a little bit on the discrepancy, or the continual tension between one's relation to everyday politics, or what Isaac calls the "pulp of politics" on the one hand (those metaphors that Ethan mentioned, or that symbolism, however dangerous, are sometimes necessary to sustain us), and, on the other, how we can find life in them to continue these concrete political actions and to kind of save ourselves from the numbing that Lucy mentioned, that can occur with a kind of purity politics surrounding a cult of values in a really bad way.

BELLA

Ethan's turn to the orchestra playing in the streets of Chile, and Isaac's talk of the art and books that carved a path between the "mundane grit of struggle" and the experiences and projections of solidarity: I see these as momentous experiences of collectivity, which come closest to being captured and kept alive after they pass by art. They provide an access point into the longue durée of time, but not in a way to extract stories for a particular narrative of political history as unfolding towards a penultimate, or as Lucy said, a direction of unwarranted optimism—either in Federici's narrative or Hegel's dialectic. Rather, in a communion with history and political action that knows no end, or at least struggles but does not need to be in the name of a certain end.

GABE

There is a piece near the beginning of this week's selection from De Beauvoir's *Ethics of Ambiguity*, where she talks about the negative attitude being easy. She writes, "In one sense the negative attitude is easy; the rejected order is given unequivocally, and unequivocally defines the revolt that one opposes to it...The return to the positive encounters many more obstacles." In the very next paragraph, she talks about how an "antinomy reappears as soon as freedom gives itself to an end too far off in the future, and every construction implying the outrageous dictatorship of violence."[6]

That seemed to share the sentiment that you expressed, Lucy, in terms of easy frustrations, or the ease with which we sometimes make comrades in opposition to things which are easy to oppose, like capitalism and imperialism. When there is a time for a positive construction of that opposition, such as the Sanders campaign, that's where it gets complicated and difficult, because of the ways that people oppose positive construction of new alternative orders, while others don't see those concerns as a threat in the same way.

LUCY

I think De Beauvoir is talking about the same thing that I was talking about. And Max Weber does too, or at least makes the distinction between the ethic of conviction and the ethic of responsibility.7 On the one hand, one may claim to understand the service of an idea or, rejecting the same principle, may, on the other hand want to serve external everyday life. I read Weber differently than De Beauvoir, though, because I don't see this dichotomy as something that's easy— it's tragic and a function of incessant defeat.

COLIN

This is also related to a conversation that we were having about *Cradle Will Rock*, and the problem of the left not having a sense of humor or being too serious sometimes. And I think it's related to this purity politics that is the end result of a lot of wear-and-tear or jadedness. Where does one go from there with those comrades that aren't interested in a diversity of tactics or possibilities, or don't have that refreshed spirit? It kind of puts you in a position—like you said, Lucy—of awaiting a reckoning for some sort of betrayal. There's no easy way to deal with it and that was a lot of the sense I got from Isaac's masterfully pulled quote, "These ambivalences, these problems, these issues are a part of the history of these movements of the left, that we're claiming and living with." There is a generational difference in addition to the wear-and-tear of certain activist circles.

From a discussion of *Cradle Will Rock*, 24 March 2020

COLIN: When you said that there's ambivalence about the mistakes or the faults of the left in this time, as portrayed through the critiques delivered by some of the characters, my takeaway from that was the constant refrain from Bill Murray's character, the communists are just not funny and what they do isn't funny. And his frustration with the proletarian nature of this act. And then finally, him doing his communist bit at the end, I feel like that was just classic liberal self-hatred, Oh, I don't like myself, and that's the substance of his critique. Was there something else?

ASMA: The left certainly does have a problem with irony. I don't think they like being the brunt of jokes—I know that for a fact. It's just the history. The Orson Welles character has a weird sense of irony, and the grand artist isn't ironic, Welles is not not ironic, certainly not self-ironic. So there's a certain way the left and the artist do share this lack of self-ironization—I think all ideologies do. And of course in the Liberal, you're right, it takes the form of a kind of self-hatred, feeling the burden in a certain way that just needs to be expressed and channeled outward. If you just think about it, there is an expectation that left politics failed because they weren't perfect, and that's what we have to deal with today, that Bernie made that particular mistake. But the right is never held accountable to a perfectionist stance (for lack of a better term). At the same time, of course, the liberals and conservatives are very unfunny people (to us) because they are murderers. But in terms of "our people," there's an exacting expectation and touchiness around portrayals that aren't certain about something—that's my feeling: the aesthetics just don't hold up. You have to make "good art," something that just isn't interested in plot of any kind. But how do you tell an actual story and keep it somehow clean?—as if we have to be cleaner than others.

COLIN: The portrayal is the simultaneous building and destructing of art or collectivity or sociality. And the production of this film in 1999 or now, I feel like this is a classic strategy used for us to defend ourselves in whatever we are doing, hiding in a legible illegibility of a work in progress. Oh we're just rehearsing this thing, it's not done yet. And maybe that's the critique of the Bernie campaign in general, a continual rehearsal. About the end product, for years we have struggled on and off, how we do it and with what kind of posture of confidence we try to do things, and how it's taken terribly sometimes, even by our friends, by the well dressed gentlemen who won't play.

DAN

In thinking about Lucy's observation in a lot of different fields in which I have some capacity to act right now, I've been wondering how to steer sympathetic people towards recognizing what it would mean to get to solidarity in one way or another? In these conversations, it feels like these are people, in general, with good intentions, but who wouldn't consider themselves leftists. They have some kind of goodwill and the desire to do the right thing, and the desire to connect, and maybe also some kind of institutional power—or at least there's some lever that they are in a position to move. I've been thinking a lot about how to talk to people who are in that situation and to get them past attachments to their own sources of power, their own comforts in some cases, or their own denial in others. There's a need for them to let go of what they're holding, but they're not quite ready to do it. So it's easy to feel impatient with these folks.

ASMA

That actually connects nicely, because one thing I've been thinking about is what Federici doesn't consider. Lucy, thanks, for even signaling to that, because that got me thinking of temporality. When Gabe had introduced Federici, there was a sense of the longue durée—of this place called "history" where somebody comes out of and goes back in to. Federici has a facility with the longue durée of history and revolution that allows her to tell a story in a strange way. We barely think about how much the question of purity is connected to one's capacity to have faith in "capital H" history. Where is the place for those of us who don't have that faith? What's this sort of trick that allows those of us who are completely marginal to that faith in History to then perform a purity politics? So that's a kind of ill-fitting clothing type of thing that just doesn't suit you, for those of us who feel this kind of detritus of history and constantly pick up the rubble that Benjamin tells us about, as if we could ever have historical unfoldings as a place to be in, or a vantage point from which to see things. I don't get moved by Federici as much as I try to, because I'd rather see *The Crucible*. There's something *The Crucible* does that takes Federici a whole 500 pages to do—I know that's unfair, but I am really not trying to disrespect. I'm just putting it out there for consideration.

The De Beauvoir moment is not about negativity and positivity as much as it is about *what do you think you are doing?* in place of what do we think we are wanting? What's the capacity? And I have avoided the turn to the ethical that ends up completely shunning the question of desire by forcing the hand on a particular kind of political act or the "right" political act. But, again, speaking from a place that has history looming above us, whatever we call politics becomes these little spaces, microcosms, or these very tiny Leibnizian monads. So I'm wondering whether what De Beauvoir is talking about is politics as a kind of account-giving that is different from that thing that asks you which side were you on, or what kind of H/istory. Maybe she wants us to think not of which side, but whose side.

The conversion of the who into the what is like the giving up of, or the conversion of, politics into capital-H history or morality. I wonder what it means to give anybody the permission to ask us that question. It's like asking for an account of what you did for Bernie. What did you do? Were you enough of a traitor? Is Bernie anti-imperialist enough? I mean, there's just something about that that feels disingenuous, and De Beauvoir says, "In the first place, it seems to us that the individual as such is one of the ends at which our action must aim. Here we are at one with the point of view with Christian charity, the Epicurean cult of friendship and Kantian moralism, which treats each man as an end. He interests us not merely as a member of a class, a nation, or a collectivity, but as an individual man."[8] I think what she means by individual man is different from what we think of as the liberal individual—we have to give her that much—and this speaks to a slight complication of man of conviction versus man of responsibility, that Lucy brought up from Weber.

Beauvoir goes on to talk about this "joy of existence," which Ethan brought up. What does it mean to run into Colin at the antifascist protest? I'm just placing these things out here because I feel like perhaps we don't clarify what it means to be speaking about the political because we are constantly blackmailed into speaking what we want rather than who we want it for. I think that people like Wendy Brown and all these contemporary post-Marxists really screwed us up in that way, because there was just this sense that somehow articulating someone's desire correctly was the answer to this, and I just don't believe it. I just don't believe that's how everyday life feels. I don't think that, at any time, thinking about justice can only be about the what part of what we are vetting and what we are. I think the reason some of us have difficulty engaging in forms of political solidarity is that we don't trust that, because we just don't encounter any sort of attentiveness to the who that hasn't been converted into a thing, and I'm sorry if I'm sounding super existentialist, I don't like *things*.

ISAAC

I think this idea of converting the "what" into the "who" is a perfect dovetail into what I saw and gained from reading *The Romance of American Communism* by Vivian Gornick.[9] By the time the '70s came around, and Gornick was a part of the women's movement, she was in her forties and had long since left behind the politics of the old left or the Communist Party, which she was brought up in. When she was called a reactionary in the midst of Second-wave feminism, her immediate response was to reflect on her time in the Young Communist League when she was in her teens, and, in her early twenties, the death of her father, the 1956 collapse of the Communist Party, the disillusionment that was experienced at the kitchen table. She says it wasn't until she experienced this dogmatism in the second-wave feminist movement in her middle age that she had this perspective change about the Communist Party of her past. She has this beautiful line, "I thought they had been in a calm sea but it turns out that the sea is an ocean and they had been doing admirably just to keep themselves afloat."

That becomes the prompt not just for an anecdote, but to go on a road trip and interview all of these people who had been in the Communist Party in the United States in its heyday in the thirties and forties, and to revolt against the kind of simultaneous quieting of those histories and experiences, both from people who themselves had been broken by that experience, and from the erasure during the Cold War. I don't think that it presents enough of an answer, but I think that she gets to a place where we can start to say that this is something that is wide and expansive; and we can study it and we can mine it; and we can produce art out of it and produce political understanding from it. That is what I loved about the essay about blessing and how these experiences are part of the history of movements, maybe with a lowercase h, but in order to force them into an "uppercase H" history. I think that it's through reverse engineering—that existential conversion that you spoke about, Asma—that maybe we have for some people a sense of beginning. And I'm grateful to people who have laid out those tracks.

CHARLIE

I'm curious about the role that the "who" plays in determining an individual articulation of desire—the people one is surrounded by, so to speak—and what impact that has on one's interest, for lack of a better word. Are there ways to make that transparent? And what is the transparency of who is determining what one cares about in these situations? Is it what one is looking at? What does that do in relation to this question of what is mobilizing a force towards the positive as opposed to the (too-easy) negative?

CHRIS

Ethan's comments about defeat, which is a serious issue to deal with, really got me thinking in particular about Alain Badiou's *The Communist Hypothesis*.[10] The entire preamble is called

"What is Called Failure?" and it begins with the idea that communism as a hypothesis has been a complete failure, and yet, it's a correct hypothesis, so it's not something that we can just abandon. The entire history of the left will be a history of failure until that last moment when it's not anymore. And I think one of the texts he has in mind whenever he is outlining this is the essay by Mao, "Cast Away Illusions, Prepare for Struggle!" and the lines in particular he's thinking along are the lessons from the imperialists. The logic of imperialists is "make trouble fail," "make trouble fail again until they're doomed," and then later on, the logic of the people is "fight, fail, fight again, fail again, fight again until their victory." That's kind of the text to which Badiou is responding.

Badiou is writing at the end of the twentieth century. The "big lesson" of the twentieth century was the defeat of communism. And yet, we can't just abandon it, because the communist hypothesis is a true hypothesis, and we need to continue to work it out. But with Benjamin we're talking about a longer history, the last 6,000 years during which there have been classes and states, and that's a big context in which to think about struggle and failure. The powers that be are who we allow to determine what is considered success, what is considered failure, and we allow them to call us failures for not having achieved what they have prevented from happening. I also think of all of this rhetoric from liberals from within the Democratic Party saying, "Well, what did Bernie achieve in all of those years as a senator?" What he achieved was to be able to say things that are true, and to continue to say things that are true, when others would be completely shutting down any kind of proposal at every step of the way. It's a history of failure until it's not a history of failure. Then the whole notion of "purity politics" shows that the movements that we are participating in are filled with contradictions, but these are the contradictions of the moment we are in.

It's a moment that's filled with contradictions, and there's no shortcut. We can't choose the ideal moment that doesn't exist in order to participate in it, and every single movement we'll ever be a part of is an imperfect movement full of contradictions. If you can't accept that, if you can't live through that, then you're just going to be criticizing from the sidelines and not actually participating in any actually existing movements. I just wanted to say I enjoyed this so much last week. And I think I needed to be a part of it again, so thank you all for letting me be here in this space.

HEIDI

It's really lovely to hear you all and be with you here in this way. I've just been thinking a lot about desire and I really appreciated the Kollontai piece in thinking about a love that's political and that exceeds, or is outside of, or away from, a bourgeois love, which I think in being anti-bourgeois is also, in a way, always already queer. So I was partly interested in what you were saying, Asma, about desire because I think it's related to, some of the things I've been thinking through in sick, and chronically sick and disabled communities, and in queer communities during this particular moment. I've been trying to think through intimacy, desire, closeness and love as a practice in the material world, especially in a time of pandemic-related physical distancing. I've been thinking a lot about Karen Barad, what she's doing with quantum physics and the sort of like quantum-level social theorizing of closeness and distance, as well as thinking about Moten and Harney's idea of hapticality, but these are just things I wanted to bring into the conversation that are shaping a lot of the thinking and the practices that are happening in other communities that I'm in and just trying to parse through what is different about this particular moment and what does it require differently as we're all being forced to relate in this digital manner?

ZIBBY

My heart! Speaking of this counter to a cold heart—you've definitely succeeded in doing that, so my heart may fall out of my chest. I'm here in London studying theatre and in my program a lot of the actors in this moment want to say, "Okay, so we do not have our space anymore, so we're no longer going to perform, and we no longer know how to interact with this." But Lucy's question of impossibility reveals how even the most intractable problem arises with its own set of renewing possibilities. At the same time, it goes back to the question of Adorno asking, "how can we steer the alternatives of spontaneity and organization?"

My undertaking in the theatre doesn't consist of any kind of reliable interpretation of events, or show a way out of a vice that we feel trapped in. I think that it's assumed that the theatre has the aim of communicating, and I think it can be true only to a point. I don't know exactly, Milo, what you wrote about a "bounded politics," but I think this communication is true only to a point. For whom? Are we doing this for the actor or for the audience?

Isaac, I'm so moved by what you said. I'm working on a piece right now about Ezekiel, because Ezekiel is the actor of his prophecies in a very physical way, and there's this one moment in which he eats a scroll which Hashem wrote the words of mourning and woe on them so that he can speak of this kind of post-exilic history, although he's told that no one will listen. And in terms of this idea—if all the seeds were inked and they're still insufficient, they're still insufficient.

Yet, this unquantifiable space is not something that isn't a possibility...for me, I think that we need to create a theatre from these shipwrecks which are not synonymous with any kind of destruction but are actually a kind of mutation so that we are not giving ourselves to a dissolving sea, but some kind of sea of metamorphosis. We need to be thinking about regeneration. I think we need to think seriously about what theater and politics have to teach us about the possibilities and perils of summoning the incorporeal. You know, to what end are we seeking an escape from our bodies, and what are we mourning when we're fleeing the catastrophe? And this kind of exhilaration of embodiment.

In terms of what a lot of people have brought up about history—is this because performance is threatening? This kind of captive remains which is dictated by the archive of history—is this why the logic of the archives scripts performance and theater as disappearing? Does performance disappear this physical action in favor of History, and is it favoring, in some ways, bones over flesh? So in the Jewish Old Testament, maybe we are expectantly waiting for this absent God, but I'm seeking a place in which language and our conversation right now is not an ineffable absence but an effable presence. So the question is really about, like, what is our freedom? What is our freedom politically and theatrically to enact our histories? And why do we think it's impossible? And is this a kind of freedom from history or can it be a freedom for history?

Going back to this question of why the archive is predicated on loss...maybe it's from fear of these traces, and fear of memory, and a fear of the present. As we know, admittedly, being able to live in the present in this instant of time is nearly impossible.

ETHAN

There's a video of an interview with Ghassan Kanafani from 1970 where he was meeting the PFLP (Popular Front for the Liberation of Palestine) in Beirut.[11] And this was a moment when the PLO (Palestine Liberation Organization) was fighting against King Hussein in Jordan. They were quickly defeated, and the journalist who's interviewing him says, "You know what's the point of all of this? You're losing—what have you possibly achieved from that?" And Kanafani's response is basically, "We proved that we're right, that we have the correct case of fighting against imperialism and proved that Palestinians will not be defeated and will continue to be there and fight."

Especially thinking about that moment and the Palestinian struggle, which is something that I've been involved with, a lot of my organizing in the past few years has been so much defeat—so much defeat, and so much of the world just not caring, at least those with power not caring, but continuing to struggle and still see some positivity, maybe not so much in trying to spin defeats as victories, but in seeing the fact of resistance as something to keep looking to, and as the thing to to keep giving hope. Through all those defeats there's still something about being on the right side. There's a quote by Rosa Luxemburg that says something like "the history of revolutionary struggle is the history of failure, but you also only have to win once."[12] So, nevertheless, people still continue to struggle—there hasn't been some final defeat either.

COLIN

I was thinking about the Kanafani interview as well, which I had never seen before. It was at once fascinating and really hard to listen to. Because, on the one hand, he's doing everything that Ethan says about the cause of the Palestinian people. But while he's showing every way that this movement could proceed, the interviewer is instead fixated on this differentiation between violence and non-violence. He keeps pressing Kanafani: "Why can't you just talk? Why can't you just talk?" And every time the interviewer tries to ask a question, you just see this intense dissonance between interlocutors where the grammar of what is being said introduces a barrier of incomprehensibility. The journalist asks, "why can't you talk?" and Kanafani says "To who?" You know, "Why can't you not fight or stop the bloodshed?" And, Kanafani is, like, "For whom? Who are going to be the ones that won't die in that situation, and why?"

He refuses to have a conversation between the sword and the neck, and the literality of that is lost completely on the interviewer who says, "Well, but what if everyone just kept their weapons outside?" He ends by saying, at the end of the day we, the Palestinian people, would rather die standing, and these things you keep making up—about citizenship or paperwork or some sort of peace treaty—it's all capitulation. And so that was an alternative to the moment that we inhabit which Lucy showed us, which is clinging to values in a different way. With Kanafani, there are these beliefs in commitments that say, "Yeah, I'm sorry, at this point we can't proceed any further. At this moment everything is lost if we do anything that you're suggesting."

ASMA

Ethan, you said something about "we only need to win once," right? Could you say more about what that one victory looks like, and then is this just an experiment—I'm just wondering who experiences victory, right? Ever? I'm honestly wondering whether diehard conservatives or white supremacists move through the world thinking they won anything, right? Because for the past at least five years, I keep thinking that unless we completely create a situation where everyone is speaking in completely bad faith… For a second, if we have a space to think about whether your white supremacist student in the class actually thinks they're winning anything, you know? We will talk about battle victories later on, but I'm just thinking around failure.

There's this beautiful poem—I went back to it about a week and a half ago—by Faiz, which in Urdu says something like "neither is our victory new, nor their defeat."[13] And there is a certain way that I always seem to mis-remember that line as its inverse: neither is our defeat new, nor their victory! It's as if I am literally the spawn of those whose lives were saved by a mix of deep dialectical materialist fantasy and…All terrible things were seen as leading to justice for someone, which gave complaint a different taste than it feels in this country, this culture…

Thus, I'm just wondering who thinks they have won anything? It's an honest question. Do we actually think victory is a modality in which even the worst conservatives experience the world? I mean, there's certainly something going on with the gloating, right?

So, there's Adorno in "Education after Auschwitz," and he says, look, there's a certain way they keep thinking that those of us who are suffering are happy. That's what the fascist is moved by—this bizarre feeling that people like you and me, who sit in a classroom talking to each other and actually feel blessed by the presence of another who is with us, and who would read a text with us, are somehow happy.14 God knows we have experienced that, but I'm wondering whether even for Nietzsche, ressentiment from anybody—from the right or wherever—is based in any assumption of their victory. One, what is that victory for? I don't say it in a tragic pessimistic way, that's not my mode, but what is this "one victory" we need; and, second, who are we taking it from?

COLIN

To this question about victory and defeat, there's this: In certain experiences that I've had with movements, I get caught up in this burden of a promise that you can deliver something for someone else—you know, a stranger, or someone you know that maybe you don't agree with, or maybe you care about a lot. But then there is this feeling that defeat or failure, or the conditions of victory, rely solely on the achievement of that promise, or upholding that promise that you made at the beginning of the movement, or something like that. That's what I think about when I think of the script of liberalism that the left gets kind of tortured into. Or maybe about someone who joins because they think, like, there's no way we're not going to get this victory. But, then, it's a self-fulfilling prophecy of contract and domination where that's the basis of one's engagement with other people in a certain political context that becomes the entirety of one's political engagement with other people. That feels really close to my heart recently, going back to my hometown, which is a company town. The company owns all the houses and all the jobs, and there's no such thing as political speech really. And, then trying to organize around things like immigration. How do you have those conversations with people that don't involve some sort of victory-or-defeat discussion? Because there's no concrete victory besides being able to protect each other a little bit more, or being able to say things to each other that we actually want to say and hear, rather than what we can say in front of the boss.

PHILIP

Going back to the need for metaphor and symbol, and also to the discussion of possibility. In the Alexandra Kollontai piece, she says, "Collectivism of spirit can then defeat individualist self-sufficiency, cold inner loneliness,"15 which reminds me of what I've been reading in Mark Fisher's *Capitalist Realism*.16 He makes a point about how individualists are trapped in their own feelings, their own imaginations. So I think, then, that this individualism, which traps us in our own feelings and our imaginations, leads us to this present sense of there being no alternative to capitalism. He's speaking here post-2008 where the banks fail and we bail them out, and we're in the year zero post these catastrophes; we're in the year zero post-coronavirus or during coronavirus, and we bail out the banks and there is no alternative. This is just the way things are.

So I want to ask: how does a collective emotion allow us to conceive a world that better suits the collective? And how does that become material? We can talk a little bit about victory here because I'm not asking this rhetorically. I'm genuinely asking this: are tenants organizing rent strikes making material collective emotion? Is that victory? When the waste disposal workers in Philadelphia refuse to work without hazard pay under unsafe conditions, is that a victory? Is that collective emotion? I am genuinely asking. We participate, we organize. One thing Fisher talks about is that we must keep the priority on class and not the neoliberal calls that Biden represents—calls for normalcy and decency—very abstract things that don't mean anything and don't feed anybody. We have to refuse to remain detached spectators to the coronavirus, to corrupt business. Otherwise, we remain isolated individuals, isolated workers who can't escape our own singular imaginations in favor of the possibilities offered by the collective.

ARI

I've been thinking about what's happening with coronavirus and other things in the UK versus in the US, and about the fact that, naturally, the rallying cry here is to defend the National Health Service. I think that it puts a different slant on the idea of a politics of purity when you actually have liberal institutions of some kind that might be worth defending. And, then in conjunction with that, the different volunteer efforts that have come up. Like elsewhere, there's mutual aid networks, but then there's also now, in the same sort of war mobilization vein that's going on in other places, a nostalgic Blitzkrieg kind of thing. There is a national push for volunteers now also, and they've had something like three-quarters of a million people sign up to do that. There are debates going on in online fora about which mutual aid program to volunteer with.

This gets at whether it's humanitarian sentiment that makes you do it, or do you also have some commitment to the principles of mutual aid that you want to enact by doing that? Are you somebody who can trust the official organization to deliver food to your house, or can you not give your address because maybe after whatever amnesty, you'll also be deported?

We're talking about defeats. It's funny how much of the world is invested in Bernie's campaign. I mean there isn't really a global left, but the symbol of that is important for a lot of people. Was the symbol of Corbynism important? And what was that importance?

ISAAC

The Adorno piece heated up for me when he talked about the bankruptcy of solidarity, of the ability to say, "this is the same struggle as mine."[17] A lot of my thoughts about this conversation have been predicated on the writing that I've been doing with activists who were a part of the New Left. And I'm particularly interested in the navigation and forging of a Jewish radical politics in the '70s that was informed by the dissipation of the secular Jewish radical project from the old left, from the pre-war generation, and the transfers and transitions from this generation. I am interested in people who are able to still stay sharp after decades of activism. Particularly people who in the early '70s were a part of a political movement for peace in Israel and Palestine that was definitely dead on arrival. But, it didn't feel that way to them in the decades to come.

I was interested in the people who are able to keep moving and continue to innovate in their political vision and connect and who are interested in me as a person of a different generation and give me a lot of generosity of spirit, and a lot of chances to listen and learn. So that's something that I've been bringing to a lot of this thinking. Okay, we can't get fifty years back; we see that we got most of this stuff wrong, and that we were disoriented and scared about the present. And, we're still worried and scared about the present. It's not like as a younger person I don't share the same kind of earth as people who are older who have more experience.

ETHAN

Maybe just some closing thoughts on Asma's question about victory and what that is, and this idea of only having to win once. So, to base it in two quotes, there's this quote in the opening of "Reform or Revolution" from Luxemburg, where she's criticizing Eduard Bernstein's socialism when he says, "The ultimate aim of socialism is nothing, but the movement is everything."[18] She goes on to say, "But since the final goal of Socialism constitutes the only decisive factor distinguishing the Social Democratic movement from bourgeois democracy and from bourgeois radicalism, the only factor transforming the entire Labor movement from a vain effort to repair the capitalist order into a class struggle against this order, for the suppression of this order the question: 'Reform or Revolution?' as it is posed by Bernstein, equals for the Social Democracy the question: 'To be or not to be?'"[19]

And, so I think having some vision of something beyond that maybe constitutes a victory, right? If capitalism is actually abolished, that seems like maybe some kind of victory, and that actually what distinguishes communism from other forms of politics is that there's some vision of something beyond capitalism and not just continuous struggle against it.

Another quote that I was thinking of as a sort of complement is from Marx and Engels in *The German Ideology*. They say, "Communism is for us not a state of affairs which is to be established, an ideal to which reality [will] have to adjust itself. We call communism the real movement which abolishes the present state of things. The conditions of this movement result from the premises now in existence."[20] There's some vision of something beyond capitalism. Some predetermined thing that we're walking up the stairs of and at the end we'll enter. We're on a new floor where there's something else. What the thing beyond capitalism looks like is determined by people still struggling. I think the finality of victory is questionable and I don't think there's something that we just win and then everything's fixed. I don't have that sort of messianic vision of what socialism is.

COLIN

Isaac and Ethan, you both speak of a kind of intergenerational exchange, that interaction and interest in one another that comes from different times and spaces, and tries to learn together to share certain long-standing desires, but then also learn to entertain new ones. This seems so, so important to me. It has echoes of what Heidi and Asma were talking about earlier, bringing us back to conversations of hapticality and queerness and being together in a different way under quarantine and beyond. If I zoom out a little bit, one of the things that really surprised me when the four of us—Lucy, Isaac, Ethan, and I—were talking earlier this week was the way that movements also necessarily must do that. Whether it's Palestinian solidarity activism, or Ferguson and Black Lives Matter, or Sanders or mutual aid, or opposing femicide in Latin America, how they move together and learn from each other is essential as well.

Hopefully, we'll see you all next week. Invite your friends, invite your Mom. We'll be here.

On the Interregnum : Ejeris Dixon with Gramsci

I first stumbled across Gramsci's quote on the interregnum during a period of time where I was deeply attempting to make meaning of the political conditions. And this concept that there was a political space with profound opportunity, instability, and challenges was simultaneously illuminating and grounding. This quote helped anchor an essay I wrote, " Fascists Are Using COVID-19 to Advance Their Agenda. It's Up to Us to Stop Them," in Truthout. This piece was was my attempt to analyze and name the rise of a global fascist movement, and how it was impacting the strategic goals for US organizers, particularly Black, Queer, and Trans organizers.

I wanted to use my vantage point as an advisor to multiple social movement leaders, and the fact that I've been organizing for a few decades, to support an analysis of our strategic opportunities. I followed the idea of interregnum to a class at the Brooklyn Institute for Social Research, which brought me back into a place of study. I thought so much about Gramsci's state of mind, health, and the psychological and physical impact of the surveillance of Mussolini's government. I thought about what it meant to be writing as a political prisoner with your sickness and disability progressively increasing.

Recognizing that we've already seen reports of activists disappearing. And organizations that I work with are experiencing white supremacists and white nationalist threats. Knowing how so many of us are sure that we're being monitored by the state for our political work. I felt a kinship with Gramsci's determination to put out strategy and analysis, to be useful, to do everything possible to fight fascism.

Here I am trapped inside my house, under a pandemic, as a Black severe asthmatic, with chronic joint pain. I've known multiple incredible BIPOC organizers who've died due to COVID19. And I recognize that breathing the wrong air could kill me. But despite the limitations of the societal conditions, and while I'm not imprisoned by the state, I certainly feel trapped by state negligence and the knowledge that my Black Queer, Trans, Disabled communities have been left for dead.

When I came across Gramsci's writing on a "war of position," on building struggle and power over time, recognizing the relative power of state hegemony, it felt clear, needed, and useful. It allowed me to also think about what our organizing goals are in these times. So my connection to Gramsci is both about the content of what he wrote, and the experience of writing knowing your existence is subversive, and your writing is threatening, and doing it anyway. And humbly offered, here is the essay that I wrote.[21]

Notes

1. *Cradle Will Rock*, directed by Tim Robbins (1999; Touchstone Pictures, 2000), DVD.

2. Alexandra Kollontai, "Make Way for Winged Eros," 1923, accessed December 26, 2020, https://www.marxists.org/archive/kollonta/1923/winged-eros.htm.

3. Silvia Federici, *Caliban and the Witch: Women, the Body, and Primitive Accumulation* (New York: London: Autonomedia; Pluto, 2004).

4. Alain Brossat and Sylvia Klingberg, *Revolutionary Yiddishland: A History of Jewish Radicalism*, trans. David Fernbach (New York: Verso, 2016).

5. Katie Endicott on a panel of striking teachers in West Virginia, WeAreManyMedia, 2018. 21:54-26:13, accessed December 26, 2020, https://www.youtube.com/watch?v=_cYpsDXXdHo&feature=youtu.be&t=1314.

6. Simone de Beauvoir, *The Ethics of Ambiguity* (New York: Philosophical Library, 1948).

7. Max Weber, "Politics as a Vocation" in *The Vocation Lectures: Science As a Vocation, Politics as a Vocation*, David S. Owen, Tracy B. Strong, Rodney Livingston, eds. (Cambridge: Hackett Publishing, 2004), 80-85.

8. Simone de Beauvoir, *The Ethics of Ambiguity*.

9. Vivian Gornick, *The Romance of American Communism* (New York: Basic Books, 1978).

10. Alain Badiou, *The Communist Hypothesis*, trans. David Macey and Steven Corcoran (New York: Verso, 2015).

11. Ghassan Kanafani, interview by Richard Carleton, Beirut, 1970. 2:21-4:07, accessed December 26, 2020, https://www.youtube.com/watch?v=3h_drCmG2iM&feature=youtu.be&t=141.

12. The Luxemburg quote is not in her writings, but found in, of all places, the congressional records of 1969 under a section titled "Comrade Women." A UCLA Doctor of Philosophy named Marlene Dixon quotes Luxemburg as saying, "The history of revolutionary struggle is the history of failure, but you only need to win once." Source: A US government propaganda film, *Communists on Campus*, which is full of archival material from the United Front Against Fascism conference in 1969 (the archival material makes it worth watching). Last accessed on December 27, 2020, an audio recording of Dixon's words begins around the 32-minute mark: https://www.c-span.org/video/?463374-1/communists-campus.

13. Faiz Ahmad Faiz, *Nuskhaha-e-wafa* (Delhi: Educational, 1980).

14. Theodor W. Adorno, *Can One Live After Auschwitz?: A Philosophical Reader* (United Kingdom: Stanford University Press, 2003), 19-33.

15. Alexandra Kollontai, "Make Way for Winged Eros."

16. Mark Fisher, *Capitalist Realism: Is There No Alternative?* (United Kingdom: Zero Books, 2009).

17. Theodor Adorno, "Marginalia to Theory and Praxis," in *Critical Models*, trans. Henry W. Pickford (Columbia University, [1969]2005).

18. Eduard Bernstein, *Evolutionary Socialism: A Criticism and Affirmation*, trans. Edith C. Harvey (New York: B. W. Huebsch, [1899]1911), 202.

19. Rosa Luxemburg, *Reform Or Revolution*, trans. Integer (Three Arrows Press, [1899]1937).

20. Karl Marx and Friedrich Engels, *The German Ideology* (New York: International Publishers, [1932]2004).

21. See Ejeris Dixon, "Fascists Are Using COVID-19 to Advance Their Agenda. It's Up to Us to Stop Them.," *Truthout*. May 6, 2020, https://truthout.org/articles/fascists-are-using-covid-19-to-advance-their-agenda-its-up-to-us-to-stop-them/. The full text of this essay has been reprinted in this collective work under "Second Interlude | In Our Bones."

second interlude

IN
O U R
BONES

The Love for Ruins

Silvana Carotenuto

...the end is beginning
– Maurice Blanchot

The apocalyptic scroll ends by revealing the joy of "a secret garden." What will grow in its fertile earth? What will be produced by its soil? What is inaugurated in its enchanted survival? Might its germination be the flower, the flower of rhetoric, flores retorici, the metaphor of the flower? In *Glas*, Derrida reads Hegel's "religion of flowers," countersigning it with the "practical deconstruction of the transcendental effect" operated by Jean Genet, his name already consisting of flowers.1 On the double page of the book's textual event, the journey of the sun, burning on one side, as the heliotrope in its holocaust, meet and dialogue with the side of the cinders left on the earth, most proximate to the ground. *Glas, Cinders, Memoirs of the Blind*: in ideal semence, the metaphysics of the rhetorical flower turns into the ashes disseminating among the ruins of the earth. The flower of rhetoric descends towards the below, leaving its ruinous trace among rests, stops, dwellings, remains, residues, and vestiges.2 For Derrida, the devoted poetics of the remains allows the gaze that originates the ruin, to mark its own ruinous origin: "In the beginning there is ruin. Ruin is what happens to the image from the moment of the first gaze."3 What rests is the testimony that substantiates its possible love, the only possibility of love, by touching and being touched by the fragility and finitude of the flower, in its never-ending oscillation between birth and decay, the ruin as the rest of what was and is not any more, the image of ourselves in the face of our inescapable mortality.

> Ruin is not a negative thing. First, it is obviously not a thing. One could write [...] a short treatise on the love of ruins. What else is there to love, anyway? One cannot love a monument, a work of architecture, an institution as such except in an experience itself precarious in its fragility: it has not always been there, it will not always be there, it is finite. And for this very reason one loves it as mortal, through its birth and its death, through one's own birth and death, through the ghost or the silhouette of its ruin, one's own ruin – which it already is, therefore, or already prefigures. How can one love otherwise than in this finitude?4

Born and dying in finitude, the love for the ruin does not search for an object, a theme, a representation or a sense, in order to express its affection. It just opens the eye to memory, beyond intention or finality, and signs the ultimate surge of "experience:"

> The ruin is not in front of us; it is neither a spectacle nor a love object. It is experience itself: neither the abandoned yet still monumental fragment of a totality, nor, as Benjamin thought, simply a theme of baroque culture. It is precisely not a theme, for it ruins the theme, the position, the presentation or representation of anything and everything. Ruin is, rather, this memory open like an eye, or like the hole in a bone socket that lets you see without showing you anything at all, anything of the all. This, for showing you nothing at all, nothing of the all. "For" means here both because the ruin shows nothing at all and with a view to showing nothing of the all.[5]

The "treatise on the love for ruins" would need a space and time of reading different from what is allowed here. Yet, its page might, possibly, inscribe the singularity of the visual poetics of Cai Jin, the Chinese artist who dedicates her entire activity of creation to the series "Beauty Banana Plant," the four hundred and more paintings of Meirenjiao, the Chinese word for "canna genus," the plant or phyein that, insistently, as an obsession, haunting process or state of trance, shows its floral decay.[6] From the beginning, the flower comes to Cai Jin's aesthetic world in the intoxicating materiality of its "gamey odor." Originally, she is struck by a nameless sensation, which continues in the following days, intoxicating her with uncertainty and unpredictability. The sensation tells of its involuntary flow: "... something familiar was coming out of me when the sticky paint began to move, invading the canvas of its own accord." In another statement, Cai Jin insists on the permeating 'odor' that comes from the red paint:

> The color red drives me insane. Whenever I use it, I wield my brush with extraordinary sensitivity. This is a matter which dominates my experience... the red on my brush gives off a gamey odor which pervades my mind and my sense. The odor flows from my brush, and even more so, from my mind, and congeals in my paintings.[7]

The "cinder/incense" comes out of the painted flower from what Derrida, in *Glas*, associates with "coloring, smearing, gluing you, making you sensitive, transforming you."[8] In Cai Jin's experience of life, the color red is reminiscent of her adolescence spent during the Cultural Revolution. More generally, the red belongs to blood and to its global vicissitude;[9] in creation, it corresponds to the splash of matter. History, the body, and art, all appear in ruin; under the spell of their remains, the artist's passionate love goes to the painting of the same and unique flower, transforming, insisting, and repeating hundreds of images that are then obsessively glued on canvas, cushions, cycles paddles, found objects of all sorts. The flowers sometimes remain within the limits of their inscription; some other times, they overflow the confines of the "mattress" which absorbs, surfaces, and, at the same time, disseminates its bleeding flow....[10]

Is the repeated flower rhetorical or metaphorical? Does it make a sacred religion of its semence? In truth, the sumptuous and encrusted matter of the hundred paintings reveals no transcendence, but materially inscribes the "experience" of the ruin representing "nothing at all," "the nothing of the all." The eye is simply allowed to see, growing and grafting its gaze in the act of seeing. In Cai Jin's carrier, gradually, slowly, inexorably, the "efflorescence" of the banana plant expands, glues and transforms the insistence of the "Beauty" series into the future of "Landscapes," the recent work that incorporates the colored blossom of the red flower by chancing, developing and enlarging the form of its ruining matter into the future of new visions-to-come.[11]

Notes

1.   Jacques Derrida, *Glas* (Lincoln: University of Nebraska Press, 1986), 105b. The philosopher continues his sentence by adding that the practical deconstruction of the transcendental effect "is at work in the structure of the flower, as of every part, in so much as it appears or grows as such." For the name of Genet, the philosopher explains: "Genet/ginestra is the name of a plant with yellow flowers (*sarothamnus scoparis, genistra, genette, genet-à-balais, poisoning and medicinal…*)" 191.

2.   Derrida, "White Mythology," in *Margins of Philosophy* (Chicago: U. of Chicago Press, 1982); Derrida, *Cinders* (Minneapolis: U. of Minnesota Press, 2014); Derrida, *Memoirs of the Blind: The Self-Portrait and Other Ruins* (Chicago: U. of Chicago Press, 1993). On "cinders," see my "Derridean Cinders/Sacred Holocausts," in *Darkmatter,* in the *Ruins of the Empire* "Impossible Derrida," edited by S. Carotenuto, May 2012, http://www.darkmatter101.org/site/2012/05/18/deriddean-cinderssacred-holocausts/. On "ruins" in female contemporary art, see my "A 'Treatise on Ruins:' The Loving Work of Lida Abdul" in *Re-enacting the Past: Museography for Conflict Heritage* (Siracusa, Italy: Lettera Ventidue, 2013).

3.   Derrida, *Memoirs of the Blind*, 68.

4.   Derrida, "Force of Law," *in Acts of Religion* (London: Routledge, 2002), 278.

5.   Derrida, *Memoirs of the Blind*, 69.

6.   See the catalogue of the exhibition "Against the tide" organized by The Bronx Museum of the Arts, 1997, with the participation of Lin Tienmiao.

7.   Cited in Patricia Eichenbaum Karetzki, "Time and Love: Cai Jin's New Work," *Yishu. Journal of Contemporary Chinese art*, nov-dec. 2013, vol.12, n.6, p.47.

8.   Derrida, *Glas*, 105b.

9.   Among the themes of life, death, spirit, glory, the proper of man, for the Deriddean "*history of blood*" that is at the centre of *Glas* and that remerges in The Death Penalty Seminar, see Michael Naas, "*Derrida Floruit*," in *Derrida Today* 9.1, 2016.

10.   See Carol Archer, "Womanly Blooms: Cai Jin's Beauty Banana Plant Paintings," *n.paradoxa. International Journal of Feminist Art*, vol.30, n.48, 2012.

11.   See Chambers, "Beijing: Cai Jin,", *Art in America*, October 2013, www.chambersfineart.com/. See also J. Goodman, "Cai Jin: Return to the Source," Chambers Fine Art, Beijing, 2013.

It's Up to Us to Stop Them

Ejeris Dixon

The COVID-19 crisis is a story of a predictable pandemic. It is a result of the willful ignorance of the impact of the climate crisis and unsustainable expansion, a failure of multiple governments and the intentional under-resourcing of public health and medical systems. It results from our societies' ignoring of the conditions for poor people, the unhoused, disabled and chronically ill people, sex workers, migrants, communities of color and street-based communities, and the exploitation of this crisis by a rich, privileged and powerful fascist minority. Our government had the information, the resources, and the ability to prepare for this pandemic, including supporting those most at risk. We could have had the tests, the masks, the ventilators, the resources and emergency plans.

These are not mistakes. These are choices. We have been left for dead, and it's not the first time.

Over the past few years we've watched the rise of a global fascist movement in the U.S., Russia, India, Brazil, the United Kingdom and many other countries. And, while scholars and writers currently debate whether to call Trump an authoritarian, autocrat or a fascist, it's clear that he's not a fan of democratic institutions, and he often uses a fascist playbook. Fascist and authoritarian governments often exploit, accelerate, or create crises to increase their power and further their agendas.

Here's the fascist emergency playbook:

- Use the emergency to restrict civil liberties—particularly rights regarding movement, protest, freedom of the press, a right to a trial and freedom to gather;
- Use the emergency to suspend governmental institutions, consolidate power, reduce institutional checks and balances, and reduce access to elections and other forms of participatory governance;
- Promote a sense of fear and individual helplessness, particularly in relationship to the state, to reduce outcry and to create a culture where people consent to the power of the fascist state;
- Replace democratic institutions with autocratic institutions using the emergency as justification;
- Create scapegoats for the emergency, such as immigrants, people of color, disabled people, ethnic and religious minorities, to distract public attention away from the failures of the state and the loss of civil liberties.

These steps are currently in progress. In the past few weeks, multiple cities have started to arrest people for "violating" stay-at-home and physical distancing decrees. Under Trump's current emergency powers, the federal government has the right to detain people if it's determined that their "illness" could cross state lines. Federal and state governments are currently laying the foundation for further repressive actions. In Florida, their government is considering detaining and isolating sick people without their consent—for "public health." In Louisville, Kentucky, COVID-19 patients are being placed on house arrest. The Department of Justice is seeking to use emergency powers to detain people indefinitely without trial. In some cities people are being charged and detained for "terroristic threats" after concerns they had attempted to intentionally spread COVID-19. And Trump persists in calling COVID-19 the "Chinese virus," foisting responsibility for the global crisis onto a particular group.

Trump's use of fascist strategies is present, and accelerating. We must pay attention.

A Pathway Toward Liberation

Despite these grim circumstances, fate has handed us a society-changing opportunity wrapped within a tremendous challenge. We must think in terms of Antonio Gramsci's concept of interregnum, a time period in which "the old (world) is dying and the new cannot be born." In this liminal space, we have the opportunity to define that new society, and call it forth. Time is limited and the opportunity is precious. So, where does the left go from here, in terms of both addressing increased repression and moving towards a more liberated future?

Creating an Emotionally and Spiritually Captivating Vision

Fascists have a worldview and a clarity of purpose that can be alluring to their supporters. Using actual or exaggerated scarcity and naming themselves as societal "victims," they use promises of restoring society to a mythical past to override their followers' sense of morality. Sound familiar? Scarcity, real or imagined, fuels fascism. And COVID-19 is creating an abundance of actual and perceived scarcity, from rising unemployment, reduced access to hospitals and shortages in medication, medical supplies, groceries, and cleaning supplies.

Yet, systemic failure can give birth to systemic opportunities. To resist how COVID-19 is being used to justify a potentially permanent loss of civil liberties, we need to solidify and amplify a vision of liberation that is emotionally and spiritually compelling. We need the kind of vision that gets people out of bed, and inspires them to take bold actions, while navigating an ever-increasingly terrifying world.

Historian Timothy Snyder talks about how a sense of inevitability increases complacency under tyrannical governments. Inevitability means that people believe that nothing can truly be done to make change, and therefore they become both complacent and complicit in the shifts of political terrain. To move toward the type of vision that topples fascism, we need greater clarity of purpose on the left. Here are the questions that I think we need to answer, in order to move forward with a visionary organizing agenda that not only survives emboldened authoritarian movements, but moves us towards liberation.

- How will we address harm and violence within our communities? What is the role of the state (if any) in navigating harm or violence?

- How will we build movements with space for all of our people—those who are currently sick, chronically ill, disabled, survivors, those who are poor, Black, Indigenous, and people of color, queer and trans people, currently incarcerated folks, migrants, those who are targeted and criminalized, and so many more? How do we make room to discuss issues of power and privilege, and move through conflict, without it suspending or ending other forms of political work?

- With "in-person organizing" radically shifting or temporarily stopping—what does mass resistance, mass protest, and base building organizing look like? What new tactics will we use to create the sense of community that in-person movement building has created?

- Do we believe in governments? If not, what systems do we propose to create more equitable change and redistribute resources? If so, what is liberatory governance, what does it require of us as individuals and of the state?

- With so many people on the left disinvested and dissatisfied with both the Democrats and the Republican political parties—is it time for another party? Should we be building more power within the Democratic Party? What is our connection to large-scale political struggle and independent political power?

- How will we push ourselves to build the movements we need and increase time for rest, collective care, and our health? How can we do this and increase our discipline, rigor, and accountability to each other?

Building Deep Relationships to Strengthen Our Movements

Earlier this week my neighbor said to me, "I know that you have asthma. I know the folks in Apartment 3 have a child who is immunocompromised. So I have decided to mop the hallway, wipe down the elevator, and wipe down the garbage chute, as often as I can because I want to make sure that you all are alright." In the past, my neighbor and I had commiserated when our building didn't make repairs or when other neighbors acted out. But this pandemic has transformed our relationship to a place of deeper interdependence. This crisis presents an opportunity for all of us to build stronger, life-saving relationships that also strengthen our movements. I feel incredibly inspired by the increase in mutual aid organizing that's occurring all over the country. I'm particularly moved by the potential of mutual aid to deepen our relationships with friends, family, and how those networks can become interconnected to create a web of resistance.

History shows us that under repressive governments, people need to take big risks to resist and dismantle state oppression, and those risks must be supported by strong relationships. Whether it was non-Jewish people supporting Jewish families to hide and escape during the Holocaust, or people joining underground resistance movements under occupied countries during World War II, people took big risks to resist authoritarian governments, often when asked by people they knew well and trusted. Deep relationships allow us to build the solidarity we need, and to address targeting of communities that's already occurred.

Fascism relies on scapegoats. Fascists and authoritarian governments use emergencies as justifications to take quick and extreme steps to further oppress marginalized communities. With Trump currently blaming China and migrants for the coronavirus, we need deep forms of cross-community solidarity so that as people are targeted based on their identity or based on having COVID-19, we will show up in solidarity, with protest, and other disruption strategies. Scapegoats also require public complicity. The public needs to ignore and simultaneously participate in this oppression. While physical distancing is making it difficult for people to build, maintain relationships, and show up for each other, people will be most likely to disrupt these actions through their trusted relationships.

Sustaining Consistent Resistance Through Many Tactics

Within this global pandemic, life is increasingly more complicated for many people. We now have to figure out how to shift our lives to regularly check our temperatures, overcome barriers to getting groceries, and check on our sick family and neighbors while maintaining a safe distance. And we must do all this without touching our faces and while adapting to new work conditions or confronting our lack of employment—and mobilize. The inherent multi-dimensional juggling that living within this crisis requires offers us the strategic blueprint for our movement work.

Trump will be moving to entrench and consolidate power, escalate the crisis, and further criminalize dissent. To push back on these strategies, while navigating taking care of loved ones and ourselves, we will need to increase our political power, engage in a wide range of strategies, and engage a broader set of political allies. It will take a show of force to contend with and defeat Trump's agenda. History shows us that broad alliances, even temporary ones, are required to defeat autocratic and fascist forces.

To survive this, we need to let go of "either/or thinking" and embrace the complexity of this moment. I've noticed many folks get into a mindset that one tactic or strategy will create change, and is inherently oppositional to the others, especially when talking about healing, organizing for policy change and mutual aid.

We cannot allow this pandemic to re-solidify our separation from each other within progressive movements. Policy-based organizing won't singlehandedly transform society. Mutual aid, in isolation, won't be able to feed all the folks that need food. It's necessary to pool our strategies and work together to support oppressed people in living longer, and we must connect this work to the organizing we need to create structures of liberatory governance.

The "real work" will involve organizing for policies that increase resources for the most vulnerable within our communities, while creating networks of care and support, while pushing the federal government to increase access to medical supplies and resources for low-income communities, while also taking care of ourselves—our health and our spirits.

Holding Pain, Grief, Sickness, and Discomfort

Organizing against authoritarian, fascist and autocratic governments is often done while people are simultaneously surviving and grieving the violence of those systems. Holding grief and sickness while building political work is something that is no stranger to disability justice, to HIV and AIDS movements, racial justice movements, to movements against police violence, to survivor-led movements, to trans and queer organizing, to sex worker organizing and many other struggles. We must draw from these movements' lessons in the current movement.

We must integrate a healing justice framework deeply to support us in navigating trauma, grief, care taking and boundary setting within our organizing spaces, so that we can continue to have vibrant movements that are not harmful to ourselves in their pacing. As named by Cara Page and the Kindred Southern Healing Justice Collective, Healing Justice is a framework that identifies how we can holistically respond to and intervene on generational trauma and violence and to bring collective practices that can impact and transform the consequences of oppression on our bodies, hearts and minds.

Simultaneously, we will also need to push back on fear and disdain for discomfort within our movement building. Some of the people that we love and know will die, and their deaths will be directly connected to the failures of the U.S. government to manage this pandemic. While our work should also center joy, we are entering a time period that we will need to do especially hard, uncomfortable and painful work—as survival often necessitates. At the same time, people who were not previously involved in activism will be willing to take action now, seeing the dire circumstances in their lives, families, and communities. In order to support new people in our movements, we must navigate their material needs, their health and their grief.

This moment offers a grim opportunity. Yet it also creates the conditions for the rapid expansion of our movements that we will need to contend with the right wing's agenda.

The Road Ahead

While things feel devastating now, there will come a time when these conditions will feel normal to us. Remember back when the Muslim travel ban felt improbable and extreme? Two weeks from now, arresting people for leaving their houses could be the new normal. Under normalization, people can preemptively give up, or decide not to protest, or react to repressive actions. Organized, politically-engaged, communities can resist normalization.

We have a moment of opportunity. And the right has the same window. As you read this article, right-wing strategists are likely also figuring out their next steps—they're determining how to use the COVID-19 crisis to quickly move an agenda of privatization, criminalization and anti-immigrant sentiment, in the name of public health and safety. I believe that we have everything we need to oppose them and to move a liberatory vision, but we need to build more political power, increase our engagement, and find healthier ways to sustain our activism and organizing.

Naomi Klein recently noted, "The future will be determined by whoever is willing to fight harder for the ideas they have laying around." These times are asking so much of us. It is terrifying, yet possible, to build the society we want from this moment. These times require us to find a way to balance our commitments to ourselves, our families, and our communities. And I truly believe that we can win, as long as we do not give up on ourselves. Fascists can't win without our concessions, our normalization, our inaction, and our complicity. The old world is dying, and a new more liberated society, lies just beyond our current vantage point. Let's give it everything that we've got.

Cráneos Rotos

Edgar Flores Noriega

Dices que resguardas el orden	You say that you keep the order
Solo nos violentas más	Only you do us more violence
Dices que vas a cuidarnos	You say that you are going to take care of us
Pero nos vienes a aniquilar	But you come to annihilate us
Cráneos rotos por botas militares	Broken skulls by military boots
Cráneos rotos por fuerzas policiales	Broken skulls by police forces
Cráneos rotos, cráneos rotos, cráneos rotos!!	Broken skulls, broken skulls, broken skulls!!
Fuerza bruta, corrupción	Brute force, corruption
Falsa ley tu profesión	False law, your profession
Robas al pobre	You rob the poor
Protejes al rico y al influyente	You protect the rich & influential
Cráneos rotos por botas militares	Broken skulls by military boots
Cráneos rotos por fuerzas policiales	Broken skulls by police forces
Cráneos rotos, cráneos rotos, cráneos rotos!!	Broken skulls, broken skulls, broken skulls!!
No más represión, no más represión,	No more repression, no more repression
No más represión, no más represión	No more repression, no more repression
No más represión, no más represión,	No more repression, no more repression
No más represión, no más represión	No more repression, no more repression

Who Cares About Care If Care Is The Alibi: A Lamentation in 3 Fragments and 7 Songs

Bonaventure Soh Bejeng Ndikung

Epigraph by M. NourbeSe Philip from "The Ga(s)p"

We all begin life in water
We all begin life because someone breathed for us
Until we breathe for ourselves
Someone breathes for us
Everyone has had someone—a woman—breathe for them
Until that first ga(s)p
For air

We begin life in a prepositional relationship with breath: someone breathes for us. We continue that prepositional relationship, breathing for ourselves until we can no longer do so, and it appears that this most fundamental of acts is always a contingent one—breathing for, with, instead of, and into. Survival demands that we learn to breathe for ourselves, but the sine qua non of our existence is that first extended act of breathing—a breathing for and being breathed for in utero. We can, perhaps, call it a form of circular breathing or even circle breathing. Are there wider theoretical and possible therapeutic implications to breathing for someone and allowing someone to breathe for you? Further, how do the prepositional modifications change these implications—is breathing for the same as breathing with or instead of? Finally, while "i breathe" is semantically complete, its completion would not be possible without that original, prepositional act of breathing for.
— M. NourbeSe Philip, "The Ga(s)p"[1]

*"Who Cares About Care If Care Is The Alibi," serialized in this volume across the second, fourth, and sixth interludes, was first published by Archive Books in *The Delusions of Care* (2020).

FRAGMENT 1

Rest Assured / Bodi No Be Fayawood: A Space. Of Solace. A Sanctuary. At SAVVY Contemporary

The last weeks have been tiring. Indeed the last years have been exhausting. Indeed some existences—especially for Black and Brown peoples in certain societies—are exacting and debilitating. The struggles seem to be endless. Whenever one watches the news these days, there is news of another Black man executed in broad daylight in the USA, or another case of femicide in South Africa, or another journalist killed in Cameroon, or how the COVID-19 pandemic has ravaged within Black communities more than all other communities. The news of police brutality against people of color—be it in France, Brazil, India, or Cameroon—increases with the minute, and every now and then we are reminded of the fact that our breaths or the mere act of breathing, for some, is in a permanent state of precarity. In the past weeks, months, and years, we have all wondered what we can do at our various levels, and besides thematizing these injustices, racism, dehumanizations in the works we do as artists, curators, theoreticians, some of us have heated the streets in protests, written letters to politicians, advocated with forces in power, supported those in difficulties, and tried a plethora of ways to organise ourselves and care for each other. But even this too has been depleting—to say the least. A few weeks ago, while on one of the #BlackLivesMatter demonstrations against the cold-blooded murder of George Floyd and against systemic racism in the police and other institutions in front of the American embassy in Berlin, overweighed by the burdens and adversities of our times, I sat down, lost in wondering, watching in contemplation. Resigned. In the middle of my thought, a young Black woman walked up to me, started a conversation, asked how I am, what I do, where I am from, etc., and we noticed that there were many common denominators. After that conversation, I felt uplifted, cared for, seen. It felt like a recoil. Someone seemed concerned and felt like sharing the load on my shoulder, despite the fact that she obviously had her own burden to carry. It felt like she had come to say, "It is ok. Please take some rest. You have the right to be tired. Rest. And then carry on." In the middle of that sea of distress, revindication, and dissent, an island of radical care was built, and strength and spirit disseminated to carry on.

In the past days, I have found myself coming back to one particular song by the great South African singer and songwriter Letta Mbulu with the reassuring title "Carry On" from her 1996 album Not Yet Uhuru.2 The song was of course composed for a specific context and time, but that context and time of 1996, just two years after SA's first real democratic election, echoes with the histories and contemporaries of Black and Brown people all over the world. In the song "Carry

On," Letta Mbulu sings, "They will tell their lying stories/ send their dogs to bite our bodies/ they will lock us in their prisons." This is the present continuous. The past continuous. There is so much familiarity in the imagery she evokes and how that has become the fate of many Black and Brown people. Then she resists and with her resilience, "All their dogs will lie there rotting/ Dintsa tsa bona, di tla shwela naheng/ all their lies will be forgotten/ Mashano a bona, will be forgotten/ all their prison walls will crumble/ chakane tsa bona, will crumble." Her singing is a convocation of the spirits, the higher beings to protect and guide. But what I am most interested in is her persistence and prospicience when she sings "If you can't go on any longer/ take the hand held by your brother/ Every victory will bring another." And in the very beginning of the song she sings "There's a man by my side walking/ There's a voice within me talking/ There's word that needs saying/ Carry on, carry on."

Song 1³

I am interested in the figures of the voice within and that hand you can cling to. At that moment of despair, and almost resignation, the woman was that voice and hand that came on, in her way saying "Carry on, carry on." A few days later, the lady I met at the demonstration came by to SAVVY Contemporary. This time with four other Black women. As we sat down for a tea, they talked about their art, about the histories of African peoples on the continent and in the diasporas, they talked about spirituality and resilience, about what is in a name and how we carry our names in the world, and most especially about love. Radical love. With all the pressures, and the wish to stand our grounds in the face of adversities, we forget to retreat, to find ways of rejuvenation, to rehabilitate, to recoil. And especially, how do we stand our grounds, how do we fight back in the contexts of prolonged adversities?

Rest Assured / Bodi No Be Fayawood is an effort to take a break. To rest. A possibility of claiming the right to retreat as a possibility of invigoration. In times when being and breathing, when walking, working, playing while Black has become most perilous, we need to create spaces in which we can find solace, we need to create sanctuaries of and for resuscitation. The proposal is that to be able to "carry on, carry on" as Letta Mbulu so thinly sings, we must be able to afford ourselves time and space to retreat. This is the "rest" in the title Rest Assured, which must also be understood in the imperativeness of the statement which means "To be certain or confident (about something)." That imperativeness is felt when Letta Mbulu sings "It will be hard we know/ and the road/will be muddy and rough/ We will get there/ we know just how we will get there/ we know we will."

Rest Assured / Bodi No Be Fayawood is a get together for Black and Brown artists and art workers. A few years ago, I wrote an essay with the title "DEFIANCE IN/AS RADICAL LOVE—Soliciting Contact Zones and Healing Spaces" in which I wrote, "Art spaces could become spaces of radical thinking. Of radical love. Of protest. So, at stake is how can we create spaces where people and society could show their wounds? The process of turning to each other and acknowledging that we all have some kind of wound is a crucial step. For it is only by acknowledging that vulnerability that we can really see each other, converse with each other and heal each other. Protest is such a possibility of presenting the wounds of our times and then a possibility of individual and collective healings. The healing is in the protest itself as cathartic processes and moments."4 With Rest Assured / Bodi No Be Fayawood, the emphasis will be in sharing space, in seeing each other and getting to know each other, it will be in acknowledging each other's presence. Like the Black nod. It will be about listening to each other. Closely. As that possibility of communion. It is not about performing anything (even while doing performances) or striving for anything. But of creating space to be able to listen to that "voice within me talking," and collectively so. It is about "taking the hand held by your brother/sister." We will eat, drink, dance, watch videos, share our practices, sleep, laugh, dance. Do nothing else, but be. It will be a simple effort to inquire into each other's well being. In some parts of the African continent, when you are asked "how are you?" People answer, "I am fine if you are fine!" In other places, when you say "Good Morning" people respond, "My morning is good if your night was good." It is this idea that my well being depends on your wellbeing that guides and frames Rest Assured / Bodi No Be Fayawood. But most of all, it is a space where we claim the right to rest□ especially because truly, Bodi No Be Fayawood. The hope being that we will be able to carry on after that weekend of retreat.⁵

Notes

1.   M. Nourbese Philip, *The Ga(s)p* https://nourbese.com/wp-content/uploads/2020/03/Gasp.pdf accessed on Dec. 27, 2020.

2.   Letta Mbulu, "Carry On," track 6 on *Not Yet Uhuru*, Columbia Records, 1998, compact disc.

3.   "Carry On," YouTube. 6:12. Letta Mbulu-Topic. https://www.youtube.com/watch?v=EyHT9PQIg3w Accessed December 26, 2020.

4.   I am interested in this twist of the contact zone as conflict zone. I am interested to think of conflicts as frictions. And if my sense of physics doesn't fail me, when there is friction there are 2 possible outcomes: (1) The kinetic energy of the friction, i.e., work is converted to thermal energy, and (2) there could possibly be an effect of wear and tear due to the friction in place. Both effects of friction are what I am interested in. If there is something art and art spaces should/could do in our complex times, it should/could assume the position of the 'friction zone,' in which discrepancies in aesthetics, power relations, prejudices, complex issues of identities, notions of nation states, states of refugeeness, challenges of neoliberal economic tendencies, and complexities of socio-political, racial and class disparities can be investigated, negotiated, and challenged. This inthe hope that upon the friction, the issues at stake are transformed into some form of useful energy, and at the same time, problems might wear

down in intensity. Art spaces could become spaces of radical thinking. Of radical love. Of protest. So the issue at stake is how can we create spaces where people and society could show their wounds? The process of turning to each other and acknowledging that we all have some kind of wound is a crucial step. For it is only by acknowledging that vulnerability that we can really see each other, converse with each other and heal each other. Protest is such a possibility of presenting the wounds of our times and then a possibility of individual and collective healings. The healing is in the protest itself as cathartic processes and moments. So how can art and art spaces be spaces of "Auseinandersetzungen," that is to say the possibility of setting apart, engaging with the entities to be able to reshuffle them, but which also means confrontation, debate, quarrel, fight... if just to result in the transformation of negative energies to more conducive ones, and otherwise abrogate through wear and tear? How can art and art spaces become spaces for Social Healing, which one must understand as "an evolving paradigm that seeks to transcend dysfunctional polarities that hold repetitive wounding in place. It views human transgressions not as a battle between the dualities of right and wrong or good and bad, but as an issue of wounding and healing. Thus a key question driving the work of social healing is how do individuals, groups and nations heal from past and present wounds?" We need to care for each other by engaging in "Auseinandersetzungen," by being defiant, by protesting and initiating processes of making and unmaking or becoming sound again— cognitively, emotionally, corporeally, societally and humanly.

5.   This project was also inspired by Black Artists Retreat [B.A.R.] in Chicago, IL. Initiated by Theaster Gates and Elize Myrie in 2013.

Toward a Political Education of Mutual Feeling

Zara Anwarzai & Colin Eubank

I

"I think there is a role for organizers. I know quite a few people who are good organizers. They know how to talk to people, they know how to talk to a crowd, they know how to keep up the momentum of a protest.

But what they're wrong about is the overall role that they play. They are not the architects of action. They move in a kind of dynamic tension with the action that is unfolding. They don't build it. We have organizers who think that you can talk yourself into a movement one by one with each participant. All you have to do is talk to enough people for long enough and you'll get a movement. That's not true."
— Frances Fox Piven in an interview with *Jacobin*[1]

Over the past few months of the pandemic and the George Floyd Rebellions, millions across the globe have autonomously initiated and sustained powerful challenges to the oppressive system of racial capitalism. This has been done largely without (and often to the vexation of) professionalized political experts. Whereas the value of the professional political expert could be said to have been to "talk" both the language of the people and the market, the seemingly spontaneous organization of today's political actions have operated at a level of experience and feeling which explicitly contest traditional organizing strategies that emphasize incremental consciousness raising through language.

The politically educative force which has sparked a political consciousness with a determined abolitionist bent in today's collective political actions we would call "mutual feeling." But what is mutual feeling and how or where does it function? Following Rousseau's notion of common sense as a kind of moral sense (which is placed alongside sight, smell, and other sensory perceptions prior to language and reason), mutual feeling can be described as the experience of feeling that another is feeling your process of feeling.[2] It is a conscious moment of sensing the collectivity and co-implication of others in the interior infrastructure which a political subject reckons with as their own self. While at first this might seem quite basic, the experience of mutual feeling requires a few clarifications so as to avoid serious confusions:

1. Mutual feeling should not be misunderstood as a realization that another subject is feeling (or capable of feeling) what it is that you are feeling. This is not a moment of (presumed) recognition that multiple subjects are feeling the same thing (for example, sadness or outrage) in response to a shared experience (for example, the murder of Michael Brown).

Mutual feeling does not presume the identicality of subjects nor does it presume that subjects converge in relation to each other in the exact same way. This is not a moment of gross recognition, wherein one concludes that, because I am feeling them and they are feeling me, the other must be just like me (that they are a subject instead of an object).

2. Rather, mutual feeling indicates the precise and difficult experience of a collective relation. By feeling that another is feeling your feeling, the experience of mutual feeling implicates subjects in a shared, albeit oblique, co-inhabitation of each other. Herein lies a profound moment of self-understanding wherein the subject comprehends that a part of their own "self" is shared by the dissonant, strange, and unknown forces of others. One is sensitive enough to understand that the actions and desires of others (or at least, which cannot be reductively called one's own) exist within their own self, and vice versa. This co-implication does not clarify how subjects relate to each other so much as insist on the infinite complexity of mutual relation which cannot be consciously initiated.

3. The experience of mutual feeling, the collective relation it makes conscious, provides an analytic for conceiving of structural relations in a world wherein one may act not merely for oneself or others. One instead acts as from a notion of self which is not motivated selfishly, understanding one's goals and desires, one's feelings, as co-implicated with and for the world. The analytic of mutual feeling, however, also makes immediately apparent structural relations built to thwart and suffocate the experience of collectivity provoked by it. White supremacy and the structural machinery of racial capitalism cannot ever be integrated into this dynamic of collectivity. The logic of possessive individualism, interest, and economized value (to name a few) actively cauterize this mode of relation and understanding which articulate the world and self through mutual feeling.

We might say that mutual feeling illuminates the abolition of white supremacy and its corollary structural machinery not so much as a final goal, but instead an irreducible antagonism with which the world and the self cannot co-exist. Any moment wherein mutual feeling is felt is an instance wherein the abolition of white supremacy has been enacted. While it might be said that mutual feeling sketches the pathway towards a new world wherein white supremacy has been successfully dismantled, concretely speaking it is more accurate to say that moments of mutual feeling incite the inhabitation of a world wherein white supremacy no longer and does not yet exist. To proceed from the experience of mutual feeling in collective political action is to sustain (or proceed) in the building of such a world.

II

On what basis do we build this world together? Collective action requires that we first share some intention and then act in concert to advance the intended goal. Mutual feeling lends itself to sharing such an intention, as our ability to understand that both we and our co-actors possess a common endpoint relies on understanding our desires as tied into those of our co-actors and seeing our feelings as bearing weight on the web of our collective experience. In realizing our collective relation, we make it possible to share an intention.

If we want to act together, mutual feeling ought to take ethical primacy and political priority over other ways of responding. Of course, mutual feeling distinguishes itself from the experience of merely feeling others to share your feeling, which has proved itself useless for the purposes of abolition. Because mere feeling has rendered mutual interconnectivity impossible, some have turned to language to incite the foundation of mutual understanding needed for collective action. In *The New Jim Crow*, Michelle Alexander claims, "A new social consensus must be forged about race and the role of race in defining the basic structure of our society, if we hope to ever abolish the New Jim Crow. This new consensus must begin with dialogue, a conversation that fosters a critical consciousness, a key prerequisite to effective social action."[3] This arguably overestimates language's ability to motivate, awaken, and allow actors to fully understand their agency and capacities, especially in light of tools like mutual feeling. In making language a prerequisite for collective action, this view places an overly didactic burden on language as the sole generator and caretaker of political consciousness. Further, the expectation that we should first reach a language-based consensus before acting places a dangerous constraint on projects of abolition, delaying them until the right sort of consciousness has been fostered, namely, the sort of consciousness that we presently rely on to parse out the world as we already know it. Under the current conditions and the current regime of knowledge, any such consensus about abolition is unlikely to be reached.

Thus we cannot depend on language alone to activate political consciousness, or at least we cannot trust it to activate political subjects for the right reasons. While language does, of course, help us in certain crucial ways (by developing mutual feeling further, enabling coordination, etc.), it hinders our efforts when it dissociates the weight of the words from the weight of the lives it describes. Piven's figure of the organizer provides a cautionary tale of just this sort: As self-regarded "architects of action," it would seem that the specialty of organizers is not in the production of knowledge, but in the appropriate dissemination of it. The organizer provides a political education by choosing the right language to instill in individuals so as to raise their consciousness in a way that promotes an effective action, and thus increase the likelihood for victory. But this mistaken formulation is illuminating for a number of reasons. The circulation of knowledge between these realms is configured as a one-way street: it flows from the academic to the organizer, from the organizer to the organized. Thus conceived, language covers over the experience of life in an effort to render it legible, rather than working in conversation with the experiences occurring.

Working in tandem with mutual feeling, language helps give hermeneutical justice to our experiences, allowing us to produce knowledge about these experiences by contextualizing and collectivizing them. Language gives the conceptual framework to help understand the extent of our involvement with others. In this way, it becomes a better tool for communicating precisely what our goals are and narrating how our desires have led us towards those goals. Further, it unlocks our capacity for attending to the different ways in which language is used for creative political intervention. Our capacity to experiment with language, with our voice, as expressive and passionate in a poetic sense, becomes available to us. This capacity enables us to build a new language, a language needed for building a new world. In turn, the possibility of another world is itself necessary for rejecting the notion that our interpretations are limited by a certain set of permissible perspectives. And as we strain ourselves to rethink familiar interpretations of actions––actions understood as property destruction, walking in the street, making graffiti as well as yelling and talking to others––from new perspectives, we push ourselves to reimagine what it means to learn: We don't need anything new to produce knowledge. We just need to use our existing tools in the right way.

III

Yet even if we wish to use mutual feeling, our access to it has been restricted. The labyrinth that constitutes the world as we know it has been designed such that its walls twist and constrict our pathways towards mutual feeling. Sometimes, our laborious, consistent, passionate chipping away results in a break, allowing us to see and feel one another in a new light. This is the light cast by the possibility of collectivity, of a mutuality of feeling that emerges in the rarest but most valuable of moments. White supremacy and racial capitalism—both fundamentally incompatible with any true sense of collectivity—have enforced these divides, as the realization of our collective relations to one another threaten to undermine their most basic principles and most loyal followers.

Even when faced head on with opportunities for mutual feeling—when the walls have been pushed down, by either the force of others or the unsustainability of their own foundations—we see so many people turning away from the collective relation. Why might this be, beyond the obvious illicit desires offered to them by white supremacy or racial capitalism? Perhaps it is that mutual feeling, though crucial to our rejection of the ways of responding and relating that we have found inadequate to serve our purposes, also involves the somewhat terrifying realization that not only do we owe something to another, but we are also owed something in return. We might say this is the terror of understanding a debt that can never be repaid; The revelation of a relation which can never be severed transforms the given old political economy of relation in surprising ways.

Mutual feeling asks us to give ourselves over to a different organization of the senses, and thus a different way of knowing and experiencing the world. Doing so forces us to reject our current body of evidence accumulated about political possibility in favor of more generous interpretations, even when we have been failed (and have failed others), precisely because it understands that past sabotages and failures were rooted in a crass and selfish mere feeling. Thus the monopoly of mere feeling as feeling is perhaps the most dangerous tool employed by white supremacy and racial capitalism, as it thwarts possible ways of knowing any sort of relation outside of the marketplace. At its core is a cold individualism, which tells us that our feelings are ours alone, our responsibilities, hopes, and goals, all following in suit. Mere feeling is more than dangerous—it is a trap, with grave implications for what we think we're capable of knowing. By repressing this relation for ourselves, mere feeling fosters an unimaginative breed of understanding that prevents us from ever fully or correctly interpreting the actions of others. Mere feeling denies us of understanding our most basic way of relating to ourselves.

To recall, because language gets similarly operationalized to obscure this relation, we cannot afford to place it prior to collective political action. If we are engaged in the project of world-building, then we must consider how a new world necessitates new ways of knowing. As more opportunities give way to widespread understanding of our collective relations, mutual feeling offers a viable foundation upon which a new sort of political education can be formed in conjunction with the ongoing production of knowledge.

There are certain dangers of being a political actor who represses mutual feeling (or has it denied of them). She who acts without mutual feeling lacks an accurate picture of her own condition and the condition of those around her. As such, she lacks the means to respond appropriately to this condition. This is why the methods of the white ally, the uber-organizer, and the bureaucrat all suffer the same demise. These figures subsist on an economy of recognition (of some discontent, of some unfulfilled need, of some vague aim towards progress), which itself takes for granted a surplus of emotional energy from those around them or entities like the state which have already extracted and preside over its circulation.

But if we settle at such recognition, our political education is at a real risk of underdetermination, leaving us epistemically stunted. Our political education would refuse the construction of any new knowledge and instead opt for an efficient discipline of old forms. This kind of austerity petitions for a less murderous distribution of life/death, rather than refusing to negotiate with questions which did not ever even have us in mind.

Mutual feeling relieves us from the draw to recognize and be recognized, a draw which very often disguises itself as genuine political participation. Learning and becoming together are the constitutive actions of abolition, always squeezed out of even the smallest gestures, which would otherwise be overlooked in the pursuit of recognition. In making our claim to mutual feeling instead, our goals and desires become a way of understanding and relating to the things we don't know rather than merely settling for that which we can already see. With mutual feeling and the desire for intelligibility over recognition, we abandon the sovereign dreams of recognition and its ideal forms.

Notes

1. Mie Inouye, "Frances Fox Piven on Why Protesters Must Defend Their Ability to Exercise Disruptive Power," *Jacobin.* originally published on June 17, 2020. https://jacobinmag.com/2020/06/frances-fox-piven-protests-movement-racial-justice.

2. We are thinking in particular of a strain of thinking which can be picked up in a number of Rousseau's works, but especially: Jean-Jacques Rousseau, *Essay on the Origin of Languages and Writings Related to Music* (Dartmouth, 2000). Also see Jimmy Casas Klausen, *Fugitive Rousseau: Slavery, Primitivism, and Political Freedom* (New York: Fordham University Press, 2016).

3. Michelle Alexander, *The New Jim Crow: Mass Incarceration in the Age of Colorblindness* (New York: The New Press, 2010), 15-16.

Sadia Salim, *A Roaming Aesthetic III* (image by Humayun M.)

third dialogue

TO KNOW
& TO JUDGE,
POLITICALLY

4 April 2020

Companion Texts for Studio Session

Blanc, Eric and Jane McAlevey. "A Strategy to Win: A Conversation with Eric Blanc/Jane McAlevey." Jacobin, April 18, 2018. https://www.jacobinmag.com/2018/04/teachers-strikes-rank-and-file-union-socialists.

Chatterjee, Piya and Sunaina Maira. The Imperial University: Academic Repression and Scholarly Dissent. University of Minnesota Press, 2014.

Denver, Dan, host. Grace Blakeley, guest. "Coronavirus Economics with Grace Blakeley." The Dig (podcast), Jacobin, March 27, 2020. https://www.thedigradio.com/podcast/coronavirus-economics-with-grace-blakeley/.

Denver, Dan, host. Mike Davis, guest. "Mike Davis on Coronavirus Politics." The Dig (podcast), Jacobin, March 20, 2020. https://www.thedigradio.com/podcast/mike-davis-on-coronavirus-politics/ Fisher, Mark. Capitalist Realism: is there no alternative?. Winchester, UK; Washington [D.C.]: Zero Books, 2009. 17.

Gandhi, Leela. The Common Cause: Postcolonial Ethics and the Practice of Democracy, 1900-1955. Chicago: University of Chicago Press, 2014.

Gebrekidan, Selam, "For Autocrats, and Others, Coronavirus Is a Chance to Grab Even More Power." The New York Times (New York, NY), March 30, 2020. https://www.nytimes.com/2020/03/30/world/europe/coronavirus-governments-power.html.

Khalili, Laleh. Time in the Shadows: Confinement in Counterinsurgencies. Stanford: Stanford University Press. 2012.

Ray, Tarence. "A Way Out." https://popula.com. Popula, November 18, 2018. https://popula.com/2018/11/18/a-way-out/.

Said, Edward W.. Orientalism. New York: Pantheon Books, 1978.

Smith, Rogers M. "A Discussion of Jessica Blatt's Race and the Making of American Political Science." Perspectives on Politics 17, no. 3, 2019: 801–2. doi:10.1017/S1537592719002445.

Zerilli, Linda M. G.. "From Willing to Judging: What Arendt Found in Nietzsche." http://blogs.law.columbia.edu/nietzsche1313/ . Nietzsche 13/13, November 9, 2016. http://blogs.law.columbia.edu/nietzsche1313/linda-zerilli-from-willing-to-judging-what-arendt-found-in-nietzsche/.

Hosts | Ciarán Finlayson, Ari Fogleson, Gabriel Salgado, Milo Ward

Speakers | Asma Abbas, Isaac Brosilow, Colin Eubank, Ciarán Finlayson, Ari Fogelson, Isabella Lee, Dan Neilson, Gabriel Salgado, Milo Ward, Philip Zorba

Scribes & Annotators | Safi Alsebai, Colin Eubank, Jody Leonard, Hannah Walker

ASMA

Today we take the thread of the sources of legitimation in the realm of political knowledge. We are trying to find a way to connect the disciplining of political action that we spoke about a little bit last week (this uncomfortable relationship between politics also gestured to in strange ways in these moments of victories of striking workers) to the disciplining of political knowledge, whether in our access to that knowledge as truth and expression in the public sphere—which some of our speakers from today have explicit relation and experience with as writers and in editorial capacity—or in the spaces of its histories of production inside the Academy and the University. Of late, we have been thinking very much about the manner in which political affect, post-our thinking about fascism, is made both scrutable and immediate, and we're hoping to find in the sources of affirmation certain kinds of validations, aversions, and invitations that were long-held (and some long-rejected), to see what kinds of knowledges have been fostered to produce and affirm the failure—the ostensible failure—and irrelevance of any politics we brought to the table that did not conform to what political scientists, professional politicians, and equally professionalized organizers and nonprofit entrepreneurs report on our behalf. Many intersecting tracks here, and we will find their way as we go. I'm going to pass this on to four very able navigators and storytellers, Ciarán Finlayson, Ari Fogelson, Gabriel Salgado, and Milo Ward, who will take us and map with us the space of being and thinking together.

Introductions (in)to Political Knowledge

GABE

I wanted to start by sharing thoughts that I've had about a couple of different forms of political knowledge that I find suspect, and which came to mind immediately when I was starting thinking about how I've encountered the meaning of political knowledge. The first one is more related to the discipline of political science, and specifically its attempts to lay claim to itself as a science. I included a couple of reviews and short responses to a recent book by Jessica Blatt, *Race in the Making of American Political Science*.[1] I really like it because of the way that she traces this history of political science's drive to establish itself as a science, and the context of that kind of expertise that they were drawing on in the late nineteenth/early twentieth century, which was incredibly bound up with race science. Blatt argues that the role of race in the founding of the discipline of American political science cannot just be waived away as "what was in the air." She's making a point that it's much more deeply significant and impactful for how politics was being thought at the time. I believe Rogers Smith's review highlights this, talking about how race was a sort of pre-political ground on which politics was then built, so that the notion that we lived in a world divided up by racial groups, some more gifted and ready for democracy than others, was one of the fundamental assumptions from which a scientific approach to politics could then proceed.

What I found significant and wanted to bring to the conversation today is how this drive to produce more rigorous, precise scientific knowledge about politics runs counter to the way that maybe a lot of people would have imagined it would, in terms of its approach to race. It's not a way of combating racism. This drive to a more solid epistemic basis for the study of politics was not to find race and wave it away as any kind of illusion. Rather, it actually seized upon it as the very solid ground on which it would then build itself as a science.

So, I wanted to talk about this figure of the organizer and this approach to politics through the figure of the organizer as another locus of political knowledge that I'm also somewhat suspicious of (but much less so than political science's claims to itself as a science). I first encountered this figure of the organizer when I was working to unionize grad student workers. The Jane McAlevy interview we included in today's readings,[2] is an example of this kind of "organizer approach" that sees organizing as a science, and lays out concrete steps toward accomplishing goals or winning.

There's something about the certainty of what a "win" is that is one of the things that has always got to me. I found this figure of the organizer incredibly helpful to have. They present a very step-by-step way of accomplishing specific goals, and certainly there are skills of organizing that require a thorough understanding of the social totality and relationships that few people have. But that is not often what is emphasized. What I most want to push back on is how the question of what it means to do political work in our contemporary moment has been entirely subsumed by this language of organizing. So—at least for the folks that I talk to—no one wants to be an activist, everyone wants to be an organizer. We certainly need way more organizers and we need to be way more organized, whatever that means. But, we cannot let "organizing" exhaust everyone's imagination of what *doing* politics is, especially if this is also meant to counter the way the "politician" exhausts the meaning of politics. That's where I feel the real danger of the science of organizing asserting itself, and an opportunity being missed.

Picking up the conversation on the Rent Strike in the coronavirus moment itself, the way that I have seen all of the discussions play out around that is in three stages. First, a lot of people got super excited and said, "Oh, we need a rent strike. Oh, we're going to do a rent strike. There's going to be this huge rent strike coming now because no one can pay their rent." Then, there was an immediate backlash from this place of the organizer ideology (for lack of a better term) that said, "Well, you're just being ridiculous. You're not being serious if you're just calling for a rent strike. What it means to do a rent strike means you have to, you know, do XYZ things. You can't just say, we're doing a rent strike and expect it to happen. There's a lot of work that needs to go into that." Which, again, I think, to a certain extent, is true as well.

We've built our ideas of what these progressions look like, and what these sort of tried-and-true methods are, derived from the very specific political contexts in which they were tried, and then became true for. So, thinking about the knowledge that's genuinely been helpful for those kinds of movements (kinds of twentieth-century labor movements) serves a purpose. That's maybe the third stage in thinking about organization and political knowledge: how to not allow those predeterminations to become outsized, or proclaim a form of political knowledge which is used to silence, discipline, and shackle other kinds of political action.

So those were the two directions for exploring pitfalls of disciplinary political knowledge and professionalization that I've been thinking about. But at the same time, and especially with the organizer piece, I've been grappling with, and wanted to put to the group, the consideration that there are some forms of knowledge that we do want and are helpful. Organizing models have certainly been incredibly helpful to the work that I've done, and projects like the Tricontinental that are set up to produce knowledge in ways that I think we do want to foster, and are truly helpful to the left. So, how to encourage and make good use of those things without the pitfalls that I've articulated?

CIARÁN

What are our own interests as people who are interested in, or who claim, a materialist method, in terms of the sources of our own political knowledge and the sources of our own political judgment?

I've been looking back into the history of Marxism and its different claims to being scientific. It seems, generally, that the springboard for that is Engels, with the distinction in *Socialism: Utopian and Scientific,* but it's there all throughout the ending part of the *Manifesto,* as well.[3 4] The Manifesto ends with the rigid distinction between all the different types of non-communist, utopian, conservative, or bourgeois socialisms. What in particular are we claiming today when we claim to either be materialists or to be Marxists? Especially because all the main signposts of the "scientific" element of scientific socialism have fallen by the wayside or mostly been disregarded as precisely that which is least scientific within it, its most dogmatic elements, especially as it took shape in the Soviet Diamat, or in the Second International.

Last session, Rosa Luxemburg's Reform or Revolution came up—the quote about "the final end." So I wanted to return to that because Reform or Revolution is a polemic against Eduard Bernstein. It's mostly a defense of what's scientific in scientific socialism. I want to read a small part of that aloud. She's quoting Bernstein writing against the ideas of the necessity or inevitability. He's arguing against revolution, but against revolution because the people who agitate for the need for a revolutionary party or specific revolutionary organization believe that it's something mechanistic, and he believes what we should be cultivating is man's free will. Quoting him, she says:

> "Why represent socialism as the consequence of economic compulsion?," he complains. "Why degrade man's understanding, his feelings for justice, his will." Bernstein's superlatively just distribution is to be attained thanks to man's free will; man's will acting not because of economic necessity, since this will is only an instrument, but because of man's comprehension of justice, because of man's idea of justice. We thus quite happily return to the principle of justice, to the old war horse on which the reformers of the earth have rocked for ages, for the lack of surer means of historic transportation, we return to the lamentable Rosinante on which the Don Quixotes of history have galloped toward the great reform of the earth, always to come home with our eyes blackened.[5]

She goes on to say:

> The greatest conquest of the developing proletarian movement has been the discovery of grounds of support for the realisation of socialism in the economic condition of capitalist society. As a result of this discovery socialism was changed from an 'ideal' dreamt by humanity for thousands of years to a thing of historic necessity.[6]

Then, the main thing that distinguishes communism from all sorts of "bourgeois democracy and bourgeois radicalism" is the "decisive" moment, the shift from "...a vain effort to repair the capitalist order into a class struggle against this order for the suppression of this order," which is "the conquest of political power and the suppression of wage labor."[7] The quote is:

> ...the final goal of socialism constitutes the only decisive factor distinguishing the Social-Democratic

movement from bourgeois democracy and from bourgeois radicalism, the only factor transforming the entire labor movement from a vain effort to repair the capitalist order into a class struggle against this order for the suppression of this order which is defined as "the conquest of political power and suppression wage labor."

There's this long history of some of the extremely important efforts, especially centring Marxism as a revolutionary theory in the context of actual class struggles. The need to distinguish its predictive power had a different status then, maybe, than it does today. There's this John Holloway essay where he's deciding against scientific socialism, or a dogmatic Engelsism, where dialectics is a natural law—and not, as Adorno says, "the consistent sense of non-identity."[8] These scientific Marxisms believe they have a theory of society, which implicitly means they believe that they stand outside of society. They also have a certain relationship to academic disciplines, which prioritizes Marxist economics. And then, as a kind of a complement to this, people see the need to invent a Marxist political science, for example, or they need to invent a Marxist sociology in order to understand classes. Holloway thinks that none of these efforts basically amount to much because they either reveal the weakness of Marxism's categories when applied to these disciplinary formations for which they don't make sense, or they end up actually undermining the disciplinary formations to which they're hoping to contribute.

So, I was thinking today, just as a general question, what is it that we all personally are interested in, or wish to claim, for ourselves?

The John Clegg and Aaron Benanav piece from the first week on crisis ends with these three tasks of theory today: First, "...[T]o examine class struggle, not merely as possessing a theoretical framework, but as itself theoretically productive." It's not there to instruct movements, but to basically follow all the existing struggles and try to keep up with them and see the theoretical work they're already doing. The second is "...[T]o examine forms of the unfolding crisis of capitalist social relations, which provide the framework or context within which class struggle takes place." So, basically, to do a certain type of economic analysis. And then the third is, "...[T]o gesture toward the communist future, a task which has become much more difficult after the end of the labor movement."[9] It seems that a lot of the parts of this history that have the most claim to scientificity today, are those connected to some kind of predictive power. For instance, to return to *Capital* Volume III, "The Tendency of the Rate of Profit to Fall," and these types of things.[10]

One other thing I've been thinking about consistently is the first few pages of Cedric Robinson's *Black Marxism* (I haven't spent much time with *Anthropology of Marxism*) with its polemical negation of any kind of specificity toward the Marxist project in *Black Marxism*. Or, not even just the specificity of Marxism but the specificity to the capitalist era, where Robinson says in Chapter 1 that European civilization "...passed with few disjunctions from feudalism as the dominant mode of production to capitalism as the dominant mode of production." This is in total contrast to what you find in the *Manifesto*, where capitalism is a type of permanent revolution of destruction and creation.[11] So, there's a total dismissal—or at least a real thorn in the side—of claims to a specific kind of objectivity or scientificity as one particular mode of anticapitalist theorizing among others. Those claims end up being incorrect, in their determination of laws of motion (or any of these other laws or determinations that we think of as central to like *Capital* Volume I for instance).

So, these are my questions: Do we think we have any unique apprehension of society, or predictive capacity, or organizational capacity, when we turn to this movement? Or, are we more interested in the general terrain of historic anti-capitalism and workers' movements?

ARI

I think some of the questions that I want to raise really relate to what Gabe was talking about in terms of how race forms the basis of political science, and it's crucial to the kinds of questions that Laleh Khalili is also trying to ask. Furthermore, I think that her work is also an interesting counterpoint to what Ciarán's highlighting about the tasks of theory today. Maybe Khalili's project locates itself more within the tasks of pushing back within the Imperial University— also one of the readings for today—by positing a different active theorizing that's also done by spending a lot of time in the archives of this really repulsive world of the "soldier-scholars" of counterinsurgency.[12]

So, I tried to frame what my interests were for this topic in terms of another news piece that I was reading today. Since the lockdown began in the UK, like elsewhere, there have been discussions about how or when it will be able to end. Some of the media articles have dealt with the idea of immunity passports, community surveillance, contact tracing, and new powers in order to confine people who test positive or who have contacted somebody who tested positive. In *The Guardian* today, Anthony Costello criticizes the Tory government's approach as having not, in fact, moved beyond their initial proposals for mass sacrifice which they call "herd immunity." Costello raises a contrasting proposal for community surveillance and contact tracing. He says, "Finding these viruses is like guerrilla warfare. If you don't know where the virus is hiding you cannot control it. We must use a bundle of measures to chase it. We must organize teams of friendly community workers to find people with symptoms, test for the virus, isolate and treat them, and trace their contacts. Workers must check on them in their homes every one or two days."[13]

I want to back up for just a second. I started thinking about the two selections that I added to the readings from Laleh Khalili and Leela Gandhi at first, just because of wanting to return to critiques of Giorgio Agamben, seeing his work as an important shaper of left conceptions of crisis and emergency. And also because Agamben, at the end of February, put out a really short blog post called "The State of Exception Provoked by an Unmotivated Emergency" that made the argument that the Italian response to the epidemic was wildly out of proportion, and calls it "...states of collective panic for which the epidemic once again offers the pretext."[14] He links it to his past analysis by saying that, "We might say that once terrorism was exhausted as a justification for exceptional measures, the invention of an epidemic could offer the ideal pretext for broadening such measures beyond any limitation."[15] He's since partially recanted, but I don't think he's really going back on saying that it was an over-response.

I was really surprised when I went to read the actual article, just how insubstantial it is given how many people I had seen responding to it. I've been doing some work for an organization here in London that works as an advocate for people targeted in the war on terror, which has led me recently to Laleh Khalili's work, and at least to be thinking over various critiques of Agamben.[16] Furthermore, I think his work resonates with public understandings of law and exceptions to law that I think are important to push back against. One of the surprising things for me is that underneath all the disagreements about whether his analysis applies to this moment or not, is a strange consensus on the fact that his analysis, continuous with that of the "war on terror," actually holds water.

One thing Laleh Khalili does is show us in detail where Agamben's—but also a broader—understanding of the War on Terror as somehow lawless is empirically wrong, and is part of a specific liberal fantasy about it that misses how it has been carried out, and relentlessly legalized and proceduralized. It's also worth noting that if you pay attention to the ways in which Khalili highlights how liberal counterinsurgencies are carried out, then it would not be possible to say, as Agamben does, that terrorism has been exhausted as a justification for repressive measures. This is so both because there have been attacks that have served to rapidly gain and regain new powers of detention, and also because the broad shift has been specifically toward a community policing approach that draws in community elites and deputizes all public employees, including teachers and healthcare workers. It is the case in the UK at least, that a mandatory duty to inform on people in one's care is based on assessable, scientific, markers of extremism. So, in other words, specifically liberal counterinsurgent response is seen in the current form of the war on terror.

With these things in mind, I want to highlight the following: the question of how to calibrate a human response to the pandemic, the purely technical framing of these, and the irony of a "more humane" approach to the pandemic being framed in terms of guerrilla war or counterinsurgency. This makes me really curious about where the institutional habits and the knowledge to put that into practice are coming from and, subsequently, where the expertise and knowledge to enforce lockdowns might come from. For instance, are the military planners of Fallujah or Gaza involved? We've already seen in places like Israel, which has a well-developed capacity for limiting movement and for surveillance, just how they put that expertise into practice. So I find Khalili's highlighting of the circulating soldier-scholars, and treating counterinsurgencies as case studies for the "welfare state" to learn from, to be really important. It also raises a basic question about what kind of critically-engaged scholarship to do, and what to spend time reading.

I want to briefly turn to Leela Gandhi's *Common Cause* as well.[17] I know that it's strange, maybe, to jump straight into talking about this "saintly politics of descent," not knowing where that's coming from, but it raises the question of the secular in Agamben's work, and of unsettling, also, a Eurocentric history of democracy. In that vein, it's really important to point out the idea that "bare life" is connected for Agamben to the idea of the secular. Even in his recent commentary, the idea that people suddenly can't participate in religious rituals plays a major role in his hatred of lockdown. And if we do find that people are resigned to being sacrificed, what then? That's not the end of politics. It doesn't just mean, Agamben, that you go out and refuse to wear a mask.

MILO

I've been thinking—and maybe this connects both to Ari's critique of Agamben and to the conversation in our first dialogue on crisis—about Rousseau's response to Voltaire's response to the Lisbon Earthquake.[18] This earthquake happens in Lisbon—decimating nearly everything—and many Enlightenment thinkers and philosophers, including Voltaire, take the opportunity to assert that either there is no God, or if there is a God, He must be quite cruel to have allowed for such massive destruction. And Rousseau responds by saying that approaching Lisbon in such a naturalized or theological way is preposterous, because what happened was also due to material circumstances. Someone like Voltaire doesn't look at the infrastructures and poverty that produce a place as destructible. And I think that there's a really interesting thing about what Agamben does in these moments, showing that this is a moment of crisis that can suspend a legal order to allow new things, when—especially with the readings that Ari brought in—really law is always out there on the frontier.

There's this rich history of politics as something that has to be protected, in the views of classical political theoretical texts, including those of Arendt and Schmitt. I'm interested in that exact language, of political science and political knowledge as things that have to be preserved, as inherited. That framing makes it possible to draw certain conclusions about who is building political space or who has the right character to become a political subject. Not to mention the process—which becomes a scientific process—of developing political sensibilities. So, ultimately, there are those who don't have the right dispositions, and whose characters need to be formed, and so on.

These theorists who begin with the idea of politics as inherited, they can really return to an idea of justice as something that can only be viewed with an Aristotelian distance from everything else. And part of that distance is knowing that, in some ways, we can't change anything. Taking the example of a classroom, this looks like a professor who believes that students can't be helped. Or, perhaps, there might be ways to help them, but that requires shaping them to fit the world that exists today, without ever thinking about the conditions that make the world what it is. Ultimately, the conditions that we live in today are ones that are unchangeable. What is changeable are people's characteristics in living in that world. That seems to be the focus of a lot of political knowledge, especially in asking what education is supposed to do, in the dissemination of knowledge.

Another twist to this knowledge is the relation between community policing, and a channeling of local democracy and participatory knowledges into "vigilantism." In my work on community policing, I find that the most rich democratic practice that people have brought their sensibilities into is barking at their neighbors—in community participatory violence, defense of community-led property values, and the policing of values. That is something that I'm very concerned about in this particular moment—in a way that is not going to be picked up by Agamben, who is going to think about it in terms of the state, or as a state of exception. I see it as a participatory and legal development of a violence, via a "democratic sensibility" in cahoots with racial targeting and policing of the poor, criminalizing poverty in all the ways that have nothing to do with changing the circumstances that produce a Lisbon or a pandemic.

Vigilantism is both organized and disorganized. John Stuart Mill basically argued that a population isn't ready to rule themselves, and has to be ruled despotically, until they are ready to catch criminals on their own and turn them in, until they're willing to refuse safe harbor to criminals of their own community—until they are, as it were, less ashamed of an execution than they are of an assassination.[19] Interestingly, it's a kind of home-rule idea. In this long history of the idea of community policing, you have both the involvement of the community who wants to rule, and those who you are ruling over in that project. That's a way for that relationship to work. There are great examples all throughout settler-colonial states (and just colonial) states: the Aboriginal guard, the Aboriginal troopers (basically police), called the Native Guard or something in Australia who weren't the officers, but the actual soldiers and policemen committing most of the genocides. That history is really interesting because of the way that happened also with indigenous tribes in the US. The development of policing structures—of bringing Irish into the police force, and of black police officers—has this long history, that runs alongside political theory and political science advocating for the best mousetrap for your own people. Political scientists came up with broken windows.

Counterinsurgency, Judgment, Accountability, Inheritance

ISAAC

I have some thoughts about what Ari and then Milo have brought up. I would say that in Israel and Palestine, the way that the counterinsurgency by the Israeli government is working, as far as I can see it, has been either an intensification or an acceleration of what's already happened and what's already been set up. Particularly with the way the labor market works, with Palestinians in the West Bank, working either with permits—which are incredibly restrictive as many know—or working illegally inside Israel's '48 borders. That has really gone into disarray. It was already intentionally incredibly difficult and confusing and dangerous, but it's just intensified with the shutdowns of checkpoints in the Palestinian Terroritories. (The Al-Sahlah checkpoint is still running.) But it's intensified the alienation of Palestinian workers, within the Jordan Valley, particularly Area C, where Israel occupies both the civic and the military aspect. And then you have all these people who are living under the PA in Area A, who are on lockdown that conflicts with the hours of the checkpoints and the lockdown times of other Areas.

The government here inside the '48 borders of Israel has been using this incredibly draconian monitoring of cell phones, and things like that. And there's always been a really vulnerable population—now more and uniquely so—who are asylum-seekers, mostly from Eritrea and Sudan. About 40,000 of them. They don't have healthcare, they don't have citizenship, and all of them worked under the table. So I would say that, as we think about counterinsurgency, we already know which populations are the most at risk, and the way that the state and the market function to subjugate and alienate them. But it now has these new variables to it. That's what I've been seeing. So, not a huge insight, but those are the particulars of it, at least what I can see.

ASMA

In the first dialogue, we gestured to the fact that while we want to be able to give the state up as the focus or the starting point, we are painfully aware of the path dependencies already in place for the current states of, for example, India or Israel. The tragedy is that elite knowledges keep affirming that starting point, so everything reinforces that which must be undone.

ISAAC

I think that's what hasn't happened, the giving up.

CIARÁN

Would you be willing to share some of the Arendt stuff on political judgement that you spoke about before the session?

ASMA

I mean I wanted to put that in there because I feel there's something, like one particular way that she gets appropriated by the right wing or most of political science, to make an argument for particular forms of speech and also for a sense of politics as permissiveness, or, just this kind of masochistic tolerance of fascists. I worry it might be too much of a divergence from the excerpts you have read aloud and the conversation that has ensued. But, quickly, since you ask, I think I was trying to signal to a possible departure from the discourse on will (but not the discourse on freedom, to be sure) that we find in the turn to judgement as the right sort of province of politics, which is why I placed it here for our conversation about the disciplining and "unfreeing" of political knowledge. I think that that's something very contrary to how people read her and use her, and how some of them are literally, I feel, eating off her body.

As far as I can tell, she just doesn't think of political truth like any other kinds of truth, and there is some very explicit invitation to forms of perspectivism that are not liberal, and that are not in love with a kind of transparency, but rather give room to each other to constitute a democratic community on the basis of this other capacity to judge, drawing on the forms of aesthetic judgment she finds in Kant (also corroborated by Adorno). I wonder if, then, this particular free will that sort of the left invokes, or actually renders, comes into conflict with that. So I just wanted to do something with that distinction, in a way that helps us think not only about political truth but about political knowledge.

I just wonder what forms of accountability—let alone discipline—come from an emphasis on will versus an emphasis on judgment. It seems that the difference between refusal and failure might also fall along those lines as well—just to continue some of the really great thinking we encountered last week in our conversation around the calls to politics.

One thing that becomes really crucial, reading even Piya Chatterjee and Sunaina Maira around The Imperial University—as well as just thinking of people like Gayatri Spivak or Edward Said—is the manner in which they will constantly bring home the fact that all forms of expertise that the ostensible "West" produces are always referencing something that is not in the West, and that there is absolutely nothing that claims to have a ground that is without a ground—especially the political grounding—in the spaces called "the Orient."[20] I think that that's really important in even being able to talk about different countries and their capacities to emerge out of the virus and the pandemic. I just want to be aware of that constantly. I'm not thrilled that I find a clear blindness around religion and secularism even in a kind of gushing leftist hope in this moment; that's just sort of where I live affectively. That's also why the discourse of neoliberalism or that of cruel optimism seems too total in that way — it's always connected to the claim to some kind of knowledge by somebody that is grounded elsewhere but won't declare it! I'm not a crazy follower of anyone really, but there is just this small question of the entire edifice of political knowledge resting on those who have been colonized, and whom we continue to colonize.

BELLA

This goes back to what Milo was talking about: the conception of politics as this passed down inheritance, something to be preserved on the one hand, and law, as Khalili talks about it, as constituted by a body of precedent also to be preserved on the other hand. However, law is set aside by the liberal order with a counterinsurgent penumbra. In times of crisis at home one body of laws is cast aside for another that's always lying around—the one that will grant emergency powers in terms of legal precedent and contestation. A lot of the law that is constructed in counter-insurgency and through, and for, policy lacks the contestation that law usually does in the judicial system.

For example, you have John Yoo, who wrote the "Torture Memos" that came from the Office of Legal Counsel. This Office is where the President goes to vet the legality of executive orders, acts of war, and such. The only precedent they rely on is their own precedent, and that precedent doesn't go through the courts in the same way other legal precedent does. When they say "no" to the executive branch, that's not published. So the only precedents that are published are the times that they say "yes." This other body of law, that lacks the same contestation, is what grants authoritarian power. So counterinsurgency happens not just abroad, but here too. I think that in this crisis, we will see those kinds of laws enacted at home. So, in the same way that this body of laws is cast aside, I think about the kind of politics that we inherit, or of this idea of a politics that's inherited and preserved, or of legitimate political knowledge. How does that emergency power call for, or demand, the casting aside of those inherited politics?

Fanaticism always seems ludicrous to us, because it has no voice to make itself heard among us. Our fanatics, even, aren't true fanatics; they're just rascals or fools. In lieu of inflections for the inspired, they only have cries for the devil-possessed.
— from Jean-Jacques Rousseau, *Essay on the Origin of Languages*, Chapter XI (trans. Safi)

"Turning to the sensorial accounting happening in Rousseau's passage, there are some interpretive possibilities embedded in his claim of the fanatic going unheard. Among relations that allow the fanatic to emerge as fanatic is the sensorium that will not listen, and Rousseau suggests that there might be a connection between us 'not having learned how to see things in all their relations' and the impossibility of hearing the fanatic that follows—or even as gestured to in the previous paragraph, even regarding someone as a 'true fanatic.' Here, 'true' appears to me to be an issue of verification (a la Rancière) very much implicating the political sensorium. It reminds us not only that something becomes listenable within certain relations, but also that listening itself is relational and locational (the fanatic has no voice among us), and certain sensoria can only verify certain realities and truths. It could be said that this particular lack of listening is essential to the project of the kinds of learning liberal Enlightenment sponsors and rewards. It behooves a democratic impulse to be suspicious of what amounts to listening, voice, and being heard in this sensorium. Indeed, that is what constitutes democratic politics.

"For Rousseau in the passage, the fanatic asks to be held differently, not placed beyond judgment or finalised in the present to determine what the fanatic is and what he will do. In linking our inability to hear the fanatic to our disregard for the totality of relations that produce our judgments, Rousseau is not arguing for a partiality to or sympathy for the fanatic, but proffering a different way of problematizing that figure for politics, wherein the enfoldings of history and politics manifest in the body that speaks and forces us to listen, allow us to be close and to betray, and even suggest a place and role for us. Voltaire has certainly missed an opportunity to consider certain kinds of relations, as he imagines a form of political life managed by sectioning off, excising, or pretending away, the hold of the fanatic on our imagination. He refuses to consider the entwinement of sentiment and imagination that might allow him an imagination, or to see himself as someone also telling a story of prophecy and vision not unlike those he is railing against."

—from Asma Abbas, "The Fanatic and the Case for an Inefficient Politics"

Capacity, Affect, Imagination

CIARÁN

I wanted to ask more about Gabe's comparison, between the kind of spontaneity-oriented leftists and the cautions of the organizers. We were talking with Hannah Black earlier about the rent strike, which tries to overcome some of these divisions, wherein it's not about picking at the knot of organization and spontaneity.

ASMA

Thinking about Ciarán's question in relation to Gabe's question of the organizer, while perhaps bringing in the vigilantism in the realm of politics itself: are we in a position or a situation where we have the potential for a unique access to a predictive or organizational—not only possibility, but—capacity? For instance, when Hannah Black discusses the rent strikers' tool kit in her contribution on the Rent Strike Movement, that makes me wonder about what kinds of knowledges—not only predictive and organizational kinds—are relevant and which are irrelevant? What do we have no need for in order to do what people are doing?

CIARÁN

There is an argument that the scientificity that Marx claims is a purely negative science; it's the immanent critique, or the determinant negation of the errors of the aspirations of clinical philosophy, when it doesn't formalize itself into a positive content. And that it was Marxism's formalization into a positive science that led to the errors that actually undermined—that have done more to undermine—revolutionary activity and theorizing than state repression. This is one of the arguments—in one of the surveys of scientific socialism, by John Holloway[21]—that is interesting in relation to the question of overcoming the division between the ultra-left claim to the rent strike or call for the rent strike, and the justified reservations of the organizers. It cites the potential for a broad-based unity, the conditions of overcoming divisions, and then the act of pointing this out, as being the examples of the tasks of communist theory today. How do we claim a certain insight into reality? I'm not sure what relation that claim has to science, but maybe it functions as its own type of non-specialist political knowledge or something. I think this is one of the things that we've all sort of been gesturing towards today.

SAFI

As you noted, Ciarán, in your introduction, when a discipline makes a claim to being a "science," we might think of it as making that claim with some assumed standard of objectivity, reproducibility, predictive power—something a scientist would be wont to call "rigor."

At the same time, in their introductions, Gabe and Milo highlighted the way that such claims to scientificity as imparting certain assumptions and claims regarding the subjects of such a science. That is, claims of certain senses and sensibilities, limits and excesses of imagination, capacities to remember and forget, etc. that ultimately inform these subjects' capacities to act within what is deemed by these same original scientists to be political space—to know and to judge and to act politically.

Milo also noted that juridical law makes a move of seeking not only to be enacted—at the border, as the shadowy penumbra—but to be educated and internalized—on the one hand, where a professor might foreclose on what all a group of students will ultimately be able to learn in order to be "productive citizens," and on the other hand in the "cops in the heads" of vigilantes at the same aforementioned borders, taking up the work of law as their own to claim.

Maybe the understandings of capacities and limits that claims to "science" make are more telling than how predictive they imagine themselves to be.

ASMA

Even the "self-evident" framing of neoliberalism as a thing has done a lot of work in making conversations on the left very paltry. If you read earlier critiques, say of the university, from people who are trying to protect the university from neoliberalism, you find a commitment to a production of the citizen that is just using the same skills of "neoliberalism" but in the service of organizing, or in the service of good things, rather than the state and the corporation. It just seems, perhaps, that we never quite understand how turning to neoliberalism as an explanatory system itself had consequences. We bought into an imagination that wasn't imagination at all. I wonder if the university used neoliberalism as the thing to kill all imagination.

I have a hard time with students constantly saying, neoliberalism did this or that—you've really got to say more, right? And I think that there's something about just what was supposed to be defended at the university level or in terms of community organizing against the market in this particular form. It invaded everything. And it has a lot to do with what we thought we were teaching people and what they were supposed to become—what good use of knowledge and skills would be. I think that there's so much that the university has done to produce the monster of neoliberalism as the thing we circle and circulate around. Why aren't we talking about imaginations that are not tied to undoing this thing that's just there because we call it something? What is the predictive power of these namings? What ways do each of us have to name the commitments we constantly make, even in the realm of knowing things and critiques, not merely holding or becoming a negative space.

DAN

I have a lot to think about, but I want to share just one quick observation, which might help tie together in a relatively material way some of the ideas that have been put out. One of the things that became obvious, which was quite revealing and synthetic during the 2008/2009 financial crisis, was that the mechanism for the crisis really exposed the relationship between housing and labor, especially. I'm referring to the US system here; it connects to other places in interesting ways, but the thing is that, in the US, the prevalence of the thirty-year fixed-rate mortgage as a financial instrument allowed work and the home to be connected through the financial system in an important way. Of course, what then developed was precarious labor on the one hand and what you might as well call precarious finance on the other hand. They broke down together in an important way during the crisis.

The fracture along which that broke down began within the financial system and had a big impact on labor. But, there was a comparatively quick restoration of the "normal" labor order because, for the most part, it was the financing arrangement that had gone wrong. I say all of this because I think in the sum of the conversation so far about rent strikes in particular and the figure of the organizer, we can see already that this moment ties together work and the home in a way that is once again absolutely essential: namely, that there's a call to shelter, and the request or the imperative to work. Whether that's because labor relationships afford the privilege of bringing work into the home, or in other cases show an inability to work—that distinction is obviously critical—we're seeing the close relationship between shelter and home on the one hand and work on the other, as a focal point for this crisis itself. So, where do financial relationships show up and where could they be severed or incapcitated under current circumstances in these moments of organizing? Maybe there's something about how the refusal or failure would spill over into working relationships as well. How else might that show up? Maybe around a loosening, a natural loosening, of the restrictions of the quarantine weeks or months in the future.

Communication, Common Sense, and the Political Work of Materialism

COLIN

One of the components of today's conversation that I was thinking about which hasn't yet come up explicitly—but I think is really present in what everyone has been saying with questions about knowledge and its production, political education, and disciplining—is kind of the element of media and/or mass communication more generally. What Asma was just speaking about with the deep complicities of the university and the violences of neoliberalism, for me, also connects to a question about the role of public education or community conversation or the sharing of one another, which might be a different kind of thing that could fall under the heading of what I think Ciarán called the non-specialist knowledge of being able to communicate with others, that has the chance to circulate at this moment. I think this speaks to what Gabe was talking about with the role of the organizer today, or our critiques of the primacy of the expert in the age of neoliberalism—or the one who knows market logic the best and uses it as a common tongue to translate desires and make appeals to our frenetic, broken subjectivities which deeply mistrust but still, inexplicably, have a modicum of faith in making arguments that are legible to the systems that destroy us.

At least in my community, there is this stronger than ever dissonance, or a dissonant realization, between what is being talked about 24/7 by media outlets and then the knowledge that people need in order to survive and be with each other in this immediate moment. This seems relevant for the pandemic or something like burgeoning rent strikes or mutual aid organizing, though I'm sure we can all agree that this configuration of contestation over information and its legitimate dissemination has inundated the public for at least over the past half-decade. What becomes interesting to me, though, in the time of the pandemic, is that more folks seem aware that these contests over words are important not because words are (or were) important in and of themselves...but that words matter because the lives of our loved ones, or the lives of others, always hang in the balance. So the Democrat that relishes fact-checking Trump just to demonstrate that Trump is lying is kind of exposed for the fact that this is all still only a game for them. For the rest of us, it seems, some sort of collective negotiation with that stuff precedes or evades language, yet always makes us strive to use it in more creative and less austere ways. So, this dissonance manifests itself in my conversation with my mom, where she'll say, "Yeah I'm so tired, I spent my whole day listening to the live updates on the pandemic. I listened to Trump's daily speech, and then the Governor of California gave his, and then you know Mayor Garcetti from Los Angeles gave his speech." But it seems evident to her that their rhetorical power only lies in that they might be able to convince her neighbors and community members to do one thing or another. Beyond that, they have no real power for her at this time. So she takes to these other things: Facebook discussion groups, or phone trees from a local mutual aid group, or WhatsApp message groups, which actually move fast enough to avoid just mirroring the same soundbytes or memes that are going to circulate the airwaves of major news channels for the next twelve hours. Anyway, I think this has been really eye-opening for people because it is the first time in a really long time that traditional media has not been able to dominate all means of communication and keep a uniform message by framing the terms of discourse for the duration of the crisis.

It could be said that the use of TikTok as a nimble international digital organizing tool for disrupting Trump's rally and the subsequent threats by the President and other governmental agencies to shutter the platform demonstrate precisely this combat between new technological modes of communication. But the point here is less technological differentiation—as we know the real estate of a person's social media feed was always for sale—than identifying a shift in where trust is placed: a shift from trusting institutions to trusting people in carrying out collective survival.

A similar sentiment is found in Frantz Fanon's essay on the radio in Algeria's anti-colonial struggle, which demonstrates how the adoption of a particular technology helps us realize the deep utility of communal communication networks that pre-exists and pervades the birth of what he calls Algeria's national voice. If the radio was mostly considered a tool of colonial administration before 1955, the announcement of the revolutionary Voice of Free Algeria gives Algerians a reason to bring this technology into their homes and listen.[22] But, just as the colonial narrative is contested by the broadcasting of revolutionary counter-narratives across the airways, so begins the "soundwave warfare" of systematically jamming Algerian signals. Thoroughly engrossed in the battle of the waves, the listener would keep his ear glued to the receiver and reiterate those small moments wherein information could be deciphered. But even equipped with the new technology of the radio, the Algerians utilized what was referred to as "the Arab telephone" to negotiate, decipher and ultimately disseminate this collected information. Originally used as a pejorative by the Europeans, the Arab telephone referred to the rapid speed at which information filtered through native society and crossed incredible distances. With time, both colonial and anti-colonial forces referred to this as a formidable infrastructure, almost a secret weapon. The technology of the radio announced the voice of the nation, but what turned a single voice into a formidable cacophony accumulates in the retellings and reformation of fragmentary information in the company of others.

What was yesterday written off as gossip, chisme, or the fanciful rumor-milling of a small community becomes essential infrastructure for the transmission of social life during the long days of a state-sponsored pandemic. It doesn't take very long to realize that the success or failure of counterinsurgent ops rests upon control of the attention economy. But old and new technology teaches us to keep company in the words and stories of our neighbors. — Colin

In his essay, "Boredom," from *The Mass Ornament*, Siegfried Kracauer derides the advent of the radio on the basis of its ability to distract, interrupt, or wedge itself into moments of genuine interaction and being with the self and others. Kracauer saw it as a tool for social isolation, explicitly at odds with any sort of collective feeling, writing that it "vaporizes beings....Silent and lifeless, people sit side by side as if their souls were wandering about far away. But these souls are not wandering according to their own preference; they are badgered by the news hounds."[23] He also acknowledges its inherent imperialistic qualities and bent towards the dissemination of Western news ("Should the Chinese imbroglio be tactfully disembroiled, one is sure to be harried by an American boxing match: the Occident remains omnipresent, whether one acknowledges it or not"). Taken next to Fanon's writing on the role that radio played in Algerian anti-colonial struggle a mere three decades after Kracauer so thoroughly bashed the technology, this understanding of the purpose of radio is useful for helping us situate the role of more modern technologies in contemporary struggle. I've been preoccupied with the contradictions inherent in the new ways of using social media for certain types of organizing, which is a much more lateral, horizontally disseminated way of sharing information. Social media for organizers, activists, and workers alike has been a saving grace during the pandemic and for the ongoing Black Lives Matter protests throughout the country, yet it is only recently that these platforms have begun to take on this role. Social media's usefulness or even legitimacy as a tool, or anything other than what Kracauer might imaginably call a "cult of distraction" (his contemporary language for cinema and film) is constantly called into question along generational lines and by people not participating in the current rebellions. The idea of receiving and trusting news and information that is often crucial to one's safety in a certain place or moment from anywhere other than more formal, top-down, organized news sources automatically disqualifies the legitimacy of the information to many people. But it is pretty unimaginable that coordinated, though often spontaneous and unorganized (but not disorganized) movements and moments could have taken place without the real time sharing and boosting of essential information across multiple platforms. On the other hand, perhaps somewhat ironically, in my limited experience, organizing across social media and other digital platforms has sounded a death knell for more traditional routes of organizing. There are few things more likely to instill active disinterest in organizing workers than the insufferability of Zoom DSA subgroup meetings. This brings us back to the larger questions of the role of the organizer and what types of political knowledge we rely on. It seems apparent, now, that we are witnessing a marked shift in

Maybe this conversation about budding forms of communication gives us a different perspective on what Mark Fisher narrates from World War II, when there's an explosion of really cool communist or radical works that Channel 4, BBC, and other public broadcasting entities end up commissioning during this moment of crisis (even though, we know, the backlash and purges that will follow).[24] I've got a friend here in Oaxaca who is a screenwriter and works with film. He suggested to me that a similar thing is happening again in the UK right now—all the regular sitcoms and TV shows can't film so the studios and companies are looking for new, creative programming, and, in a way, are actually clamoring to give people the chance to take what Fisher would call the risks that the social fabric is willing to get on board with.

This is interesting because it presents an opportunity for mass access to moments of public education on topics that were until only yesterday written off as too experimental for the profit margin, or too red for public sensibilities. But, at the same time, I think our earlier comments on media demonstrate that these new openings are attached to the invitation to play no small part in the recovery of this market, and working to deliver it a stabilized, resilient form.

PHILIP

I wanted to get back to the strikes a little bit, and maybe answer one of Ciarán's earlier questions that I thought was really good. What are we claiming when we say we are materialists? I'm gonna hop around in the reading so bear with me, but I'm thinking back to this point that Fisher makes about how in individualistic society, we're all trapped in our own feelings, our own imaginations. I think this connects really nicely with Tarence Ray's point that the union traditionally activated working people's imaginations and how this can't work with the liberal theory of change.[25] That further connects to the Leela Gandhi piece, where she has this point about self-sacrifice—voluntary disenchantment for the sake of solidarity with persons and properties that have been stripped of value by historical circumstance.[26] One of those properties, you could say, is unions. When we get into the Jane McAlevey interview, she talks about how one of the benefits West Virginia had over Oklahoma and their teacher's strikes is (or was) their labor tradition.

So, now, with things like tenants and Chicago's Amazon workers striking, I'm wondering how those things become material, or how these things become labor traditions? Tarence Ray, at the end of this piece called "A Way Out," makes an appeal about how we can do this because we've done it before. I'm asking how do we do these things? I'm asking this genuinely again, and I apologize if this is naive, you can tell me so, but in the future will Amazon workers say, "we can do this, we've done it before" if they are victorious now? And, to kind of answer Ciarán's question, and you can tell me if this is naive as well, about what we mean when we claim we are materialists: I think, in part, it's Fisher's point in *Exiting the Vampire Castle*—how we have to re-orient around class instead of these neoliberal ideas of decency—and one of the things McAlevey says, which is that, "there's no way out of the current crisis...other than taxing corporations and the wealthy," and how successful strikes give workers confidence in their power to make political changes happen.[27] I'm just wondering how this becomes a labor tradition.

ISAAC

Philip, I like the question of how these practices become labor traditions and felt histories. Also, going back to Ciarán's question about materialism: I immediately thought of my frustration with someone who said that something wasn't materialist enough, that someone's analysis wasn't materialist enough. And I thought, this is sort of a ridiculous thing to say! How does someone get more or less materialist? Isn't it that you are or you aren't?—maybe that's really crude. But, there's something to that way of making it an "aesthetic" that I find really bothersome. I think it's also important to consider this in the context of the readings that are culled from the teacher's strikes from the past year, which began as wildcat strikes. I think it's really important that, outside of the Chicago Teachers' Union, which has a very militant leadership, the wildcat labor strikes worked in tandem with more militant shops. I think these things are crucial.

That goes back to the rent strike conversation of "Who gets to strike?". On the one hand, those who can't afford to pay rent at all don't pay, and that becomes the strike—the crisis of failures as we called it. And, then, on the other hand, those who are ideologically-driven, but maybe not striking out of necessity. The real answer is: both. Both of those people support each other; you see people through the two types of organizing, which feed off of one another. And as far as the people that articulate this binary, I was thinking about a piece about the 1956 Hungarian Revolution, by C.L.R James, Grace Lee Boggs, and Cornelius Castoriadis, called "Facing Reality." It's very much that strain that tries to seek out a kind of felt history of autonomous uprisings that take on both the party orthodoxy, as well as a stance towards socialism. But, I also think there are some pitfalls in trying to say, "Let's put this all into an autonomist history, and that'll make all our problems go away," because, ultimately, I think it's a dialectic between the people who have the history of struggle, but who have it packaged into a more ideological place, and those who don't. And I think that there's a lot of listening happening.

I've been thinking about Sudhir Mishra's film, *Hazaaron Khwaishein Aisi* that we watched together.[28] At the end of it, one of the characters, Siddharth raises the question of whether or not the mysteries of the (medical) body are more or less confusing than the mysteries of revolution. He is writing this in a letter to his former wife, Geeta, with whom he spent many years in a village in rural India sowing the conditions of revolution. And he is writing this at a point when it is clear that revolution is not going to happen according to a regimented Naxalite view of things. He ultimately decides to trade one "science" for another, to leave India for England and go to medical school.

I have a suspicion that constant attempts to avow this or that method as "scientific" might, in part, be borne out of a deep-seated fear of letting oneself go to that method. As much as making a claim to science includes making certain assumptions about one's own capacities as a subject, the constant re-evaluation of methods on the basis of, for example, predictive power and objectivity and applicability to as many cases as possible, that might just come down to a timid distance and some lack of faith. Distance, in case you might see yourself in the images that method ultimately throws up at you, on account that the image may be frightful, impure, unsavory. Lack of faith in case you might lose yourself in that method and find yourself somewhere you didn't wholly expect. —Safi

CIARÁN

I'm thinking about this idea of the lockdown as a strike emptied of its social content that Chuang writes about. I was wondering what makes something a strike versus a lockout, and it seemed that it has to do with the specific way in which it's politicized. I'm wondering how one gets to that specific kind of political distinction without a claim to scientificity or correctness? How to move forward in a specific direction, I guess, remains my question. What if all the movement is happening independently of our movements, or leftists' movements? If we're seeing the nationalization of healthcare systems or hospitals, and these types of things independent of political movements, then again what is the specific task of anything that we're trying to do? Is there any specificity toward it beyond the general affirmation of the already existing movement of workers or something, which would not necessarily have to be either Marxist or materialist, or any of the things that we generally work through or towards, except that they are maybe a part of our broader political inheritance. But, that wouldn't have the same specificites of method, would it?

ISAAC

This reminds me of this anecdote a friend told me. In the 1960s, when some of the representatives to the U.S. anti-war movement met with the Viet Cong, the first thing they asked was, "Oh, we're having this big debate: what should we do? Should we do draft resistance, or should we get drafted and then do G.I. resistance on the military bases?" This had been a really intense debate of strategy, and had divided a lot of people in the U.S. anti-war movement. To which—and this is all anecdotal—the Viet Cong guy responded, "Oh that's easy: the people who want to do draft resistance should do draft resistance, and the people who want to get drafted and do G.I. resistance should do that." I think that that's an interesting paradigm to some of these debates that you see with the renter's strike: we should do this, or we should do that. And a lot of the time—and this goes back to the kind of crude point about Edward Said—a lot of the things that seem like they're really complicated strategy debates amongst people maybe aren't. A lot of it responds to this politics of scarcity of revolutionary tactics, and I think that that's always something to push against and move beyond.

ASMA

I really appreciate that, Issac, because I do wonder how much we have also learned from a kind of austerity politics for many years, to somehow enact it as obligation. In my recent experience here with mutual aid stuff—I'll be honest—I do resist compulsions of any kind, and I feel that somehow I have to protect the students who I am trying to help be engaged with the mutual aid group, which is actually not built on mutual aid principles, but a kind of survivalism. I feel a need to protect them from the violence of the survivalist mode, with all due respect, since I don't approach life and death in a certain way, and I think that that's really where certain differences in modes of secular materialist thought, and meanings of life and death appear. Is this my "bias"? Language has played a role in that for years; whether it's people writing necropolitics, or Rancière doing his stuff, there's just a way that I think some of us feel the stiff fingers, reprimands, and burdens, of all those forms of theorizations implicit in people's reactions now. I feel nervous, not about militancy by any means, but by forms of secular moralisms that do not involve me, and that do not involve the people they will affect. So how do we, without duplicating efforts, play a role in reproducing an alternate notion of mutuality and reciprocity built on rural white, liberal, ruling class understandings of made-up scarcities of a certain kind, that make us unable to take the discourse of scarcity seriously ever? So, that's my reaction. I will die before I engage scarcity as the premise of organizing, but I probably would do that if I were in Pakistan, so I don't know. I think that there it's a different thing, because of a not-yet-fully neoliberal or philanthropic idea of charity, because there are only so many rich people (and those who are, are very wealthy and exhibitionist), and lots more who don't have anything still give a lot. And speaking about these poorer countries where more people will die: the fact that certain places have infrastructures for mutual aid has everything to do with how many poor people have already been there, and know how to do that for each other anyway. And, so it's all these rich people here who have no idea how to help each other, because someone else has been looking after them (and we'll see how that plays out in November). How do we articulate these things without ending up fighting the same old fights, as if it's just a matter of "bias," or one's place in the world, or one's claim to spaces? Who ends up taking charge in these spaces where many of us will be marginal to the economies of life and death because who we are doesn't matter, and somebody else's perceived half-life can always prevail and silence us.

Notes

1.   Rogers M. Smith, "A Discussion of Jessica Blatt's *Race and the Making of American Political Science,*" *Perspectives on Politics* 17, no. 3 (2019): 801–2.

2.   Eric Blanc, Jane McAlevey, "A Strategy to Win," *Jacobin* Magazine, accessed on August 23, 2020. https://www.jacobinmag.com/2018/04/teachers-strikes-rank-and-file-union-socialists.

3.   Fredrick Engels, *Socialism: Utopian and Scientific*, trans. Edward Aveling (Progress Publishers, [1880]1970).

4.   Karl Marx and Friedrich Engels, *The Communist Manifesto*, (Penguin, [1848]1985).

5.   Rosa Luxemburg, "Co-operatives, Unions, Democracy", in *Reform or Revolution* (London: Militant Publications, 1986).

6.   Luxemburg, "Economic Development and Socialism."

7.   Luxemburg, "Introduction."

8.   John Holloway, "Why Adorno?" published 03 Jul 2011, http://www.johnholloway.com.mx/2011/07/30/why-adorno, citing Theodor Adorno, *Negative Dialectics*, trans. E.B. Ashton (London: Routledge, 1990), 5.

9.   Aaron Benanav and John Clegg, "Crisis and Immiseration: Critical Theory Today," in *The SAGE Handbook of Frankfurt School Critical Theory* (SAGE Publications Ltd, 2018).

10.   Karl Marx and Frederick Engels, "Part III: The Tendency of the Rate of Profit to Fall," in *Capital Volume III* (New York: International Publishers, 1894).

11.   Cedric J. Robinson, *Black Marxism: The Making of the Black Radical Tradition* (University of North Carolina Press, 2005).

12.   Piya Chatterjee and Sunaina Maira, *The Imperial University: Academic Repression and Scholarly Dissent* (University of Minnesota Press, 2014).

13.   Anthony Costello, "Despite what Matt Hancock says, the government's policy is still herd immunity," *The Guardian*, originally published 3 April 2020. https://www.theguardian.com/commentisfree/2020/apr/03/matt-hancock-government-policy-herd-immunity-community-surveillance-covid-19.

14.   Giorgio Agamben, "The State of Exception Provoked by an Unmotivated Emergency," *Positions*. February. 26, 2020.

15. Agamben, "[...] Unmotivated Emergency."

16. Laleh Khalili, *Time in the Shadows: Confinement in Counterinsurgencies* (Stanford: Stanford University Press, 2012).

17. Leela Gandhi, *The Common Cause: Postcolonial Ethics and the Practice of Democracy*, 1900-1955 (Chicago: University of Chicago Press, 2014).

18. Jean-Jacques Rousseau, *Correspondance Générale* (Paris: Colin, 1924-34), 20 vols., II, 303-24.

19. John Stuart Mill writes, in Chapter 1 of *Considerations on Representative Government*, "...a people who are revolted by an execution, but not shocked at an assassination—require that the public authorities should be armed with much sterner powers of repression than elsewhere, since the first indispensable requisites of civilized life have nothing else to rest on. These deplorable states of feeling, in any people who have emerged from savage life, are, no doubt, usually the consequence of previous bad government, which has taught them to regard the law as made for other ends than their good, and its administrators as worse enemies than those who openly violate it." Published in *On Liberty, Utilitarianism and Other Essays*, ed. Mark Philp and Frederick Rosen, Second edition (Oxford: Oxford University Press, 2015), 184-185.

20. Piya Chatterjee and Sunaina Maira. *The Imperial University.*

21. cf. John Holloway, "The Tradition of Scientific Marxism," in *Change The World Without Taking Power. The Meaning of Revolution Today*" (London: Pluto Press, 2002); Also Rob Lucas and Andy Blunden, eds., Marx: Myths & Legends, accessed on December 27, 2020, https://www.marxists.org/subject/marxmyths/index.htm.

22. Frantz Fanon, *A Dying Colonialism*, trans. Haakon Chevalier (New York: Grove Press, 1994).

23. Siegfried Kracauer, "Boredom," *The Mass Ornament: Weimar Essays*, trans. Thomas Y. Levin (United Kingdom: Harvard University Press, 1995), 333.

24. Mark Fisher, *Capitalist Realism: Is There No Alternative?* (United Kingdom: Zero Books, 2009).

25. Tarence Ray, "A Way Out," https://popula.com (*Popula*, Nov. 18, 2018).

26. Gandhi, *The Common Cause.*

27. Eric Blanc and Jane McAlevey, "A Strategy to Win." *Jacobin*, Apr. 18, 2018. https://www.jacobinmag.com/2018/04/teachers-strikes-rank-and-file-union-socialists.

28. *Hazaaron Khwaishein Aisi,* directed by Sudhir Mishra (2003, PNC Film). Netflix.

third interlude

AESTHETIC ARCHIVES, POLITICAL POSSIBILITY

The Call for Future Oeuvres

Silvana Carotenuto

> ...rose
> bitter
> semence ...
> The mirror in pain
> – Jacques Derrida

Gradually, slowly, inexorably, the "events of thought" crossing Deconstructive reading with Chinese female practice of art, reach the "landscape" of their final grafting. After having thought the 'end' of "the end of the world," and expressed his love for the experience of ruins, Jacques Derrida thinks of the (im)possible future for the world which survives the apocalypse and grows out of its disseminated rests. In 2001, following his interpretation of the apocalyptic Biblical text and the "blind vision" of drawing, the philosopher turns his inspirational attention to the work of art. The word and the meaning of *oeuvre* stays at the core of his 2001 speech "The University without Condition,"[1] where his thinking deals with the future of critical thought, the task of the Humanities-to-come, the idea of academia in the time of its mundialization.

Jacques Derrida's deconstruction is simple and complex at the same time, inspired and informed by aesthetic practice. According to his reading, the university is and must be unconditional, without conditions. Even if we know that this is not true, due to the rule of times, our task is to vindicate the 'as if' or profession of faith in its absolute unconditionality. The "as if" of literature, fiction, creation, imagination, signs faith in the unconditionality of thinking, of critical thought, and of the deconstructive praxis. For Derrida, the future of intellectuality lies, nowadays more than ever, in the praxis of absolute belief in the freedom of literature to say everything and the contrary of everything. This gift inspires our responsible engagement in "affirmative" and "performative" yes of Deconstruction, overcoming dialects, refusing the separation of thinking and praxis, translating the privilege of *phoné* into intervening acts, creating, both in thinking and in action, and beyond all horizons of expectation, certainty, control or sovereignty, the just conditions for the event to come.

The legacy of this interpretation rises from the historical critique of the canonical "Work," passing through the redefinition of the "text" offered by the science of semiology in the sixties, calling now for the production of oeuvres within the order of faire la *verité*, "make" the truth. Specifically, Derrida refers to the Anglo-Saxon custom of inviting artists and resident writers within the academic premises, asking them to produce works of art during their residency. For the philosopher, the practice might inspire the responsible call of the unconditional, affirmative, and performative "as if" of creation into the invention of the Humanities-of-the-future, where to celebrate the coming of oeuvres of unforeseeable "thinking" and "making." This promise has no assurance of success, no guarantee of safety, and it can possibly remain only inspirational; in truth, Derrida himself is uncertain of the "event" of his own discourse:

> I especially do not know the status, genre, or legitimacy of the discourse that I have just addressed to you. Is it academic? Is it a discourse of knowledge in the Humanities or on the subject of the Humanities? Is it knowledge only? Only a performative profession of faith? Does it belong to the inside of the university? Is it philosophy, or literature, or theater? Is it a work, une oeuvre, or a course, or a kind of seminar?[2]

In Derridean uncertainty, what stays on is the notion of writing as a textile, the weaving of marks, signs and traces on the page of their inscription. In "A Silkworm of One's Own," devoted to the text "Savoir" by his friend Hélène Cixous, both included in Veils, Derrida refers to some nuances of his philosophical enterprise: the obsessive presence of veil, the "unveiling" of truth, the memory of his taillih, the desire for the textual embroidery's to diminish its stitches...[3] This infinite work of weaving finds its Chinese Penelope in Lin Tianmiao, the "apartment" artist working in Beijing in the '70s, who emigrated to New York in the '80s, and who came back to China in 1995.

Born as a textile designer, Lin Tianmiao supported her exile with embroidery work, gradually turning her craft into art. Today her exhibitions are seen at the Asia Society Museum and the MOMA in New York, and in other prestigious institutions in Europe and in China.[4] Among her performative creations, "Bound/Unbound" is the piece presented in her first solo at the Asian Society, an immense work consisting of threads and strings, white silk weaving and sewing, embroidering and embossing. The work has, at its core, the word of "lace," evoking rarefaction, absence, and permeation, that here turns into the concrete matter of covering up million balls of different size with thick covers of wrapping. The color is given by the infinite layers of white, washed so thinly as to be rendered vaporous, tenuous, and transparent, producing a figure so fine in its threads as to open its spectacular weaving to a true "aesthetics of lightness."

What is extraordinary is that the work's light, tenuity and rarefaction go together with the strength of their flowing out of the bare, hollow and black hole at the origin or at the end of the work. Who will ever be sure if the cascade of threads "go to" or "return from" the void center of 'Bound/Unbound'? The oeuvre remains, stays on/in/to/from the empty space of its centrality, simply enjoying its infinite "series," the word that, as Derrida reminds us, comes from the Greek seira, meaning "cord, chain, lasso, knotted cord, that which interlaces, a lineage."[5]

Framing Events of Thought

In the philosophy of Derrida, some "events of thought" practice the gathering of thinking and praxis, the ideality and the materiality of writing, that proves relevant to sensitive concerns of the global present.[6] These "thinking events" are associated with the philosopher's reflection on "the end of the world," with his love for the "ruins," and with his deconstructive—inspirational and prophetic—thinking of the "future."

The Apocalypse, rests and relics, the call for future oeuvres: Derrida is interested in the structure of apocalyptic discourse, producing intense reflections on the human love for the remains, and engaging his responsibility in indicating critical perspectives to confront l'à-venir. These interests, reflections, and engagements are not the outcome of abstract reasoning, but emerge always-already in specific acts of deconstructive reading. In "Of an Apocalyptic Tone Recently Adopted in Philosophy,"[7] Derrida interprets the Biblical text by the apostle John. In *Memoirs of the Blind: The Self-Portrait and Other Ruins*,[8] his writing is exposed to the ruins historically rendered by the teknè of drawing; in his late text "The University without Condition," he finds inspiration for his thinking of the future in the singularity of art....

Here, it will be the question of the singularity of Chinese female art. What follows would try to prove that the visions or inventive poetics signed by some female Chinese artists materialize, today, on the scene of national and international art, the "events of thought" that are resonant with the Derridean interpretation of the "apocalyptic tone" spreading through the globe, crossing their love for ruins with the intimate passion expressed by the philosopher, announcing, in their way, which is the way of art, their call for future oeuvres. In the milieu of experimental art in contemporary China, the works calling back at Deconstruction identify here with the scroll "Apocalypse" realized by Bingyi, the series "Beauty Banana Plant" painted by Cai Jin, and "Bound/Unbound," the installation that Lin Tianmiao's mesmerizing insistence on weaving and embroidery constructs as oeuvre of the future par excellence.[9]

Future and Female Art

Derrida dedicated three important essays to the aesthetic puissance (un)contained by the works of art of Colette Deblé, Michaela Heinich, and Camilla Adami.[10] Supported by the critical insights of his reading of these female oeuvres, connecting them with his deconstruction of "the end of the world," his love for the ruins, and his thinking of l'à-venir, this article reads the artistic practices of Bingyi, Cia Jin, and Lin Tienmiao as the countersignatures—in terms of resonances, points of intensifications, and echoes of inspirations—of the thought of the event, the eventful thinking, the "Events of Thought" whose invention, as their art testifies, is urgent and necessary—for China, for the globe, for the planet.[11]

A question finally resounds: could it be a "female" lineage that survives, flowers, and makes oeuvre? When interviewed on the "gendered" nature of her work, Lin Tienmiao states, "If the audience sees female traces through my oeuvre, it is because I am "une" artist and not "un" artist. It is natural."[12] The women artists whose works have been read here as deconstructive "Events of Thought" are not necessarily feminists. Yet, through the scroll of allegorical writing, in the loving obsession of ruining insistence, threading handmade female passions, their works hear the apocalypse "tone" resonating all over the globe; witness the precious instances of survival and growth with the techné of their artistic insistence and persistence; weave the urgent and necessary exposure to the intense materiality and resistance of their oeuvres.

These female artists are both creators and academics, scholars and inventors. Their aesthetic operations inscribe new thoughts on the scene of contemporary art, inside/outside/bound/ unbound to the reception of global publics. Under the bliss of Deconstruction, the spacing of their writing with ink, color, and matter embodies, materializes and grafts in the eyes and in the minds of these audiences, the powerful invention of "Events of Thought"-to-come.

Notes

1.   Jacques Derrida, "The University Without Condition," in *Without Alibi*, Peggy Kamuf, ed., (Stanford: Stanford University Press, 2002). See also Derek Attridge, "The Humanities without Condition: Derrida and the Singular *Oeuvre*," *Arts and Humanities in Higher Education*, 2014, vol.13(1-2), pp.54-61.

2.   Derrida, 237.

3.   Derrida, "A Silkworm of One's Own. Points of View Stitched on the Other Veil," in Hélène Cixous and Jacques Derrida, *Veils* (Stanford: Stanford University Press, 2001).

4.   See "Weekly Highlight: Chinese Female Artist @ MOMA - Lin Tian Miao" 專題： 紐約現代 藝術館的中國女畫家林天苗, October-2010, http://carrieartdesignjournal.blogspot.it/2010/10/weekly- highlight-chinese-female-artist.html

5.   Derrida, "At This Very Moment in This Work Here I Am," *Psyche: Inventions of the Other*, Volume 1, (Stanford, Stanford University Press, 2007), 165.

6.   In the interview "The Spatial Arts: An Interview with Jacques Derrida," in P. Brunette and D. Will (eds.), *Deconstruction and the Visual Arts*, Cambridge, Cambridge U.P., 1994, the father of Deconstruction assigns his privilege to the word "'gathering' (in English), the being together, the assembly, the now, the maintaining together. Deconstruction does not consist of dissociating or dis-articulating or destroying, but of affirming a certain "being together," a certain "*maintenant.*"

7.   Derrida, Jacques, and John P. Leavey. "Of an Apocalyptic Tone Recently Adopted in Philosophy," *Oxford Literary Review 6*, no. 2 (1984): 3-37, accessed December 28, 2020, http://www.jstor. org/stable/43973661.

8.   Derrida, *Memoirs of the blind: the self-portrait and other ruins*. (Chicago: University of Chicago Press, 1993).

9.   For Bingyi's scroll, see http://www.inkstudio.com.cn/press/27/. For Cai Jin's artistic career, see http://www.artnet.com/artists/cai-jin/biography. For Tienmiao's oeuvre, see http://asiasociety.org/new- york/exhibitions/bound-unbound-lin-tianmiao-0.

10.   Derrida, *Prégnances: Lavi de Colette Deblè. Paintures* (l'atelier des Brisants, 2004); *Mille e tre, cinq:*

Lignées par Michaela Heinich et Jacques Derrida (William Blake & Co, 1996); Camilla Adami and Jacques Derrida, *Primati. Corpi che ti guardano* (La casa Usher, 2011).

11. For the ecological question that undermines the interest of this article, the critical movement from the "globe" to the "planet" finds its specific articulation in Gayatri C. Spivak, *Death of a Discipline*, (New York: Columbia University Press, 2003), where the scholar proposes "the planet to overwrite the globe…the planet is in the species of alterity, belonging to another system; and yet, we inhabit it, on loan… When I invoke the planet I think of the effort required to figure the (im)possibility of this underived intuition."

12. Lin Tianmiao, "An Interview: Bound Unbound," Asia Society Museum, https://www.youtube.com/watch?v=9JyiY9J6bHY, accessed December 28, 2020.

Trump Threatens To Defund Education If Schools Refuse To Open Amidst Global Pandemic

Ashna Ali

for four months they place our bodies
in shells and fail to notice as we pick
at the stitching. discover the flesh.
capillary root network. soil vibrations.
we have begun to talk amongst ourselves.
track body time. the sun rises even when
we do not pay to rent our limbs from
ourselves. yet, even all alone this exhale caress
smacks of stealing. in this country
where they sell us our own skin,
place us in the window for the children
wearing comparable faces, ask us
to teach them how we serve ourselves up,
quietly. in a deep spoon. palliative.
in this country that taught our fathers
to hold their heads low as survival wisdom.
in this country that taught our mothers
to play so much pretend that they knead
truths and lies into the same daily bread
we still eat to live. the swallowing
that makes us of this place.
what if we concoct of this flesh
some new medicine. what if when
they wrench us back, new beasts
made from nerve endings,
skin turned inside out, programming
exposed, we magic the spoons
to hold gasoline, matches, fire.
make new bread of these bodies
feed the children
so that their skin
tells no lies.

No Mammies on Saturn

Sy Klipsch-Abudu

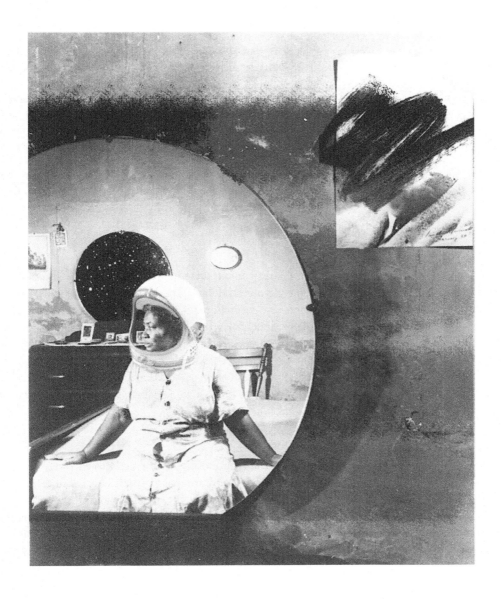

Letter to a Colleague on Struggling with COVID-19

Lewis R. Gordon

This letter was written in response to a set of questions posed to me by a friend—Michael Paradiso-Michau—who was completing his spring 2020 semester of teaching at the Art Institute of Chicago when he learned I was convalescing from my struggle with COVID-19. He said he was sharing accounts of "survivors" of the disease. I place the term in quotation marks because of my critical writings on the concept. Survivor consciousness often garners problematic attitudes toward those who didn't survive. When brought to national levels—as it did in the United States after 9/11/2001—it results in the sickness of "survivor-identity," a form of consciousness in which there is a search for affirmation and justification for surviving. It's a problematic consciousness parasitic, for its identity, on the production of casualties, those who supposedly "shouldn't" survive. Think of how many people killed globally for the sake of continued U.S. survival. This, too, is a mentality growing in many countries in which a swing to the right is accompanied by a near-divine sense of survivability. That said, this is what I sent my friend.

5/10/2020

Dear Mike,

Your questions offer much for reflection. I'll just conjoin some in my response. I will also offer a lot of detail since that may be helpful to some of your students and others who may be suffering from COVID-19 (the disease brought on by the new coronavirus SARS-CoV-2). Since so many people are quarantined and are thus out of sight, much of what goes on—especially among the most ill—must seem mysterious, or worse, fictional. The eeriness of empty stores, streets, parks, and isolation makes everything surreal and leaves many with enough doubt to become reckless. All this is worsened by governing officials invested in misinformation and disinformation. The invisibility of the virus and the afflicted will no doubt lead to unreasonable efforts to root out concrete and tangible "causes" in already noxious societal commitments.

I

Although I have argued this philosophically, the reality of living is acutely so each day at a time. The short of it is that my antibodies have kicked in and are making their effort. But the damage done through the period of severity was worse than I thought. The healing process is going to take some time. Although I'm no longer formally suffering from COVID-19, I'm struggling with its aftereffects. It's still being determined whether the post-COVID-19 process is a continuation of the disease without the problem of viral transmission. Thus far, my experience is that it may be so.

The illness has three stages for those in my position. There is infection followed by the full-blown symptoms and then the matter of the lingering effects. For some, there is simply infection. For others, they don't get past the second stage. They are the casualties. And then there is my lot. We're just grateful to be in stage three. There is, of course, possibly a stage four, but that, as of this writing, is still to be determined and understood. The damage may be like a repaired car after a terrible collision. It's no longer the same.

Given my penchant for allegories and metaphors, I've been describing COVID-19 like this. Imagine you have a nice house with many rooms. Imagine it's the kind of house in which each room functions well if it is locked and only open to pass things through the corridor from one room to another. Similarly, the windows should not only be shut, but also locked.

Now, imagine that one day you left the front, back, or side door open. For the most part, passersby will ignore it. But let's suppose a nefarious group that was prowling the neighborhood, checking each door, finds one of yours open, and enters the house. The group starts searching through the house to get into one of the rooms but is unable to do so. Let's say there is another group already there, and its task is to protect and clean the house. That group of protectors and cleaners is in a special room. As the prowlers move through the house, members of the protectorate are alerted and subdue the prowlers. If they can't kick the intruders out, they at least cordon them off. That's what we call a "healthy" house. Let's call that *scenario 1*.

Now, imagine a similar scenario, except that the protectors were busy dealing with some other prowlers in different rooms while trying to keep the other doors shut. The prowlers come in and notice that there are some open doors. They head in to see what havoc they can wreak. The protectors see it and intervene before much damage is done. That's still a fairly healthy house. Let's call that *scenario 2*.

Now, imagine a similar scenario, but in this one there are many open doors, and there may be vermin or mold or other things going on in their rooms, and the protectors and cleaners are at the moment a bit tired from trying to contain and clean things up. The prowlers now come in, and they notice not only those shabby rooms but also that the time spent on them left a few other rooms open. This new set of prowlers announce to their buddies that they're going to have a serious house party. They bring in their disco ball, turntables, crazy friend with the lampshade on his head, wrestlers, some gun-toters shooting up the place with M-16s, and on and on. They begin to party so hard that they are not only breaking furniture but also breaking windows and the roof, and thus other critters and prowlers begin to come in and the whole place begins to fall apart. If the protectors are able to contain this situation and eventually kick those uninvited guests out—and if not, simply keep them at bay in a closet or part of the basement—the big task now is to patch up the place. They'll have to fix the roof, the windows, clean up the rooms, fix the toilets, and lock the doors. Let's call that *scenario 3*.

And then there is *scenario 4*. The partying makes the house collapse.

At this point, you get the picture. Scenario 1 are the carriers. Inhabitants in the rest of the rooms may be unaware there were ever any prowlers. During the conflict, some of the prowlers may even gather enough energy to move on and may unfortunately break into your neighbor's home next door to continue their antics.

Scenario 2 should be obvious. They are the mild cases. They, too, may have let some prowlers out, who then promptly started seeing what damage they could do to the neighbors' houses. Scenario 3 are the critical cases. And scenario 4 are the casualties.

Thus far, I'm scenario 3. My D-dimer level (measurement of blood clotting) should be .5 or less, but it is as of this week (2 months since infection) 4.3 (8.6 times the level it should be). The research hematologist with whom I spoke said it would have been interesting to see what my levels were at the height of my illness. He estimates it could have been 50! The thing is that at 4.3, I face the after-effect of clots in my blood that could lead to strokes. At the height of the illness, that was obviously a greater possibility.

What many physicians are saying is that a weird dimension of COVID-19 is that a lot of the rules are being broken. There are people with blood levels that should mean they shouldn't be standing, speaking, breathing—in short, they should be either unconscious or dead. Physicians look at such people with wonder.

The pulmonary specialist observed that I have scattered COVID-19 scars throughout both lungs. That signifies I was suffering from COVID-19 pneumonia. What he found shocking but now unsurprising (as he has now seen patients with this many times) is that I was able to breathe, speak, and walk throughout. I'm fortunate. The infection didn't get to the lowest part of my lungs where oxygen and carbon are exchanged. About three weeks into the illness, I had felt the virus growing in my lungs and then retreat when I took certain measures against it. That part of the illness was, in my memory, going on for no more than two weeks. I had no idea of the damage it achieved in that short time. My lungs looked like I had inhaled broken glass.

The pulmonologist said my blood is now a precious commodity. I not only have antibodies but also, given my genetic diseases, those suited for people with rare and some not-so-rare conditions. Added to all that, my blood-type is O-positive, which makes me, but for my condition, a universal donor.

II

With regard to when I learned of my illness, I didn't notice I was sick until a week after my initial symptoms. I learned this later on while in the throes of the most intense manifestation of the disease. I first experienced lower back pains. I thought it was because of my wearing inappropriate shoes—Timberlands—when my wife Jane and I had taken a long walk on the beach a few days after our return from New York City. We had driven there to move our son Elijah out of his dormitory. Given my pre-existing conditions, I stayed in the car as Jane and Elijah got his stuff and packed them in our vehicle. I had attributed the lower back pain to what turned out to be about six hours of driving followed by walking with inappropriate shoes. A day later I felt very cold. I attributed that to the fact that I had recently lost some weight. My experience of weight loss during the winter is that it results in my feeling colder. This went on for five more days. Then—and I remember this with great detail—at 5:20 PM on March 23rd, after a wonderful Zoom meeting with some colleagues (since the lockdown was in effect by then), I reached to pull down the blinds, and it was as though I were hit by a bus. My head felt like it was exploding; my eyeballs seemed as if they were hard-boiled eggs; I was suffering from the rigors (shivering, covered in sweat, etc.) and pain that reached all the way to my toes.

I immediately went to bed in a warm cardigan and wrapped myself in three blankets, but I was still cold. So I turned on the heater fan in Jane and my bedroom and also turned up the room purifier since it has a hepa filter and would thus catch small particles stirred up from the fan blowing hot air onto me. Yet I was still cold. At that point it was clear I was pretty ill. I at first didn't conclude it was COVID-19. The symptoms that followed, however, were nastier: diarrhea, a weird slime with little bubbles floating over my eyeballs, oversensitive skin, earaches, chalk-white tongue, extraordinary fatigue (just walking to the bathroom about ten steps from my bed would wipe me out), a loss of appetite, and more. I fainted twice, and—yes—I experienced hallucinations. I have memories of conversations with friends that I have since unfortunately learned never occurred. At a certain point, there was no sensation in my left thigh except deep down near the bone, where it felt like I was being stabbed over and over by a serrated knife. When I touched that thigh, my skin was so numb it was as if it weren't being touched by my fingers. My thermometer was broken, and I didn't have an oximeter, which meant I had to order them online. The demand was so high that I didn't receive the thermometer until I was three weeks in, and I received the oximeter at the fourth-week mark. So I don't know what my highest fever was, but my temperature at the point of receiving the thermometer was typically 105 F/40.5 C, with a good day as low as 102 F/38.8 C. Since those were readings when I was actually feeling a little better, my suspicion is that my temperature was higher during the worst period. By the time I got the oximeter, I was measuring oxygen blood saturation levels as low as 70–80 percent but eventually (when I was on the mend) in the mid-90s, with an occasional dip to 68 (which might have just been invalid readings).

Something to bear in mind is that given the unique medical history of each patient, some symptoms are absent. For instance, I never vomited. This is because I rarely vomit. In fact, the last time I vomited was at age eighteen under forced circumstances (long story). But more, my other genetic conditions are such that I never lose my sense of smell. My olfactory sense is unusually high. Even in the past when I would have my nose stuffed up from a cold, I could smell perfectly well. This, I suspect, is connected to the cause of my multiple epilepsies (which are neurological). Thus, in my case, instead of loss, my sense of smell became wolverine-level. I could smell things at levels that even I found abnormal. For instance, cinnamon, a spice I love, became unbearable. I could smell a few sprinkles of cinnamon on the kitchen counter, which is approximately 45 feet from Jane and my bedroom. At its height—when I was sleeping about twenty-two hours each day (waking periodically to roll over because of a lack of circulation) and couldn't walk much farther than to the toilet—I was able to smell animals moving through the yard and discern their species (deer, bob-cat, rabbit, groundhog, rabbit; owls, hawks, small birds, etc.) by their odor, and I always knew where Jane and Elijah were in the house because I could smell them.

Our house has three levels. Our quarantining effort involved my being confined to the bedroom on the second floor; Jane was in our daughter Sula's old room on the third; and Elijah was in his on the first or basement-level. Our having a house with all those bedrooms is from our being a family of six in which at one point all the children were home. It turned out our separation on different levels was pointless, since we had all contracted the virus from NYC; Elijah, as a college student, had been doing what college students do—from dorm to dorm, neighborhood to neighborhood, hanging with friends and partying. So, he was scenario 1 (a carrier); Jane was briefly ill for three days (most likely scenario 2); and I had my ass kicked (scenario 3).

Since I had become ill during the initial stage of national hysteria, it was difficult to get tested. I could only get virtual appointments. This is where I also was dealing with the racism of how healthcare is administered in our society. For instance, the medical consultants rejected my request for testing because I wasn't vomiting. I could tell they were lying, and I concluded at that point that I didn't want to go into hospital because I noticed that, as the saying goes, black people go in, but we don't get out (except, for the most part, in body bags). Although that wasn't absolute, it was clear that something serious was going on. So, I decided, given all I learned from dealing with my preexisting conditions and also what I learned from my grandmothers, great-grandparents, and other relatives from my early childhood in Jamaica, that I would focus on home-care. I resolved to study my illness while suffering it. I concluded that COVID-19 is not simply a respiratory disease, as was being reported at the time, and that patients must differ according to their medical and genetic history. Not vomiting shouldn't rule it out. I knew I had it from the moment I saw bubbling slime flowing slowly over my eyes.

So, I took action. I made a spray mist of 80 percent rubbing alcohol to catch airborne droplets (although I didn't experience coughing and sneezing until week 3); I learned that fecal matter carrying the virus floated through the air, so I made sure not only to flush right away but also to spray the air over the toilet; I learned about how soap dissolves the protein through which the virus maintains itself, so I not only washed my hands but also lathered my face and washed it with warm water, which quickly rid me of the slime that was growing over my eyes; despite having no appetite, I forced myself to drink soup and consume small quantities of highly nutritious foods and drank lots of boiled ginger-root water (because it's an expectorant, an anti-inflammatory agent, rich in antioxidants, and has mild amounts of unprocessed sugar) and sterilized water with some lemon juice; added soup and foods rich in Omega-3 (cod fish, salmon, anchovies, sardines, dark-green vegetables, avocadoes, etc.) and high-antioxidant bush teas (such as cerasee); and I continued sleeping a lot. I instructed Jane on how to make the ginger-root drink and at a certain point, when I was a little better and able to eat more, a super spicy chili with bitter dark chocolate and other items rich with nutrition and antioxidants such as a fish curry.

I also noticed that I would be gasping for air at any moment the ambient temperature in my bedroom went below 72 F/22.2 C. I concluded that breathing warmer air would deter the growth of the virus in my lungs. So I tried 73–75 F/22.7–23.8. I actually felt the virus receding in my lungs over the next week. I also concluded that the fevers and pain were my body fighting, so I did my best to bear it as long as possible and minimized the amount of pain relievers (whether aspirin or acetaminophen) I took to facilitate the build-up of antibodies. Finally, I noticed that stress facilitated the increase of symptoms, so I tried, whenever I was awake long enough, to watch something entertaining and informative such as updates from Trevor Noah, Seth Meyers, and John Oliver, on my laptop. Noah was especially helpful, as his talents transcend comedy, from which he achieved his fame. He is an amazing journalist and cultural critic. He is also an intellectual with extraordinary compassion, a proverbial kind soul. His colleagues and he offer so much of what was lacking, in rare exception, from the country's highest leadership.

This reflection on relieving stress reminds me of how I experienced one of the symptoms at the height of the illness, when my fever was most severe. As I already mentioned, I suffered hallucinations. Mine turned out to be visits from deceased loved ones—my mother, my grandmothers, my father, my stepfather, grand uncles and aunts, my maternal great-grandparents. We would have conversations during which I was aware of what was going on because of the timbre of their voice and the odd quality of light in the room. Despite knowing this, it occurred to me that I should enjoy such visits because I missed each of them, especially my mother and grandmothers, and their presence was comforting. We should never underestimate the power of endorphins. An amusing moment was when I recalled something I lamented when I used to dream about deceased relatives: they would leave whenever I reminded them they were dead. I did the same during the hallucinations, but my visitors didn't leave. For a moment I panicked, wondering if I had already taken my last breath.

When I was eventually able to stay awake longer, I, as strange as this may sound, took advantage of the time to watch horror films to update myself since philosophy of horror and the fantastic is one of my areas of specialization (and, as the saying goes, guilty pleasures) and then, as I got better, transitioned into classic rom-coms with Jane and Elijah, and, eventually, some of my favorite off-beat comedy such as Rick and Morty and Curb Your Enthusiasm. I focused on audio-visual media because I couldn't read or write because the illness exacerbated my preexisting condition of convergence eye insufficiency syndrome; basically, everything I see from a distance under three feet is doubled. With COVID-19, this became everything under about five feet, and instead of doubles, I sometimes saw quadrupled images. The condition is still pretty bad even as I write this letter; my typing speed affords the feeling of words in my fingers with little ability to read what I am writing.

When my fever finally went down to 99 F/37.2 C, I decided to try a common practice in Jamaica from my childhood, which I learned from my maternal grandmother. I drank lots of water and took an herbal laxative. This is no doubt counter-intuitive to most readers, since I was, after all, suffering from diarrhea. My reasoning was that viruses use our large intestines as a highway system. The diarrhea is our body trying to expel viruses that use the large intestines to do more damage. After flushing toxins out with the assistance of the laxative, my temperature went down to averaging 97–98 F/36.1 –36.6 C within several hours. That temperature range went on for about two more weeks, with an occasional rise to 99 F / 37.2 C, for another two weeks, and I'm now steadily in the 98s F/36.6s F.

At that point, I noticed that I had lost much muscle and fat. My weight loss was about 30 pounds/13.6 kilograms. As it's dangerous to lose a lot of weight so quickly, I forced myself to eat enough to stabilize myself from withering away. The problem with the left thigh, however, continued. After some research, I decided to do some gentle yoga exercises and meditation to increase blood-flow in my legs. As of this point, that course of action has proven very effective. I have most of the sensation back in my left thigh, and the swelling just above my kneecap is almost gone. Perhaps also the yoga breathing exercises helped my lungs, since it expels moisture from them.

I should like to mention that I had a medical physical examination back in December 2019. I insisted, because of my preexisting conditions, for my physician to give me an anti-pneumonia vaccination. I suspect that had also helped me since it reduced the chances of a bacterial infection on top of the viral infection in my lungs. (Remember the metaphor of the other invaders coming in from the virus breaking the windows and roof.)

One of my conclusions is that had I buckled and called an ambulance, thereby going to the hospital, I would probably have died. My reasoning is this. First, they would have put me in a COVID-19 ward. Had I not had the virus, I at that point would have got it. Second, given the racism of U.S. society—especially in the administering of services—it's unlikely any medical professional would have listened to me. Third, even if they weren't responding from racial biases, there was simply a lot that healthcare professionals didn't know about the disease at that time. They were learning on a case-by-case basis, pretty much as I was learning through studying what I was going through. Well-intentioned though they may have been, the results for many patients were catastrophic. Fourth, given my discovery about ambient temperatures, a hospital would have been a deadly place. They tend to be air-conditioned (since western medicine is premised on the idea that cooler temperatures are more sterile), and had physicians X-rayed my lungs and seen the havoc, they would have probably put me on a ventilator pushing in cool oxygen. With that tube down my windpipe and my being probably sedated, there would have been no way for me to tell them that they were making me worse. One of my Chinese doctoral students recently informed me that his medical researcher friends in Wuhan informed him that they realized by February that the temperature of the actual air the patients were breathing needed to be warm as a preventive measure against the growth of COVID-19 pneumonia.

III

A terrible memory is the traumatic sound of ambulance sirens. It was worse, of course, for people in New York City. I live in a far less populated town, but even here, one could hear, from late March through to mid-April, ambulances every twenty minutes or so. Eventually it was every hour. And then eventually once a day. Until now: hardly ever.

There were moments, at the height of the illness, when the pain was so bad and the rigors were in full force, that I wondered, "Is this my last breath?"

I was relieved I had prepared a "death file." It's an important thing to do for one's loved ones. I learned this from having to handle the deaths of too many relatives and friends over the past twenty years. Thinking about others, of course, extends beyond one's immediate family and relatives. I wondered about those people in those ambulances, their families, their friends, and so many more. New York City, as an example, went from approximately forty home deaths per day before the pandemic to more than 200 each day. On some days the number was as high as 450. We can add to that the many dying not only in this country but also across the globe without being placed into the demographics and statistics of COVID-19 fatalities. This is similarly so with the many asymptomatic people spreading the virus. The actual number of the infected is clearly many more times larger than official reports. So, too, are the number of deaths. We see here a social scientific quandary, where science and truth don't meet.

The convention now is to sign correspondence with "be safe and healthy." My existential commitments make me add: "...and, despite the dire times, find moments of joy."

Here we get into philosophical conundra. For me to have such reflections, for me to be in the position to be writing this correspondence, brings me thirty years earlier than my maternal grandmother was at the point when she used to respond, when I used to call her in her late eighties through to her ninety-first year, to asking her how she was doing. Her response was always the same: "Still here."

I, like many, lost quite a few people over the past few months. Among them was a student, Walter South, whom I last saw in January in New York City at a doctoral defense of another student on whose committee Jane served. I met Walter going on four years ago in Maribor, Slovenia. He was such a kind, beautiful soul. He was also a person of extraordinary intellect. I said to him, after a brief hug, that I was looking forward to the draft he was to send me so we could be on track for his doctoral defense, which was to take place at the (now canceled) Global Center for Advanced Studies meeting at Oxford in August. The news of his death was devastating. Additionally heartbreaking was that I hadn't participated in the virtual funeral for him because I myself was locked in the throes of the worst period of the same illness. I learned of the funeral a week after it was held. Additionally difficult is what my popping up on screen as another afflicted member of the community would have meant to everyone involved. I have come to the conclusion that it was best that I wasn't able to participate. The funeral, after all, was about Walter and our collective grief in losing him, not me.

There are so many people with similar stories. For the living, there is the problem of not being able to be with deceased loved ones in those final moments and the process of their internment or cremation. My good friend Sonia Dayan-Herzbrun is still in sorrow at her ex-husband-and-lifelong-good-friend dying alone because no one was permitted to visit him in hospital. They and she were permitted only to stand outside at physical distances in front of the crematorium to watch the smoke rise into the air as his corpse turned to ash. You could imagine her trauma, as an Orthodox Jew in her youth, also because she went through Shoah (the Holocaust)! A student of mine lost her best friend, whose father then passed from the illness on the day of his son's internment. The list goes on.

Not all of us understand the significance of being able to say: "Still here." The high from the initial rush of oxygen from feeling better leads some recklessly back into the outside world without understanding that feeling better is not identical with actually being well. The wreckage on their insides make rushing back out into the world a dangerous thing to do. Many are reporting supposedly being "re-infected," when in fact they are most probably suffering relapse or simply damaging themselves from premature activities interrupting their antibodies' efforts to patch them up from the inside out.

So, I'm still here.

Reality never waits for us. There's still so much to do. With humility—because there are so many things greater than us—we press on. Being alive, we face the continued opportunity and—as expressed in Judaism—mitzvah of living.

I hope your students and you find this account useful.

Continue being safe, healthy, and, of course, try to find moments of joy,

—Lewis

Morbid States, Struggling Bodies

Dresda Emma Mendez de la Brena

Each society has its own particular diseases, and those diseases speak the truth of its society. The scenario we are facing today locates life, any life, "between the implosion and the outbreak,"[1] where there is no distinction between life and death but debility as a continuum. Between the implosion and the outbreak, there are bodies in exhaustion. Bodies that not only show the debilitating aspects of neoliberalism, but the economies that sustain it;[2] that is, a vitalist extractive system that places fatigue, illness, weakness, and debility, at the service of capitalist accumulation.

The symbiotic interrelation between neoliberalism and the etiology of recent epidemics is that "capitalism produces the virus that then re-uses itself to control us."[3] Its side effects (isolation, exploitation, suffocation, disease, deaths, etc.) are essential for imposing a standardized state of emergency. Capitalism is a morbid system that gets aroused by provoking sickness and debilitation. We are in the presence of what I call a "Morbid State," that is, a system that feeds on the paradox of living an unlivable life with the hope of continuing to live it. In order to live this life, some bodies are made to medicalize their vulnerability. Bodies are forced to manage their weakness and in doing so, their illnesses and weaknesses are transformed into vital commodities on which capitalism not only depends, but benefits from.

Therefore, the concept of "Morbid State" presents itself as a twofold condition of living. On the one hand, illness, debility, and exhaustion become an individual responsibility, and one based on a neoliberal sensitivity that turns self-weakening processes into an everyday commitment. This is a "necro-empowerment"[4] system that functions as a generator of morbidity. On the other hand, it refers to the "necro-administration" of suffering through State structures such as productivity, effectiveness, efficiency, mobility and temporality that enable the production of the disease itself. The physical and mental undermining of bodies is, therefore, the result of a structured necropolitical complex that cynically encourages impossible fantasies of happiness, while reducing the exercise of personal sovereignty.

Although "Morbid State" is an appropriate theoretical tool that reveals the perversity of the neoliberal system directed upon some bodies, it also makes it possible to find spaces to generate more agential corporeality, where morbidity can also be seen as an affirmative category. I refer to the active participation of morbidity in processes of agency and in the creation of the meaning of life itself. In other words, morbidity as a material-discursive process of difference. Bodies that develop contingent forms of agency may not be so spectacular, obvious, or evident. However, these can be seen as forms of self-realization and resistance within the slow death processes. These forms of contingent agency, which Laurent Berlant calls "lateral agencies"[5] describe the experience of all those bodies that live in disease, that have the intelligence to live with the disease, and that develop daily strategies in disease. Lateral agencies are, therefore, ways of doing/being/sensing where the body has no choice but to stop, pause, interrupt the movement, hide or modify its behavior as ways of survival.

We are struggling bodies striving to achieve living in the face of annihilation. Bodies "desperate for change, as [they] are both in illness and insurrection."[6] Bodies that share illness, debility, militancy and revolution "absorbed in the acutely human experience of encountering one's limits at the site of the world's end."[7] Bodies whose time-action is different but no dissimilar to what we believe action is. As Hedva mentions: "We tend to place illness and revolution opposite each other on the spectrum of action: illness is on the end of inaction, passivity, and surrender, while revolution is on the end of movement, surging and agitating. But maybe this spectrum is more like an ouroboros: one end feeding the other, transforming into, because of, made of the same stuff as the other."[8]

Struggling bodies have always known the potentiality of tiny forms of resistance: acts of rebellion from impossible bodies that do not work, that oversleep, retch up, rest, and struggle to get out of bed. Bodies whose vulnerability generates states of revolt and seditious times. In other words, such bodies ephemerally generate micro-states of sabotage. These are bodies that know that revolution can look like desperation, suffocation, exhaustion and agitation. And when illness spreads through the system, it soon roots itself and radicalizes, revealing its insurrectionary power, in tiny acts of micro-activist bodily protests.

Notes

1. Santiago López Petit, *Los hijos de la noche* (Barcelona: Bellaterra, 2014).

2. Jasbir K. Puar, *The Right to Maim: Debility, Capacity, Disability* (Durham: Duke University Press, 2017).

3. Santiago López Petit, "El coronavirus como declaración de guerra." *El Cuaderno*, 30 (March), par. 3. (2020), accessed on August 1, 2020, https://elcuadernodigital.com/2020/03/31/el-coronavirus-como-declaracion-de-guerra/.. .

4. Sayak Valencia, "Economía: Cuerpos en Negocio." *Universidad Internacional de Andalucía* (2010), accessed August 1, 2020, http://ayp.unia.es/index.php?option=com_content&task=view&id=649.

5. Lauren Berlant, "Slow Death (Sovereignty, Obesity, Lateral Agency),"*Critical Inquiry*, 33(4), 2007, pp. 754–80.

6. Johanna Hedva, (n.d). Get Well Soon!., parr. 3. accessed on August 1, 2020, https://getwellsoon.labr.io/.

7. Hedva, parr. 4.

8. Hedva, parr. 8.

Spring Summer 2020 Writings

Zohaib Zuby

The following is an edited collection from my journal entries. I have maintained this writing practice for a little short of two decades now. It has been a source of my healing, but paradoxically, has also cemented my pain and loss as ink on paper—that I carry as baggage off my heart; but in my cabinets.

23rd July 2018

It is not the most obvious skill to acquire → the skill to align yourself with what's happening for you, around you.

We don't know; and we can hardly see it → there is a wavelength of actions/demands of the universe individually tailored for us all.

And we have to stick to it – by finding it. Stop saying no. Asking yourself again and again – "What do you want to do?" "What do you value most?" "What do you want to do till you die?" And these difficult questions lead to difficult answers; angsty attitudes; delirium, and sometimes indigestion!

It's not easy to love. Then it's not easy to sacrifice things for what you love. And then it's not easy to take risks for what you love. And then to pay the price. And sometimes – to risk it all. Or break down and cry.

There is no beginning or end. There is just the convoluted repetition of routine, or "everydays." And hours that are spent – withering you away.

There is only imminent death; but a today full of joy and ecstasy. Glee. And it's ok. Don't complain. Don't twiddle that thumb either. Don't lose hope. It'll all be ok.

What hurts, subsides – what elates, deflates. What you believe makes you stronger. Align to the universe. It makes all the difference!

12th April 2020

Now that I am not going for PhD, I'm wondering what to do with my mind! With all the intense work I did for so many years, and all the vivid visualizing this past year or two – I'm just lost. It's an odd sensation.

There is a bench outside in my verandah. We had dreamt of it right when we shifted; then later when I went to Ahmed's house and saw his log in his lounge; and then when we cut the

Eucalyptus tree; then when I gave those pieces to Zain to make; and then I finally got what he made home, and got it polished. This took many years. But it took its sweet time to happen! But – it did happen. What was a desire became an idea, and then took tangible existence. What I can "foresee" can finally be "seen." As an architect – this is normal for me...

I am confused about what to do with my mind!

→ How should we think?

A. Keep trying to fight the "hurdles" and "obstacles." (To achieve your dream.)

B. Chill out! No "trying."

For (A) we can say. "Are you trying to fight your destiny?"

For (B) we can say, "Are you being complacent?"

I want to do neither! I don't want to force upon myself a desire (because it may be coming from a dark internal place) to do/be something. And I don't want to sit thinking the only way to move "forward" is to commit to stasis and allow things to unfold.

Why can't I see progress in doing what I believe I should? Why can't that bench start getting made?

How does the world work?

30th May 2020

Zeeshan has tested positive for COVID-19. How sad and odd. What kind of world is this becoming? My kids are growing up in a different world from mine. Well – I don't have a choice in this. These days the best advice can come from Seneca + Epictetus + Aurelius...

What do we really control? Maybe all of this really is a game. We play our part. We exit the stage. Keep your expectations low. Smile often. Hug and Kiss every day!

Remember God – in your prayers, and otherwise. Sleep on time. Wake up with no desires or dreams. Just doing your thing!

God. I pray for all these COVID-19 patients. We all need your Mercy; your Grace. We need recovery. We need life. We need Love. Keep all the patients safe.

6th June 2020

Our drawing room has changed a lot! It's been changing since Ramzan because we put the large carpet and white sheet. It looks "sacred" suddenly. Then I got the TV and it became a lounge. Today I officially set up, actually Zayaan did—set up my IVS Desktop in the corner [[for his online school]]. Now it is officially an apartment lounge : TV room : Working room. You can even sleep here!

Life has changed radically; and we're still trying to understand it.

Dear God,
You've seen it all. I don't understand You. But you surely understand me.
I think You can see that I mean well. You can see my heart.
I carry noble intentions; and dreams of goodness. They are all that's mine.
I hope you allow me to do some of those things here. And you help me out of trouble –
and help me keep myself out of trouble!
Cheers!
Zohaib Zuby

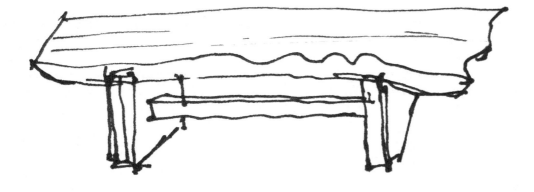

Zohaib Zuby, *Bench*

Defense Strategies

Heidi Andrea Restrepo Rhodes

The U.S. Department of Defense (DOD) National Defense Strategy emphasizes the need for the US to reclaim and maintain its once-uncontested global superiority, and advance an international order conducive to its security from threat and through economic prosperity via access to international markets. Key to its capacity to do so is its ability to strengthen its Joint Force relations, domestically and with alliances abroad, and develop the US Military's "force posture"—its ability to deploy lethality in "contested environments."[1] The defense machine of war in the service of capital is a matryoshka doll of force within force, defense within defense. The state seeks alliance, but what it means is that it seeks collaborators in the work of lethality, the deathwork of architecting the globe as its necrotopic fantasia for capitalist glee.

When Foucault, in his *Society Must Be Defended* lectures traces a genealogy of society's defense, we see a relevance of legacy—state appropriations of defense of the nation from the barbaric outside, and later, "[T]he emergence of the idea of an internal war that defends society against threats born of its own body." Further, "[T]he idea of social war makes, if you like, a great retreat from the historical to the biological, from the constituent to the medical."[2] Eugenics and its precursors projected onto the body politic the need for racial self-defense as a preservation of the white Western I/eye bound for the bourgeois enjoyments for which the world's "wretched" have bled, continue to bleed. "Racism justifies the death function in the economy of biopower by appealing to the principle that the death of others makes one biologically stronger insofar as one is a member of a race or a population, insofar as one is an element in a unitary living plurality."[3] This is also "defense strategy" of the state—the lethal force posture in a contested environment 50 states wide. And planetary.

The lethal force that in the spring of 2020 obliterated the life out of George Floyd, Breonna Taylor, Tony McDade, is "defense strategy" in the afterlife of slavery. The lethal force of incarceration—of undocumented migrants in Homeland Security Immigration and Customs Enforcement (ICE) Detention Centers, and of black and brown cisgender and transgender people in federal, state, and private prisons—is "defense strategy": an insidious corollary to policies weaponizing the desert at the US-Mexico border or the streets in any-town, USA. The lethal force of murder of indigenous women, in the ongoingness of this country's foundation on genocide, is "defense strategy." Every death function in the economy of biopower—from racialized poverty; to healthcare inaccessibility and the run amok function of the autoimmune in disease, dis-eased by the world; to overwork in the toxic landscape of factory, field, and office; to the militarization of the police—all constitute "defense strategy." Capital's conscription of the masses into the "American

Dream," which packages historical, bodily, and socio-relational trauma in a pretty bow and names it happiness, is "defense strategy."

You and I, in our black and brown skin, our queer desires opening us to the yeses of the world and each other, our critical dissent to every epistemic and material violence, render us a threat to imperialism's fantasia. I am a contested environment. You are a contested environment. The (non) space between us, how we touch and flow together in study and love, is a contested environment. All subject to the slow and quick lethal forces of liberal-fascist clockworks. Racial Capitalism is the bedfellow of the Law; impunity is their spawn. Which is what Foucault means, really, when he says, "[T]he blood has dried in the codes."[4]

Fight and flight are sibling defense mechanisms. We, and the contested environments of our nervous systems, have collectively been in fight or flight mode for five hundred years.

Aside

It is not a mistake that my body, with autoimmune disease emergent from sustained traumas wrought by racial heteropatriarchy, now fights itself. An overdrive of defense as a limitation on my capacity to defend against the defense strategies of the state and of capital. I could never keep the world out of me, and so I spill over with its wreckage. Look: an angel of history in the cytokine storm of conquest, the Age of Extractive Discovery still bubbling at its feet.

Also/And/Or

My body defends me against the "liberal eugenics of lifestyle programming" of hyperproductivity.[5] I inflame if I do not slow down. My overdrive of autoimmune defense is psycho-somatically produced (which is not to say, fake, but emergent from the entangled nature of psyche and soma, mind and body, history and present, ecology and political economy...) It is my system's limitation on my ability to participate in, be conscripted by, the defense strategies of the necropolitical Joint Force lethality. My defense against the Defense Strategy of the state. My will to endure, and undo the endless estrangements of capital's defense against our solidarities, our togetherness, our fugitive planning and politically haptic affections. Capital wants our alienation, desperately. The contested environment of my body says to me: you were never a separate or singular being. There is no estrangement. My body says to me: I'd rather eat you than feed you to the hungry mouth of the lethal.)

Defense as a practical mode and language for liberatory political work and thought, may both be a position of (flight) refusal and negation of Joint Force Lethality, as well as the active (fight) protection of the weak and wretched, the stronghold of the sacred-profane of place and being, and being out of place. How we (un)belong, how we (un)be longing for. Joint Force defense is a lethal combination in the service of Apollonian purity. Solidarity is our shared defense, the Dionysian instinct we have for survival, the thinking-feeling with each other. The music in the cacophony.

Arm, its etymology in both our limbs of embrace and weaponry, is ar- "to fit together." How do we arm ourselves, arm together in limb-linkage against invasion, neo-conquest and gentrification, eviction of mind and land? What is our defense mode? A haptic and dreamed transfer of collectively borne pain and delight, wonder and want in the viscera of flesh and word. How we shield each other from injury, bring open arms and doors and books as invitation to refuge. How we protect the earth from drilling and hacking, the fracking oil shed of these Mother veins. How we scheme and plan and question and laugh our way out of the contested environment into the cross-pollinating decalcification of our spacetimemattering.

Our grammar of defense in the work of assembling the future-tense is rooted thus: in "the joy of wanting to destroy whatever mutilates life."[6] This is defense strategy against our estrangements: open your arms. (This isn't liberalism's multicultural group hug.) Open our arms. Be/holding. The instinct is not monumental. It is a shadowdance of the not-yet. We defend the indeterminate. We defend the yes, the together-yes, in the chaos and kaleidoscope of we. We arm ourselves with the yes in defense of life.

Notes

1. US Department of Defense, *Summary of the National Defense Strategy of the United States of America: Sharpening the American Military's Competitive Edge*. 2018.

2. Michel Foucualt,"*Society Must Be Defended": Lectures at the Collège de France, 1975-1976*, London: Picador Press, 2003, 216.

3. Foucault, 258.

4. Foucault, 56.

5. Jasbir K. Puar, "Coda: The Cost of Getting Better: Suicide, Sensation, Switchpoints," *GLQ*, Vol. 18, No. 1 (2012): 153. Pp. 149-158, doi: https://doi.org/10.1215/10642684-1422179.

6. Gilles Deleuze, "A New Cartography" in *Foucault*, trans. and ed. Seán Hand (New York: Continuum, 1999), 21.

Sadia Salim, *A Roaming Aesthetic IV*

fourth dialogue

(WHICH) SOCIETY MUST BE DEFENDED?

11 April 2020

Companion Texts for Studio Session

Possenti, Ilaria. "Is the Social Anti-Political." *Soft Power*, vol. 4, no. 2. (2017). http://www.softpowerjournal.com/web/wp-content/uploads/2019/10/21-possenti.pdf

Berlant, Lauren. "Thinking about feeling historical." *Emotion, Space, and Society*. vol. 1, iss. 1 (2008): 4-9. https://lucian.uchicago.edu/blogs/politicalfeeling/files/2009/01/berlant-thinking-about-feeling.pdf

Jaffe, Sarah. "Social Reproduction and the Pandemic, with Tithi Bhattacharya." *Dissent*. April 2, 2020. https://www.dissentmagazine.org/online_articles/social-reproduction-and-the-pandemic-with-tithi-bhattacharya.

Lepore, Jill. "What Our Contagion Fables Are Really About." *The New Yorker*. March 23, 2020. https://www.newyorker.com/magazine/2020/03/30/what-our-contagion-fables-are-really-about

Hoffman, Amy. "Love One Another or Die." *Boston Review*. April 2, 2020. https://bostonreview.net/gender-sexuality/amy-hoffman-love-one-another-or-die.

Wilson, Amanda. "Moving from Abstinence to Harm Reduction in the Age of Physical Distancing." *Université Saint-Paul School of Social Innovation*. March 31, 2020. http://innovationsocialeusp.ca/en/crits/blogue/moving-from-abstinence-to-harm-reduction-in-the-age-of-physical-distancing?.

Smith, Justin E.H.."It's AllJ Just Beginning." The Point. March 23, 2020. https://thepointmag.com/examined-life/its-all-just-beginning/.

Roy, Arundhati. "Arundhati Roy: The Pandemic is a Portal." *Financial Times*. April 3, 2020. https://www.ft.com/content/10d8f5e8-74eb-11ea-95fe-fcd274e920ca.

Hamilton, Robert Omar. "Irreversible Shift." n+1. 2019. https://nplusonemag.com/online-only/online-only/irreversible-shift/.

Martin, Nick. "Against Productivity in a Pandemic." *The New Republic*. March 7, 2020. https://newrepublic.com/article/156929/work-home-productivity-coronavirus-pandemic.

Odell, Jenny. *How to Do Nothing: Resisting the Attention Economy*. New York: Melville House, 2019. http://93.174.95.29/main/458F2B1B772D16ECE13A45DDBC0A44AA.

Hicok, Bob. "A Primer." The New Yorker. May 12, 2008. https://www.newyorker.com/magazine/2008/05/19/a-primer.

Hosts | Sara Mugridge, Daniel Neilson

Speakers | Asma Abbas, Safi Alsebai, Isaac Brosilow, Christopher Carrico, Starling Carter, Ciarán Finlayson, Ari Fogelson, Nathaniel Madison, Sara Mugridge, Daniel Neilson, Jody Leonard

Scribes & Annotators | Colin Eubank, Zibby Glass, Sanya Hussain, Isabella Lee, Heidi Andrea Restrepo Rhodes, Yashfeen Talpur

Part One

On what is to be defended

What can we learn from indigenous defense collectives for example, in Latin America, who are there to protect land against invasion/conquest/developers/extraction economies. How alternative epistemologies of defense might be meaningful, or if there is another language we want for what it is we seek to do. Thinking iterations of "defense" as shielding/protecting (the earth, each other) from injury; as constructing places of refuge; as survival tactics; as war mechanisms. — Heidi

ASMA

We have been on a strange journey and continue to weather time and space and our own isolations in certain ways. Welcoming you all this Saturday before Easter. I don't know if you've been watching any Easter movies, but I'm right in the middle of *The Greatest Story Ever Told*,[1] so I hope not to make too many references to neighbors, and premature failures, and leaders we love but who have absolutely no political sense. But that's something we suffer throughout, and I've been spending a lot of time thinking how.

These past weeks confronted us with yet another moment of abandonment or betrayal or failure or defeat, any and all of those, in relationship to the Bernie Sanders campaign. Even if it isn't just shock, something still reverberates. A reverberation that is just an unnecessary repetition of something that we could have done without. It is also, yet, an occasion to reflect on our conversations so far around the sufficiencies and insufficiencies of the category of the political in order to explain what goes well and what, well, doesn't. This will be some of our work together today.

I've also been thinking about the conversation we've had around having to justify defeats as some kind of victory, and not feeling quite in that mood right now. At the same time it's worth asking, what does one do if failures of politics cannot be translated into any other kind of victory? Since it's a brutal question to ask, I ask it with love and kindness toward the people for whom I feel a lot, including historical figures who have meant a lot, and who led us but constantly lost. While I don't feel any kind of grand comfort in that, it is true that people we love quite often lose. And then you wonder why you love them, or if that is why you love them! A good politician does not always have good politics, and the other way around, and how is one supposed to deal with that!

So here we are, four weeks into our effort, having moved from our conversation of crisis, to an attempted interpretation of our own political moment, to the meaning of our investments in political action and the lengths and places we go to in order to understand ourselves. We had the first session—to repeat for those who are here for the first time—interrogating categories of politics and crisis. Then we moved on to hear from several friends who are engaged in political activism about how they deal with questions of callings and legitimacy of political action, and in whose courts they are to be adjudicated. This led to the third conversation last week, around the tasks of knowing and judging politically, but also modes of valid proclamations around political unfolding, and the question of the future in relation to the question of history that we've been dealing with for three weeks, that capital-H history within which politics must make an appearance in order to be valid. So, really, we've been thinking of these various scenes.

Today, we step back from the scene a little bit. We are moved to ask now, what is the prescribed way forward? That requires returning to that place where some of us do find a little more comfort outside of rehearsed scripts. Maybe it helps to step away from proclamations, into the space of inquiry and reading and thinking together. In that sense, we go one step deeper into the circles of our own political hell, and try to read and listen and write together today.

As for "society" and its defense, we are indebted to that formulation in the first set of Foucault's *Society Must Be Defended* lectures.[2] We are not engaging that text closely but remain responsive to it as a provocation to re-read, and to think about the relationship of the social to the political if what we're experiencing is a complete abandonment of certain expectations of certain roles and certain forms of reliances on social systems, or the realization that they never existed, beyond our conjuring and our desire. What are we to be defending, if at all? There must be something to be defended, so here we are.

We will be moving a bit slowly today through texts, and the goal is to break out into smaller groups. Dan Neilson and Sara Mugridge will be the facilitators of this space and we look forward to working with each other in a slightly different key than the past few weeks.

DAN

Sara and I have organized introductions to each of these breakout conversations, which we'll share now. Maybe, while you're listening, you can form a sense of which one you might like to join. We'll do that for a little while, and then come back together and reassemble as a full group and see what we have to say to each other. I'll start with the first grouping of texts, to which we have given the theme, *The Social is Essential Work.*

In the US, state governors' offices are rushing to post lists that clarify which businesses are delegated as essential in the midst of pandemic. Such lists, like the one here in Massachusetts, include the categories of defense, industry, base, which place healthcare and public health above all others, but food and agriculture below the oddly condensed "law enforcement, public safety and first responders." In the clarity of our moment (but not only in this moment), we know that work that creates and sustains us in our social world—"care work" in all its forms—is essential. We cannot survive without it. We know that for all its enabling of life, it more often than not denies a sustainable livelihood to those who do this work. Overwhelmingly, and historically, this work is gendered and racialized. In the pandemic, we see clearly the enforcement of an old and horrific correlation between "essential" and "expendable" as care workers doing essential work are being forced right now to labor in more and more dangerous conditions without access to safety nets, or safety equipment for that matter. Without, that is to say, care.

In a recent interview, Tithi Bhattacharya observes that the coronavirus has clarified what social reproduction feminists have been saying for a while, which is that care work and life-making work are the essential work of society. According to Bhattacharya,

> [R]ight now when we are under lockdown, nobody is saying, "We need stockbrokers and investment bankers!: Let's keep those services open!". They are saying, "Let's keep nurses working, cleaners working, garbage -removal services open, to keep food production ongoing." Food, fuel, shelter, cleaning: These are the essential services. The crisis has also tragically revealed how completely incapable capitalism is of dealing with a pandemic. It is oriented toward maximizing profit, rather than maintaining life. [Capitalists argue] that the greatest victims in all this are not the countless lives that are being lost, but the bloody economy. The economy, it seems, is the most vulnerable little child that everyone from Trump to Boris Johnson is ready to protect with shining swords. Meanwhile, the healthcare sector has been ravaged in the United States by privatization and austerity measures. People are saying that nurses have to make masks at home. I have always said capitalism privatizes life and life-making, but I think we need to re-word that after the pandemic: "Capitalism privatizes life, but it also socializes death."[3]

Today we ask, how do we reclaim "essential" from "essential to capital"? How do we care about care work rather than protecting policing and death-making work?

SARA

I'm offering an invitation to the section titled *Reading Around Emotional Labor, or Thinking about Feeling in Crisis.*

Today, we'll be flooding the term "emotional labor" against the advice of its originator. For now, we remain less interested in the expressive gesture, not inclined to delineate what feelings are managed for what pay. Instead let us ask how we think about feeling in crisis. What we take to be the work of affect, how we approach modes of feeling that bring us into an intimacy we might come to know, and solidarity. What is the feeling of labor and making it possible to live together, to live? How are we feeling this urgency, as Amy Hoffman borrows from W.H. Auden, to "love one another or die," in times of heightened anxiety and enforced isolation? As always, we ask: what solves, salves, provides refuge, without retreat?

Lauren Berlant thinks about feeling through close readings:

> Let us now tell something. We don't have to think about it, we don't have to feel anything. We don't have to express our deepest self and wait for recognizing a response. This nascent solidarity is solipsistic first and not performative. Telling is a state of bodily practice, whose performance opens intuition to surprising rehabituations. Though by making where you are from into something you can rely on only if you tell someone. If you tell about it, someone hears it, and produces your thereness as a warmth of presence in a historical present. Solidarity happens prior to intimacy, or the contents of your auditor's subjectivity. This is not about recognition, letting in the other, etc. But in fantasy there will be transactions of telling and hearing in the genre of sound, streaming.[4]

On the notion that solidarity happens prior to intimacy

Intimacy is contingent on solidarity, solidarity is prior to intimacy, and needs to be prior to "legibility" of the life with which or with whom one seeks that solidarity and intimacy. "Telling" may also deviate from its confessional mode which announces a self to be made legible and therefore deemed worthy of politics' salvational attention. Telling may emerge as a speculative form of relation threading the future-now in and as intimacy with each other: what selves, what worlds we may draw into becoming as we expand toward each other. What can "the encounter" (as solidarity, as intimacy, without retreat) be in a context of enforced isolation? What can we learn from other contexts of enforced isolation, without appropriating claims of the violence from which those contexts are born?

COVID has changed, is changing, what general public intimacy means, looks like, how it is imagined. There is a collective enforcement (and/or ignoring) of imagining public intimacy with a kind of defensive framing right now, for better and worse on both sides, perhaps. — Heidi

DAN

The third breakout session is called *Against Repackaged Normalcy*.

We will not go back to normal, but where will we go? Importantly, what do we take with us? How do we begin to do so without enacting or repurposing old cruelties? First is a quote from Arundhati Roy's "The Pandemic is a Portal":

> Whatever it is, coronavirus has made the mighty kneel and brought the world to a halt like nothing else could. Our minds are still racing back and forth, longing for a return to "normality." Trying to stitch our future to our past and refusing to acknowledge the rupture. But the rupture exists. And in the midst of this terrible despair, it offers us a chance to rethink the doomsday machine we have built for ourselves. Nothing could be worse than a return to normality. Historically, pandemics have forced humans to break with the past and imagine their world anew., This one is no different. It is a portal, a gateway between one world and the next., We can choose to walk through it, dragging the carcasses of our prejudice and hatred, our avarice, our data banks and dead ideas, our dead rivers and smoky skies behind us. Or we can walk through lightly, with little luggage, ready to imagine another world. And ready to fight for it.[5]

Angela Davis, too, suggests that we seize this moment. It is one forged, not only by crisis but by organizing, and we can think back to last week's readings, the calls from Joshua Clover to let go of demands that organizing look only one way.

On refusing the notion that organizing looks only one way

What organizing must look like is so often defined through ableism and logocentrism. I have been encouraging peers, colleagues, to understand organizing expansively. I think it must mean we get to work, in constellation with each other, knowing that light takes time to travel distances. In "No Place for Self-Pity, No Room for Fear" (2015), Toni Morrison writes of the artist's responsibility in times of dread: that this is precisely when we get to work. This will not only mean fists raised in the streets, or surging forces toward the polls. It will be thousands of little fires everywhere, flickering, flaring, fueling something so much larger than we, here, now. — Heidi

Perhaps optimistically, Karen Russell reflects in the *New Yorker*,

> Nobody crosses the six foot barrier; you might argue that humans have never been less like a flock, than at this moment of voluntary isolation. But I also feel that our stasis itself is a kind of secret flight. Externally, we are all separated from public spaces, cancelling weddings and graduations, retreating into our homes. This physical separation belies what is happening on another plane: people are responding to the crisis with a surprising unity. More swiftly than I would have thought possible, hundreds of millions are heeding a difficult call to stay at home. It's the way of soaring into formation. And yet, "murmuration" seems like the right word for the great

convergence of humans traveling through this time together, listening to the latest news with our whole bodies, alert to subtle atmospheric changes, making constant recalibrations in response to the fluxing crisis at speeds to rival the dervishing starlings. How rapidly we are adjusting our behavior, to protect one another.[6]

SARA

The last section, we're calling, *Out of Productivity in and from Home.*

Headlines give us new and awkward permissions. The *New York Times* commands, "Stop trying to be productive." *The Washington Post* soothes, "it's okay not to be productive during the coronavirus pandemic." *Huffington Post* politely begs us, "Please don't be guilted into being more productive during the Coronavirus," and there are others. So, we ask, what should we refuse in failing to comply with capitalism's call to order?

On what we must refuse

In relation to the notion of "essential care work," how, when productivity is simply equated to putting in the hours at a job, it renders invisible the essential work of caring, life-making. What does this essential work look like under different conditions of visibility and sanctioning? How do we think about the "productivity" of care-work, or the refusal to be productive in that context? What requires being available to, being 'cared' for and in what manner?— Yashfeen

In 2016, artist Trisha Hersey began the "Nap Ministry,"[7] a project that reminds us that the longstanding rest deficit has always been weaponized, and that the revolutionary act of restoration, in particular for systematically oppressed people, is a holy and wholly radical stance. Jenny Odell too, has been thinking about how to do nothing.

Gathering all this together what I'm suggesting is that we take a protective stance toward ourselves, each other, and whatever is left of what makes us human including the alliances that sustain and surprise us. I'm suggesting that we protect our spaces and our time for non instrumental non commercial activity and thought for maintenance or care for conviviality, and I'm suggesting that we fiercely protect their human animality against all technologies that constantly ignore and disdain the body. The bodies of other beings and the body of the landscape that we inhabit.[8]

What radical nourishment, and what protective stances, are we offering against enforced productivity in and toward ourselves in and from our homes? What postures do we take toward and with each other, across and against assumptions about hope when so many live in places that are not refuge but literal or figurative prisons and sites of abuse and inadequate shelter? What alliances will sustain and surprise us?

On willing refusals

There is an abrupt and very uneasy coexistence at best, but mostly active opposition, between working at home, which includes things like affective, emotional, and reproductive labor, a maintaining of life, yours and of those with whom you live, and working from home, which includes a poor imitation of what is imagined to be productive labor. (I mean "poor" in the sense that it is obviously lacking in its effectiveness and productiveness, but not as something that we should mourn. On the contrary, it becomes a site or a moment for the possible refusals and failures that keep cropping up in different threads throughout these Dialogues.) — Hannah

ASMA

Thank you, Sara and Dan. This was really lovely. Thanks for the work you've done to put your thoughts in, bringing all these coordinates alive, to get us going. What we now would like to do is to just recommend that each person, find a room, click into a room that corresponds to each of these four prompts and provocations that have been put forth. We will all talk about everything together after we've met in small thematic groups.

Anna Poplawski on *Women Talking* as Abolitionist Method

Reading *Women Talking* by Miriam Toews as a work of abolitionist literature implies both a provocation and a method. The 2018 novel, based on true events that came to light in 2011, is Toews' fictional imagination of how the women of a Bolivian Mennonite Colony called Molotschna respond after discovering that years of sexual attacks they experienced were not nightmares, fabulations, or punishments ordered by Satan, as they had been repeatedly convinced, but drug-facilitated rapes executed by their fellow colonists. A group of eight men directly perpetrated the attacks by spraying sleeping families with animal sedative before entering their homes to commit acts of sexual terror against women and children as young as three. Most of the men in the colony both enabled the attacks and committed their own routine domestic abuse. *Women Talking* envisions what the women of Molotschna would discuss if they secretly met in a barn for two days in order to decide whether they will leave, stay and fight, or do nothing in response to the attacks and broader reality of pervasive sexual abuse.

The novel reads like a dialogic work of political theology; the women cite parables and invent their own, consider producing a radical manifesto, and theorize the nature of authority, forgiveness, and the soul. Considering what it would mean to stay in Molotschna and try to change the society whose most basic logics produce sexual violence leads to extensive deliberation: How are the women to defend themselves if they, as Mennonites, believe in absolute pacifism? Will being in close proximity to their attackers and other abusive men lead the women to develop reprehensible violent thoughts? And how are the women to initiate social transformation if they are all illiterate, speak only Low German, and their concrete knowledge of the world is limited to what they are told by the Mennonite elders who enabled systematic rape?

Ultimately, the barn meeting delegates decide that all of the women (apart from those who were not interested in fighting or leaving) will leave Molotschna, along with their relatives under twelve and the elderly or disabled people for whom they are responsible. In the process of deciding to leave, particularly while discussing who should leave with them, the women of Molotschna collectively examine not only their religious and cultural beliefs, but also their feelings toward the husbands, brothers, fathers, and sons they have loved, cared for, resented, and feared all their lives. Breaking ties with one's abuser who is also an intimate partner or relative is, of course, one of the foremost defining and difficult aspects of ending any situation of domestic violence, but *Women Talking* offers a thoughtful and unique vision of that process that sees political, ethical, philosophical, familial, and emotional commitments—and how we might opt to betray them—as deeply connected to each other and rooted in broader social existence.

At first glance, the women's decision to leave their home appears to be a politically separatist move. However, given that Molotschna is a remote Mennonite colony in Bolivia, leaving means the negation and refusal of their society's original separatism, along with its debilitatingly authoritarian, violent, and patriarchal conditions. It is methodologically important to note that organized departure has a different significance for these women than it does in the broader world because separatist movements, particularly Christian ones, are often historically and conceptually incompatible with abolitionist politics. Far from rejecting the world and their imbrication within it as subjects, the women of Molotschna leave their colony in order to escape immediate violence, but also to emancipate themselves and their children from an isolated and repressive way of life.

It is on this basis that I glean from *Women Talking* a contribution to abolitionist political method despite the intense particularity of its setting. Toews' narrative models a mode of collective study that makes the transformation of social life to the point of non-recognition its goal, and is remarkable for its recognition that all of one's relations must be considered and potentially dissolved in order to overturn the present state of affairs. Willing an end to our historical reality, although it differs substantially from Molotschna, similarly involves bringing a materialist eye to all aspects of experience, paying particular attention to lived contradictions of loyalty and affiliation as they arise in domains like the family or other intimate enclaves, including left intellectual and/or activist spaces.

Why do we have the affinities—to particular forms of relation, to institutions, to values—that we do? And, what must happen when we find that those attachments or perceived obligations contribute to the reproduction of violence? Reading Miriam Toews tells us that abolishing society as we know it requires addressing that question by thinking and struggling together. — Anna

Part Two

DAN

Hi, everyone. We're back together again. I hope that was nice! In our group it felt like we could speak a little bit off the record or around the coffee table or something. I don't know, it felt a little more informal, maybe! I would like to welcome everyone back. So, at the risk of being a tiny bit artificial, maybe we could just go around the groups in order and hear a little bit back from someone from each group, or a couple people from each group? And, then see where we are?

SARA

Re: "The social is essential work."

In our conversation we spent quite a bit of time hearing and thinking about agricultural work, but certainly were not limited to it. We discussed the meaning—the what and the how—of "essential." We also came back around to the notion that policing is actually listed as an essential activity. Of course, "essential" not to life-making, but to protecting the system protecting property. But how is that brutality, that violence, being used to enforce essential work right now?

On productivity

How have we also internalized the police as a function in the context of productivity, what brutality do we perform on ourselves and each other either out of misinformed "investment" in capital, or out of the need to survive the brutality of the system?— Heidi

SAFI

Re: "Reading around emotional labor or thinking about feeling in crisis."

We started off our discussion by turning to Berlant's "Thinking about Feeling Historical," and her reading of Bob Hicok's poem "A Primer," and thought about the distinction between reading drama and poetry in this moment, as one where drama sometimes pre-scripts certain ways of making dialogue. So, in poetry, we can sort of figure out how to make conversations outside of that prescription. Right now it seems easier to read poetry than to read drama.

What is it to be/hold, to let inquiry be a practice of love, of patience, carework, long-haul labor beyond our individual lives, and into the always-present not-yet?
Jill Lepore writes in her March 2020 article, "What Our Contagion Fables are Really About:"⁹

"The literature of contagion is vile. A plague is like a lobotomy. It cuts away the higher realms, the loftiest capacities of humanity, and leaves only the animal. 'Farewell to the giant powers of man,' Mary Shelley wrote in *The Last Man*, in 1826, after a disease has ravaged the world. 'Farewell to the arts—to eloquence. Every story of epidemic is a story of illiteracy, language made powerless, man made brute.'[10] But, then, the existence of books, no matter how grim the tale, is itself a sign, evidence that humanity endures, in the very contagion of reading. Reading may be an infection, the mind of the writer seeping, unstoppable, into the mind of the reader. And yet it is also—in its bidden intimacy, an intimacy in all other ways banned in times of plague—an antidote, proven, unfailing, and exquisite." – Heidi

ASMA

Forms of literature and expression also have their own built-in contagion, or forms of thinking about what is heard, versus what voices we are asked to release from those among those always captured in bodies that are so removed from us. It's much harder than the nebulous imagination of the poetic. So, we brought up the enduring "poetry after Auschwitz" moment and just these small things that could be helpful in thinking about something like the task of availability. So, it's not a matter of what's harder to express or unable to be captured in language, but what it is easier to be available to, and what is asked of us socially, and the social labor of being available to each other. That's sort of where we were trying to complicate the question of cultural expression, and collective feeling by that name.

ZIBBY

I think this is related to the Ilaria Possenti piece this session started with, speaking to the transformation of the "society," into "civil-society," "with space for civil liberties but not the experience of political freedom".... She goes on to say that "it is specifically the liberal perspective that frames community life in a way that neglects this kind of freedom and conceptualizes "the social" in a way that begins to be anti-political."[11]

COLIN

I really like this line at the end of the Lepore essay: "Reading may be an infection, the mind of the writer seeping, unstoppable, into the mind of the reader. And yet it is also—in its bidden intimacy, an intimacy in all other ways banned in times of plague—an antidote, proven, unfailing, and exquisite."[12] It seems to echo the sentiment that the group took up and worked with.

In her book, *Cloud of the Impossible*, Catherine Keller opens with an epigraph by Nicholas of Cusa: "And the more that cloud of impossibility is recognized as obscure and impossible, the more truly the necessity shines forth."[13] What is to come, the future, is always a clouded form entering the sphere of visibility, vaporous, morphing with the weather, which is, following Christina Sharpe, the condition of the atmosphere climatologically as well as figuratively-politically, constituting "the totality of our environments"[14]—the total climate that is antiblack, the storm of progress, the tempest of capital's unfolding in the palm of coloniality. Keller's second epigraph, from Edouard Glissant's *Poetics of Relation*, offers the following: "[A]t the bow there is still something we now share: this murmur, cloud or rain or peaceful smoke. We know ourselves as part and as crowd, in an unknown that does not terrify us."[15]— Heidi

NATHANIEL

We also brought up comparisons between HIV/AIDS and COVID-19 and talked about the reversal and difference between the stigma and the valorization of these two events. You have this kind of intense stigma and homophobia, out of AIDS, and the general social reaction to it. That's brought up really well by Amy Hoffman, in "Love One Another or Die," and makes me think of the current valorization of care work despite the class issue underneath, where people are deemed either essential and not paid, or have to work in conditions where they don't really have means to protect themselves. At the same time, it is being treated or seen as war, and the same people are being monumentalized.

> Because AIDS was defined early as a disease of homosexuals, Haitians, and junkies, nobody in the political, medical, or social service establishments felt obligated to do anything about it. We had no choice but to do all of it ourselves—the caregiving, the treatment, the research, the public education. Our organizing, to be effective, had to take on the epidemic from all sides: the racist, homophobic way it was framed; the challenge it posed to the health care system; the indifference of politicians; the scientists who saw people with AIDS as juicy experimental subjects; the religious leaders who saw the disease as divine retribution for sin, a blessing in disguise.[16]

ASMA

The other thing Hoffman also does is bring up the class context in relation to who was supposed to be dying of AIDS, and extrapolate from that. So, the primary construction of homophobia is there, on one hand, but then, on the other hand, AIDS isn't considered an epidemic or something to defend against by looking at sex workers! The entire city got basically wiped out, but we always have to associate AIDS with a different kind of epidemic than this one. Because, right now, we are as yet uncertain as to who can be marked for slaughter on this bench of history, as compared to the meticulous construction of the pariah and stigmatization of certain kinds of intimacies marked for sacrifice.

But, they weren't deemed, even then, as "essential." I wonder if this "essential worker" category could be translated into sex workers in India, wanting to have protection against AIDS. So, I think that that's maybe a related point. I think from there we were just talking about the fourth point: even though we are testing vaccines in Africa or elsewhere, there is still a certain way that we are not certain. Right now the people marked to be killed haven't quite been determined, right? So there's an unseemly failure of a kind of war imagination that hasn't explicitly figured out who needs to be sacrificed, and to what eugenicist form it is committed this time. So I think that's connected with this, the question of knowledge.

ARI

I just have a quick question, since we're discussing it. What is the role of an expert here? How is knowledge about the disease accrued, and who has that knowledge? You know, the use of a medication without having that necessary background is termed "compassionate use."

ASMA

I know, and in our group, we were connecting this question of expertise to Bernie too. What allows us to pretend we know nothing? What is the "epistemology of ignorance" in its specific connection to marginal bodies that allows us to not think that the history of AIDS informs the present, and our responses to the pandemic? If, as I have said before, that this present has a past, who gets to decide what history counts and when, and what knowledge counts, when, and for whom? Especially if it is, as we literally see, being produced over bodies who are dying and those on whom the vaccine will be tested. Familiar bodies, no?

It's as if my use of the term "eugenics" is for a reason! As if somehow the evolution of knowledge has its own Darwinism—interesting knowledges that could have helped somebody else are decimated, erased, stored as moral advice in theatre productions. So, how come thirty years of being a politician didn't prepare Bernie for what was going to come, right? Was it the problem of our professional politicians or the lack thereof? Or, as in the case of the virus, what exactly was not known? So I'm not at all engaging in conspiracy theory, as much as asking, what is the natural life-cycle of knowledge around these things that we've come to not count on? All of this knowledge seems to have existed and we have gone through this before. In the context of such overproducing knowledge factories, is this, then, a typical capitalist crisis of overproduction, putting your own workers in debt, dumping knowledge elsewhere to make room for more on your own shelves, and "crisis"? This drama of lacking knowledge and resources, being lost, needing to know, feels like gaslighting right now: they, all of them, should have known better. But, seemingly nobody knew better. That's trauma plus abandonment that I think people are feeling, besides isolation.

On the evolution of knowledge and its own Darwinisms
I have been thinking about this in various ways, too, with the 1918 flu, and the plague in Europe.
What forms of knowledge, expectation, practices, have we inherited, and how consciously do we
relate to those forms, with what sense of epistemic Darwinism that assumes evolution and adaptation across time (often violently, through imposed universals), and with what sense of having
learned something valuable to collective well-being?— Heidi

JODY

Our group started off talking about how, in a lot of ways, and in ways that seem kind of
surprising, there are so many aspects of life that are still normal for us. The quickness with
which we have been able to adapt to this kind of environment, even though it is clear that there
is a crisis going on for so many people. And then we talked about the experience of trying to
help people out, through mutual aid or something else. At one point we talked about how it
feels like the groups that were most successful in delivering aid were the ones that already had
existing relationships in the community, and how that ended up triggering, for me at least,
without trying to shoe-horn everything into observing electoral politics, the role of institutions
in how things happen in the world.

So, if you look at the recent Democratic primary in the US, in the end it came down to
the candidate who had, with his campaign, tried to construct, at least as far as US politics are
concerned, the definition of a grassroots campaign, with lots of field offices, lots of participation, lots of small-dollar donations; versus a candidate who had none of that—who didn't have
field offices or excited volunteers or small-dollar donations—but had instead a decent amount
of media support and the institution of the DNC behind him. And I think one take away from
that election is that the guy who had the institutions—the long-term institutions—crushed it.

"I thought, too, that when I grew older I would no longer understand the city's language.
That the beats of the future would be as incomprehensible to me as drum 'n' bass to my mother,
that the city would wear a new lexical snakeskin—shiny, fresh, full of charm and warning.
But, the strange thing is, nothing really changed.
— from Omar Robert Hamilton, "Irreversible Shift"[17]

Turning to the topic of normalcy, I'm lamenting an idea or a set of principles that have existed
and been made real in the world through institutions or whatever else over a long period of
time, which are more powerful than the righteousness or the correctness of the idea itself. That's
kind of trite, because things that have been normalized are powerful. I think it's something to

reflect on while we think about what to undo or redo or try to take advantage of. Our group also tried to not feel as depressed about that. We drifted towards talking in our little session, not about repackaging normalcy, per se—or if normalcy has been repackaged—but the fact that in a lot of ways, even in a moment of crisis where you might think things have been undone, or there's an opportunity just to be changed, a lot of normalcy has continued.

"Is it any wonder that in a century dominated by surveillance, paranoia, terrorism, rendition, financial collapse, and hard borders our language has retreated? Our reality, for years now, has been of individual survival under austerity[...]. Of course the language has stopped growing: where are we even supposed to talk to each other now?"
— from Omar Robert Hamilton, "Irreversible Shift."[18]

COLIN

The discussion of repackaged normalcy, or lack of necessity for the repackaging, brings me to political education and the need for a rethinking of how it occurs—contra the opinions and traditional knowledge of experts—in a way that actually does not necessarily require incremental consciousness-building and hand-holding by expert organizers. People come together and learn by doing. They learn with what it is that they have at hand.

STARLING

I wanted to add that we were discussing mutual aid networks, and talking about how these networks of assisting one another have already existed for certain communities and in certain places, either out of necessity or something else. So what's happening now could be seen as an example of people who are not historically marginalized communities having a similar experience of realizing what will and will not be provided by the state and the powers that be, and how that provides a jump start to get a lot of people moving. Even knowing who's in their community and reaching out and doing some activity and some organizing as well: I expect that will be totally necessary in a second Trump term. So, thinking a little bit about how a lot of people have been forced into action in a way that I hope will lay some groundwork for continuing to protect and know our communities into the perhaps difficult and dark future times. But that's a hopeful thought.

ISAAC

Re: Out of productivity in and from home.

From my perspective, I think we had a scattered but really informative conversation about the need to kind of put an exterior value onto forms of labor, especially with respect to notions of emotional labor. And that reminded me of the kind of impulse to create an actual invoice for emotional labor as a way to "wage" it and the role that autonomous feminism and similar movements have played in those strategies.

On the term "emotional labor"

I want to consider the policing of affect itself, of the worker under capitalism, how affect is seen to serve or undermine capital and the worker's productivity, how it becomes something else for capital to appropriate/expropriate to produce symbolic and material value. Is it useful to ask if there is a kind of emotional and affective eugenics at play along with the sociobiological inheritances of eugenics that linger and haunt this present moment?— Heidi

ASMA

I am someone who has been suspicious of the category of affective labor as separate from other kinds of labor—carrying a kind of sneaky secularism—and also of the manner in which, especially within academia, a seemingly liberatory category becomes a category that produces new kinds of hierarchies. For whom is labor ever unaffective, especially if it is true that it is always laced with questions of survival and of having to build, work, as a means of life, rather than the other way around? I'm thinking about the insufficiency of existing forms of acknowledgement of both political resistance and labor, which really runs counter to, or at least puts into question, the validity of a particular model of even recognizing labor. I'm thinking about what your conversation about this invoicing of emotional labor was, because I wonder if the form of value is the form we should uphold through this time, or if it's the thing we have to break, which doesn't solve the problem of how we're going to feed ourselves and have a shelter over our head. I think it's a question worth asking because I feel that our ways of thinking about essential and non-essential labor have had everything to do in the past few years of trying to shift conversations about women's labor and the labor of people of color, so that there is a particular impasse now. It has always existed in feminism around, like, Oh is all work value or does work counter the production of value? I want to know more about this, because I do think some of us have attachments to these notions of retributive uses of emotional labor that just almost give too much credit to the oppressor in a certain way. I'm wondering what you feel about that.

ISAAC

This reminded me of an interview with David Ranney, who is now a professor but was a factory worker, and a member of the New Left group called Sojourner Truth Organization from the '70s and '80s, based in Chicago. There is a quote about work stoppage and wildcat strikes that he was part of in Chicago. His organization was criticized by New Left groups, as well as Maoists, for not taking over the factory and organizing production better, during the strike. Instead he had to stop work and told the management and the bosses to fuck off. And he basically made this distinction that because they hated the job, they hated the work they were doing, then for them the radical act was in the refusal of work, and, we kind of made this point: that it really is kind of a hybrid conversation when it comes to tactics and stoppages and the form of value and labor that we take. And, in some cases, it's something that depends on the situation, but I think there are ways that it can be really radical.

ASMA

I wonder if there is a different way to desegregate the conversation about work from this question of affect and feeling, and to demarcate the work of dismantling from the work of building and imagining. I fervently believe that the value-form is the problem, not just kinds of value, but I don't think this is really a discussion about that. I do wonder what happens if we bring in the other pieces around the production of society that could be imagined as working outside of categories of work and labor, and not feel like we have to hammer out once and for all the categories with which we must all work from this point forward.

Trying to think about forms of human experience and their translations, I'm feeling a little bit directed into clarities that I think might forestall a creative, collaborative, sense of different senses of being in the world or working. Maybe I'm just too abstract or formalist for this … but I guess because I do think that there is a searching that isn't gratified by just finding a better category for my work. So I just wonder if we can actually be *more* messy, you know, rather than *less*—and see where might that take us. I honestly don't think that it's a luxury. I start to feel suffocated when I don't have that room and the whole world feels really suffocating right now and I just need a little bit more room, and I think people have to make categories together to breathe better. I think building-work requires different categories than dismantling a system does. They go in tandem but I don't think they're all constantly engaged in the same act. I think that there has to be room for the stopping that's not refusal, and that doesn't need to be interpreted and given a value right away. I'm nervous about both the desire to give value or a decision to withhold it. Where to go from there? What words to make and language to deploy? I just want to confess that in this space that we are building. Thank you, thanks for listening.

On expanding what counts as subversive arts

What is made possible in understanding the "work" we do in constellation, in entangled flows that create meaning and transformative experience and relation, without needing to be catalogued as legitimate organizing, or legitimate work, by whatever status quo or value system we concede to? We need the risk of the abstract right now, the risk of messiness, an art of not-knowing....while also maintaining rigor. And also, re. Audre Lorde's "Poetry is Not a Luxury," the subversive arts, the exploratory and imaginative and questioning work we do, I think has to be seen as necessary. As soon as we let it be seen as luxury, we let that work enter into that value system, and expect an accounting of input → output. But the more abstract, imaginative, artistic, poetic, intuitive kinds of work are not immediately traceable to outputs of capital value (please let them never be!). If we see them as luxury, they become disposable in times of urgency and crisis, and we lose vital space for germination, surprise, wonder, experiment, joy, yet-unimagined possibility. — Heidi

SARA

In your reporting back, I'm hearing throughout that these threads are not very naturally pulled apart into these four sections, although we did want to do that to give ourselves some time to be in smaller spaces. Maybe now would be a good time to open this up and find where these threads are naturally overlapping—between social and emotional labor, between feelings, between waging or refusing productivity.

It is a little tongue-in-cheek but I am just thinking about the term emotional labor itself and how actually, the policing of the term's use is something that makes it really difficult to think with it about affect and emotion existing simultaneously with the essential work that we're talking about.

CHRIS

I was thinking about how under quarantine, where value-producing wage work and the work of social reproduction are all in the same space at the same time and the categories break down, in terms of what we're doing and what we're responding to at various moments. This is an exceptional circumstance, but it speaks to something that is a lot more general than that. In one sense we're called now to respond to all sorts of things having to do with wage work outside of this tightly circumscribed time when we're supposed to be at our jobs. But then we don't experience them as separate. I do think that it is useful to make a distinction between two very different senses of what we mean by value. Things that are value-producing in a capitalist economy aren't necessarily the things that are valuable to people in terms of what is useful to them and good for them. We're constantly in this space of: "I've been told by economists that value isn't a category that has to do with something's moral worth, and yet we live in a society that actually does ascribe value to your ability to produce value." I think it is useful to begin to kind of make an analytic distinction between those usages.

ASMA

That's really helpful. And it speaks to the distinction made earlier in the conversation between productive and reproductive labor to complicate the one between essential and nonessential work, the initial frame. There's something you point out that's at the core both of the subjective experience of labor, and of the analytic categories with which we approach it. I think that might be where we are landing, and perhaps that's what the quarantine is highlighting or illuminating. Just this juncture, or that produced disjunction, much more than it usually would be, and I wonder if that can be taken advantage of rather than hidden away from. I'm also thinking of Bourdieu, and I think that connecting reproductive labor to social reproduction itself highlights the requisite arrangement of spaces, as well as categories that organize the space of thinking as a space and in those spaces. I wonder if that's maybe where quarantine challenges us further.

DAN

I guess we're coming towards the end. I wanted to return to one thread that had been in the conception of this session—the calls to maintain, the calls to normalcy, against any sense of reality. This instruction to do your job as best as you can, or these banal institutional requests to submit this piece of paper or that piece of paper, which nobody needs. They come from the usual people at the usual times, and they simply make no reference whatsoever to how much more work it will all be, or how extreme our circumstances are. I find it to be a kind of terrifying clutch for normalcy that is maybe a grinding of teeth: "None of this is happening, and I'm going to hold to the past as long as I can, and then as soon as I can I'm gonna switch over to the future, and all of this in-between will never have existed."

On banal institutional requests and the mandate of normalcy under crisis

I witness the requisite of "Keep Calm and Carry On," as well as neoliberal rhetorics in university settings. For instance, with online teaching, so many educators are experiencing a major increase in hours of labor required to teach, and are utterly fatigued by it, some dealing with pay cuts or job precarity—all while being told that labor is "for the good of the [insert university name] family." So educators (mostly women and transgender professors I am witnessing facing this) are placed in roles of labor and reproductive labor; the university becomes a heteronormativized site of nuclear family defense, being asked to sacrifice for the better of their children (students) and of the family (the institution), which translates to "ignore your needs" such that "your body/wellbeing matters less as sacrificial mother." Those who are not holding up well under these added demands on their own temporal, physical, and mental health during this time are seen as failures, are seen as selfish,

As Chris was pointing out, our roles and relationships cross and overlap in quarantine. While we've been on this call we've been fighting for bandwidth with our children who are trying to stream a movie, and so I feel that overlap intensely as I'm trying to be with you folks right now. The thing is that during this time, what we have in here seemed to me like not quite ghosts, because I think they could be maybe some kind of zombies that could still be reanimated: the impressions, roles, arrangements and hierarchies that we brought into the quarantine with us. They're not gone, obviously. I'm resistant to the urges to rearrange them, or to bring them all back in more or less the same form—unsure, yet, of how we sort through the things that we brought into this time with us. How do we sort through and figure out which ones still serve, which ones might serve, suitably altered, and which ones never served before and will never serve in the future and so should be abandoned? Active work during this time to distinguish among them seems imperative.

appearance of an event, not a structure, a place which is not bound to compromise or bound to reproducing a system...
a place which can escape infernal repetition... — Zibby

It seems like maybe we have all entered into a meditative slumber—who can blame us? Next week, Karl Marx will be joining us, live, in person, for our conversation about institutions. I appreciate your willingness to experiment with the multiple channels here and we welcome feedback or suggestions or concepts for discord-based pedagogy at any time. There's a lot more to be said, of course, so we'll turn off the recording now, and once the recording is off you're welcome to share whatever crazy ideas you've been holding on to for the last little while. Thank you everyone for joining us, much love to everyone, and we'll talk to you again soon.

Notes

1. The *Greatest Story Ever Told*, directed by David Lean, George Stevens, and Jean Negulesco. (UK, 1965). DVD.

2. Michel Foucault, *"Society Must Be Defended": Lectures at the Collège de France, 1975-76*, trans. David Macey (London: St. Martin's Press, 2003).

3. Sarah Jaffe and Tithi Bhattacharya, "Social Reproduction and the Pandemic, with Tithi Bhattacharya," accessed on December 23, 2020, https://www.dissentmagazine.org/online_articles/social-reproduction-and-the-pandemic-with-tithi-bhattacharya,

4. Lauren Berlant, "Thinking about Feeling Historical," in *Political Emotions: New Agendas in Communication*, edited by Janet Staiger, Ann Cvetkovich and Ann Reynolds (London: Routledge, 2010).

5. Arundhati Roy, "The Pandemic is a Portal," *Financial Times*, Apr. 3, 2020, accessed on December 23, 2020, https://www.ft.com/content/10d8f5e8-74eb-11ea-95fe-fcd274e920ca,

6. Karen Russell. "How the Coronavirus Has Infected Our Vocabulary," accessed on December 23, 2020, https://www.newyorker.com/magazine/2020/04/13/a-temporary-moment-in-time.

7. Tricia Hersey, "The Nap Ministry," accessed on December 23, 2020, https://thenapministry.wordpress.com/about/.

8. Jenny Odell, H*ow to Do Nothing: Resisting the Attention Economy* (Melville House, 2019).

9. Jill Lepore, "What Our Contagion Fables are Really About," *New Yorker*, March 2020.

10. Mary Shelley, *The Last Man* (London: Colburn, 1826), vol. III, ch. 1.

11. Ilaria Possenti, "Is the Social Antipolitical?" *Soft Power* 4(2), (Jul.-Dec. 2017), 329.

12. Tricia Hersey, "The Nap Ministry."

13. Catherine Keller, *Cloud of the Impossible: Negative Theology and Planetary Entanglement* (New York: Columbia University Press, 2014); Nicholas of Cusa, *On the Vision of God*.

14. Christina Sharpe, "The weather," *The New Inquiry*, January 2017, accessed December 23 2020, https://thenewinquiry.com/the-weather/.

15. Édouard Glissant, *Poetics of Relation*, translated by Betsy Wing (Ann Arbor: The University of Michigan Press, 1997), 9.

16. Amy Hoffman, "Love One Another or Die," *Boston Review*, April 2020, accessed December 23 2020, http://bostonreview.net/gender-sexuality/amy-hoffman-love-one-another-or-die.

17. Omar Robert Hamilton, "Irreversible Shift," n+1 (2019), accessed December 28, 2020, https://nplusonemag.com/online-only/online-only/irreversible-shift/.

18. Hamilton, "Irreversible Shift."

fourth interlude
SPECIES/BEING/FALSE/WORK

Who Cares About Care If Care Is The Alibi: A Lamentation in 3 Fragments and 7 Songs

Bonaventure Soh Bejeng Ndikung

FRAGMENT 2

Ti Manno

Like many of you, I have been lamed by and with rage since the violent murder of George Floyd, 46 years old, in Minneapolis, and the fact that this is nothing new, not the first time and probably not the last time a Black man was/will be cold-bloodedly murdered by a police officer—white or black, in the USA or in Cameroon—in broad daylight. Maybe the most terrible thing about this kind of rage is the feeling of helplessness. A feeling not to be able to do something. Yes, we are organising and will go out to protest. Yes, I will write something like many of you, and will vent. Yes, I will call friends, and I will cry in private. But all these won't bring back the life so brutally taken from someone I don't know and never met, but who like the other Black men and women murdered before him, could be my brother, my sister, or even me. Yes, we shall share speeches by Baldwin, Davis, Finney and the many others who have warned us of the many evils out there, but that feeling of being conscious but unable to act, that feeling of being half-awake and half-numbed so akin to sleep paralysis still reigns and envelops like a straightjacket. Indeed in the past two days I have revisited some of these voices—to seek solace, to mourn, to find reassurance, to escape. Nikky Finney's lecture "Sipping Kerosene at the Refectory" for the "Breath>Body>Voice" conference was one of such.[1] Breathing took centre stage in the lecture and Q&A. Beyond this, I have had to think of the non-obviousness of breath. Sometimes when children are born, the midwife has to hit the baby for it to breathe. The uncertainty of breath in such perilous times, and how that uncertainty is so much related to one's race and class. I have been more conscious of, and hail, every exhaling and inhaling. Also, in the past two days, I have been rummaging in a maybe not-so-obvious sonic space. Rather than go to Bob Marley or Gil Scott Heron, I went to the great Haitian Compas and Kadans artist and man of the people, Ti Manno a.k.a. Antoine Rossini Jean-Baptiste a.k.a. Emmanuel Jean-Baptiste. One particular song from his 1982 album "Gemini All Stars De Ti Manno" completely caught my attention, and with each hearing I try to dissect even deeper.

"Nan Danje" is what one might call a typical Ti Manno song: deep, very consciously speaking to his people, politically anchored, and still danceable. It is a song that tells of contributions of Black peoples/ Haitian people in the making of, the development of, the freedom of, the world we live in. But everywhere we go, we are in danger.[2] In general, Ti Manno sets up a sonic and poetic discou discourse on poverty, discrimination, exploitation, humiliation, stigmatization of the Haitian in particular, and the African in general.

Song 2[3]

Ke se noumenm ki sove anpil lot pep
— We are the ones who helped liberate many other countries,
Menm lezetazini ki premye pwisans di mond
— Even the United States, the greatest power in the world.
Nou te rive edel pou-l pwan lendepandans
— We helped them become independent.
Len-n fini sove Venezuela
— When we finished liberating Venezuela
Nou ede la Bolivi
— We helped Bolivia.
Nou libere le Perou
— We freed Peru.

Kote-npase nou gen pwoblem	Nan danje
— Wherever we go we have problems	We are in danger
Nou rive Mayami	Nan danje
— We come to Miami	We are in danger
Nou rive Nou Yok Siti	Nan danje
— We come to New York City	We are in danger
Travese la Gwadeloup	Nan danje
— We cross over to Guadeloupe	We are in danger
Monreal Kanada	Nan danje
— Montreal, Canada	We are in danger
Toutkote nou pase	Nan danje
— Wherever we go	We are in danger

If Ti Manno was here with us today, what would he have written about the brutal murder of Mr. Floyd?

The thing is, we are also faced with our own incompetencies in relation to organizing ourselves, building structures to care and protect each other, as well as avoiding being caught up in the same capitalist fantasies that tell us that if we as individuals are fine, everyone is fine. One thing Ti Manno couldn't stop pointing out was our own responsibilities and failures towards stopping the violences against Black people all over the world. In almost every song he sang he discussed the human condition, criticised power misuse of the Haitian government and other governments, sang against racism, sexual harassment and all forms of discrimination. It's worth listening to the song "Sort Tiers Monde."[4]

Song 3[5]

This is a particular critique of the Black middle class that is trained in the big universities, but still confuses faculty (as in sense) with university, and is still caught up in an inferiority complex. These same middle class that perpetrates the violences of class, racial, language discrimination on other Blacks is what he criticises, not by pointing fingers, as in YOU, but as in a WE. An autocritique:

> Nap viv avek yon konpleks denferiorite
> — We live with an inferiority complex.
> Sek feme, klib pwive swa dizan distenksyon de klas
> — Closed circle, private clubs give an air of class distinction,
> Anpeche inite egalite fwatenite
> — Which prevents unity, equality, and fraternity.
> Toutmoun konplekse Toutmoun sou manti
> — Everybody's puffed up, Everybody's pretending,
> Pale franse vin tounen metye
> — To speak French becomes a profession.

To be honest, my favourite piece on this album is "Neg Kont Neg," a song in many gears.[6] It starts with an almost funeral procession-like, but groovy sound. That kind that calls for a collective swinging and stooping. The shoulders have to move. Then the piece drives into a middle upbeat: Kompas gear with more bass, drums and whistles and leads to the Ayibobo transition. Then it drives over to a version of the great Makossa classic by Bébé Manga, "Ami Oh," and in place he sings "Afrique Ohhhh." Bébé Manga had just released the song (composed by Manfred Ebanda and Eyoum Nelle already in 1962) in 1980, and it is one of the most sampled Makossa pieces (by Henri Salvador, Manu Dibango, Monique Séka, Papa Wemba & Angélique Kidjo, Nayanka Bell, etc.). Ti Manno transforms the love song into a protest song about injustices and the policies of divide and rule in the African world. Though satirical and ironical in his singing, Ti Manno puts the finger in the wound and points out the complexes that divide Haitians in Haiti and abroad, and Africans on the continent and in the diaspora. He sings about how Haitians living in Queens feel superior to those who live in Brooklyn, and Haitians in Port-au-Prince despise those who live in the provinces, he sings about self-hate amongst us, how some babies are discarded or insulted for being too black like burnt cake or for having flat noses. "Neg Kont Neg" is a very difficult pill to swallow. It's a beautiful song that hurts. While you dance to it, you feel your knees weaken.

This album has come back to me because, as we mourn the violent murder of Mr. Floyd, we must remember that we can only be valued if we value ourselves. In the past days, photographs have been circulating online of Cameroonian soldiers choking Anglophone protesters in Bamenda, Buea, and other cities of Anglophone Cameroon in similar ways. There is a violence in these images that hit like a tsunami. At the same time, I have read many posts on social media asking Africans in the Diaspora to come back to Africa. While this is a very good intention, it begs the question if this alone is the solution? Every human should be able to feel free and move around the world. While we use our last energies to fight racism, we must also tackle all other violences in our societies. They are so intertwined with and in each other. They produce and inform each other, and we must fight racism, classism and sexism and other forms of violences, oppressions, discriminations and abuse together, and this to me seems to be what Ti Manno is proposing. We must fight our other ills to be able to fight for each other, put our forces together to be able to care for each other, and stand up against these violences like we just saw in Minneapolis and other places.

Ti Manno himself died rather young, and I still wonder what he would have written today. I do not really have a problem with death per se, except when a life is meaninglessly and so brutally aborted prematurely as is the case with Mr Floyd. In general, though it might sound as a platitude, I do believe that we all come to this world for a particular purpose, and when we are done with what we were to do, we can journey on and make room for others to breathe. Though Ti Manno went too young, I think he had accomplished what he had come to this world to do. But in the past days, I have thought the world so much needs the intelligence and compassion, prudence and love, wittiness, razor-sharp critical tongue, and poeticism of Ti Manno to help us understand the tides we are navigating. To help us dance while we think and while we solidarise. To help us through our storms of rage—not to calm the storms, but to serve as a compass as we navigate the storms and high tides.

Ti Manno's death at the age of almost 32 in 1985 wasn't sudden. It had become known in 1983 that he had a terminal illness. A crowdfunding effort by the Haitian community in the USA brought together more than $15,000 to help save his life, but to no avail. The rumour machine has it that he died of AIDS. It is said that his funeral in NYC brought together one of the largest gatherings of Haitians and other Africans as his brother presided over his funeral. On his dying bed, Ti Manno wrote a poem to his people, which I found translated online (by SONY SAUVEUR):

> Even if you didn't have anything to give, your prayers are worth more than money
> Your passion, care, love, effort, good faith, and sincerity showed me that your loyalty is stronger than a nuclear weapon
> Because the Missile can only destroy

Every time you released your love, your prayers, and your courage to this untreatable disease
For somebody who is going through difficulties that is a beautiful rose you put in your life
The nuclear bombs destroy life and our weapons of love rebuild it
I don't have the power to give the Haitian people what they deserve
I submit all positive feelings and thoughts I feel about you people to God
Only God knows how to repay you
I don't have the rights to give you my heart; you Haitian people dwell in my heart.[7]

Notes

1. Finney, Nikky. Performance keynote, Breath > Body > Voice: Humanities Futures Capstone Conference, Durham, NC, September 14, 2017.

2. "Nan Danje," on *Gemini All Stars De Ti Manno*, Chancy Records, 1982.

3. "Ti Manno Nan danjé," YouTube video, 7:52, June 26, 2015, https://www.youtube.com/watch?v=DmeJRwrGDkg, Accessed Dec 26, 2020.

4. Ti Manno, "Sort Tiers Monde," on Gemini All Stars De Ti Manno, A1, Chancy Records, 1982.

5. "Sort Tiers Monde," YouTube video, 10:05, Dec 17, 2011, https://www.youtube.com/watch?v=7KiySdhL0Io, Accessed Dec 26, 2020.

6. Ti Manno, "Neg Kont Neg," on Gemini All Stars De Ti Manno, A2, Chancy Records, 1982.

7. Sony Sauveur, "Antoine Rossini Jean Baptiste "Ti Manno" was born in 1953 in Gonaïves a province in Haïti." 2016, https://www.snsfm.com/copy-of-info-13.

Nature who never lies

Miri Davidson

Marx says we're still living scattered in the primordial forest.
This is what I take him to mean, anyway, when he says that
the end of prehistory coincides with the end of our world.
I don't disagree. After all, if we were not, would there be any
use in speaking about "essential work?"

Essential work exists only because of the tower blocks and dark
gleaming complexes and vast storehouses of unessential work
in the dark stairwells of which essential work lives.

Curious to find it there, and suddenly humbled in its presence,
we try to drag it out. Once every Thursday night we drag it out.
When it is on the street in front of us, we come out of our houses
onto our front porches and clap. We clap for it from our doorways,
leaning out from our balconies, hanging our heads out of our
windows in a sudden show of great joy for it.

In the one to two minutes of our great joy, essential work
shuffles into the light. We turn to one another to share the moment,
look back and find it gone. We put up a sign in our window:
Essential work, come out from that stairway! Come into the light!

Sometimes unessential work comes out instead dressed up
as essential work. No one is sure what to do then.
The clapping stops for a bit. Some regret this; others feel it's
natural. Applause has a beginning and an end,
that's what applause is, after all.

(untitled)

Hannah Walker

I feel like it's important to note the position from which I'm thinking about these things. Living on a small farm in New England has certainly shaped my ideas about labor during a pandemic in many ways, but is also a narrow lens, not by any means wholly representative of agriculture in the rest of the U.S. or globally right now. One thing that I've been parsing is the convergence of productive, reproductive, affective labor that was present in farm work long before the pandemic. One of the goals of a farm is obviously to generate profit, created through the labor of apprentices and workers (and on some farms, animals), as that's how the farm sustains itself. But the fruits of the labor, if you will, literally and figuratively, are life-sustaining, so arguably they are also a form of reproductive labor. These two things are indelibly intertwined, as is labor and dwelling, so it is also a form of working at home, albeit not one that is commonly recognized as such, as opposed to things like childcare or household chores. When the pandemic hit, certain parts of the market for small farmers ballooned, while others diminished drastically. There was a significant loss of revenue through restaurant sales; however, for many, individual retail through farm stores and CSAs increased dramatically. There was a marked shift in how people view farms and the food systems in which they participate daily but rarely acknowledge; suddenly farm workers were "essential workers," as people realized in a more conscious way that food comes from somewhere and it is, in fact, essential to sustaining life. Yet that designation seemed comically at odds with, say, the proposed cuts to immigrant farm workers' wages. These drastic changes happened all around the farm on which I live, but on the farm itself the days seemed to plod along. There was no disruption—animals and plants still need to be cared for, people still need to eat—but there was also no increase in production, no push to work harder or longer than farmers already do, in response to meat shortages or increased sales in the local market. After all, you can't force a pig that takes six months to grow to slaughter weight to miraculously grow large enough in three months instead.

The Convivial Animal
Notes Towards Decolonial Ontologies in Indian Cinema
Bindu Menon Mannil

The long, protracted, veritable war around the figure of the "cow" in India and its violent contemporary resolution by the "gaurakshaks," the fascist Hindutva cow-savers, brings to sharp relief the tortuous history of the foundations on which the "human" is erected. The fateful power of the figure of the cow, on the far side of Indian modernity, realigns the two terms "human" and "animal." The affective contestation of these interlocked terms "brings together caste1 and religion with the anxieties over the moral and physical status of the body of the nation."[2] The Indian present, haunted by the cruelty of humans and the unquantifiable violence against other humans, is riddled with questions of ethics and suffering. What about humans, we may ask. In the multiplicity of blood-soaked images—of Muslim cattle-trading men who are lynched, and Dalit men, who are the leather workers, flogged and stripped in public—is the anchoring of those acts around the figure of the "pitiable cow." The spectacularity of these violent acts and the audience for them, not just the ones who are present at the scene, but the rest of the nation which consumes them, poses challenges to our reading of the images. In the avalanche of lynching in India since 2015, many Muslim and Dalit men have been lynched as a pair.[3] Reflecting on a series of lynchings across history and in different social contexts, Megha Anwer unravels the semantic constellations that emerge between the couple who witness each other's suffering, yet suffer parallelly in isolation and the rest of the citizenry who got away.[4] Thus, for Anwer, the primary semantic charge of these visuals arises from the communion in suffering, emerging in these images.

This "human suffering" visits us with force, traumatic enough to fuse animalized humans and dehumanized animals in one swoop. The rediscovered pity for the suffering of the cow can be fully comprehended if we focus on Giorgio Agamben's call to recognize that dehumanization and animalization are entwined processes. He writes, "The total humanization of the animal coincides with a total animalization of man."[5] This discourse of animality functions as a critical strategy for humans to oppress other humans, the force of which depends on the traditional ontological distinction between the human and the non-human animals and the ensuing ethical divide.[6] Inimical to the workings of such coercive power, cinematic imaginaries located in the margins have explored novel vocabularies, cinematic language and techniques. A number of Indian-language films in the last decade have embraced the non-human animal and centralized the figure of the animal through the tropes of ontological parity, confrontational relationality, and convivial togetherness: *Fandry* from 2014,[7] *Chauthikoot* from 2016,[8] and *Pariyerum Perumal* from 2018.[9]

The Elusive Sparrow and the Filthy Pig

These ontological distinctions between "upper caste" and "lower caste" and human-animal is at the core of the chiasmus of relationships in *Fandry*, a Marathi film by the Dalit film maker Nagaraj Manjule. "Fandry" refers to the "pig" in the dialect spoken by the "untouchable" Kaikadi community of Akolner, the village where the story is set. Living off garbage and filth, the pigs run amok interrupting daily life in the village. Jabya, the teenage protagonist of the film, has his heart set on his attractive, dominant caste classmate Shalu and an elusive black sparrow that darts across the nearby woods. The black sparrow is a figment of folklore that enters his life via his friend and mentor Chanakya, who leads an anarchic and outlandish life outside the mores and rules of the caste-ridden village. Spending most of his time in the woods, Jabya's slingshots at the bird are futile.

Figure 1. In search of the elusive black sparrow. Screen shot from *Fandry*

The pigs and their movement across the village send the villagers in a scurry to bathe. The Kaikadi community, on the other hand, lives isolated in the outskirts of the village and are expected to touch the pigs (in order to get rid of, or to eat, them). This animal-like placing of "untouchable" communities is inherent to the caste order of Indian society.10 In the highly unequal world of caste hierarchy, the Kaikadi community and the pigs are placed in the framework of an ontological parity, bound in relationships of touchable/untouchable. Distinguishing between literal and figural touching, Aniket Jaaware has shown that the symbolic aspects of figural touching works as the source of "material regulation of bodies" in the social ordering of caste.[11] Jabya and his family's everyday life in the village is populated with hurtful words, and physical and mental abuse.

In an abrupt and violent interruption, Jabya is brought to confront the reality of his existence as an oppressed caste human towards the end of the film. In an extended sequence, set in the pig's roosting ground, in the rubble next to his school, Jabya and his confront the pig that troubles the village. Jabya, reluctant to participate in catching the pig, is beaten up by his father publicly, as his schoolmates watch. The sequence extends itself to a wild chase of the pig, as his school mates including Shalu who watches and jeer, casually licking a lollipop.

The dominant caste hooligans, shout obscenities, shoot the chase in their mobile cameras and air it as "*Fandry* match" on YouTube. Amidst the mounting humiliation, Jabya's world comes crashing down on him as he realises that he is invisible to Shalu, and there is no miracle that would dissolve the invisible boundaries of caste. The family catches the pig and carries its carcass mounted on sticks across the school courtyard; in the backdrop of wall paintings of the key figures in the history of Modern India. Seething in humiliation and anger, Jabya is further taunted by the dominant caste thugs as they walk through the village road, carrying the carcass. In a fit of anger, a crazed Jabya performs an act of defiance and disavowal and throws a rock into the camera. The rock comes crashing at a regime of looks, a force of habit and choice, a compulsion to not "see" both the pig and the "untouchables"as living beings.

The film creates an intersecting text that weaves poetry, history, and memory, to replicate the shock and awe of both the quotidian and spectacular violence of caste system that is suffered by Jabya and his community. The film's lyrical-poetic voice in the first half transforms into a resounding silence when the possibility of political speech or even speech in language is erased. In the long sequence of confronting the pig, a mighty chasm opens between the caste subject and the animal. We find ourselves not on the side of the pig, but the human. The encounter with the animal, its look, has set off some of the contemporary philosophical explorations into human-animal relations. For John Berger, this exchange of looks is central to man's recognition of his ontology.[12] The separation between animal and human being is within humankind and humanism. For Jacques Derrida, the same encounter is the source of the logocentrism of human beings.[13] Jabya, in his encounter with the pig, arrives at the sharp awareness of his ontological parity with the animal, a state of being he must alter by confronting it.

The dismissal and non-recognition of sentient conditions of the animal leads to the subsequent reduction of individual humans to the status of "mere" animal life and engenders the bestialising of social and political others. The abjection of human others made possible by the human/animal opposition then forces the "other" to insist on their humanity as a mode of resistance. This insistence, one may argue, can end up in inscription of the species logic, which in the first place initiates an exclusion. Yet, in *Fandry*, the knotted relations of species logic entangle itself with caste and deconstructs these relations by placing both the humanized animal and the animalized human in a framework of ontological parity. Though terms such as animal, caste, gender, class, and religion have characteristics that signify inferiority here, they function jointly within a discursive system that appeals to hierarchical animal taxonomies, and relegates life-forms into fixed, hierarchical categories, such as animality-caste and animality-patriarchy.

Fandry reconstitutes caste system's disavowed animality as central to the ethics of memory. While *Fandry* explores dehumanization as a test case of the deployment of the human, it simultaneously deploys a conviviality when Jabya seeks the elusive bird, in the outskirts of the village and in the general textual geography of the film, where Jabya, his mentor, and his friend often leave the village and embrace the wild nature outside its bounds. Conviviality with animals has solidified as a powerful exploratory frame in film making from the margins. In the lack of long-established traditions, tropes, and techniques for film-making from social margins, a trope of animality has indurated as a powerful exploratory frame in such film practices.

The "Messianic" Dog

Pariyerum Perumal (The God mounting a Horse), set in small-town Tamil Nadu, the southern Indian state, narrates the story of a young Dalit man, Pariyan, who struggles against an oppressive caste system and poverty to study law, following the model of his leader Dr B. R. Ambedkar. The film opens with the violent death of Pariyan's beloved canine friend Karupi (Blacky), abducted and tied to the railway track and left to be run over by a train. The death of his dog Karuppi is a constant source of grief and dream for Pariyan in the film. However, Pariyan's struggle against multiple challenges, lack of mastery in the English language, lack of cultural capital, and an apathetic education system. Helping him in overcoming much of these is his classmate Jo, a girl from a wealthy dominant caste family. Suspecting an affair between them, Jo's family physically torture and humiliating him, creating many misunderstandings between Jo and him. Pariyan, driven by stress, and humiliated and taunted by his dominant caste classmates, openly confronts and challenges them. These events take him to the college principal, who summons his father for a meeting. The father, a drag performer in the traditional theatre, is publicly humiliated and stripped of his clothes by the dominant caste men. Jo's father, suspecting an affair between Jo and Pariyan, commissions a henchman to murder Pariyan. The henchman is none other than someone who pretends to be a friend of Dalits but stabs them from behind. Through an act, drawing from a recent case of honor-killing in Tamil Nadu, the henchman tries to kill Pariyan by pushing him to the railway track, inebriating him forcefully and letting him die on the tracks. Pariyan, woken up from his dazed state by the caressing tongue of Karuppi, manages to pull himself out of the stupor, tries to escape and in the process kills the henchman. The film ends, where Jo's father apologises to Pariyan and says that he looks forward to a brighter future. Pariyan, in the closing shot of the film, replies, "As long as you remain the same and expect me to remain a dog, nothing will change." The turn towards the compassionate and convivial animal is in response to the water's edge between human and animal, manifest in the dehumanizing aspects of caste practice referred to in this closing sentence of the film.

Fig. 2 Pariyan and Karuppi in an embrace. Screenshot from *Pariyerum Perumal*

The entanglement of human and animal lives is centralised on the relationship between Pariyan and Karuppi in the film. In a song sequence that is part lament and celebration, Pariyan yearns for his beloved companion. The structure of the song vaults between rap, poetry, and death rituals to invoke a new sonotope for the performative song culture of Dalit life worlds, retaining the semantic charge and sensations of such life worlds.[14] Bereaved Pariyan raps on, "Now, I want to see you now/rub my nose against yours/let your tongue cleanse all the dirt in me/where can I meet you?" The song pushes forward the boundaries of human and animal when it asks, "Who lays broken to pieces in the woods/is it you or me/is it you or me." The rap monologue continues, "Why did you go? Whose call did you respond to/How many times have told you to not trust all humans," and seeks a greater definition of humanity. However, the dimensions of connectivity in the film do not exist in a linear, derivative sense of human compassion toward nonhuman others, but represent an open terrain of life, a trans-species connectivity.[15] The nonhuman animal is bestowed with qualities of purity and empathy. Yet, it is not this screen animal overwritten by political meanings, but the fabulous qualities of the animals that creatively trouble the anthropocentric boundaries constituting human-animal connectivity. In his inebriated state, and at the edge of life and death, it is the fabulous political animal that wakes up Pariyan in a dream sequence. The dog in this sequence is blue in colour, a rich palette symbolic of the Ambedkarite Dalit movement. The animal here evokes feelings of wonder, charm, enchantment, curiosity, and a general suspension of certainty. The animal has a stubborn persistence in the imagination of South Asian popular religion and public culture.

The film's subtle manipulation of the gap between human and animal results in a poetic voice that swerves from the singular, humanistic voice of the first half of the film and crosses species boundaries to craft an embodied, multiply voiced utterance across these boundaries. The film thus incorporates distinctive experiences without assimilating their difference. Although caste and species are independent ideologies, they have been logically and historically enmeshed. This relationship in *Pariyerum Perumal* is more than an analogy between the nature of animal suffering and human suffering.

In *Corporal Compassion*, Ralph Acampora develops the notion of "embodied conviviality," by which he means "a specifically somatic core of the cross-species moral experience."[16] Acampora develops this in response to a specific affective/somatic deficit in animal ethics approaches. In Acampora's reckoning then, besides vulnerability, it is conviviality that allows inter-corporal cohabitations and forms the basis for human-animal relations. In the South Asian context, Radhika Govindarajan maps the embodied and affective dimensions of human-animal interaction in the western Himalayan region.[17] She argues for the agency and quality of animal behaviour and bodily reactions as equal participants with human actors in shaping material, cultural and spiritual life worlds of communities. The affectation for the animal and compassionate living in both the films insert relations between into the frame. A tantalizing question that emerges here is one of the workings of animality for human relations. Dehumanization as a strategy of oppression, many in critical race studies have observed, has a long and immoral history. The decisive and negative machineries of dehumanization in Holocaust are some of the most widely recognized events of the twentieth century. Working on complex markers of difference like caste and gender, Indian filmmakers from the margins call upon this strategy again and again.

End Note

A veritable critique of posthumanist thought is the charge that critical animal studies/posthumanism eluded questions arising from the broader contexts of colonialism, race, and slavery. Positing such a continuous link between poststructuralist and posthumanist theory potentially presents a Eurocentric tendency, and erases the genealogies of similar thoughts that might have anticipated and constituted the field of enquiry. For example, the terms "Human," "Humanity," and "Humanism," have been variously claimed, invoked, and challenged by oppressed caste reform movements in the South Asian context. Some of the oppressed-caste reform thinkers sought admission into the category of "Human" while attempting to reform it from within. Aime Césaire, Sylvia Wynter, and Frantz Fanon interrogate enlightenment essentials and broadens the normative category of "Human."[18] How can we re-signify and revalue such knowledge that not only questions the metaphysical essentialism of enlightenment that is "Man," but also breaks with Imperialist and Brahminical ontology as well? Can we propose a decolonized animal ethic that finds legitimacy in indigenous cosmologies? How can we work toward a decolonization that disrupts the power apparatuses of anthropocentrism in their totality?

Notes

1. Caste system is a hierarchical system of ordering society in Hindu religion. A scripturally sanctioned order, it places groups of people in an order of vertical hierarchy where the Brahmin castes are placed at the top of the order and the shudra castes at the bottom. I have mostly used the term Dalit, which literally means "broken" or "shattered," to refer to an agential identity and political gesture of self-recognition. The other terms currently used to refer to the relationship among castes are "oppressed caste" and "dominant caste."

2. Shivani Kapoor, "'Your Mother, You Bury Her': Caste, Carcass, and Politics in Contemporary India," *Pakistan Journal of Historical Studies,* 3(1), 2018, pp. 5-30.

3. *The Quint* webpage dedicated to tracking lynching in India, lists about 113 cases of lynching, accessed December 28, 2020, https://www.thequint.com/quintlab/lynching-in-india/.

4. Megha Anwer, "Three Photographs, Six Bodies: The Politics of Lynching in Twos," *Kafila* Online, published June 5, 2016, accessed on December 28, 2020, https://kafila.online/2016/06/05/three-photographs-six-bodies-the-politics-of-lynching-in-twos-megha-anwer/.

5. Giorgio Agamben, *The Open: Man and Animal,* translated by Kevin Attell, (Stanford: Stanford University Press, 2003), 77.

6. See Cary Wolfe, *Animal Rites*, (Chicago: University of Chicago Press, 2003).

7. *Fandry*, directed by Nagraj Manjule, (2014: India), DVD.

8. *Chauthi Koot* (Fourth Direction), directed by Gurvinder Singh, (2015: India), DVD.

9. *Pariyerum Perumal*, directed by Mari Selvaraj (2018: Neelam Productions, India), DVD.

10. See Note 2 above.

11. Aniket Jaaware, *Practicing Caste: On Touching and Not Touching*. (New York: Fordham Univ Press, 2018), 25.

12. John Berger, *Why Look at Animals?* (London: Penguin, 2009).

13. Jacques Derrida, "The Animal That Therefore I Am (More To Follow)," Trans. David Wills, Critical Inquiry, 28.2 (Winter, 2002), pp. 369-418.

14. Jacob Smith, *Vocal Tracks: Performance and Sound Media* (Berkeley: University of California Press, 2008).

15. Wolfe, *Animal Rites.*

16. Ralph Acampora, *Corporal Compassion: Animal Ethics and Philosophy of Body*. (Pittsburgh:

University of Pittsburgh Press, 2006), 96.

17. Radhika Govindarajan, *Animal Intimacies: Beastly Love in the Himalayas.* (New Delhi: Penguin Random House India Private Limited, 2019).

18. cf. Aime Césaire, *Discourse on Colonialism,* (New York: NYU Press, 2000); Anthony Bogues: *After Man: The Critical Thought of Sylvia Wynter* (Ian Randle Press, 2006); and Frantz Fanon, Frantz, Jean-Paul Sartre, and Constance Farrington. *The Wretched of the Earth.* Vol. 36, (New York: Grove Press, 1963).

Sadia Salim, *A Roaming Aesthetic V*

fifth dialogue

JUST INSTITUTIONS:
WHAT, WHERE,
& HOW TO BUILD

18 & 25 April 2020

Companion Texts for Studio Session

Césaire, Aimé. *Discourse on Colonialism*. Translated by Joan Pinkham. 1950; New York: Monthly Review Press, 2001. 72-73.

Hanchard, Michael. *Party/Politics: Horizons in Black Political Thought*. New York: Oxford University Press, 2006. 3-6.

Martin, Dawn Lundy. "The Long Road to Angela Davis's Library." *The New Yorker*. December 26, 2014. https://www.newyorker.com/books/page-turner/long-road-angela-davis-library.

Marx, Karl. *The Eighteenth Brumaire of Louis Bonaparte*. Translated by Saul K. Padover and Friedrich Engels. (New York: *Die Revolution*, 1852). marxists.org, 1999. https://www.marxists.org/archive/marx/works/1852/18th-brumaire/index.htm

Melamed, Jodi. "Proceduralism, Predisposing, Poesis: Forms of Institutionality, In the Making." *Lateral*, Volume 5, Number 1. Spring 2016.

Moten, Fred and Stefano Harvey. *The Undercommons: Fugitive Planning & Black Study*. New York: Minor Compositions, 2013. 20, 26, 32-33.

Spivak, Gayatri Chakravorty. *An Aesthetic Education in the Era of Globalization*. Cambridge, MA: Harvard University Press, 2012.

Hosts | Colin Eubank, Gabriel Salgado

Speakers | Asma Abbas, Isaac Brosilow, Colin Eubank, Ciarán Finlayson, Ari Fogelson, Gabriel Salgado, Philip Zorba

Scribes & Annotators | Asma Abbas, Safi Alsebai, Jody Leonard, Nathaniel Madison, Coco Marcil, Gabriel Salgado, Philip Zorba

From Sociality to Institutionality (and Back)

ASMA

We are in a moment that keeps shifting, every week interrupting what we thought it was, its increasing monumentality being that it could be infinitely so much else. Minimally, our showing up here for ourselves and each other through this affirms the many dimensions of learning to work together and inside a moment structured by various necessities and contingencies. It just drives home the failure of tested ways of prophecy and prediction within political and social sciences that we have been discussing. It also clarifies for us that the lag between event and comprehension isn't just the old "Owl of Minerva" issue, but can be attributed to the very fact that we, as inquiring subjects shaped by what we are trying to know, also go through our own shifts in capacity to recognize and call something knowledge or understanding. In another way, it is also this sense of being inside this moment, an extension of being inside a problem that is living and not dead, that makes the task of knowing inseparable from being. It also, thus, makes it inseparable from thinking about institutions which structure and organize our capacities and incapacities, needs and desires, proximities and distances, accesses and availabilities, and so on.

Our goal in these conversations has been to come at the question of futurity from a place that didn't seem too already given over to the future as already prescribed (or foreclosed, which are both often the same). It is no surprise that part of our effort in engaging with movements and possibilities in the current moment is perhaps, to be generous to all of us, shaped by a kind of hope, and also a deeply felt sense that not all is as it should be, even in those spaces that promise us that possibility, and promise us—to recall Arendt—the "promise of politics" itself.[1]

So, with Marx shaping so much of our thinking around the question of relations and the totality which we impute to the composite of realities we confront at any given time, along with the sense—in a Kantian way—that we are responsible to and for that which we assemble and inquire into, there is inarguably a different kind of responsibility to the object of inquiry when it is summoned by us. And the summoning is, in a materialist and relational way, really a response to being summoned, and that's the way that some of us already do understand the question of voluntarism vs. necessity, to which I will turn shortly.

Our work together is inspired by a commitment to politics as a living and not a dead labor, and it is inspired, additionally, by a relationship to knowledge and institutions in the name of something that has long been forgotten, and that does not find any pleasure in making or answering to reactionary calls to order. One major piece of this is challenging how and by whose design knowledge-production and pedagogy get sundered inside various institutions such as the university. This includes the university with all its problems and complicities, but it also includes those spaces which, apropos our conversation today, are constantly committed to a work of repair, and the facilitation, production, or midwifery of justice in whatever form.

We have been thinking for a while about this question, often framed in terms either of reform or revolution or of one's location inside or outside of institutions. But these seem too pat and too merely "academic" to capture exactly what we do after we have been thus mapped, and the substances and lived impasses of our relations to institutions and institutionalities (on the heels of our conversation about socialities in the last dialogue). We hope to make our way there today, because it seems like we are at a point where we do need to address our various kinds of disillusionments in institutions, in order to have a chance to shed some old traps and find different ways of framing the choices ahead of us.

Thus, we begin thinking in earnest about the how, why, and what of just institutions, tackling the necessities, pitfalls, and possibilities of "thinking institutionally." Or, one might say, thinking politically about institutions. Earlier in this series of conversations, we have touched on which histories of institutions must be taken into account in our attempt to make something else right now. Of course, we understand that almost all of this requires some sort of disconnection from the immediacies, as well as from a presumed sublimity, of this situation in which we find ourselves.

Today, we will try to splice together our multiple struggles and their plural dimensions in order to hold institutions and subjects together in a fully political inquiry. As before, our hope is that the readings invite us to come back to each other, and that attempted relation to others in this space—a glimpse of incipient community or even figmentary "minor institutionality" that frames some part of every week for us right now—might be the tether that allows us to turn to the text if we don't find something in each other. Taking this time is a gesture of love and kindness toward each other and thank you for being here for that. A lot of this feels extremely important and futile at the same time, so thank you for coming along. Please bear with me as I will try to set up the conversation by way of some of the texts we posted, and then I'm going to pass it on to Colin Eubank and Gabriel Salgado to take us forward and back, between ourselves and texts, as needed.

One, the poetry of institutions, and misreading to go beyond the phrase.

There is a quote from Marx that is present in the naming of this collective—this loose collection of aspirations that we call our collective, a performance of building something bigger than the body in order to lift the weight off certain bodies—which can be read for some clues about what it means to perform and build something. It is a moment in Marx where he misreads Hegel, willfully, who has himself willfully misread the Greeks. It's the familiar passage of, "men making history, but not in the circumstances of their own choosing," that ends with something like, "until the circumstances call out, 'hic rosa, hic saltus'" (instead of Hegel's deployment of "hic Rhodus, hic saltus"). Marx then goes on to translate the phrase into "here is the rose, here let's leap/dance."[2] So, we remain genetically and politically in awe of empowered but not necessarily cocky and all-knowing misreadings. I am myself drawn to acts of reading that will be seen as misreadings, which allow us to marvel at the power that is exchanged in the utilization of texts, and in seeing texts as utilizable, given the ecologies of reading and recitation we each hail from.

The need to misread, and that freedom to misread that is necessitated by circumstance, and a kind of sympathy for that misreading, make possible a promise of a future that wasn't already predicted in any scripture, secular or not. It is, not surprisingly, the same section of Marx's text which also touches on the prosaic vs. poetic nature of the future, and Marx, clearly connecting prose to present or past, and the future to poetry, adumbrates, "here, the phrase went beyond the content, there the content will go beyond the phrase." This is after he has talked about how the revolutions of 1848 borrowed their poetry from the past. With us having discussed in our First Dialogue the "global" 1840s even prior to the *Communist Manifesto*, and the confluence of struggles in the pre–civil war moment and abolitionist moment in the US, it's really important to think of the poetic gesture that is already present in that moment, a gesture to a kind of internationalism that has not yet been defined.

And, so, this—a mix of misreading and the poetic as something that is yet to be materialized, determined, and which has not been scripted—has been really important to me and I trust many of us here. Even this thinking about assembling the future involves this relationship in Marx between the content and the phrase. This idea of the content going beyond the phrase signals an impetus to theorize political desire, that is not valorized for being free of necessity and hence simply willful, but something that is linked to a necessity, a necessity understood in very close connection to how Marx will talk about needs, and in turn their close relationship to our powers.

I just want us to bear those things in mind as we talk about power today and about desiring and prospecting the future. Another problem is our inheritance of the problem of institutions, especially when we, as people who think about politics, think of an institution as an assembly of problems, what it puts together, what it severs. And this, very much, has to go to the conversations last week around sociality, and really thinking about where we need to think deeper about the social in order to think better about the political, even where Marx fails to do that. We have to do that work, and this is a plea to move in that direction today.

Two, institutions as need, availability, power, and promise.
So, when I am asked what I do, I mostly say I study politics and institutions, worried that if I say "political scientist" or "political theorist," I would be considered an expert politician qua colloquially misunderstood Machiavellian manager, or a caricatural Eichmannish bureaucrat who will follow all rules as ethics—rather than someone who thinks too desperately much about institutions as a way both to avoid thinking about redemption, as well as for us to do together for each other what we cannot do ourselves and for ourselves.

Far and away, however, we find ourselves constantly having to opt for one over the other, where relations to power get tainted the moment we give in to the managerialist imperative over any lofty "leadership" ideas. So, those of us who often know how to build and run better institutions are often sabotaged by our own deep disinterest in, even revulsion toward, seeing ourselves as "administration" or "management" or your local cop (or maybe I speak just for some of us). But, where must we place and claim a real important interest in power, and the organization of power, that allows a democratic self-determination of the human being, and not hand it over to the others who are only able to think of power as pathology (their own or others)?

If we just take up the simple phrase from "Critique of the Gotha Program"—"from each according to ability, to each according to need"[3]—what we have is a formula for the institution that remains coextensive with the social. So, yes, there is a way that, my constant attempt to not let the political devolve into the ethical (a righteous boundary-maintenance that is flailing nowadays, I must admit), is really a signal, maybe even just a plea, that the political must hold itself to and be vested in something bigger than the ethical imperative, and "defend" and redeem the social as more than an "externality." Here, the issue becomes thus: we need institutions, because we can't do everything ourselves, and we need institutions even more because they have to exceed ourselves and allow our bodies to, as Marx would later say, "find labor because we want it, not because we need it." So, the burden to think about institutions is a simple one; it's a question of "How does one square ability and need?" and the production of a collectivity and a community that has a memory, on the one hand and, on the other hand, a relationship to responsibility and authority that has learned from the question of space and a history of organizing spaces and people.

Here, I'm informed by the very close relationship in early Marx between need and power, which goes on to inform his way to labor and labor power in *Capital*. When it comes to thinking about institutions, it is not enough to affirm that things relate. We have to think of various kinds of relationalities and to acknowledge and summon something other than transactional logics, so that we are pushed to de-normalize and de-naturalize exchange and the value-form as the dominant templates of relation. Hence my wariness in relying on the value-form in any descriptive understanding of what we build, lest the descriptive slip into the normative, and because there isn't an easy way to stop once you start there. So, when we call out institutional racism and institutional capacities, and when we engage in institutional critique, then we need to unpack what that pronouncement entails—that is, identifying what is twisted together in the institution, in order to make room for thinking beyond the value-form, and beyond transactional administrative and managerialist logics.

To connect back to the Fourth Dialogue, and staying with the question of the social, we must tackle how Marx, weirdly, secularizes it—I say weirdly because of his rich suspicion of the secular in his early work that he just sets aside later on—in order to understand what he is able to theorize, what he cannot theorize, what he refuses to theorize, and where that leaves us. I think we are in a familiar space, responding to a weighty pedagogical invitation to engage with Marx in a really creative way. I think this is something that happens with all those folks like Lenin or Gramsci, for instance, who are seen as ancestral to a tradition, as if they were simply consistent or continuous with whatever preceded them. Don't many of these people take on the mantle of interpreting Marx from the place of having been written outside of history, eve out of mere historical possibility, by Marx? Or, perhaps you feel invited to something that is not yours? And, perhaps the disciplinary and professional US "socialists" of today are just too presumptuous about owning, in order to do the work involved in being invited to a history where others also live.

Three, from the memory of institutions, to memory-as-institution and institution-as-memory. So, any institution, to take from Tracy Strong's understanding of politics, braids together the logic of the community and a collectivity as a claim over a particular arrangement of beings and spaces, and the logic of authority that allows a temporal continuity that makes responsibility possible.[4] Nietzsche comes to mind here, in terms of "the right to make promises," as a way to think about responsibility.[5] And, this is probably the one time in my life I will use Nietzsche's discussion of the "sovereign individual" to an end other than undermining the modern subject. For our purposes today, I do think there is something else there, beyond the idea of the contract, and beyond debt, and I wonder if it has something to with this question of authority understood as responsibility to another—to bring responsibility and community together. I think that keeping those things in mind, and keeping them in mind as different things, helps reveal the shortcomings of the prescriptions available to us, whether ensuing from sectarian Marxist spaces, or from creative entrepreneurial ones. As political thinkers, we need to grapple with why they're not the same, and where they meet, and I think that determines what we make of institutionality and the strategies we make.

To that point, we read Jodi Melamed's "Proceduralism, Predisposing, Poesis: Forms of Institutionality in the Making" for today, which nicely unpacks the way institutions occur to those contemporary thinkers who have bemoaned the death of institutions.[6] Melamed shows that those institutions that are bemoaned, and whose corruption is blamed on neoliberalism, were not really ever to be found in that pre-corruption stage. They weren't sullied by neoliberalism; they were just kind of there, and neoliberalism merely exposed them. To state the obvious, I take from this that we have to think about institutional racism or these other things not as having just descended upon us, but that they were always there, and that the neoliberal moment really gives a moment for them to unleash without cover. In other words, confronted with institutional evils of all kinds, we would do well to acknowledge the dead labor—involved in the production and sustenance of and upheld monumental (and not merely monuments to) slavery, genocide, colonialism, capitalism — that is already part of these institutions. And, then, we have to take those complexes and do the work of disaggregating the questions of community from those of authority to assemble a politics in between, with, and within those.

The question has to evolve away from "should we stay inside these spaces or leave them?" because almost no one I know experiences it as this question of voluntary entry or exit, or of voluntary stasis or motion. (I recall Hannah Black's invocation of not-refusal here in an earlier conversation.) Often, the best we can do for each other is remind each other that it isn't ever a matter of whether but how our work will be appropriated, assimilated, and repurposed as weapons that have nothing to do with our intentions. Most of the time those of us who are trying to bring about institutional change are wracked with questions of what could be possibly safe from appropriation, and what remains after our labor is accumulated to produce another monstrosity.

But, it's never just one thing that happens in the time of our labor and its appropriation, not just one thing is produced, and we cannot be convinced of the monotheistic myth brought to life in our too-earnest commitments to saving institutions! Or, maybe that is just a consolation. Here, we usher in Stefano Harney and Fred Moten, and their, literally, "pro-lific" writings on institutions[7]—but even this language of the in/out of institutions, how we use them and how we abandon them, is (as we have gestured to in earlier conversations) a simplification of the problem of necessity and of production and reproduction, drawing a strange line between those who cannot (afford to) leave institutions, or who cannot, try as they may. Our memories are not reducible to institutions or their memory, for better or for worse, and that has to be remembered.

Thus, I want to think about strategy that is plurilateral, and prioritizes building a sense of the community that is a corralling of—a con-viving with—a particular relationship to history and to the present moment that isn't confessional, that doesn't entail constantly professing our relationship to history in every act. We must be honest and accept that it is possible to give almost too much credit, and too much of ourselves, to institutions to foster an earnestness that ends up extending indiscriminately to authoritarian Marxism, or to bureaucratic fascism, or to managerialist neoliberalism, in a way that allows each to override, instrumentalize, and betray the social. I want to be able to talk about that at some point.

Four, institutions as "means of production" of agency, and all that might entail ...
If we work backwards from Gayatri Spivak's working definition of agency as "institutionally-validated action," we can arrive at thinking of institutions as those spaces or those structures which validate human acts qua agency or as agentic, with entire epistemologies in tow. (To stretch the metaphor, if they indeed transform action into agency, are they where action comes to be produced as agency, and where that social labor takes a particular form? There is much to say about that, which is not possible now.)

Inverting that frame might allow something else in, as a way to shift the constructed and contingent faultlines between necessity and contingency, so that something else might appear, or so that spaces are created within or alongside mandated performances. Might we have the chance to turn around and look at each other and conserve the conversations in which we are not beholden to categories, but where categories are beholden to us? This returns us to the question of summoning and confessing and, outside of those mandated and compulsive labors, populates a language of action that is not indiscriminate, but rather honest and discerning about what the summoning is, who's summoning us, and what are we summoning in return. This is where we wrest some dignity in place of the shame of our incessant earnestness and exposure in the wrong spaces.

If all an institution is that which validates, even inflects or produces, action as agency, why cannot we accrue to ourselves our own mode of thinking institutionally—counter-institutionally, but yet counter–institutionally—that allows us to not be naive about power, and to understand it as something which both enables as well as emerges (produces and is produced) in that shift of orientation which ultimately repartitions the necessary from the contingent. In this sense, authority becomes accountable to power and not the other way around. That sense of appeal to the institution is quite something, and I know it's very tricky for many of us to have to pick one side or the other. I'm not saying we need to do that at every turn, or as the constant act of establishing legitimacy (in a way that ultimately grants the institution legitimacy). But, I do think that, in refusing to profess or confess to just one space in a liberal topography of politics rife with unitariness and sovereignty, we might feel the need to turn to another. I'm just honestly wondering what would happen if we radically refused to confess anything to anybody who even vaguely resembles the boss or the priest, but that's just me.

Now, to the matters of solidarity alongside those of power and institutionality. I think we can't separate those things and this is where I feel that when categories precede the question of solidarity, we are often in a bind where we do not know whether we can ever fully understand authority and necessity in a temporal way, and not just in a way that's about discipline or domain, disciplining or colonizing. I would like us to think about what it means to produce authors, which is my way of saying that my point of entry and exit here is the question of education, whether it is in terms of thinking about the university or the spaces of our labor, political or otherwise.

I'm realizing more and more why I don't even think of "academic labor" as quantified knowledge production or credit hours taught, since that quantification—and the myopic, reductive, and isolationist frame of capitalist social reproduction of which it is a part—elides and occludes the colonial elements of the qualitative nature of the work of reproduction. I am beginning to find that what is common to every situation in which I feel that certain normative relationships to knowledge aren't being upheld is the absence of a necessity (epistemic, ontic, existential) to think about colonialism, and how that becomes part of the blueprint of institutions. So, while materialism deals with concrete experience and its taxonomies, it needs to imbibe the history of the colony in its method if it is to be applicable to institutions—understanding them and building them. This is why I included an excerpt from Aimé Césaire's *Discourse on Colonialism* in our readings for today, really just a way for me to cry over something. Of special note is the paragraph in which Césaire talks about this ethnographer who offers a particular way of thinking about the equality of people in the eyes of the law without having to actually believe in the equality of people in fact. That person makes a case that the task of leadership and responsibility must lie with the people who are racially superior. This applies to both the colony and beyond it, to supremacies wrought under the sign of race but by no means limited to it.

We would be remiss in thinking that our problems with Occupy Wall Street, or Bernie Sanders, or whatever else are exclusively with class reductionism or insufficient attention to race. It's not the object, it's the method, which is to say, system or institutionality! In my way, they are entirely connected to how colonization inflects the problem of authority in these spaces and movements. I cannot emphasize that enough. Coloniality, then and now, corroborates responsibility with inequality of races, and we cannot proceed without accounting for that concretely. The question of the subject, left open by Marx, is not far behind—the subject that will be able to hold, one might say with Spivak, the public use of reason towards the social good. I believe that why Marx stops where he does after having solved the problem of the appropriation of capital for social production, and social productivity, is because he hasn't been able to address the problem of the human without taking stock of its colonial determinants.

This speaks to the notion that there are problems—"problem[s] of the human"—that cannot be solved with only a focus on capital, or some other economic attenuation. The typical critique of views that obsess over economics is that they are class reductionist, but this instead centers the problem of colonialism, which I find instructive. — Jody

I will insist that we, as educators, respond to such an inheritance of the colonial question, because it makes its way most evidently to us in the realm of knowledge and education—and not merely the production of scholarship which seems to be increasingly what the academy is a site for.

A question we have been probing these past weeks, but especially in the Third Dialogue, here adding the dimension of coloniality to the very form of knowledge sought and accumulated uprd in relation to colonialism. — Safi

But, an epistemological shift is possible, whereby thinking of social freedom and social subjectivity requires centralizing the relationship between formations of class and racial subjectivity, and showing how colonialism enables and disables the otherwise segregationist process that produces beings that will actually never be able to be free and equal. It is impossible to exclude the question of potential fascisms that are bred in the formation of the individual, especially the responsible individual in colonialism. If we do not think of power in the company of those problems, I'm not interested in thinking of power at all.

Misreading "Strategic Essentialism": Essential Labors, Non-Essential Institutions, and Strategies of Snails

COLIN

I think that while we're all here trying to practice different ways to think and help each other in this time, it is important to not just take up a question but maybe try to answer it in certain ways. So I've got a little thing to read that riffs on the questions posed to us in Asma's opening statement and the texts, and then Gabe's going to do the same thing in relation to some of the texts in the mix, and then we'll open it up for general conversation.

Moving away from the comfortable, antiquated question of "within or without the institution?" challenges us to think about a strategy, or comportment, toward institutional participation which could begin (or end) without recourse to the confessional. While confessing relationships—to history, to the present, or to the dreams of tomorrow that sustain us in the twilight of today—often feels like the most earnest way to build a real sense of community inside hollowed-out institutions, the difficult truth is that dire consequences seem to so often ensue from the confessional strategy, and any faith we might have in bureaucrats and institutional custodians on a good day is bound to shift in the other direction on mediocre ones. Like all those cop shows, the confession becomes a signed death warrant, where any discussion of intention goes out the window, questions of justice seem entirely forgotten, and so begin the squabbles for the consolation prize: the best plea-bargain to be squeezed out of a now lost situation.

What I mean to say is that, unfortunately, if we acknowledge that we are living in institutions, odds are that our confessions come to be fashioned into our own nooses—waiting to be tightened when our institutions need another sacrifice. And in these images, I am not referring to the death of our bodies, or our own economic livelihoods (those are often already jeopardized). I am speaking of the mutilation of our relationships—to principles, commitments, and ideas of sociality—which could have allowed us to become something together. Once confessed, these relationships become the next piece of celebrated fat to cut in times of austerity, or the next pet project to be zombified in a marketing scheme to make the institution successful or relevant again. This seems as true today for our political parties as it is for our universities and factories.

So, we're looking for another strategy, one beyond the confessional. But, whatever this strategy looks like, it must be honest about who and what is being summoned in an institutional endeavor, if we really believe in each other, or claim to understand the importance of the social, as a community that has a sense of responsibility as it organizes and rethinks things like needs, abilities, and powers, while leaving behind the collusions of capital and colony in its performances of fascism or liberal development.

I don't really have an answer to what a strategy beyond confession concretely looks like, other than to note that many institutions today have made gestures which themselves can be construed as confessions. Connecting to histories beyond the pandemic, they disclose something of themselves and their relations to the people. The question of strategy, for me, seems to be less of how not to confess or what institutional building would look like if we did not confess anything, but what to do with the institution that confesses itself to you? What maneuver might be made here that does not fall into the trap of the perfectly fashioned subject, willingly offering its hands to share in the blood stains of shared culpability for a crime we had no part in? Or, if nothing else, might we learn from this moment that an institution's commitment to a mutually recognizable history—at least—makes available the possibility for restorative justice as a substantive catalyst for the generation of new relations, whereas the best that could have been sought in our own confessions were tired promises and deliveries of procedural justice? This seems to me to be the other side of the bind of confession which we need our strategy to be able to maneuver.

GABE

I wanted to turn to the readings so I'll be trying to connect some of the preceding discussion with the Spivak and Césaire selections in particular, which I've just been thinking through.

So, Spivak insists on institutions being at least partially about a responsibility to an other. As she works out Marx's discussion of socialist community in Volume III of *Capital*, she makes her way to this question of why people as a whole would want to exercise freedom to arrange for the upkeep of other people (and notes that this is what government as an institution was sort of meant to address). So, I guess, the question that I have is this: what does it look like to posit that responsibility to others around, through, or as, an institution, without reducing the other to a problem or an object to be managed? What does it mean to be attentive to the needs of others without engaging in a form of pathology or risk management, which may be the most familiar form of institutional engagement many of us are familiar with? How does one not turn this responsibility into a sort of white man's burden which Césaire discusses in that first selection that we read?

Spivak's sense of responsibility to me charts a different course, obviously, from what Césaire is speaking against; it's not a "speaking for others" but, as she puts it, the imperative to imagine the other responsibly. I think that the solution can't just be to return to one's own needs in the form of some popular invocations of the universal—which I think some parts of the socialist left in the United States have really taken up as one of the solutions to that question. One example of this is how framing universal solutions or universal programs and institutions seems to be the way out for some people on the left today.

One can identify institutions with one's own needs and that can do a lot but I don't think it's really the solution that I'm looking for. Because those are workarounds that, instead of engaging the question, say, "Well, there is no real need to engage with a responsibility to others because we can transform that responsibility towards others into simple self-interest and see our own needs in other people's needs." There's something unsatisfactory about that but I do think that's the logic behind this push from that certain sector in the US left for saying, "everything must be put in the language of the universal," because it allows that easy identification. Ultimately it requires a kind of translation of every other need into one's own need; it leaves unattended those needs that can't undergo that transformation. I don't think that's fully satisfactory for me. I don't think it actually answers the question.

Now, to the matter of not engaging with institutions in a confessional mode. So, what happens if we radically refuse to confess anything to anyone in our institution-building? Is there another way that institutions and needs can meet each other that's not in that confessional mode? Not to mention Césaire bringing up the white man's burden, which is clearly one way that institutions have engaged with that sense of responsibility. But that is not the sense of responsibility which we're speaking of here.

As I think more about this, while it seems like it does not directly address the issue of responsibility to others, I do think it might be part of the way out of that question. It takes head-on the way in which the confessional mode of engagement with institutions, and the structuring of relations between their constituents, is exactly part of that procedure through which institutions take the expression of needs and turn those into problems to be managed.

So, that's what I've been working through and want to put forth as a charge to everyone: how to hold institutions to be attentive to needs, and how to avoid the confessional way of engaging with institutions that is often just a plea that institutions attend to our needs?

COLIN

I've been thinking a lot about drug cartels as institutions, but I won't talk about that quite yet. I think we'll open it up. I'm excited to hear what other folks have to say and maybe I'll rant about the cartels later.

GABE

Yeah, Colin, you can't just drop that in here. That's all that's going to be on people's minds now!

COLIN

I will say that maybe there are moments right now where institutions aren't taking that risk management approach to needs. I think that the drug cartels are actually asking a question that allows us collectively, whether they intend to or not, to re-evaluate this question of not just needs but also abilities and I think that it's not unique to the drug cartels. I think institutions that aren't the state have the capacity right now to open up that question about ability, where they can self-reflect on what they're capable of doing in tandem with what people actually need as a real conversation, whereas I think that the government or state apparatus right now is completely locked in to what Gabe beautifully described as that risk-management mentality. So I kind of feel like the parties right now, as appendages of the state, are playing the same exact game. Weird organizations and syndicates right now seem to be opening up a space, at least visually if not verbally, for conversation. So that's what I was thinking about there.

ARI

I really liked Colin's framing about institutions right now that are also doing the confessing. That got me thinking about some news that was out this past week about the U.K. government being worried about people isolating and not being in schools and not engaging with normal state services. This is because, for instance, they're seeing a huge drop-off in the number of referrals to the government's Prevent program, which is the counter-radicalization program that has been integrated within all schools and all healthcare systems. So it's like saying, "Oh, we've seen Prevent referrals drop off like 50%, so we don't know if we're catching people or not," which is completely absurd. It's reported as if it's a real thing. It just speaks to how they actually view the purpose of schools and healthcare.

I'm curious about how another institution and practice of care for others might play out: I am thinking of puritan imams in Pakistan calling people to come back and pray for Ramadan, portraying this as if it were not about their dependence on contributions for the month. I think there's a lot of problems with that but I'm curious how practices of Zakat, which are a big part of Ramadan, might be different and I'm thinking also about how it all opens up different possibilities of surveillance, then, of those acts of giving, because I know there are some activist charities that are largely reliant on cash donations given during Ramadan.

It becomes impossible to organize and you're subject to a different sort of surveillance.

CIARÁN

I was just listening to Vijay Prashad on Doug Henwood's podcast this morning. He was reflecting on the Bernie Sanders campaign and the cultural transformation aspects of it, the parts that he was interested in, the longer timescale: the 30-, 40-, 50-year goal of movement-building and the transformation of social being. That wasn't the term he used but it seemed to be what he was getting at—that it wouldn't actually be in the institution of Medicare-for-All. He was doing some comparisons of countries that have longer histories of Communist governments, especially in their recent past, and how they responded differently. And, how without the state sending out masses of people to respond to the pandemic, the youth organizations and women's organizations have been able to turn out tens of thousands of people to immediately meet other people's needs. The relation to social totality or to the universal is still there but it's not an automatic function of winning a policy called Medicare-for-All. That would be a useful part toward getting there, but the ostensible universality of the policy itself isn't the actual social transformation.

ISAAC

Earlier, Asma was talking about "right to make promises," and I was thinking about what Ari was saying about the pandemic sort of rendering obsolete, as I understood it, the way that institutions rely on the normal working of things. Then, Colin brought up risk, and Ciarán direct, mutual response. How can we think about the relationship between institutions and the perpetuity that they promise, and the way that it mitigates and transforms subjecthood and responsibilities?

Here in the Not Holy Land, I am studying the *Talmud*. We are currently on the part about the responsibilities of the Apitropim, of the guardian of an orphan. That's my direct tie-in to the ongoing discussion: when is it the responsibility of the guardians, and when is it the responsibility of the orphan who has been inheriting the property from his deceased family members? There's this distinction that they draw: the care provider is responsible for immediately and directly feeding the child, but when it comes to food that's stored for many, many years, the responsibility falls upon the child when he comes of age. So, because we're in this time period which has these long-term and short-term ramifications that are playing out in institutions around us: How can we think about our responsibility if it's beyond confessions, or if it's moved in a more radical way? How are we thinking about promises and time, and the way that institutions are all wrapped up into that or unraveling around it.

On Electoral Punctuations and Constituting Mo(ve)ments, with Brianna Pope

BRIANNA: I currently work for a political consulting firm that calls itself the "Electoral Firm of the Movement." To me it appears that there are multiple movements going on, just as there are multiple forms of and calls to electoral politics. The area of electoral politics I work within is electoral justice. The firm works with Black women candidates, though we did not work with any candidates for this particular election cycle, and are focusing on the VP choice, hoping to get somewhere with that.

One might ask: did the Sanders campaign really learn from its first go? (I ask this after having worked for one of the lead strategy firms for the Sanders campaign in 2016.) I would say not necessarily so. While he was leading his own movement, the grassroots organizations, or at least Black grassroots organizations, were perpetually trying to get him to intersect his economic platform with the current social needs of our people. Given this pandemic, and everyone feeling economic pressure, there is a big opening here to intervene in the debate on who is an essential—and who an inessential—worker (on what labor is socially necessary), and allow for a substantive and thick definition that takes the entire social structure as its basis. After all, we know that even economics is more than just economics!

Anyway, you would think that his economic policies would be spot-on for this moment, when everyone is realizing that if there is one thing that connects us it is the fact that we are scrambling in urgencies and scarcities. My partner works for Amazon, and so every day there's a decision to make. Do I need to go to work? What is the risk? What is the benefit? Do you want to harm someone for the sake of your own security, which isn't even that secure in the first place? In professional spaces, or at least in organizational spaces, there's been a circling around the question of the way that we do protests and demand change. In Texas right now, there are protests demanding re-opening. I'm thinking about how we want to shift our ways of protest and our ways of being heard for the benefit of our larger communities.

I will say that, in the Sanders campaign, the strategists had to make a decision on whether or not their values are the values that must lead in this particular moment in time. Is the need for Sanders to be elected greater than the need for a particular firm to insist that they actually only work with Latino candidates, or that they only work with candidates whose values are in line with the values of this or that firm? I think that is where the disconnect between Sanders and many communities came from: there was just this feeling of not being heard, or the feeling that we're only heard up until a certain point, in order for a campaign to get as far as they can before their constituents—in a quite real way, as in those who constitute the movement being called upon and being invoked—are forgotten.

Right now, I think a lot of frustration comes from the knowledge that Biden is going to pick a VP, and this whole time he's been signaling that he's going to pick a Black woman. (In my ideal world, the Vice President would be Stacy Abrams, just for clarity.) But, as he moves forward in his candidacy, there's talk that Gretchen Whitmer might be the VP—or at least there's a shifting away from Black woman to just woman, which I think is just telling of how generally politics in these campaigns go, which is where the firm comes in. They try and interject into that moment, to be like: actually "No, you have to have a candidate that is like this, this, and this"; these are the demands of a collective moment and organization; we have collective demands like "this is who we want to lead us, and it's a non-negotiable."

So, I think there's frustration there.

I think there's also the frustration of being involved in an institution—going back to Asma's question of what are the continuities and discontinuities between the campaign and the movement as institutions—that might be committed to ideas but never fully get there. There is, sometimes, a lack of creativity that isn't neutral in its effects—we slide backwards! For instance, Biden is now the nominee, and immediately there's an instinct to get behind him, instead of figuring out how to disrupt it, like in 2015. I protested against Sanders back then, saying, "Actually, you have to say her name, you have to say that Black lives matter." So it can seem cyclical—even a spiral downward—when you come back to the campaign trail and you come to terms with the fact that the campaign has heard, but hasn't absorbed or changed. I think there's also a lot of hope, especially in this pandemic. There is a real chance to have a moral conversation around what systems and institutions we want to keep and what is actually necessary for our growth and happiness—something in which we can all be more invested.

GABE: Brianna, I was really interested in what you were saying about feeling conscripted by certain necessities to come back and work for or towards something in a particular way. For example, feeling invested in certain questions around the Biden campaign. It made me think of one of the passages in Spivak's Aesthetic Education in the Era of Globalization, where she warns against the danger of "allow[ing] ourselves to become instruments of the crisis-management of the old institutions, the old politics," and advises on how to navigate that danger. While power, "collective institutional, political validation," is useful and should be held onto, a "practical notion of power," according to Spivak, is a limited and dangerous one.[8] So, how might we want to think about power and institutions beyond that form of collective institutional political validation? It feels like this connects to what you were talking about in terms of how we protest and demand change— what forms those political manifestations take—and how we think about power to begin with, as something beyond that "collective institutional, political validation."

ASMA: That's an interesting inflection point that connects some of the conversations even beyond the campaign, including the always looming (and often damning) question of who's going to be trusted to decide when voices are heard and not heard? And—in the kind of panoply of what's going on—what counts, and what point does the disgruntled unheard voter prefer (someone who has never really heard, or whose hearing hasn't been tested for whatever historical or other reason, or who construes hearing as simple auditory capacity). I read today, for instance, about Stacey Abrams that she loves Ayn Rand! Well, what sort of speaking or hearing is that? When we are in a situation that that counts as being heard, there's something to be said for Spivak turning our attention back to who the political subject is, rather than scripting one for us.

It's at least a relief that we don't have to take the route of "false consciousness" or the tried and tested yet boring "They are voting against their interests!" And it's a relief not because those aren't interesting names to put to certain tendencies that can be explained, but because it just doesn't quite give us a way beyond a "getting our souls right" kind of sacred idea of politics. There has to be another way to speak to these differential expectations of voicing and hearing, and to make real room for them as realities to not set straight as before or outside politics itself. This is the lack of creativity Brianna is also talking about, I believe! So, who's been tasked with determining the administration of that hearing is, I think, really crucial, because it also produces those who compel certain kinds of speech, you know, and there is that cycle that will never end.

BRIANNA: Thanks, Gabe, for sharing that passage. I think it really goes in line with something that Asma was talking about right now with Stacey and Ayn Rand, but I think also Stacey and Bloomberg and a lot of other people and Bloomberg. So, yes to this idea of not letting yourself become utilized as a tool for this institution. But the longer that you are in this, the longer you start thinking like, "Oh, what I can do with this money?" and then you start imagining.... So the values, the moral ground that we're holding Abrams on, keeps shifting the longer she's fighting this cycle. Her idea of taking money was with the intention to resource our communities, to empower, to fight against voter suppression in Georgia, which I think is a mode of thinking that a lot of people, a lot of organizations, are adopting that have accepted some form of cash. That has left my own firm asking if we want to continue to be in a relationship with these candidates or these people, or these organizations?

CHRIS: It seems like we were at a Poulantzas/Milliband moment. Are we now back to a Gramsci moment? I just feel like this is a moment where things seemed possible through electoral strategy, and all of a sudden, that crashed all at once. And we saw the same thing with Jeremy Corbyn and in Greece: Syriza was in office, but not in power. It's a series of very dramatic disappointments through electoral strategy. We're set back more to a familiar moment, one when we had to think about much longer-term strategies. So I think it's perfectly appropriate at this time to be thinking about institutions, because, then, what we're really thinking about is building a movement that is sustainable, not just from election cycle to election cycle, but over a much longer period of time.

GABE: A related question is one that came up in our First Dialogue as we were thinking about the temporality of crisis, particularly in the contemporary moment and regarding the pandemic. Chris, you are also gesturing to the temporality of struggle and the temporality of institutions, and how those two things can relate to each other. So, I appreciate this image of a Gramscian moment. That form of political struggle situates us currently to confront certain kinds of institutions as suggested by the kinds of temporality that they hold or in which they operate.

ASMA: One of the things helping me think through this is the real anger at Bernie having abandoned something that was needed in a certain way. Allowing it to unfold might have been able to channel certain things that feel nascent. So, there's a particular structural analysis of what he couldn't have accomplished in terms of the presidency, but other things that happened along the way, as you are celebrating. This movement, this energy, this sense of futurity which even—I think it's the first time I've used the word "future" in my life.

But, I also think about the other side, which is that all of this work happened. How do we utilize those same structures and that same building of things that are now there, and take heed to the demands that are absolutely there. Even the campaign structures, the mobilization structures: they're all in place, how can we use them?

Of course, there's a moment that comes where Sanders is directing this energy around the coronavirus that then falls into the mode of a kind of self-help that will always be manipulated by the state. I just wonder about the real question of what happens with the movement, even the movement structures, even the campaign structures, as actual capital that is ours, because we literally paid for it. How does one repurpose but also claim, even, anything about it that isn't now the ownership of an electoral campaign?

I think this is a good moment to even bring up this question: in our experience of the campaign, or even in the coronavirus mobilizing that each of us is part of in some way or not, where did we see a shift in the narrative of power that was being sought? If we can find it, in terms of looking for what we sustain and retain beyond this, what is it that can be gathered from the practical experience of that?

SARA: This has come up before in our conversations about how to think of success or victory. As Gabe asked earlier, if we're thinking about validation or a certain kind of recognition in electoral politics, what are other ways of going about doing that—even as a complex strategic situation? It's almost as if anything we acknowledge as a success is going to be forbidden tomorrow. It's reminding me of conversations we've had about hope, or dead hope, or of the possibility of ignoring success; or, along the lines of what Spivak is saying, ignoring validation—so maybe it's not redefining so much as a turning-away-from. But, again, can there be a strategy with that success?

BRIANNA: I just am really attached to this question of redefining what success looks like. That's something that I constantly think about, and I'm very curious about how that is defined, by individuals and by collectives.

The Pedagogies of Movements and/as Institutions

PHILIP

I keep thinking about this statement that might have been from Jane McAlevey, that a movement campaign needs movement institutions doing meaningful work in between elections.[9] Otherwise, I think we have trouble canvassing effectively. We have trouble, like Gabe brings up, with how we frame our demands. I think about the striking Oklahoma City teachers specifically asking to tax the energy corporations, a very Oklahoma-specific demand.

I really like the Spivak quote that Gabe highlighted: "Why has the imperative to imagine the other responsibly been lifted?" I think that is the difference between building a true coalition of workers versus adding demographics you can brag about as supporting you. I think there's this question of where your socialism matters — in the party name or in the community? Because, once you're in power, you have to contend with market pressure and you need institutions of labor to hold the politicians they empower in check. Afterall, McAlevey maintains that strikes change who creates a crisis for whom.

Greece was invoked last week and of course that activates me. The people who voted for troika-dictated bills in 2011 that included the termination of trade union rights were socialists in name. They were the Panhellenic Socialist Movement of Greece (PASOK). There was a harder route out of it that would have made them a lot of enemies in the banks, and they had to pass thousands of people screaming in Syntagma Square next to the Parliament building. But time and time again, with few exceptions, they went in and voted for bailouts that meant austerity that was going to strangle a lot of people and take their pensions and take their bonds. Without that labor movement, there was no way of keeping that in check. Otherwise, it is like building a bridge just strong enough to get those politicians you believe in to the other side and then watching it collapse once they're over there in two ways: you can't hold them accountable, and they're no longer thinking of you.

I believe only a labor movement can do that: really shift who creates a crisis for whom. It does not begin and end with the electoral cycle.

GABE

I think that was really helpful, Philip. Part of what I'm trying to navigate is exactly that sense: that institutions can hold others accountable in the way that, for instance, (you have spoken about before) a strong labor movement can hold elected officials accountable in particular ways, that institutions hold their members accountable, and members do the same to the institutionalized movements if they become too separate or independent from them. How to not become too accountable to certain kinds of institutions that you may not entirely want to be beholden to, perhaps even those movements that are not what they used to be? That accountability and the way that it cuts both ways is something that I'm thinking about.

COLIN

So, Philip was talking about the importance of building a movement or maintaining institutions that are substantive in their commitment to community or in actually doing some social work. That, and realizing that we don't just live around the elections, is really important. Here, in Mexico, two actions unfolding simultaneously as the country enters phase 3 of the pandemic. The government and all the major politicos have been doing the same political theater as in the US: a lot of fake news craziness and, finally, they've cobbled together some sort of Public Health program as well as loans and bailouts for the middle classes. Meanwhile, the vast majority of the major cartels started this distribution initiative where they're taking care of everyone in their towns- giving them all basic sanitary health supplies, educational information on social distancing and taking care of yourself, and basic non-perishable foods and stuff like that.

As this happens, the government says, "Oh, well, if you really want to help fight the pandemic you should stop your sins, stop killing people and selling drugs." The government says, "Confess!" and the cartels don't care because the institutional operation of the cartel, the way it interacts with the community to sustain social life is not built on the same lies and does not require the same optics as the state. They're specifically giving the goods to the chronically unemployed, the poor, and the old in their communities because they are their communities and they know who's in them. They know the people whereas the government doesn't. They don't have any funds, whereas the government has a slush fund with which the governors are supposed to be buying food for poor people in general, but everyone knows that the poor people aren't going to see the food, and that the money's just going to disappear.

The government only shows up during election times. Meanwhile, on the boxes and bags of all these supplies, there are these notes from the cartels—maybe it's inappropriate to call them love notes, but the sentiment is really interesting. They say things like, "From the lord of the roosters, Mancha, with the people," or, "In support of this town." Or, the daughter of El Chapo, who's heading up one of these initiatives, said, "We're obligated to do this work to help those that are responsible for teaching us manners and traditions." I think what's not lost is that these cartels are born of the community, in a way. They have maintained—throughout the good years, the bad years, the truces, the turf wars—a concrete connection to the community that the government or even our own ideas about the necessity of building a new institution don't enjoy. A mutuality or deep history is gestured to in these messages, and they are an actual invitation on the part of these institutions to inquire into and re-evaluate needs and capacities.

Now, don't get me wrong, obviously the cartels use these needs assessments for their own benefit. I mean the cartels are like the pioneers of the disaster capitalist brand that NGOs will steal and put a benevolent face to, right? But, I think there is a conscientiousness that actually makes a difference here as well. I think that the cartels are expressing their support, and reinforcing that they are there institutionally in a way that the government will not be, something for the community to lay a claim to. But, unlike the government they are not interested in already saying, "We know your needs, we're figuring out how to manage them" or "We know your needs, we just have to deliver."

Not that we need to say "We need to build the cartel not the party"—but what's important is that if we're thinking about community, if we're thinking about sociality, if we're thinking about what's going on around us and how we live with each other and how we live institutionally, I think there is something to learn. We can learn from the possibilities that open up with respect to these old institutions because they don't play the same game as the state, which is so good at relying on the performance of an ahistorical, ideal, relation between a structure and its subjects which has never actually existed in real life except as a model which conjures away, if only to justify, its own domestic abuse by calling it an exception or perversion of power, rather than the product of historical necessity.

> The question of ownership is super important, especially if it was the Bernie campaign that allowed or empowered the union members to act on their own behalf, in the name of that campaign, instead of the US idea of the corporate union. I think that's an important thing to think about as a collective asset, because we did collectively fund it in ways financial and more. I'm just wondering how we can start to think about what it can be used for I think we've seen something happen that can be brought back, but I just don't know if professional politicians will ever do that. — Asma

What's tough for me is that I often associate a lot of institutional behavior with state behavior—I know that's not always the case. Like Asma said, we can think about institutional logics as something other than just crass exchange and I think that's what we're seeing here and that's why I bring up the whole cartel thing. The cartel, you know, discloses that it could not have been built except by a community which was battered, bruised, and abandoned by the state. And, sure, the cartel does its own murdering and extorting of the community. But, the trajectory of its entire existence is built on the transformation of its relation to the community that spawns it. At least, it doesn't demean its people by pretending otherwise. I am really bothered by coverage of cartels that pretends that the cartel aspires to become its own version of the state in its neighborhoods, just because it creates norms and vies for legitimacy within its communities. What about the fact that the entire value of the cartel comes in the relative distance it continually negotiates with respect to the state in terms of collusion, betrayal, extortion, and infiltration? Like, how unimaginative are you? Regardless of whether the material quality of life actually was better for the community under the state, an institution like the cartel changed the material conditions of the world and does so based on the continual transformation of relations to people and institutions. To Philip's point, it pushes us to think about what our party is, if we're talking institutionally about parties, to think about it more like Michael Hanchard and some of the excerpts we read there. How do we have that dual understanding of party? How do we really think about politics in a non-procedural way, which could be through the DSA or something else?

On the Political Theology of Falseworker as Neighbor
Colin Eubank reads two scenes from *La Estrategia del Caracol*[10]

About Law & Faith

A community living in sections of a large house (Casa Uribe) in one of Bogota's poor neighborhoods decides how they might successfully fend off their impending eviction. Their neighbors, tenants in a house called the Birdcage (La Pajarera), have resisted their eviction with guns and firecrackers. After the judge sanctions the eviction and the police storm the building, all that remained were walls—vacated of the life that had made it home for so many years. As the tenants of Casa Uribe debate how to proceed, two tenant protagonists argue passionately:

JACINTO: It's possible, I tell you.
ROMERO: That's not the point!
JACINTO: The point is, if you don't trust yourself, then you certainly won't be able to trust me. You know we can't win if we go the legal route.
ROMERO: Listen, I am a lawyer —
JACINTO: A lawyer? You haven't even graduated!
ROMERO: All I'm missing is my thesis, but I was already trained to think like a lawyer.
EULALIA: Excuse me, Dr. Romero, may I ask you something?
ROMERO: Just a moment please.
JACINTO: Let's find another place tomorrow. They're sure to kick us out.
ROMERO: And why are we doing this here?
JACINTO: For our dignity.
ROMERO: Your strategy has no precedent, Jacinto.
JACINTO: That's exactly why I like it. [pause] Listen Romero, I do my job and you do yours. If your way doesn't work, that doesn't matter to me. But have some faith in people, not just the law.
ROMERO: All right, Jacinto, but I believe in the Law.

Jacinto—an exiled republican Spaniard working on the technical side of a local theatre—imagines a bold plan to beat the eviction. The neighbors living in the Birdcage were violently evicted, and no matter how formidable the tenant defense, the police eventually overcame them. So, what if the community of Casa Uribe were to pick up, plank by plank, every piece of their house and take it with them? Using an elaborate system of scaffolds and pulleys, as well as the skeletal remains of the Birdcage as a kind of secret staging-ground, the community could beat the impending eviction by walking out of Bogota with their house on their backs, like a snail does its shell.

The problem that faces the strategy of the snail is not whether it is technically possible to execute. As the argument between Jacinto and Romero demonstrates, the plan's feasibility is immediately conceded. Instead, at stake in the debate around the project are the kinds of beliefs that such an initiative solicits from the community and, conversely, those forms of knowing which risk becoming untenable. Romero represents the anxiety of many. While not officially a lawyer, he has "already been trained to think like one," and has only been able to know the world through his belief in the law. Jacinto's proposition is difficult to accept because it requires a belief, or a faith, in people. That knowledge, even when presented scientifically, presumes a certain amount of belief is not, in itself, surprising. And, yet, the pause that greets Jacinto's strategy demonstrates just how great a role belief plays in how knowledge is produced or what kinds of worlds are imagined by the projects in which we place our faith.

From their exchange, a question emerges about the relationship between belief and the project of knowledge production: What kinds of knowledge cannot afford to coexist with other forms of knowing? Or, put another way, what kinds of projects demand the monopolization of belief?

About Knowledge & Collectivity

While lacking precedent, Jacinto is certain that he has an eviction-defense strategy that will be able to save his eccentric community. All the plan lacks is the community's belief in itself as something worth fighting for. Jacinto's scientific certainty is met with the nerves of a people conditioned by intellectual austerity. What has the world given anyone to believe besides the certainty of an impending defeat? Compliance doesn't make the sting of injustice hurt any less, but a consolation prize for good behavior and the continual management of expectations just might.

After pressure to make his case for the strategy of the snail at a community meeting receives lukewarm response, Jacinto appeals to one of the oldest voices of Casa Uribe (Doña Trinidad, aka Trina) and prepares her a demonstration of the pulley systems to be used in moving their house by showing their use in the theatre to easily move heavy props and scene backdrops across the stage. Jacinto's performance is accompanied by the musicians, lighting, and the works. He finishes with a leap to center stage with his arms raised:

JACINTO: What do you think?
TRINA: Ok...[skeptical] but all of this, what is it for?
JACINTO: Doña Trina, these are the temples of music and theatre. In them, art and civilization find their most sublime forms, arousing emotions of generosity and hope. Victor Red.
TRINA: [unconvinced] I like my house better.
JACINTO: We all live in the same house. The only thing I wanted to show you was this mechanism and how it works.
TRINA: [leaving the theatre] You know what, Jacinto, let me consult the souls in purgatory.
ROMERO: Señora Trinidad, please tell them it's urgent!

While Doña Trina does not react positively to the overtures of art as a means of changing her perspective, the impasse between the performances of prayer and a play is only apparent. Even as Doña Trina is unmoved by the gestures of the theatre, she understands its point: Jacinto needs people to believe in his plan for it to work.

Although frustrating, considering the dire straits they find themselves in, Doña Trina's words demonstrate something significant as the tenants try to build confidence in the strategy of the snail: As they search for a common basis to believe in each other, these neighbors must judge for themselves (and thus each other) to whom and what they see themselves accountable in the action they contemplate. Doña Trina does not believe that the affirmation necessary to endorse the strategy of the snail can come from her. Instead, she turns to the myriad souls in purgatory, hoping that they can give her the clarity necessary to face the uncertainty of their situation. Kneeling before a painting of the Mother and Child in her home shrine, Doña Trina starts to pray. Deep in prayer, the painting falls away from the wall to reveal a discoloration on the wall in the shape of the Virgin Mary:

TRINA: A miracle! A miracle!
[Trina rushes to announce her findings. Soon, she leads a room full of tenants in a prayer of thanks]
JUSTO: [to Trina] This is just a humid spot on the wall.
TRINA: For me it's a message. A very clear message! The lord sent me his Holy Mother to answer my question. God does not want me to leave this house of ours.
JACINTO: Misia Trina, may I recommend that you use the utmost discretion. This phenomenon and everything about our plan must remain a secret. No one must hear about either of them right now.
TRINA: But I must tell my confessor. It will remain a secret.
ROMERO: Ok. All right, tell the priest.
TRINA: On your knees. [Everyone except Jacinto kneel] All of you, on your knees!
[Trina leads the tenants in a religious song: "Madre Maria, send comfort to my heart..."]
[Later, Eulalia speaks to her ailing and unresponsive husband...]
EULALIA: If the Virgin appeared here, then it is a sign that we are under her protection and have her approval. Isn't that so?
[Cut to Jacinto, Romero, and Trina. Trina is kneeling at her shrine with tears in her eyes. Jacinto and Romero are just behind her...]
TRINA: Thank you! Thank you, Mother of God, comfort to the sad of heart, thank you. [Trina clears her throat] Jacinto, Romero, I want two conditions: One, that the Virgin leaves the house first.
JACINTO: Of course.
TRINA: Two, that we use Jacinto's invention and thus commit ourselves to serve the Holy Virgin.

Up until this point, tenants of all political stripes are plagued by aporia and racked with uncertainty about whether to accept Jacinto's proposal or not. Although Jacinto has shown the plan to be objectively possible, this scientific demonstration does not transform anxiety into confidence. Like Rosa Luxemburg's description of mass workers movements in "Social Reform or Revolution," the community of Casa Uribe already has all the tools they need at their disposal. But the question that remains, and that cannot so easily be decided, is how they use these tools in the moment they face. Although the violent and legal demolition of the Bird Cage testifies to the fact that all other known strategies for eviction defense are unavailable to the tenants of Casa Uribe, the tenants have not yet let go of the idea that they might heed the eviction order and willingly abandon their community. Thus, they are left to answer the question: "We have the tools to enact the strategy of the snail, but is it the right time to use them?" Plagued by doubt, self-critique and fear, Doña Trina's discovery of the image settles her internal struggle. While the appearance of the Virgin Mary is just a water stain to some, for her it presents a message that abandoning Casa Uribe is impossible. If Doña Trina believes in God, if she believes in anything, she cannot abandon the community. Doña Trina's abandonment of Casa Uribe amounts to the complete abandonment of all that is meaningful to her world, whether in life or death.

She sees with clarity that her community inhabits a situation which "renders all retreats impossible and conditions themselves cry out: 'Hic Rhodus, hic saltus!' Here is the rose. And here we must Dance!" There is not another option but to believe in the strategy of the snail. Faced with the possibility of eviction, it is the eclectic acts of Doña Trina and other tenants which actively furnish these conditions — ensuring that no other reformist routes are feasible. As one of Casa Uribe's longest residing tenants and a pillar of its community, Doña Trina's assessment that, for her, leaving is no longer an option makes it a reality for others in the community. The function of belief in a moment as a decisive transformer of social conditions is even present in what some might read as the most scientific configurations of Marxism defended in "Social Reform or Revolution," wherein Luxemburg confirms that, yes, all revolutionary actions are indeed premature until the moment wherein the workers embark upon them and understand their results (whatever the outcome) to be in the continual service of the final aims of revolution. These things will always be untimely because they are fighting to take back their own sense of time.

But the comedic delivery of God's message might also help us become attuned to the small myriad of contingent and minute, non-rational, factors that help furnish our judgments. In other words, our knowledge is not only accountable to history, humanity, principles, and people, but to a stain on the wall, the ritual of a prayer or a song, laughter, a tone of voice, loving sentiments, chaotic commotion, the familiar gait of an old friend, a wiley grin, or a series of missed opportunities. These help to both open ourselves to a less determinative relationship with causality, and also serve as a helpful reminder of the improvised manifestations which factor into changes in belief. At this time the tale of Casa Uribe pauses and returns to the time and place of its narrator, Paisa, who recounts the experiences of himself and his narrators to a television crew which is covering another eviction in Bogota 8 years after the evictions of Casa Uribe and the Birdcage:

PAISA: [pausing his retelling to interject commentary to the news anchors] I'd even commit myself to the cause if the devil gave me permission...with all due respect to rank, of course. Doña Trina's decision inspired the indifferent, encouraged the fearful, and decided the undecided. And, ok, so the strategy took shape, right? "Everyone must participate," said Jacinto. And he organized everyone into teams and brigades and committees, even for food! And this movement of planks, scaffolding, pickaxes, spades was a veritable symphony! People rushed back and forth. Even the pessimists forgot the darkness in their hearts and the strategy glowed with their enthusiasm and love.

A true strategy!

The Pedagogies of Movements and/as Institutions (cont'd.)

GABE

So, Isaac, I was hearing you ask, "How can we think about the relationship to perpetuity that institutions provide to people and how are they tied up with promise and time?" I feel like that becomes part of how some people set institutions against imagination, but it's not necessarily so. I think part of what institutions are helpful for, or what people seek in them, is a different kind of relationship to time or perpetuity that surpasses what people are often able to do on their own. But, at the same time that "playing to" perpetuity of institutions becomes part of the problem, which people then try to resolve with this question of imagination as distinct from institutions. That makes me think of that part in the *Brumaire* where we are told that "the social revolution of the nineteenth century cannot take its poetry from the past but only from the future."[11] The sense that what has already been affirmed, and what claimed perpetuity within the institutions that we have around us now, might not be what we want to carry forward into the world. The task ahead, of making promises, of forging new sorts of relations to each other, can't be necessarily dictated by those past promises. This brings me to the need for forgetting at times, as well, and how that's a useful political skill. As much as we need institutions to forge some relation of perpetuity or of endurance we also need to learn to forget at some times, and to let some of those past claims upon people go.

ISAAC

I do a lot of research, myself, on the new communist movement and the New Left, the way historical memory functions inside the movement from within a leftist vantage point, and especially approaching millennium. The way that *Angels in America* ends right before the Soviet Union collapses is noteworthy; Louis is talking about how Gorbachev is this great political thinker rivaled only maybe by Lenin. It's a subtle irony that Kushner's putting into it (not so subtle actually). When you were talking about forgetting, I was thinking of how imagination is, for some leftists, seen as the cardinal sin or primary error—however you want to read it, or maybe not an error at all depending on your vantage point.

I was reminded of the stance of the anti-revisionist camp: various communist parties making the international communist movement's development contingent on the Soviet Union, rather than on the conditions of those countries themselves. That becomes one of the criticisms of it. Then, you see this with the New Left in '69 and with the dissolution of SDS, which is very much in my mind as members of SDS recently came out with this really cringey letter shaming DSA members for voting against the endorsement of Biden, against the NPC in particular. The way that they used historical memory, to me, was very telling. They talked about their experience in SDS, the time in which it was a formidable force on the US left, and they talked about the problems of European socialism that led to a breakdown in Germany and World War II. It was entirely convenient, it was really to be expected, and it was this moment where you see not only lack of imagination, but a refiguring of the narrative. Many of these people who wrote this letter had been involved in presidential campaigns and electoral campaigns. In Chicago, the Harold Washington for Mayor campaign in the '80s, the Jesse Jackson campaigns in the '80s. None of that was in the article because none of that fit the bill.

Back to what you were saying about the imagination. The criticisms come either from an anti-communist left perspective or an anti-Bolshevik perspective, saying, "You can't just criticize other leftists to make your politics," and I think there's a lot of truth in that. I think that it historically played out that way, especially the irrelevance in the United States of the new communist movement. At the same time, I see a real danger and a real false prophecy in constantly trying to talk about a type of freedom that might actually be non-existent or a type of engagement with politics that is undefined or difficult to talk about, or maybe opportunistic, and you can just throw it on to every form and say, "Oh, yeah, the community garden or whatever." So, I think we're really fucked and I think that in terms of political imagination, you're totally right. We need to forget a lot of the twentieth century, but maybe it should be a gentle forgetting and one that can preserve the things that should keep us up at night and should make us maybe have the dream that weighs upon the present.... You know what I mean? Maybe that should stay, that sense of foreboding that we have when we go into new leftist projects.

ASMA

I appreciate this particular forgetting that you speak of, Isaac, which is also connected to what Philip was saying. So I have a thought on this temporal question. I feel that from a very concrete analysis of the Bernie campaign over the past four years, one might say that perhaps the seeming newness of Medicare-for-All and similar demands is actually entirely consistent with the Democratic Party's complete disavowal and abandonment of the things that were, in some ways, still functioning. The current state of the US, very connected to what Isaac was saying, is not some sort of continuous declension but something that can be taken back to the Clinton era at least in terms of policy. The newness or the radicality of Medicare-for-All only betrays an enormous forgetting of what was in some ways possible for people not long ago, even in the US. When we teach US politics (or we read Edward Said, or both), and we see that there were moments within the oil boom, when there were independent Middle Eastern Gulf countries that have been shackled to a long process of their destruction (almost complete now) that ran in tandem with a forgetting and disavowal of redistributive/welfare state possibility at home in the US. It's not hard to correlate. Certain things didn't need to be remembered because they weren't absent (yet). When we celebrate how many people have gotten energized by the Sanders campaign, let's not forget that the party before, even the Democratic Party or the ostensible center-left of the country, was much more capable of asking for these things not that long ago. Right?

Reminds me about a point Mark Fisher makes in *Capitalist Realism*, that the deregulation of business today was unthinkable in the '70s. And paying for a vaccine was unthinkable in the time of polio. Realistic vs unrealistic is always a tool used by those with power. — Philip

I really want to be able to say more than the fact that what is claimed new is not new. I really love that you brought up the word "freedom," Isaac, because what gets to be proposed as demands, as hopes, as aspirations, in a given moment is very much connected with what is being denied. (Such as when we think of why and when the word "human" would have to exist, or why and when something called "freedom" would have to be demanded.) So, the question of the articulation of need and aspirations has a dialogic, diachronic, history, something that forces us to turn to the work of institutions in staging, holding, and capitalizing on, that dialectics of the "new."

On what gets to be proposed as demands. If we don't have an eye on what is being denied we lose connection to how things used to be, what we used to be "capable of asking for," and we lose our ability to imagine the future fully. We're dragged into procedural, insular change. — Philip

In other words, institutions have a role in producing their own seeming newness of discourse when it's not necessarily new, from which follow gentle or brutal forgettings, that correspond to institutions finding new ways to bind themselves. This, I think, is important in relation to the US party system, and doubly troubling. Outlets like *Jacobin*, and contemporary elite socialists in America, have taken it upon themselves to stack on the party apparatus of the Democrats. I think this is really tricky, and I'm having a hard time wrapping my head around what could have been a way, as Gabe was saying, to channel, deploy, activate Medicare-for-All such that it could have gone around these institutions, and placed itself in another longue duree.

I think it's really interesting what kind of leftist strategy it was to make Medicare-for-All *new*. What was it? Why did we buy that? Why did we come upon that as the model of persuasion? That's what I hear Gabe calling on us to do: ask ourselves why and where do we constantly cede the ground and accept the most banal, insulting, and condescending starting points to political conversations. I do think that accepting the ins and outs of that discourse as pre-scripted is also an erasure of ourselves, and of histories of asking for those things. In one stroke, claims to newness become a matter of actually disregarding history so it's no longer a gentle forgetting, and becomes strategically contrary to the strategic essentialism of Spivak. Let's say, a strategic immaterialization, or a strategic inessentialization, or a planned efficiency via erasure and obsolescence— that decides for us when we can speak and with whom (ostensibly after we have been given that hallowed and hollow right "to speak for ourselves").

Alright, if those are the terms we must accept, why do we accept them without any irony, and why do we outperform institutions and disciplines in their forgetting? Fine, we can frame it as new—but why can't we let each other know it is actually not that way? So, while the *Jacobin* and the Democratic Party common cause around a lack of ideology, their common cause around this weird self-transparency and constant confession of socialist strategy, seems wholly bizarre, it is not surprising. I wonder if that brutalized starting point makes for a vacuous, if at all, any politics that isn't scorched or evicted.

Labor and the form in which the US has inherited it, has to also, exactly as Isaac is saying, be taken for all that it carries and what it cannot carry. Hence this insistence that it must bear the linguistic and semantic burden both of a history of slavery and of struggles. I believe that the naiveté around Medicare-for-All and naiveté around labor share a particular history of not ever speaking from the inside of American history and white supremacy. This is part and parcel of a vacuous secularism, a kind of committed atheism of the US socialist left that does something really troubling—just constantly disavowing and justifying its inability to speak from the entrails of its own history. It is a creepy and ridiculous kind of self-abnegation which, if we are to believe Nietzsche, is deeply self-aggrandizing and nihilistic at once. I don't know what to do with that, but it certainly haunts my attempts at being in this country trying to build things holding the mutuality of these naivetés, and I can tell you there is no way around it. There's no way to propose a starting point that hasn't been compromised from the moment of its utterance; not because it is forgetful, but because it hasn't negotiated with its history in a meaningful way. I think these things are all connected, and it's the source of my worry about US left discourse and its exports.

CIARÁN

I feel like *Jacobin* was pretty consistent in talking about the long history of M4A and the ways it's been thwarted since before Medicare was even established.... They spent lots of money buying the *Tribune* archive and rights to lay claim to a certain heritage of the British left. But, it's entirely new, yeah.

ASMA

Thanks for that important detail, Ciarán. I am just speaking of how the re-establishment of the starting point becomes a claim to the form of resurgence in the articulation of a demand, and am wondering what comes in the way of the development of social institutions outside of the party. We know that those institutions exist, and that they have existed for the marginalized populations here as elsewhere. I worry that there is an actual supersession of that in those dicta of proper political action that cannot get over their own idealization of particular kinds of institutions, and their place in history, for the present and future. Keeping only this delusional history of ideology and progress to be necessary and inarguable requires holding those other histories to be contingent and conditional. There is a calcified left that continues to see left politics as managed charity or philanthropy, relying on advancement professionals qua politicians who set some playbook norms around how we were going to do it this time.

The manner in which race and class politics worked itself out in the UK is fundamentally different than here largely because of institutions that were struggled over or not, whether or not they were won. And, if the formalizations of that struggle in the US were already compromised by their subsumption into corporate logics—such as modes of self-narrating the movement as a company, and then various nonprofit businesses in social correction where consumer-as-citizen, "advancement," and fundraising, displace notions of membership and collectivization. There are particularly insidious ways in which the discourse of labor, of left organizing, was also impacted by this. We can't wish that away, even if all our memories of anti-fascist, communist, collectivities derive from the interwar period, where they were naturally cross-racial, international, in ways that resembled the early abolitionist struggles echoed in contemporary discoveries of intersectionality. So, from corporate social movement organization language to contemporary expertise in community organizing to social justice managerialism, the terminology has altered the landscape of organizing, so that "socialism" in those spaces of lining us up feels like a thrift store term being repurposed for some kind of cool via offputting declarative cockiness made worse by the harsh absence of the subjunctive.

GABE

Thanks Asma, that's really helpful. Ciarán, your comment, too, is helping me delineate what might be a few different processes but related to each other. That claim to resurgence, whether tied to their newness, or to an inability to recognize anything that's going on already institutionally and politically, can cause a rub with other organizations that have existed a long time and have been doing work like providing mutual aid. I'm thinking about how a claim to newness has operated around the sort of infrastructure that has been built around the push for Medicare-for-All to say like, "Ah, this is finally now the moment of the left, ah, nothing has really happened before, this is finally happening," which just steamrolls over, ignores, and pisses off, all the people who have been engaged in all sorts of other political projects before and alongside that. I guess that's how I was thinking also, Asma, of what you were talking about, how that sort of claim to newness operates within the US left.

ASMA

And maybe that's the next question, right? I have two thoughts here. First, I want to go for a moment to the Jodi Melamed essay. The last paragraph reads,

> My suggestion for thinking about pedagogy is to advocate for thinking and teaching that renews our sense of institutions as sites where the form and appearance of social being and collectivity is determined through social action and contest, even as we problematize institutions as always explicitly incorporative, as constituted out of the durable predispositions of adaptive hegemonies. Inspired by Ferguson and Harney and Moten, my call is perhaps to work for a disruptive institutionality, to work with the paradox of institutionality — which pits congealed social process against lived presence — to plan for what Audre Lorde called "a new and more possible meeting": for a broader sense of collective social being than neo/liberal forms of institutional power let us imagine and practice. Infused with the disruptive potential of illiberal discourses of collectivity, "institutionality" can be made to line up anti-intuitively with critical rubrics that empower us to try to inhabit social being otherwise (undercommons, abolition, fugitivity), while reminding us that "radical change requires structure."[12]

A question has to be framed. Given the semantics and the sort of discursive work that left movements have done in other countries, why does the US left insist on thinking through certain categories where its most immediate history has been much more terrible around unions, around labor? It has actually been compromised much more than the same movements in other and far poorer countries. What exactly is that place to come back to, and is that place even there in a Marxist or a Hegelian method? We know that in both of those, the point of return is never a place where you started from (and the other way around). So I want to ask: what is our attachment and why have we not been able to graduate from a resort to terms of discourse that are much more stained and much more problematic in this country?

ISAAC

I was thinking about this. There's a book about the John Brown Anti-Klan Committee that was formed in the late 1970s.[13] It really became a force during the Reagan era, as a national anti-fascist organizing network. They were sometimes a front group for ultra-left organizations, other times they were more grassroots. But, many of the people who had joined had been part of the New Left and had weathered the '70s to get into more focused activism in the '80s. A lot of it came out of them doing prisoner support throughout the '70s, of friends and comrades who were locked up. Basically, many of the activists who were part of it by the '80s were incarcerated, not for their works particularly in the John Brown Anti-Klan Committee, but for being a part of the more militant new left—new communist groups, like the May 19th

Communist Organization.

It was in jail, similar to what became of the Weather Underground and the Black Liberation Army, that many of these people became the frontline for fighting AIDS in prison. Kuwasi Balagoon who passed away from AIDS in prison, David Gilbert who is still in jail, and several others. A lot of this was really just the daily work of fighting against the stigma, fighting against conspiracy theories, fighting for pure counseling for resources, participating in the AIDS quilt. I was thinking about this as a moment of history that I think we shouldn't forget, that I think has been glossed over. I think that people like the late '60s rah-rah and the early '70s—because it's glamorous, it's easy to romanticize—but overlook the lives of people who spent decades fighting, who fought and are still fighting within prisons and outside of prisons. They really saw this as a continuation, albeit one that was a bit localized and narrowed, both by prisons and by just the kind of shifts of where the momentum was around them, certainly during the Reagan years and later.

I feel that some of the kind of stoppages that we have of the imagination, and the fear that we have of the stoppages of the imagination, are best approached by some of the literature I encounter in religious studies. For example, this idea of taking on the whole world to try to fix all the problems in the world—that is a perennial habit when we talk about the left or revolution. I think that we see the practical reality of this in the story of Noah, who is not able to save the world, but only a representative sample of it. On the other hand, we have the Leviathan—the sea monster—about which is said in the *Talmud* that, in the world to come, we'll be eating the sea monster and making religious objects out of it. So I think that there are these ideas, one of trying to save the world and only being able to barely salvage it, and another of things that terrify us that are subterranean which we will one day feast upon. Those are two things that, I find, nourish my way of approaching some of these political conversations that are happening right now.

ASMA

This connects beautifully to the concrete question of what is it to which the action of withholding or resistance connects—with or without imagination—regardless of wanting to neatly cohere the starting and end points, or who organizes and for whom and what. Moten & Harney also remind us in *The Undercommons* of a kind of relative autonomy that goes back to the way that Marx imagines the state in relation to its formative and precipitating forces. We haven't really talked about the state per se, because part of the history of the twentieth century that Isaac wants us to gently forget is the history of the state—what it recapitulates and the modalities it makes efficient and non-negotiable. What is this institutionality to which we might be beholden, and to what desire or problem of ours was it a response?

Notes

1. Reference to Hannah Arendt, *The Promise of Politics*. (New York: Schocken, 2007).

2. Karl Marx. *The Eighteenth Brumaire of Louis Bonaparte* (1852), Chapter 1, accessed on December 28, 2020, https://www.marxists.org/archive/marx/works/1852/18th-brumaire/ch01.htm.

3. Karl Marx, "Critique of the Gotha Program," (1875), Section I, accessed on December 28, 2020, https://www.marxists.org/archive/marx/works/1875/gotha/ch01.htm.

4. Tracy B. Strong, *The Idea of Political Theory: Reflections on the Self in Political Time & Space* (South Bend, IN: University of Notre Dame Press, 1990).

5. Friedrich Wilhelm Nietzsche, Walter Kaufmann, and R. J. Hollingdale, *On the Genealogy of Morals* (New York : Vintage Books, 1989).

6. Jodi Melamed, "Proceduralism, Predisposing, Poesis: Forms of Institutionality, In the Making," *Lateral*, Vol. 5, No.1 (Spring 2016). https://doi.org/10.25158/L5.1.10.

7. Stefano Harney and Fred Moten, T*he Undercommons: Fugitive Planning and Black Study* (Wivenhoe: Minor Compositions, 2013).

8. Gayatri Spivak, *Aesthetic Education in the Era of Globalization* (Cambridge: Harvard U P, 2012), 58.

9. Eric Blanc and Jane McAlevey, "A Strategy to Win," *Jacobin* Magazine, accessed August 23, 2020, https://www.jacobinmag.com/2018/04/teachers-strikes-rank-and-file-union-socialists.

10. *La Estrategia del Caracol*, directed by Sergio Cabrera. 1993. Colombia. 105' http://vimeo.com/6060203 http://p2p.kinoki.org/displayimage.php?pos=-54 http://cinemaanarquista.blogspot.com.es/2011/08/la- snail-strategy-sergio.html.

11. Karl Marx, *The Eighteenth Brumaire of Louis Bonaparte*. (Moscow: Progress Publishers, 1954), 6.

12. Jodi Melamed, "Proceduralism, Predisposing, Poesis"

13. Hilary Moore and James Tracy, *No Fascist USA!* (San Francisco: City Lights Publishers, 2020).

fifth interlude

STILL
LIFE
IN
MOTION

Resting Places

Rei Terada

I

Immanuel Kant's causal theory of time separates past from present agentially: mutual, subject-subject relationships—as opposed to subject-object relationships—can only exist between entities who share the present. By doing this, Kant means to limit the power that he can attribute to his mere feelings of time's flow, but inadvertently or unconsciously he affects thought about relationships between the living and the dead. While I am not yet sure how to characterize the relationships that Kant produces, I do see evidence that, after Kant, a great deal of thought about the past perceives a rift to be healed. Karl Marx's and Walter Benjamin's formulations about letting the dead solve their own problems and the dangers that continue to threaten the dead are famous political touchstones for this quandary.

A case in point is Henri Bergson, the modernist exemplar of the past's continuing agency. Like Kant, Bergson eloquently protests subreption, the interruption of the hard limits of reason by a wishfully impossible image. Space only "appear[[s]] to preserve indefinitely the things which are there juxtaposed, while time in its advance devours the states which succeed each other within it" because "we cannot hinder ourselves from asking where memories are stored up."[1] The fault lies in crossed wires that have to be uncrossed. In response to Kant, Bergson insists that his readers treat past perceptions in the same way that "perceptions absent from your consciousness and yet given outside it"— for instance, outside the room you're in at the moment—are treated.[2] Bergson seems to want to accord past entities some kind of autonomy equivalent to that of present but distant objects. Even so, he creates a special faculty—memory—to take care of them. Instead of thinking of past entities as ordinarily having existence autonomous from the subject, Bergson locates their existence in the unconscious memory of the subject. What effect does this placement have on persons of the past, who now are entities conforming to this location alone? He invents mental space for the activity of the living and the dead as though it didn't already have space—as if it could not share whatever space is normally available to matter in Bergson's philosophy. The category "memory" keeps Bergson from fully examining the separation of "things" and "states," so that he does not think of considering an ongoing past as possibly anything other than memories. In turn, this is because his interest in its activity is overridden by his conviction that "actual consciousness," "ever bent on action," "accepts at each moment the useful and rejects in the same breath the superfluous."[3] Because he believes that, he already needs the conclusion that "the past is only an idea, the present is ideo-motor."[4]

Bergson's high interest in the past, which defines so much of his reception, is only able to emerge at all because, even though usefulness is paramount for him, to his credit he is not willing to make pragmatism into a metaphysical ground. So, his complaint that "the same instinct, in virtue of which we open our space indefinitely before us, prompts us to shut off time behind us as it flows,"[5] accepts automatically that space must open before him, but protests the extension of that principle into the world as a whole that (for him) cannot be just the instrumental world. He saves the past from nonexistence by disentangling existence from usefulness. But acknowledgment of a different existence, rather than "motor" existence, is as far as he'll go. "The question is just whether the past has ceased to exist or whether it has simply ceased to be useful."[6] Similarly, although Bergson fiercely criticizes the dogmatism of viewing homogeneous space and homogeneous time as real, he excuses it to the extent that it is retained "to obtain . . . a fulcrum for our action."[7] Therefore his advocacy of an ongoing past promotes only those parts of it that are "nearest" the present conjunctures from where historical value has already been decided. However scattered and unconscious the conjunctures, their historical values are calculated from within historical bounds, and then expressed in cinematic terms: "it is in this illuminated part of our history that we remain seated."[8] This illumination is a political value, inevitably, differentiating the relevant from the irrelevant dead.

There are many examples of this pattern besides Bergson's (take a look at passages of Deleuze influenced by Bergson). Clearly, the problem that these schemes solve is that otherwise, it would not be possible to differentiate the relevant from the irrelevant past and it would not even be possible to know when the living were not sharing the present and agency with the dead. Anthropologically, not being able to know when the dead are present is a dilemma of guilt and appeasement. But, also anthropologically, not being able to know when the dead are absent constitutes a broad and indeterminate space for the living and the dead that does not have to figure as guilt and that does not enforce attachment. Instead, recognition and the obligations that go with it are distanced in favor of an uncharacterized, spatial coexistence that includes, but does not radicalize, separation.

II

The passage graves of Neolithic Europe were long rectangular chambers, covered with earth or stone, in which skeletons were interred. After interment, there will still visiting rights, so to speak: community members could enter and continue to manipulate the bones of the dead.[9] As new bones were interred, others moved further to the back. Eventually bones would have been intermingled and no longer able to be told apart. In this enactment—more than a symbolization—of gradual dissolution into community, something like linear time is both recognized and contextualized, as though linearity itself were something that appeared only close up. Speculatively, more than one kind of time, or space, is created, in proximity and distance with the living.

Standing stone monuments inspire different possibilities on a spectrum leading toward ambiguity. The locations of monuments are often associated with specific features, such as a view, or proximity to water. In the present-day Alentejo region of central Portugal, standing stone monuments "are found either singly or grouped in megalithic enclosures" in areas where granite is available. The monuments themselves are most often placed slightly outside the granitic area, however: "even where they are set in granitic terrain, locations in immediate proximity to conspicuous granite outcrops were avoided. The locations chosen for single standing stones were always open areas, free of obtrusive natural features."[10] Natural outcrops often looked like megaliths and vice versa, but the monuments were spaced away. It was common to locate remains in a kind of staging area.

Fig. 1. "A view of the summit of Carn Meini, Preseli. In the foreground to left of center is the unclassified monument."[11]

Early Neolithic monuments in very rocky regions of Scotland and Wales, however, stretch and fracture the grounds for this practice, for "all of the later Neolithic monuments in south-west Wales are located in areas that are covered with rocky outcrops."[12] In her remarkable essay "All cultural things," Vicki Cummings emphasizes that since the concept "natural outcropping" may not have existed, people who used the monuments may not have perceived the distinction between megaliths and outcrops as it is perceived now, or even at all. "If people believed that the landscape was already filled with symbolic and constructed places, to begin building monuments may not have taken a great conceptual leap."[13] Rather than becoming more distinct, in this area "later monuments . . . more closely resemble natural places" and incorporate natural features.[14] In this circumstance, later "antiquaries were unsure whether 'this particular object were a cromlech at all, and not simply an accidental formation."[15] Cummings' point is not only that the monuments were ambiguous to archaeologists, however, but that given the lengthy period over which monuments were placed in the landscape, residents themselves would not necessarily have been able to tell monument from rock. As Cummings concludes, "ambiguity seems to have been key in renegotiating relationships between living populations and the relics of a mythical past, possibly because it increasingly challenged and undermined the sense of a timeless and unchangeable past."[16]

The current circumstances of capitalist death—coerced dependence followed by abandonment—and resulting ecocide ruin the notion of natural death and make it difficult to discriminate between killed material and objects of personal sustenance. Bearing this indistinction is a different problem from that of guilt and complicity; while the capitalist class is unambiguously murderous and even individuals can meaningfully be named, everyone is coerced to live in the dead world they have killed. Even for those who want to, it's becoming difficult to stay seated in the illuminated theater of the present. A planet with a murdered ocean is living with a corpse that cannot be distanced or disposed of. It might be reclassified as aqua nullius and imperfectly forgotten—at what cost? And what else might happen? Ambiguity and omnipresence means something different in the absence of non-criminality, but so does separation. I'm not a metaphysician or anthropological prophet, but I hope it does not take one to suggest that cultural work of some kind must already be ongoing, whether it is perceptible or not, on the location and status of the living and the dead.

Notes

1. Henri Bergson, *Matter and Memory*. trans. N.M. Paul and W.S. Palmer. (Cambridge, MA: Zone Books, [1908]1991), 143, 148.

2. Bergson, 142. Although his memories "present themselves in an order which is apparently capricious," Bergson, 145; it actually cannot be otherwise that "the memories form a [causal] chain of the same kind" as perceptions, Bergson, 146.

3. Bergson, 146.

4. Bergson, 68.

5. Bergson, 145.

6. Bergson, 149.

7. Bergson, 211.

8. Bergson, 150.

9.   For this suggestion, see for example, Michael P. Richards, et al., "The Mesolithic and Neolithic subsistence in Denmark: new stable isotope data," *Current Anthropology* 44 (2003), pp. 288–295; and Chris Fowler, "Pattern and diversity in the early Neolithic mortuary practices of Britain and Ireland: contextualizing the treatment of the dead," *Documenta Praehistorica* 37 (2010), pp. 1–22. My paraphrases are far more informal and speculative than the language of the archaeological literature.

10.   Manuel Calado, "Standing stones and natural outcrops: the role of ritual monuments in the Neolithic transition of the Central Alentejo," in Chris Scarre, ed., *Monuments and Landscape in Atlantic Europe: Perception and Society during the Neolithic and Early Bronze Age* (London: Routledge, 2002) 17-35, 18-19.

11.   Vicki Cummings, "All cultural things: actual and conceptual monuments in the Neolithic of western Britain," in Scarre, *Monuments and Landscape in Atlantic Europe*, 107-121, Figure 7.10, 118.

12.   Cummings, 115.

13.   Cummings, 113.

14.   Cummings, 113.

15.   Anon., 1851, quoted in C. Barker , *The Chambered Tombs of South-west Wales: A Reassessment of the Neolithic Burial Monuments of Carmarthenshire and Pembrokeshire* (Oxford: Oxbow, 1992), p. 38, quoted in Cummings, pp. 114-115.

16.   Cummings, 119.

Choreography of the Body's Collapse: The Anti-Capitalist Politics of Rest[1]

Heidi Andrea Restrepo Rhodes

The Brooklyn-based project, "Rest for Resistance" centers rest as crucial to healing work (it is so much work to heal!), bridging the vital importance of psychological and social support; and of individual and collective wellness for marginalized communities, including "Black, Indigenous, Latinx, Pacific Islander, Asian, Middle Easter, and multiracial persons" and "LGBTQIA+ ... trans & queer people of color, as well as other stigmatized groups such as sex workers, immigrants, persons with physical and/or mental disabilities, and those living at the intersections of all of the above."[2] Published by QTPOC Mental Health, a community justice initiative, the Rest for Resistance Zine features writing and photography that foreground rest as a deeply political activity. Juhee Kwon's piece, "We Are Not Machines," reminds us that "we're more complicated than a simple input (x) à output (y) kind of linear function"—questioning the correlations between overworking one's self and how "success" is measured through whether and how we've maximized our productivity. At the expense of our physical and mental health.[3]

The exhibit "Black Power Naps" by multimedia artists and activists niv Acosta and (Fannie) Sosa (January 9-31, 2019, Performance Space New York) constructed an installation of a comfortable, restful space where people of color could show up to simply rest, reclaiming laziness and idleness as deeply political expressions of power.

To quote the project's mission statement:

> Departing from historical records that show that deliberate fragmentation of restorative sleep patterns were used to subjugate and extract labor from enslaved people, we have realized that this extraction has not stopped, it has only morphed.

> A state of constant fatigue is still used to break our will. This "sleep gap" shows that there are front lines in our bedrooms as well as the streets: deficit of sleep and lack of free time for some is the building block of the "free world." After learning who benefits most from restful sleep and down time, we are creating interactive surfaces for a playful approach to investigate and practice deliberate energetic repair.

> As Afro Latinx artists, we believe that reparation must come from the institution under many shapes, one of them being the redistribution of rest, relaxation, and down times.[4]

The poignancy of this installation's architecture rendered available specifically for downtime for people of color inside the "city that never sleeps" is also not lost on me. If what me and

Tala, as chronically sick queer non-black femmes of color are calling "bedlife" is the insistence that bedboundedness is not deathboundedness but an onto-epistemological set of differences that make possible practices of world-building; this exhibit highlights how life is made possible in and by the bed as a location symbolizing the possibility of rest: how the differential distribution of bedtimes, and time in bed, is a racially-configured violence in a political economy and national spirit founded on anti-blackness and slavery. Of black life in the wake, and black life awake.[5] How "quality sleep is really only given to rich, white people," and how the hustle has been glorified through US-American individualism that ignores the racist conditions on which our notions of independence and dependency have been constituted, while white institutions economize on the struggles of people of color. The connections between chronic violence, chronic illnesses that disproportionately affect black, indigenous, and people of color, and the structuring of work's chronicity (the long work day, the lack of vacation, the non-stop of emotional labor of contending with racism), must be attended to. Black Power Naps takes this up, noting too, how rest's threat to the order of things is a vital part of liberatory endeavor: that fully rested, fully self-possessed black life is, to quote niv Acosta, "the white man's worst nightmare."[6]

Rest is a cultivated absence, the choreography of the body's collapse. A wrench in Capitalism's droving of laboring bodies like robot machines of endless supply. Rest, like poetry, is not escape or luxury or relinquishing political life and accountability to the world.[7] Can rest be a reorientation toward modes of being that refuse the infinite sourcing of extraction? We view rest as political indeed, an evasion of what Jasbir Puar has called "liberal eugenics of lifestyle programming," to which we are subject in its intensifications of neoliberal marketization of everything in existence.[8] Under this neo-eugenic programming, every action and interaction, every word spoken, every expression of the body, every minute of every day, should be geared toward symbolic and material profit. This is how we are told to measure our value, whether or not we've lived up to the "well-born" as a constant and perpetual bootstraps birthing of ourselves into a wellness that is meant to function only and precisely for the grind of capitalism's wheel in ever-expanding profit. Rest refuses the totalizing hold of this economy on the body that is struggling to flourish in its own fleshly ruins wrought by the vicissitudes of capital's legacy—of total depletion, toxicity, and annihilative violence. Rest is preservation of individual and collective selves for a radical and undisciplined wellness; and destruction of industry as a compulsory and natural law. Rest is the reclined and purposeful disinclination to capital's insistence on our orientation toward the incline. Not limited to the bed and its reclinations, rest is also playfulness, the reach for pleasure and expressions of want outside of and away from the commodification of our bodies as perpetual and simultaneously configured labor, product, and marketplace.

Notes

1. Excerpted from Khanmalek, Tala, and Heidi Andrea Restrepo Rhodes, "A Decolonial Feminist Epistemology of the Bed: A Compendium Incomplete of Sick and Disabled Queer Brown Femme Bodies of Knowledge." *Frontiers: A Journal of Women Studies* 41, no. 1 (2020): 35-58, accessed on December 26, 2020, https://www.muse.jhu.edu/article/755339.

2. Rest for Resistance, QTPOC Mental Health, https://restforresistance.com/, accessed on January 1, 2019.

3. Juhee Kwon, "We Are Not Machines," in *Rest for Resistance Zine*, ed. Dom Chatterjee, Kofi Opam, and OAO, (QTPOC Mental Health, 2017), 4-5.

4. niv Acosta and Fanny Sosa, "Black Power Naps," https://blackpowernaps.black/, accessed on January 1, 2019.

5. Black life "in the wake" references Christina Sharpe's notion of the wake as the total climate of anti-blackness in the afterlives of slavery. Through the brilliance of Acosta and Sosa's Black Power Naps, we can also read the chronic lack of sleep for black people—the over-extension of working hours as waking hours—as another manifestation of slavery's wake. See Christina Sharpe, *In the Wake: On Blackness and Being*. (Durham: Duke University Press, 2016).

6. niv Acosta, quoted in Michael Love Michael, "If You're Black, Rest is Power," *Paper Magazine*, http://www.papermag.com/black-power-naps-2626998633.html, accessed on January 1, 2019.

7. See Audre Lorde, "Poetry is Not A Luxury" *in Sister Outsider: Essays and Speeches* (Freedom: The Crossing Press, 1984), 37-39.

8. See Jasbir K. Puar, "Coda: The Cost of Getting Better: Suicide, Sensation, Switchpoints," *GLQ: A Journal of Lesbian and Gay Studies*, 18, no. 1 (2012): 149-158.

Artist/Worker

An Exchange with Renata Summo O'Connell

CHRIS: I had a thought about this connection between creative and intellectual labor as well; about artists and musicians and intellectuals of various kinds: those of us who are doing something that capital doesn't find useful in any way. Like the artist who refuses to subject their work to the discipline of art markets, many of us in the interpretative social sciences do not do any sort of work that could be of instrumental value to capital or the state. Then again, quantitative social scientists have skills that are more easily exploitable. Those trained in mathematics or science, business, and government can find uses for you that may have nothing to do with your field of study, even if it might only be the fact that you can work with a big database and crunch a bunch of numbers.

If, however, what you're doing can't be easily instrumentalized by capital, this is another way of saying that what you do doesn't have market value. What universities have done is use this as a way to pay you as little as possible and get away with it. As a result, someone in a field like anthropology is increasingly in a position that artists have been in traditionally. There is no middle class. If you are an accountant, you don't have to be able to make the claim of being one of the world's greatest accountants in order to have a stable job. But this is the real situation for certain kinds of knowledge workers. Like most artists or musicians, the Adjunct now makes below the reproduction-cost of labor.

In the county where I grew up, I was aware of these kinds of problems from early on. At the local community college, the math and science faculty were often high school teachers before, and they started a part-time job which turned into something more. Nobody expected them to be among the world's greatest mathematicians! The local people who were really good at math or science were not working at the community college; they were working for the US Army doing ballistics and chemical weapons research. By contrast, the art faculty at the local community colleges are often world-class artists who are just brilliant!

RENATA: In Italy, and perhaps in other European countries, there is a problem with the recognition of the artist epistemologically: there's always somebody interpreting the artist. It was interesting what you were saying before, Asma, about decolonizing because it feels sometimes that we are some big body at someone else's disposal. So, there's always someone else interpreting, there's always somebody talking for the artist. I think there is a little bit of a problem, no?

We have artists who are exploited; there's a bit of exploitation, unless the artist becomes incredibly clever at making this exploitation work to their advantage. Otherwise, if a perverse relationship is established between the artist and the critic, there's real exploitation, and that needs to be addressed. It could sound patronizing, but it affects all of us working in the art world. And, nevertheless, we are not conducting a crusade for the artists here, because it affects everyone who enjoys art, the interlocutors of the artists themselves. If we don't question it and reinvent it, it's going to perpetuate itself.

ASMA: This explicative and interpretive thing is really crucial in terms of the history of what kind of worker the artist is. Because it seems to be that even more so than the worker, the artist and people's interpretation of them were already part of a commodification of "the artist" as an extension of but distinct from the worker. The market is present in the very institution of something called "the artist." In a way, the artist has always had to be that particular figure, but also separated. That is even if the shift from design to art becomes a way to keep the artist from being transparent in a way that allows everything else to make it transparent—unlike the worker who is always already transparent. It's almost as though the worker isn't even an object of study. The workers are not interesting, the workers are just labor-time. I'm just thinking about how we formulate something for our moment that learns from these histories of how particular subjects will be parlayed literally into new movements and new institutions. Do you think the "art world" can be let go of? What is the institutional space that the artist imagines to create? What do you think?

RENATA: Yeah, I don't understand why we have to talk about the "art world." We're talking about the multiverse not a universe. I don't know why we have to, in the general discourse, unify this incredibly diverse reality. When Zahabia was talking about the artist not being able to work, there's an interesting thing in English, because not in all languages do we say it's "work" as an artist. In English there's this coincidence, and it's an interesting one, between "work" and "artistic production." And what Zahabia was saying, that "we don't even have the room to work," suggests a prospect where a system exists (the "gallery system") and you are either detached from it or subject /attached to it.

MILO: There was a question of why are we even talking about the "art world." I was thinking about this in terms of Walter Benjamin's response to the art world during fascism, or the rise of fascism, his sort of response was also to say this needs to be abandoned. He was always talking about what's so cool about the destruction of the erratic function of art and all these sort of precious parts of it that would have it as a separate thing that needs to be distinguished. People are now taking these photos that intend training of political sensibilities—that's what he called it. This is not on the level of the technology of art, or the technologies that are coming into art, but about how art then is a different twist in that story where a critique such as his became about calling everything work, and it turned it into a place of labor, and these sorts of things. I do think the multiverse is an interesting place to go, but I also think about the way that the art world is responding as a sort of formal place and positionality, and that there is an "art world" to which there is an opposition such as what we are framing.

A Roaming Aesthetic

Sadia Salim

I wonder if there is something like a "roaming aesthetic," or a phenomenon where you go through a place for some other purpose but end up picking up things from the ground and look at them again and again, unable to let go and discard. And then you have a collection of stones, shells, honey combs, nests, and dried leaves, twigs, flowers and pods; the objects keep on adding and make possible to hold on to the memory of the journey, the place, the time, and the people.

During walks back and forth from a studio located in a Russian Fort in Daugavpils (now in Latvia), where most man-made structures were either destroyed or abandoned and nature seemed to be taking over/thriving in those spaces, I kept picking up dead branches that had abandoned the trees and the leaves, yet supported growth of new life on the moistened surfaces. Gradually, other plants started piling up in my studio, some were propped up on stoneware stands, and others eventually and inevitably landed in the clay bucket and the kiln. The structure of the plants held the outer layer of the clay long enough for it to harden and survive, before itself turning to ash, encased within the folds of an invisible inner clay structure, both as ash and metamorphosed into glass. The glass as it fused with clay lent to the strength of the outer shell.

I continued to make work as I experienced other terrains rich in plant life, most importantly the landscapes in Hunza, Naran, and Karachi's mangroves. The making process was not only a reminder of the fragile and threatened ecosystems but also a study of the plant forms and their uses, an occasion to engage with the communities that are sustained by these systems, and explore the politics of the land.

The ceramic pieces eventually found their way into the galleries, appreciated as works of art with little time at hand for the stories to truly unfold.

Karachi, July 2020.

Identity/Crisis
the internal conflict of an "emerging artist" in (and out of) crisis
Sanya Hussain

In a perpetual state of confusion since I walked out of the doors of my school at twenty-two with a degree that I thought, fallaciously perhaps, would be my identity from that point on. Faced with the question of what rather than who we want to be when we grow up since childhood, I don't even know when I stopped noticing the other many things that I am and want to be. We introduce ourselves by what we do. And, as someone who sincerely hates introductions, it comes from the heart, how deeply I despise the constant need to talk about my work or what I am doing in order to define my identity.

I guess we were always on our way somewhere. It seemed like a designated lane on a one-way road, or a narrow escalator only going up, that led from grade school to university without too many questions asked. Now that I think about it, I never appreciated enough the comfort the term "student" lent. It was a comfort that was so natural. We were all students. And we were all on the way, not there yet. I can no longer describe myself as an art student. I got away with "recent art-graduate," for a while. But, then "recent" wore out, and the only option left was "artist." Everyone on the internet seems to be able to use the term with complete ease. Especially nowadays. I struggle with the weight of the term. I feel burdened by claiming any kind of claim on any kind of art. I feel safer adding "emerging" before "artist," or "aspiring," as if it gives me room to justify the internal confusions, dilemmas, insufficiencies. Anyone I say this to will give me a knee-jerk reassurance by pointing out how good I am at what I do, or remind me of that one painting of mine that they love so much. But, that is not it. It isn't a question of being able to do certain things, or possessing a skill set. It is about being defined as and by what I do. And, it is about figuring out for myself what it is that I really want to do. Really, I'm not looking to be comforted.

Then comes the question of the type of artist you are. People most often ask what type of an artist you are and as you respond, carefully choosing your words to best summarize the various complexities and ambiguities your practice explores, you've most likely already lost your listener. Some listen, often with little or no interest, as you ramble on explaining what your work is about. But they've already decided based on their own notions and understandings of "artist," a term with great room for imagination, what they really want you to be. Somewhere between that dialogue you'll settle for their sake, and maybe a little for yours, at "visual artist" or better: "painter" or "photographer," etc., etc. For them to say "Ah!"and for their face to settle a bit, as their brains land, at last, in familiar and tangible territory.

This is, then, followed by them taking a moment to recall and tell you, almost as if to comfort you, that they know a certain someone whose niece also happens to be an artist. Throws in name. Waits expectantly for you to say of course you know them. Because how can two artists not, right? You lie, again for their sake and a little for yours, and say that the name does sound familiar but you can't quite put a finger on it. They relax and move on to tell you about how they also love to paint, or how well their son can draw. And how they just never had the time to seriously pursue art. Because of course. And suddenly the conversation isn't about you anymore. Phew. Anyway, it leaves you thinking about more important things. Such as why do I need to be able to summarize my varied practice and interests in one simple term. By claiming to be a painter/printmaker/sculptor, am I assuming mastery in any one field? And more importantly am I withdrawing from another? I love to write, I love to paint, and I also really enjoy photography. I also want to make those really cool coasters out of resin that I saw on Instagram and those DIY galaxy soaps on Pinterest too. But that's a hobby? Unless I sell them online. Then I'm an entrepreneur. So many of those these days as well.

As an artist who only makes work from and at home, the new-found concept of "work from home" isn't really anything new or exciting. Except that now it comes minus the guilt. Why do I feel better being "unemployed" or "self-employed" in a pandemic? Perhaps because the pandemic and the sheer helplessness it enforces on all of us, provides some strange sort of validation? As if it's not my fault anymore. Why did I feel like I was on vacation before or that I was "unproductive" unless I worked for an organization full-time? Maybe it's a fixed monthly salary thing. It is probably that familiarity and comfort of not making enough money at the end of the month, but at least having regular income. Because, where does an artist get off arguing for a higher pay? We are lucky to even get a pay of course. But was it really that regular feeling of being overworked and underpaid that made me feel "productive"? Weren't we already so done with 9-5 desk jobs before all this began? Why was I constantly always treating making art as secondary? Something I had to make time for. I feel "unproductive" when I am not making money, and in a pandemic making art for yourself just feels better, is justified. It is valid. It is needed to stay sane if nothing else. It's also fashionable. But, is it even making me feel better? Well it's supposed to. This is the first time it is beyond my control, and not my fault. To not be working full time, to be here in Karachi for an unknown period, as I wait for a pending immigration approval. Seeking approval and waiting on end for any kind of response, resonates well with us artist folks! Seems all too natural if you ask me.

When making art in the pandemic, I am constantly confronted with the question of who my audience is. Am I making this for myself? For my family? For my Instagram friends? Who am I making it for? Before the pandemic, it has always been for a show, a project, a biennale, or a buyer. Four years of art school so focused on unlearning rather than new learning, with a "self-directed" thesis project at the end that is anything but that, has really made me forget making art for myself. I have always had a mentor, a curator, an advisor tell me what works and what doesn't. But not anymore. There are no stakes at all. I imagined this would feel more liberating. But really it's just confusing.

Going back to the day I walked out those doors, if you were to ask this "emerging artist" what she'd tell that "fresh graduate" who sat there bright-eyed, listening to the keynote speaker go on about chasing dreams and limitless skies, about the "real world." I'd ask you to clarify if you mean this current pandemic-stricken world or the one before? Or the future one we can't see clearly as yet? And, as you would reply, I would tell you that it really doesn't make a difference! I don't have much say, or much to say at all.

Verdict: Mixed Feelings.

Mushtarka Khushi

Hajra Haider Karrar

Mushtarka: مشترکہ

    noun   having joints or jointed segments,
                accomplished by collaboration.

  adjective   belonging to or participated in by
                a community as a whole; public.

Khushi: خوشی

    noun   Happiness, sense of well being, contentment,
                Pleasure, joy.

Aspirations and narratives of World Class cities; physical markers of neocolonial projects curtailing local access; and erasures of the underprivileged including indigenous and minority communities through real estate development, and religious and political propaganda. Add to that, institutional corruption, censorship, and complicity. Witnessing and experiencing this personally, and through those around me, led to a growing restlessness to configure and address the stance and positioning within my community: that of the artist, academic, and cultural practitioner in the current milieu.

This restlessness and the reflections, frustrations, and limitations that resulted from working, producing, engaging, and living in Karachi through this time culminated in the conception of a project. In 2018, "Who gets to talk about whom? Collective thinking and its politics in the decolonial turn" was launched. This ongoing project is my attempt to address the complexity of representation, and recognize and interpret the ethical responsibilities and the often lacking accountability attached to it. *For whom, by whom, and how?* A framework was structured to locate the set of intentions behind cultural knowledge production, its purpose, intended audience, expected reward, and identifying the approach that is adapted to achieve these goals and its possible impacts on the knowledge produced. Alongside this, the aim is to configure and stimulate interdisciplinary solidarities through problem solving and strategy sharing and collectively imagining a desired equitable future. The project creates this premise by examining collaboration as a form of artistic practice.

The first phase of the project was structured over two components—exhibition and discursive program—to be followed by a third component known as the digital aftermath. Nine collaborative initiatives were selected for the exhibition component, each one displaying a different politics and format of collaboration. The physical manifestation of projects by each initiative was accompanied by detailed interviews with the collaborators offering in-depth information on each project's process, requirements, politics, ethics, the chosen medium, and the reflections and learnings in the aftermath. They further served as the point of departure for the discursive component to initiate a dialogue across disciplines, experiences, and demographics.

For *Falsework, Small Talk*, I would like to share a transcribed excerpt of one interview with The Tentative Collective that I conducted along with Fiza Khatri, the assistant curator. A *Pakhtun Memory* was the work selected for the exhibition and the collaborators for it are Mohammad Siddique Khan, Rasheed Khan, and Yaminay Nasir Chaudhry.

* The first and second parts of this interview were conducted in Urdu, and have been translated. The interview has been edited in length according to relevance and space limitations.

** Visuals included and referenced courtesy of the Tentative Collective.

I

Interview with Mohammed Siddique Khan

M. Siddique Khan (MSK, Chacha): The name of the song, I can't recall..

Hajra Haider Karrar (HHK): I also don't know the name of the song. But that's ok. Though can you maybe share a bit about how the planning of the project started?

MSK: We started the planning, Sister, first by taking the drums and other musical instruments (along with the musicians) to Seaview, next to the sea. There we practiced the tunes. After practicing, we got into a car and went to Sarkar Janobi known as Bilawal Chowrangi. We had just gathered there, to start the performance and have some fun and enjoy together, other people had also joined us, when the police came. The police instantly started questioning and asking us to stop the program. We requested very nicely, gently, and in polite language that we are citizens of the same country, and it's a free country, we are not terrorists, we just do fun programs, the public also enjoys them and becomes happy. We said that we will just have the program for 5 to 10 minutes and then we will leave. But they said, "No, you have to shut it down now! We have orders from the higher authorities to stop it."

I asked them again, "So we can't do it?" and they said,"No." Then I said to them, "What kind of a free country is this? This is not freedom, this is slavery. Freedom is only for the powerful and rich here. May God destroy this country." I said it this way. One of the policemen who was listening said, "I say, may it be destroyed now." To that I said, "No. it may not get destroyed just yet. You don't pray for that because it's in your favor. You benefit from it." He said, "What benefits?" I said," Lots of benefits. Whatever benefits there are, you have gained from them all." Then after a while, Sister (Yaminay) spoke to them as well. Then they said, "We will grant you a little time, you can do it for five to ten minutes, but then you have to wrap it up and leave." I said, "That is exactly what we will do, you can see for yourself. We are not terrorists. We are not robbers or thieves. We are citizens of this country and it's a free country. Our purpose is to create consciousness in the public about what is happening in our country. This is the purpose of our programs. Look at how many people have gathered. We are not here to do some random vulgar acts or use distasteful words. We do it very nicely, and politely, and it creates consciousness in people." Then we continued with our program with the musical instruments and then left.

Actually, Sister, this work is really great because one gets to create new connections and networks. For example, I didn't know the people of that area before but after this they have become acquaintances. I have gotten to know some people really well.

HHK: Chacha, how do you perceive the public reaction? Did they share their thoughts with you after the performance? How did they feel about it?

MSK: People really liked it. In fact, they wanted us to take more time and continue for even longer. We promised them to do it again sometime in the future, Inshallah. They really liked it and said things such as, "we get informed by it," and "it makes us happy," and "you should do this kind of program every day." To which I said, "Well, every day is not possible as we have to prepare and it takes time. But we will definitely do it again." They were really happy and affected by it.

HHK: Did you know the song played in the performance from before?

MSK: No, Sister, I didn't know of it. But if you want any Pashto songs, then I have some and can send them to you.

HHK: There was some planning involved in how the performance would begin and how it will attract the audience to gather together? How was it planned to start?

MSK: We had asked the drummers to stand in the lane at the back, hidden from view, and to enter one by one. First, the drummer entered then a few seconds later another one entered. People kept watching with intrigue, wondering what's happening, and started getting really excited and happy. Then from another lane, the flute player came out. They kept coming and assembling the way we had planned and shared with them in advance. A lot of people also started gathering around them. The ensemble had just gotten together that the police arrived and started disrupting. "We are citizens, this is a free country, we just have fun, life is pleasant, the country is pleasant and every person has the right to live it up," I said to them. I had promised Sister (Yaminay) that I wouldn't fight this time. But I cannot stand things that are wrong in principle. I got really angry at the policemen and said,"What do you mean?! We are going to keep at it."

HHK: Chacha, when the three of you were in the planning phase how had you imagined that the public would respond? Were you at any moment concerned that the public might not join and participate or people might not like it happening in their neighborhood? Were there any such concerns or that things may not happen the way you were all anticipating.

MSK: Before the actual performance, Rasheed, Sister (Yaminay), and I had conducted a survey for two to three days in the neighborhood. There were some Pakhtun gentlemen there, and there were some really good people there. They said, "Don't worry no one can say anything to you, we are with you and happy with you, do your program whenever you feel like it." Afterwards, they got so affected and impressed by our program that they kept asking us for the date of the next

performance. So we said, "We will keep you posted with our plans."

HHK: Chacha, how did you, yourself, feel about the performance? You had been planning and preparing for it with Rasheed and Yaminay. What did the final manifestation feel like for you?

MSK: Haha. In the beginning, Sister, I wasn't able to understand it much. In fact, I was telling Sister (Yaminay) that she should do a job or something instead of getting involved in this.

I am a daily newspaper addict. Sister (Yaminay) knows that. So I would read the newspaper and watch TV—not films or dramas, but news and critical reviews. Then, one day on TV I saw this artist, she had gotten an international award. Maybe you know her, her name skips my mind right now. There were a lot of celebrations in her family. That's when I understood what Sister (Yaminay) does and then was very happy.

HHK: When you saw people's reactions at the performance, how did that make you feel?

MSK: It made me really happy. It made me feel really good. Really happy.

II

Interview with Rasheed Khan

HHK: Rasheed, where and how did it all start? Where did the idea of doing the project come about?

Rasheed Khan: There was a clip in my mobile phone of wedding programs from my village (Buner). I showed it to Sister (Yaminay), showing her how people celebrate in Pakhtun areas. Then one day, Chacha Siddique, you have probably heard of his name, myself, and Sister (Yaminay) were watching it and she asked me,"Where can you find these people (musicians) in Karachi?" So I told her that there are musicians in the Benares colony and they can be hired to play for programs and if we hire them they would play it for us as well. Soon after, we planned that we will go to Shireen Jinnah Colony one of these days and conduct a performance there.

Then one day, Sister (Yaminay) and I went to Banaras Colony together. It was very difficult, if there was some other lady in her place she would never have come with me. Sister, you know the area of Benares. So we went together in a rickshaw and spoke to the musicians, sharing our plans for the performance and how we want it to be done, asking them if they would be willing to do it. We shared all the details with them. There were four musicians. We shared the date and time with them and how they will enter one by one in the specified location and when we say ready then they will start moving into their positions.

The day of the performance when they came, we first practiced the music at the sea. Chacha, Sister (Yaminay), and I spent an hour and a half making them understand how and what needs to be done. Then we went to Shireen Jinnah, and they followed the plan just the way we had shared with them. It was very difficult for us. Because Sister, going into an unfamiliar area, where you don't know anyone, without any formal permission, it was very difficult for us. I salute Sister (Yaminay). She is very brave and is not scared but it was very difficult for me. I was quite apprehensive and concerned.

The people instantly realized what was happening, the cart owners, rickshaw drivers, they all got really happy. Everyone got really happy. You probably saw in the video how many people gathered. Then the police came and created a ruckus. Then we spoke to them that it is nothing and quite harmless.

HHK: At first, when Yaminay proposed to do it this way, what did you think and how did you imagine it would be?

RK: When Sister (Yaminay) shared this is how the music will be played, and asked, "How do you think the people would react?" I knew it then. I know Pathans and I knew that they would like it. Even the few Baloch or Punjabis whoever was there, they liked it. I knew that if we do this program they would like it, they wouldn't mind. Everyone gathered and got really happy.

HHK: And the music is specifically from your area?

RK: Yes, it is specific to our region of the Pathans.

HHK: Yes, but Pathans are spread all over the region, from Peshawar to Waziristan, as well as in other areas, but each of these regions have slightly different kinds of music.

RK: Yes, there is a difference. As in, I can say that for people from Waziristan and Peshawar, even within Pathans there are differences, but this music and the instruments used in it are quite famous all over the region. Everyone knows it and likes it, and since they all understand and speak Pashto, they can understand the lyrics of the song and are familiar with the music. And even those who can't understand it, like there are people in the video who couldn't understand it. There was a man who was dancing, so I asked him," Did you understand anything?" Because he was not Pathan. And he said, "No. But I genuinely really liked it and that's why I am dancing on it. "There was another young child, I don't know where he was from, maybe a Punjabi from Lahore or somewhere around there, but he also said he liked it. So, they all liked it, the way Sister (Yaminay) liked it when I made her hear it. She really liked it.

HHK: Rasheed, how did you feel about it? It's something specific to your area and having it in Karachi with hired musicians from Benares, away from your home. How did it make you feel, what was your impression?

RK: You know all these people (musicians) who conduct these kinds of programs, they understand. When they came to us and we told them about the song and everything, they understood immediately. Because this is what they do. And here, as I told you earlier that Sister (Yaminay) was asking me that if we do it would someone mind in the neighbourhood? But I knew that in Shireen Jinnah Colony, 80%-90% of the population are Pathans, so I was sure that if we got this song performed there, they wouldn't mind and instead would be happy. Like the way they were dancing during the performance. Because you also know this, Sister, (the risk involved in) going into an unfamiliar area without any official permission. It was scary and made us anxious. It was difficult, quite difficult for us, but then I explained everything to the people in the neighborhood and shared our plan and how we will be conducting it. And no one questioned us. As I said to you earlier, people got really happy and it all went really well.

HHK: Rasheed, did you have any friends or contacts in Benares and Shireen Jinnah from before?

RK: Yes, in Banaras I knew some people. In Shireen Jinnah, I did not know anyone but after doing this project a lot of people asked me for my number. Then I got to know people. They were all quite happy and asked me to come visit them again and said, "You are always welcome."

HHK: When the policemen interfered, then it was unpleasant for everyone but did that also make you a bit concerned and fearful as to what they will say and do?

RK: When the police came, at that time, Mashallah, there were too many people with us. We were scared, of course, but I knew by that time that the people wouldn't let them stop the performance. Because the people had come to watch and no one wanted it to stop. Because even in the end, when we were about to conclude according to our schedule, the gathered crowd insisted that we play for another 15 to 30 minutes.

When the police came, at that time, I was scared that they would interfere but then all the public pressurized the police into letting the program continue. We said to the police, "Be calm, what is it? What have we done here?" The policeman said, "What are you doing? And why are you doing it?" To which we said," We are not doing anything wrong? It is a happy occasion, a wedding program. We are celebrating our happiness." He said, "Have you taken permission from anyone?" So we said,"Why do we need permission for that?" Then the public stopped the police. The three of us were a bit scared but the public intervened and the police realized that it would be difficult to stop the crowd. So they said, "Ok then you can continue for another 15, 20 minutes."

HHK: Rasheed, after the project completion, you and Chacha Siddique went to Shireen Jinnah again to ask people if they had made any videos (documentation). How many people made a video of the performance?

RK: The people who work there, such as rickshaw and taxi drivers who wait for their rides there, I saw a lot of them making videos. I saw that they all had a video. It made them happy. They all asked us to come again and do another performance.

HHK: Had they all made a video from their cellphones separately, or was it just one video that some had made that was being shared and circulated between everyone?

RK: No, they had all made their own video using their cellphones.

HHK: So is part of the video (compiled by Tentative as the official documentation of the performance) also sourced from one of those cellphone videos?

RK: Yes.

HHK: Who did you get that from?

RK: There is a taxi stand in Shireen Jinnah. There was one taxi driver who had made it. I took it from him.

HHK: How was the performance different from when it happens in your village to when it happened in Karachi? What was different?

RK: The difference is only that back in the village all the people that gather for the performance are all our own people (friends and acquaintances). In this instance they were all strangers. But the way people were drawn to it was exactly the same as people are drawn to it in my village. There was not much difference. The way after hearing the music people, young and old alike were slowly being drawn towards the music.

Fiza Khatri (FK): Rasheed, can you tell us what is the right place to celebrate happiness? This refers to the comment the policeman made," What kind of a place is this to celebrate happiness?" So what do you think? What place is appropriate for celebrating happiness.

RK: That is there, Sister. To celebrate happiness in our Pakistan is quite difficult. Like the place we selected for the performance was the right one but they don't allow us. Even though we all enjoyed it, none of the people in the area had any objections. Each and everyone was happy. So this was the place to celebrate happiness.

HHK: Rasheed after this event did you ever think to plan another event like this one?

RK: I did think of doing something like this because the people in that area to whom I had given my number were calling me a lot, inviting us again to their neighborhood and asking us to arrange for another performance. But then, I had to shift to Oman so didn't get the chance but if I ever come back to Karachi and have another chance then I would definitely like to do something like this again. I have thought about it.

HHK: Will you take permission next time you do it?

RK: Yes, permission I will have to take from the police. But not from the people of the area; they wouldn't have any objections, that I know.

HHK: The documentation of the performance, did you ever show it to your friends?

RK: Yes, I showed it to my friends in my village and also when I came to Oman I showed it to all my friends. A lot of people here (Oman) have asked me to share it with them. People from everywhere really enjoyed it. I have friends from India, Nepal, and Sri Lanka, who have all asked me to share this video with them. I have one friend from Egypt. He really liked it as well.

III

Interview with Yaminay Nasir Chaudhry

HHK: We would like to start from the beginning where the project A Pakhtun Memory started from. How did this idea come about and what was the idea initially?

Yaminay Nasir Chaudhry (YNC): This was a collaborative project between myself, Rasheed Khan, and Mohammad Siddique Khan. The disclaimer in this is that, the disclaimer is very important, is that Rasheed and Siddique both worked for my father and I had just come back from my grad school and was beginning to move back into Karachi. I met the two of them in my father's house and I remember, having been away for so long, relationships with house staff become slightly different when you haven't had house staff for a long time and one of the things that strikes you when you come back home is being in a strange position of power with folks who are paid to serve us. In a way I was a little bit out of it because I didn't live there permanently but yes, I definitely had a position of privilege in this situation. I was interested in having a different relationship, a working relationship with these two. It didn't actually start out with something that I had carved. It just kind of accidentally happened that Rasheed and I would talk all the time and he would show me videos of his village Buner on his cellphone. He was a really charming and super young cheerful boy, he was ten years younger than me at that time, and had just come to Karachi with all these aspirations. He would show me these photographs and music videos of musical performances from his village where they were all Pakhtun. There would be these harvest videos where the fields were being harvested and alongside, to encourage the harvesters, the landowner would invite a local music band and a dancer.

He showed me this one really beautiful video. It was a green valley with all of these people gathered around, and a particular band playing a tune and the dancer dancing away and everyone being really enthralled by it. Rasheed would listen to this on repeat all the time. In that moment of looking at this video over and over the idea came that what would happen if we were to enact this video in Karachi where he is away from his home and missing it and where I have come home, having missed my home, finding it very different and him sort of feeling out of place in Karachi where amid the sort of stereotypical classification of Pakhtuns where they are considered to have no culture, and considered to be nobel beasts in some way because of the Martial (Race) Theory that the British had sort of initiated about Pakhtun people as a race that's very violent but nobel. These kind of stereotypes stick and people now associate Pakhtuns with a lot of terrorism that's happening. So all kinds of blame is put on this community for the unrest in Karachi.

So that's how the idea began. And we thought what if we were to reenact this particular song in a place where more people like Rasheed reside. Where they're not used to listening to this music and recreate the memory of their village in a particular site of the city where maybe one doesn't feel like they belong, will that kind of musical memory create a sense of belonging? Will there be participation? Will it transform the space into some place where you find yourself kind of not really belonging but sometimes wanting to? So that's why it started.

HHK: So this was more about trying to recreate the feeling of home in a way?

YNC: More like a feeling of belonging. But in using memory, it was an attempt to reconfigure public space. When you don't belong in a place and try to reconfigure that space using music, and using memory.

HHK: How was Siddique Chacha pulled into the equation?

YNC: Chacha Siddique is also a Pakhtun. Because the project is so much about Pakhtun identity

yes they'll be able to see that a drummer and a harmonium player got dropped –but no one is going to suspect why

and about belonging. Both Chacha Siddique and Rasheed were far away from their homes in a city and finding themselves sort of put in a particular category of Pakhtun. They are both very different. They both have very different musical backgrounds. Chacha Siddique in his village would be listening to beanbaja, which is very different from Rasheed's village, which had this particular kind of dance, harmonium and tabla music. So the three of us started conversations about music. Initially when Rasheed showed the video Chacha would say, "Oh but I'm going to show you something from my village." And then he would come up with this really beautiful bagpipe music which he calls beanbaja. And so we had a lot of conversations about local music that I had never heard in Karachi. That was all of Pakhtun tradition. Our conversations went back and forth about music for quite some time before the project started. That's how all three of us became a part of the project because we were interested in listening to this music and finding a way to play this music in Karachi and not actually having access to it.

FK: What were some of the early conversations like between the three of you when you were making certain decisions about what kind of music would be played? If it was pulled from one particular tradition, from one city or town, particularly in light of the disclaimer that you just gave that you felt out of place upon your return. So how did those early conversations kind of either reconfigure that dynamic or reflect that dynamic?

YNC: I think that each of us had different things to gain from a project like this. I was interested in public space and thinking about it as an artist interested in social practice. The idea of reenacting was mine initially, it wasn't something they would have done had I not been the instigator of this idea. So that was my interest in this whole situation: can I be a facilitator, instigator, and get people together? Get together these two people I want to work with as collaborators, and ask them if they're interested in doing this idea?

Chacha Siddique was really interested in just having a musical performance at home of the beanbaja which he was trying to find for some time. Rasheed's interest in this was he was kind of bored in the kitchen. He was the cook and Chacha was the driver. And whenever we would do these expeditions, we would escape the house and go on these adventures together.

I can't speak for them, what they got out of the project. But each of us came into it such that they were free to choose to participate. I was free to be in it, work with them or not. The idea stuck enough that all of us decided that we would work together and do this thing.

I don't think we had much of a plan, how we're going to go from point A to B to C, but once the first idea came out that we're going to play this in Shireen Jinnah Colony. Rashid and Chacha started out living there. A lot of Pakhtuns live there. It was very close to our first Beyond Walls project. There was a strange kind of public-private dislocated situation happening there, since a lot of migrants live there. But then you have this hospital Ziauddin, which is very close to Shireen Jinnah Colony but caters to the elite from Karachi's residential areas that are very close to the colony. So there's this weird intersection of classes and ethnicities in this small, concentrated space.

The idea didn't get debated for very long. I proposed the idea and then we just ran with it because it seemed like a fun thing to do. There was not that much intellectualizing conversation about the idea itself. It was more about how we are going to do the process and what we are going to do. Where are we going to do it? Where do we go next? So all of that was where our conversations really took place. That's how the group formulated. Rashid said,"The bands that play this kind of music that I know of, are in Banaras, so we've got to go there. But you (Yaminay) can't go there with me because it's not a safe place for you. I'm going to go, but I don't want to go alone because I need to bargain with them and they're not going to be interested." Then Chacha would say, "If we were to bring all these musicians with their equipment into the Shireen Jinnah Colony Square, people are going to be like, what the hell is going on? So how do we stage it? How do we do it so the police doesn't stop us before we even start?" The conversations were a lot about process.

We finally went to Banaras, got these musicians to come, did a trial on the beach and then Chacha and Rasheed were like, "they are so bad they don't know how to play". And so then the conversation was about how do we make them play better. So we would convene and draw maps, sit together, discuss how to get these guys to understand the music and then the band practiced many, many times.

HHK: So the next question is about the selection of space where you planned to reenact it and you chose a roundabout. We are interested in the idea of a roundabout as a public space,how did that come about and what was behind that selection?

YNC: We didn't start out planning to be on the roundabout. Chacha and Rasheed had scoped out the site and had recommended that we start where all the mechanic shops are in front of the Masjid. There was a tiny space open right next to the parking lot of the hospital. And there was enough room to come in from four points in that space and then start playing different instruments at different times and meet right in front of the Masjid. So they figured out we're going to play right after this Azaan and it would then give us enough time to get people together. Rasheed and Chacha cued the musicians on where to start. So it started there, but nobody gathered. Musicians started playing. People didn't show up.

So we were wrong about who would consider something public space and who would come to participate in this music and respond to it by recognizing it and dancing in the same way or just participating in the same way as they would in Buner for instance. We tried for a while. I was insisting, "Let's just wait and see. Maybe something happens." But at some point, locals from the area were like, no one's going to come here. So you should move to the roundabout. There's a moment in the video where there's a kid who comes up and says, "Don't do it here.Go to the roundabout." And so then Chacha also comes and Rasheed also comes and says, no one is coming here. Let's move forward. So then the musicians kind of move to the roundabout where we've been directed.

Roundabout is the most sort of neutered kind of space, nobody can really lay claim to it. It's probably the most public space. It was completely empty. It seemed like nobody should have an issue. And according to some of the locals, people did gather there from time to time. So we start playing over there and people gathered and lots of people showed up as the little kid on the side had told us, and that's how we landed up on the roundabout. So the question of what is a public space was kind of selected by people on site.

HHK: When it was happening in the street near the auto mechanics, at that time, from what I can tell from the video, you were still sitting inside the rickshaw. But when it is on the roundabout then you are there in person with the crowd where the police also comes in. Do you think that the police would have objected if you guys were still in the street? The roundabout is kind of a platform, right in the center in a space of circulation. It gets more attention than something happening on the side of the street. Do you think the police reacted the way they did because of the attention it garnered being on the roundabout?

YNC: I would have thought the same thing, and I thought that we would disappear more easily in front of the shops and that's why we picked that place too because Chacha and Rasheed both thought that that would be closer to the colony, hence more people would come out. But it turned out that the people in that space didn't feel safe to perform or to participate there or to gather there because there was a sense of not having ownership of that space, possibly because there were a lot of police there managing the parking lot of the hospital. Things that are invisible: invisible policing and surveillance of space that I guess one doesn't know when planning something from the outside that you figure out once you reach a particular space. So even though we thought it would work there better. People wouldn't have gathered because there was a preexisting gathering in that space. I don't know the history of gatherings in that space in the past, but there must have been something that prevented people from doing this collective activity.

The roundabout at that time was completely unbuilt. It had no railings around it, like it does today. And it was a little desolate. It just seemed like there was nothing much happening. We wouldn't have picked it at all. But it was the local footfall of the area, suggesting that we go there. There's a lot of giving up of control in projects like this and you can't plan everything out. You can't plan everything out to the idea of what a public space is or should be or where you can do what oftentimes it organically kind of shapes itself.

HHK: Do you think while negotiating with the police perhaps gender plays a much larger role than class?

YNC: It's possible, I'm not sure. I mean, a lot of these things are about post rationalizing why things happen a certain way. So if Chacha and Rasheed's role was choreographing the musicians and making sure that they played in specific places, Chacha was mostly concerned with security of who was gathering and not getting people in trouble. Rasheed was more interested in getting the musicians to play the right stuff, and when to start, when to stop. And my role was documenting. I had the camera. Sometimes Rasheed would be given the camera because he had a better angle. Sometimes Chacha would take the camera. But, by and large, my goal was to be behind the camera and also to, like, I guess be as invisible as I could be because I didn't want my class as this Defence aunty to take over the whole project or the idea of the project. The premise of the project was music and belonging and configurations of space and power in public. And of course, our relationship with my class comes into it. My gender comes into it, too. But I think attempting to hide it, I don't know if that's the right thing to do. Maybe it is completely the wrong thing to do, but I was in a burka, to try not to draw that much attention to myself. Of course, the minute I open my mouth, people know, the way that my body operates in space, people know. But for quite some time the camera took away from my presence or my privilege for some part of the project, not all, and it's very visible.

With the policewala, I can't say that it was my gender that helped because it's mostly Chacha's conversation with him. That's the turning point when Chacha says, "Iss mulk mein to Khushi manana bhi mushkil ho gayi hai," and the guy at some point breaks. And then said, "I also hate this country and I hate my job. Fine, go for it." I don't know, maybe me being there some of my class was visible or my gender was visible. There was maybe one other woman there or like younger kids who were female there. But I think it was a collective conversation that got the guy to finally snap. For the police, to finally give in and snap and give us the time.

HHK: I think that moment of collective frustration is quite amazing and the way each person responds to it. So was it planned as just a one off reenactment? Was there ever conversation about doing more than one?

YNC: We never planned to do more than one, and also the sort of run in with the police was such that after this we didn't really want to do another one. We weren't expecting the police to stop us from doing something so harmless in a public space, which was used to seeing gatherings, but because the activity was like an anomaly, a musical performance without an apparent reason.

The project for me did those things that I was interested in, asked the questions I was interested in asking. But I think that the hassle of coming up against cops is not something that you want to repeat over and over again. I think all three of us were exhausted by the time it was done and we had no intention of repeating it.

FK: From starting out at the masjid and, finally bargaining with the police to get that last song and then wrapping up, how long was that duration?

YNC: From the masjid to the police, it happened from Asr till Maghrib. I'm not sure how long that is but the time preparing for the project was much longer, finding the band and hiring the band and building the relationship with Chacha and Rasheed which happened quite accidentally. The conversations about music happened for weeks and weeks before Rasheed even showed the video or I even noticed that he was listening to it in the kitchen over and over. So that process was very long. It was very organic.

HHK: What made you decide to document the entire performance? There is phone footage in it as well. How did you make the decision of when to use a DSLR and the phone? What were you thinking when making these decisions?

YNC: The DSLR was used sparsely because it makes itself too noticeable. When I was sitting in the rickshaw is when the DSLR was used or when we were doing site analysis because it was ok if it drew attention to itself where nothing was happening. But even in those cases it was kept as low key as possible because there's a tendency for camera crews in Karachi to be in your face. And it's really annoying when the documentation takes over from the conversation or the action. Why did we choose to document is a good question? I guess we could have also not documented it, but maybe that's where my being an artist came in. My professor used to tell me your project is as good as its documentation because otherwise no one else can know what actually happened.

And you could just make a claim about something without having anything to show for it. Other people would argue and say there's no need to prove your claim and just do what you did and write about it and there are other ways of documenting. But I think at the spur of the moment that made sense. We used smaller cameras where they would blend and cell phones, where they would blend in with the surroundings.

On the roundabout, there was a tiny little camera that I had. I was using that discreetly, especially when the police came the camera had to be put away. So you can feel what kind of access you have. Also, the final scene of the film has the cell phone footage of the dancing happening. That wasn't footage we took. It was taken by people who were at the roundabout. When the project finished, the video of this event was distributed to some of the local cell phone walas in Shireen Jinnah Colony. Chacha and Rasheed used their networks to find any kind of video taken by cell phones of the event. So the last bit of the video is actually taken by participants or people who gathered in the crowd to witness what had happened. I think that shifting vantage points are important in bringing this thing together that you can tell when I'm holding the DSLR which is kind of corresponding to my access to technology versus when Rasheed is holding the smaller camera versus when the crowd is holding cell phones and taking video. I think it's important for the vantage to be jumping around between different participants. So it's not a one-dimensional experience.[1]

HHK: Do you think there has been a shift in ownership of the project from where you started from to where you ended it? What was your feeling about being part of that entire process from the beginning to the end.

YNC: The hardest part of this project is my privilege and Rasheed and Siddique being beholden to me in some way because they work for my father. So, how much of them participating is because they have to versus how much of it is them doing it because they want to? And how much of it is me telling them or asking them or hoping that they will join me? I mean, you can read it in multiple different ways. Our class relations are made visible in a painful way, but I can't convey to the audience the relationship the three of us have or had at that time. I can say that there are different strengths that each of us brought. Their strength was their network and their knowledge of this way of making music. My strength was in creating an academic inquiry. So when I say that it was my idea, yes, it certainly was my idea to instigate it. And certainly they would not have done this if I wasn't there. I think that the idea is just an instigation to get something going if people are interested in it. The important part is not the idea giving. It's the process that makes it something else. So to me, my role in it is different from their role in it.. if they didn't have their networks in Shireen Jinnah or Banaras, their knowledge, the project would have been really one-dimensional, if the crowd hadn't been present to lead us. If the police hadn't come to interrupt, none of this would have happened. So I think the fact that we have these unequal class relations, made the project more complicated and complex in a good way because it reveals power relations across class where neither one is without agency. We together did something that each of us separately could not have done.

When the film was initially made, there was no introduction about who was participating in the beginning when the photographs of the team, Rasheed, Chacha, and me were inserted. It's a blatantly visible class difference and they were intentionally put in where Rasheed looks the way he looks, he's wearing the Shalwar Kameez and we talk about where he's coming from. And then you see me in a very kind of fancy backdrop with my privilege, very visible in the image. It was foregrounded in the video to alert to the power dynamics that are already in place, like a disclaimer you could say. And then throughout the video there's a kind of visibility and invisibility that is constantly there like you don't see me often. So there is the power that I have by being behind the camera. And when you see me, you see me in this burka which raises all kinds of strange questions, like why? Why am I choosing to hide? And those are questions that I still to this day haven't really resolved.

HHK: If you were to do this performance again, is there anything that you would do differently.

YNC: Again, it's the visibility or revealing class in the space. Gender you can't hide, but I could reveal my class more blatantly. And I think the output would have been completely different because I think it would have made the video a lot more about me and class relations, then about this idea of complex identities and belonging and public space and who has access to public space? I don't know. It's a very difficult thing to tackle because, you know, on the one hand, it would be more honest, but, on the other hand, it would also make the work a lot more solipsistic and it would be about me.

FK: Can you talk about your collaborative art practice with relation to the city generally over the years, how has that process perhaps changed or evolved? Have there been sort of moments of understanding or realization in this particular project or another project which have really shaped the way that you interact with the city and with the collaborative process?2

YNC: I think it's been just a very long learning process of different ways of handling and negotiating agency. I think it's equally important, like a lot of people just put all the power in the more privileged class as agency. But that's not true in engaging in some of these kind of underprivileged areas that people call underprivileged. There is agency present that you recognize and that moves you, changes you, threatens you, affects you, and changes the process in very, very, strong ways. And recognizing that agency is really important to begin that sort of collaboration, to actually think that you are not better than anybody else or have more power than anybody else. They're just different registers of agency, so I think in all of these collaborations, agency turned out to be one of the most important issues that I've thought about, which brings me back to my own neighborhood to collaborate with people who I think would have equal agency with me in some way.

HHK: The appropriate place to celebrate happiness. Those few sentences where the Chacha and the policeman are speaking about it changes the way you look at the project, because it becomes about something much more than Pakhtun memory, but more about this idea of happiness and the fact that you need permission to celebrate? The appropriateness of happiness?

YNC: It took me a while to process the answer to this, but you're right when you say that, Hajra. I think one should be able to be happy anywhere, and the thing about public spaces that annoys and infuriates me so much is that they categorize where you're supposed to do what. Like a park is where you have a picnic or a mall is where you do shopping or a ground is where you play cricket. This kind of categorization of space can be very limiting and suffocating in a city like Karachi where you have so many people wanting to do so many different things and a lot of people aren't planned for, a lot of things aren't planned for. A lot of demographics are just not considered when these planned spaces spring up. And, so, it's kind of an act of rebellion to say that I'm going to celebrate happiness where I want and outside of your designated spaces of where we should be doing it.

FK: When you guys were on the roundabout and for a while when music was taking off and people were performing what did that feel like being in a public space and being able to do that, even if for a brief moment. Were you able to move outside of your role as documenter and experience that idea of recreating this space of belonging? Did you feel it being reflected in that moment among the participants who had shown up and who were responding to the music by dancing or just standing around?

YNC: Absolutely! I think when the music broke out the second time and there was this kind of collective win, a collective victory, you could say, of having a little bit of time to do this thing together. It felt to me that there was just like joint happiness, this collective happiness. It was amazing and ecstatic, really, really lovely. Everyone was smiling, you can see in people's faces, I mean, of course, this is my perspective, I don't know how people felt, but there is a flash of a second when you feel like your body kind of becomes one of a crowd and it's a good feeling. Also because we were told that you just have one song, so in that limited amount of time it compressed a lot of emotion. And you are feeling happy that you got to do something where you wouldn't have gotten permission. Then there is this young guy who decides to do that particular dance to the music because there is only one song left.

That was the end of that public space because after that the roundabout has been totally covered by this hideous sculpture and fences that you cannot cross and it can no longer be used as public space. So it was totally the end, the final Hoorah of that space.

Notes

1. The video may be accessed on the following link: http://tentativecollective.com/pakhtunmemory.html

2. For more information on both these projects:

http://tentativecollective.com/ and https://whogetstotalkaboutwhom.com/

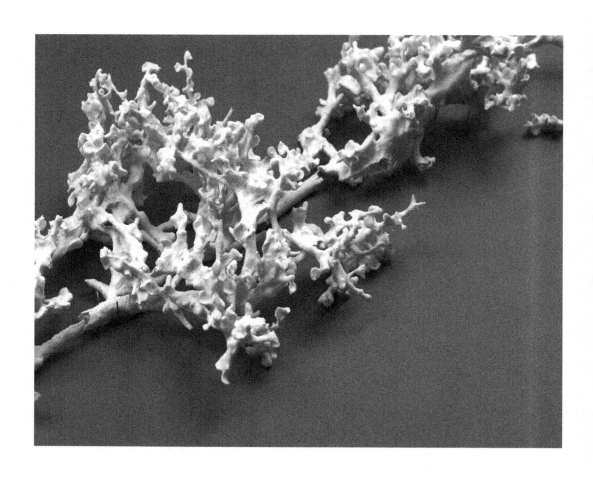

Sadia Salim, *A Roaming Aesthetic VI* (image by Humayun M.)

sixth dialogue

A C T O R S
BETWEEN
HISTORICITY
& POLITICS

2 & 9 May 2020

Companion Texts for Studio Session

Cámara, Julia, "Julia Cámara: Anticapitalist strategy and the question of organization (part 1)," Translated by No Borders, *No Borders*, May 6, 2020, https://nobordersnews.org/2020/05/06/julia-camara-anticapitalist-strategy-and-the-question-of-organization-part-1/.

Cámara, Julia, "Julia Cámara: Anticapitalist strategy and the question of organization (part 2)," Translated by No Borders, *No Borders*, May 7, 2020, Julia Cámara, "Julia Cámara: Anticapitalist strategy and the question of organization (part 1)," Translated by No Borders, *No Borders*, May 6, 2020, https://nobordersnews.org/2020/05/07/julia-camara-anticapitalist-strategy-and-the-question-of-organization-part-2/.

Dorfman, Ariel, "Chile: Notes from a Revolt," *The New York Review*, March 13, 2020. https://www.nybooks.com/daily/2020/03/13/chile-notes-from-a-revolt/

Grande, Sandy, "Refusing the University," in T*oward What Justice? Describing Diverse Dreams of Justice in Education*, Ed. by Eve Tuck and K. Wayne Yang, 60 - 62. New York: Routledge, February 12, 2018.

Hansen, Bue Rübner, "Pandemic Insolvency: Why This Economic Crisis will be Different (updated)," *Medium*, April 4, 2020, https://buerubner.medium.com/pandemic-insolvency-why-this-economic-crisis-will-be-different-841d5bbfa737.

Jäger, Anton, "It might take a while before history starts again," *Damage*, March 25, 2020, https://damagemag.com/2020/03/25/it-might-take-a-while-before-history-starts-again/

Mark, Sabrina Orah, "Fuck the Bread. The Bread Is Over.," *The Paris Review*, May 7, 2020, https://www.theparisreview.org/blog/2020/05/07/fuck-the-bread-the-bread-is-over/

Miale, Marisa, "Toward the Mass Strike: An Interview with Two Southern Organizers," *Cosmonaut*, April 29, 2020, accessed April 30 2020, https://cosmonaut.blog/2020/04/29/toward-the-mass-strike-interview-with-two-southern-organizers/.

Spivak, Gayatri Chakravorty, "General Strike," *Rethinking Marxism: A Journal of Economics Culture & Society*, 26:1 (2014): 9-14.

Hosts | Safi Alsebai, Colin Eubank, Ezra Lee, Nathaniel Madison, Sara Mugridge, Daniel Neilson

Speakers & Asynchronous Dispatches | Asma Abbas, Safi Alsebai, Christopher Carrico, Sami Chohan, Colin Eubank, Ciarán Finlayson, Zahabia Khuzema, Ezra Lee, Isabella Lee, Jody Leonard, Nathaniel Madisonsara Mugridge, Daniel Neilson, Gabriel Salgado, Renata Summo-O'Connell, Yashfeen Talpur

Scribes & Annotators | Asma Abbas, Safi Alsebai, Colin Eubank, Valerie Fanarjian, Ezra Lee, Nathaniel Madison, Daniel Neilson

ASMA

Hello and welcome this Saturday. Happy May Day everyone! Wishing you bread and roses!

Last week, we took a turn from socialities and intersubjectivities to their articulations into institutions, and to the institutions that shape, contain, domesticate and capacitate them. We are compelled to ask how institutions would have us think of the categories of political subjects that correspond to the action that institutions validate— and to the action that remains illegible to institutions, sometimes by design, sometimes by accident.

As I recall hearing about Chicago martyrs every year until I moved to the country where it happened, I don't recall the language of agency or institution, but of struggle and movement. It's a prejudice I haven't gotten over as a student of the social sciences; it either makes the category of agency seem very paltry, or forces us to stretch out the totalities which we consider and regard as "institutions" structuring certain relations of need, capacity, authority, community, memory, and responsibility.

The incommensurability of political action and institutions asks for different ways to make up the difference—adding location and motion here, locution and orientation there, bringing back the subject as a set of powers and not merely needs—and broaden the scope of what is discussed in the Fifth Dialogue. Is the worker today the same kind of subject as before, and corroborated by which institution? Has the history of neoliberalism kept the categories of work and labor unchanged? If not, how have we amended our categories and analyses in a way that actually recognizes the worker? Is it the union, the institution that is the source of our validation as workers—the ones with chains, or the ones without, though? Either way, a crucial role, but important to distinguish between the kinds of emancipations and struggles it validates in the current US context of decimation. And, what happens, especially in the context of a corporate union, or a corporatized union and its legacy here, versus the labor federations that have non-corporatist ownership of the agenda and power of left political parties in other parts of the world? To us, returning to, on the one hand, differential subjects both in struggle with, and in excess of, institutions and, on the other hand, to internationalist politics, is the same thing.

I am tempted to think that the incommensurability of the relation between actor/subject and agent in the moment is what allows us to transform and reclaim the institutions whereby one becomes the other—to be let go, and to be reclaimed. This is a moment to return to the crises— the pandemic, and the defeat of our intense investments in certain electoral campaigns—to ask what is the subject they summon. In the Second Dialogue, we discussed the "calls to politics" as the counter to the "calls to order," but we know well that the subject is constituted somewhere between them. Some kind of politics, and some kind of order. Are there transhistorical agents of history that serve a purpose of order rather than politics, and the other way around? What interpellations are we experiencing, in and from each of our locations? What are the May Day Actions across the world saying about which subjects they are calling to politics, and which to order? And which institutionalities are they taking head on, and defining which limits and totalities of political action in doing so?

Our discussion proceeds in two movements. First, we speak about "bread," since it's May Day. Then, we set the conversation up by turning to the relation between institutions and political actors, and how these crises are having us revisit the frame of the aggrieved subject being summoned to politics. Then we turn to the "roses:" to a set of dispatches from various locations to honor the spirit and practice of internationalism, and of the work of politics, to help us add crucial elements of locus and motion to the discussion of institutions that we put together last week.

We will be brought to these multiple junctures of conversation by Sara Mugridge, Colin Eubank, Daniel Neilson, Nathaniel Madison, Safi Alsebai, Ezra Lee and a number of other participants who have been requested to offer updates on what they see as inflection of the market and their lives in relationship to the pandemic, strikes, marches, and other calls to solidarity.

Bread and Roses

SARA

I'm thinking of the Paris Review essay called,"Fuck the Bread. The Bread Is Over." that came out a couple days ago. It's part of a regular column that Sabrina Orah Mark offers called "Happily," and I think maybe what I'm thinking about in terms of a connection is also how, in this piece, the writer in some ways is enacting (and this is maybe pretty trite to say, but) enacting containment in the local in terms of her own role in the Academy, her own role as a writer writing the domestic, as a woman writing the domestic. I have a quote here which is like, "What does it mean to be worth something? Or worth enough? Or worthless? What does it mean to earn a living? What does it mean to be hired? What does it mean to be let go?"[1] I guess I'm thinking about how her work is really about connecting the struggle to make sense and meaning in meaningless tasks—which is to say work—and yet being met at every turn with these questions about how worthless it all is.

ASMA

Yes, what a beautiful piece! One of the things she recounts is her meeting a string of deans on a campus visit, one of whom asks, "Where are those babies from your poems?" And she responds saying, "Yeah, you know, they don't exist. They signify voices that aren't there or won't be heard or...." It's just such a deeply funny and sad memory. I love her touch there, because it's so not self-pitying. It makes me wonder: How does one also build but also unbuild?

How can we, or where do we, put our desires to not be with people? How do we build unsociality or how do we segregate in a good way? How does one produce something that ultimately just acknowledges the non-reducibility of worlds?

What's empowering about the piece is the sense that, when we know this, then we go somewhere. How do we produce those communities or localities that do not need those same things that other institutions need—which means that they might have a chance at living? Honestly, I don't know.

COLIN

I don't think this is a direct answer, but is a riff of sorts: I was talking to someone recently about some of the most vibrant times here in Oaxaca (which is one state over from Chiapas and the Zapatista caracoles) during the 1990s and early 2000s. All of these concerts were put on all over the country in solidarity with the Zapatistas. All of the concerts were free. You didn't have to pay an entry fee. All that was asked was that you bring a kilo of something like salt or flour or whatever, and eventually that would all get delivered down to Chiapas and the autonomous communities.

My friend recalls that the most remarkable aspect wasn't necessarily the conscious- or hyper-politicization of the moment. Rather, it was the alternative form of sociality that those concerts fostered and continue to inspire in certain concerts and gatherings in the city today. It wasn't like the Zapatistas were coming to town and it was time for everyone to sit down and listen to them, or show that they were down with the cause. It was more an invitation for local or regional bands and people to get together and be with each other on different terms. Even though Oaxaca is a hub of cultural work and artistic practice—where often performance things are "taken seriously" because they are commodified and valued as authentic—this was a complete departure from that. He told me it was a moment for them to finally enjoy each other, and many folks hadn't even met before.

This inspires a memory of a sociality which radiates outward in order to maintain a healthy distance from the site of its origins. In other words, Chiapas and the caracoles do not get overrun with a kind of performance of politics. (I mean they do, but they attempt to defend themselves or ensure that they are engaging in that performance consciously.) Instead, their message seeps into other communities by inviting that community to share in a new mode of relation with itself, which is spurred by disclosing the needs that the Zapatistas have and asking the community to share part of itself by virtue of being together. We see, in a sense, a community orchestrated autonomously and yet also transmitting part of itself (or its voice) over great distances via the airwaves, allowing itself to be frank about certain needs without risking co-optation.

> "And maybe the bread, as I've always understood it, really is over. The new world order is rearranging itself on the planet and settling in. Our touchstone is changing color. Our criteria for earning a life, a living, are mutating like a virus that wants badly to stay alive. "
> — from Sabrina Orah Mark, "Fuck the Bread. The Bread Is Over." 2020.[2]

JODY

One of the things that I'm just really struck by in the essay is that she gives a lot of the tedious tasks to her sons, in a way doesn't really seem like those things are bad, really, right? It's not really bad to have these little things to do, that you learn about, or that you should take upon yourself. But, where the anxiety seems to come in is in having to measure those things against some set of expectations that were put on you for some reason—or to make them seem valuable.

There's a section at the beginning where she writes, "On the third day of the interview, the head of the creative department asks me if the courses I would be expected to teach should even exist."[3]

So, I don't think that the person is telling her she shouldn't be able to write, or that she shouldn't be able to hold classes. The problem is that they don't fit an already existing function or role. In the context of what we've been talking about, especially last week and this week, the thing that determines this "viability" is the market.

To me, the question of desire is a really tricky one. There is a section later on about all the special stuff that you get from the college job: an office, a university ID, a fancy library, and benefits. But, then, her mom just asks her "and then what?" and she responds, "and then nothing, I say as I jump off the very top of the fairytale that has no place for me." So I'm just thinking about what is it that desire really means within the context of capitalism?

ASMA

I really wish someone had written something about that over the last two hundred years, so we wouldn't be asking these questions! (Lots was, and we still are!) This is beautiful, thank you, Jody, because what you said makes clear that Joshua Clover's challenge can be interpreted in more than one way. Before getting to a "right answer," we need to know why we are even asking for something, right? I think evading some questions—not saying, "oh no, i don't have the right answer," but that, "in fact, we have a different conversation to have, you and I, but as far as you fuckers over there are concerned, there is no question here." I think this is something that we do not do enough of, and I think it's just awful and that's the unfunny part of the left: this sort of coldness, this scared coldness.

COLIN

For me, it has something to do with frustration and constant worry that what's being done is time wasted or won't be useful or effective. But, then, we continually find ourselves in these situations where things that we do engage in are bound to fail. And, when they do, and people just say "oh, well, we knew it was going to fail anyway,"or, "we weren't ready," or, "we didn't have the right sense about us to do this in the first place, so why are we getting upset or frustrated?" We see that especially with respect to electoral politics or Bernie.

The need to interrogate what is actually sought from a situation, knowing which might mediate how we engage with it, brings me back to what I've been thinking about with respect to Chile about how the protests have extended an offer of responsibility to scabs—the institutional left that has sold-out for the past decades and hasn't done anything, even though they control the popular assembly or congress or parliament or the unions or whatever other institutions. That frustration is also a frustration with oneself—that we could've done something if we were just thinking about it differently at that moment...instead of being held hostage by questions we already knew you were not interested in answering.

I think it is a great moment to speak about our motley agents of history, called in by the pandemic, and calling out when they can. In the tradition of leaps, may we not leap into the void, but instead let's study our surroundings and think about terrain differently, as well as the steps before us—even those we didn't take.

If Agency is Action Validated by Institutions, What are the "Agents of History" Supposed to be Doing, and Where Are They?

ASMA

I'm just thinking that—if we were to go back to the conversation about institutionally-validated action from the Fifth Dialogue—then even if one is acting as a union member, the agency is not validated just by being a member of that union. Right?

Isaac had brought up the New Left, and even then, the worker—an absent or disqualified agent of history, on the heels of no successful revolutions in any advanced capitalist country, and the helm of no revolutions—was asking to be replaced. The category of the worker either remained largely unrevisited— and confronted with the other emergent subjects of history, became a reactionary means to recast and preserve white supremacy—or destroyed altogether in the culturalist turn as both performative explanation and proof of the failure of the working class, taking the concept of class with it.

There are many ways of unpacking that history, but the important question is: why were the New Left, and the Marcuses of the world, imagining the student or the third world as those new agents of history? Just to be clear: I have no romance for the "agent of history," but I'm just trying to think through the fact that if there was an imperative to rethink in the 1960s, was there such an imperative after 2001, or in 2008? And, why isn't there such an imperative in 2020? Really pragmatically speaking, which category do we think will allow us to gain access to, demand, or summon something that might actually work?

COLIN

I feel like the pandemic enables us to think of the 2008 economic crisis a little differently. Vis-a-vis the shifting subjects of these "events," I think that the category of "worker," "union member," or maybe even "striker," seems a little ill-fitting today. All those people that are just surrounded by the debt that they have accumulated and just, at this moment, now that the circuits have slowed down, they just can't manage to move. I feel like the "resident" doesn't necessarily have to do with dwelling, it has to do with the fact that you reside in an area, you're emplaced there. You've congealed at this point in the circuit of capital.

CIARÁN

What's the political unity of the debtor? Or of, like, the striker without the union? I don't know what transforms it into something … I guess I'm still stuck on the question of what makes it a strike as opposed to a lockout, or something, at the moment? I'm not sure the wildcat is a rejoinder in the same way that it seemed like maybe it was being positioned as. What's the politicizing element if it's just diffused into the most general negative category?

ASMA

That's a great question, and I'm just thinking about the history of this subject that might perhaps help us. Let's look at the union per se as an institution that validates a particular act—as much as the history of the American union is something to be affirmed even through all of its corporatization, it is worth asking what it has made of the many occasions for any potential reconstitution. As far back as the Wisconsin battles as part of a long contemporary moment, chances for collective rethinking and imagination were sacrificed to a kind of survivalism that, for the union bosses, meant keeping the business going as usual, pretty much as guilds of the professional classes in capitalism. Think about how the AFT (American Federati of Teachers), how all of these big unions of educators, ended up endorsing Warren against Sanders, and how Nevada unions disobeyed the "Union" and reclaimed a collective stance for Sanders. Think also, going back to the understanding of agency as institutionally-validated action, which acts of the workers are validated as agency by the union, and what happens to those which aren't?

As we have been discussing, the union as an institution has to confess to us, rather than the other way around. So, if the subject position of the "striker" is something, as we have been discussing throughout these past weeks in fits and starts, then, in that action, one imagines an alternative. It postulates an alternative institution—to which to be accountable and which can in turn validate their action—which is not the union, that hatches a not-merely-negative category. This principle can apply to other political assemblages of subjects that reflexively bring institutions into being, and deepen a coalitional logic beyond the single-issue interest group mentality.

This is what the people in Nevada did, and not by following a logic of transcendence, but a little stretching of the political space within which their agency manifests differently. They did that. In the case of Nevada and the Democratic primary, for instance, the alternate institution was not the union! They did that, but not by rejecting the union, but leveraging themselves as workers brought together by the union, but also embedded in structures of accountability that are not just the Democratic Party establishment. It entailed local institutions and modalities. And, in all of the spaces where Sanders did win, there were structures, communities, and organizing that predated and exceeded the campaign, probably very much like what we were talking about in India or Mexico. Perhaps, I'm thinking very simplistically, but it doesn't seem enough to see alternate, extended, assemblages of political subjectivity as negations, except in an Adornian way.

The seeming consensus among people who don't agree on very much, and keep spinning in the hamster wheel of class vs. identity politics, is a set up, and has always been one, and we compulsively keep giving in to that. So I think the union's history has to be accounted for.

This is a winding turn back to Ciarán's question, but certainly not an answer. Perhaps one possible set of answers is as simple as "who needs to know?", "who is eager to determine that?", "whom does our action allow us to coincide with in this moment?", and so on. Any political action or category assembles a condition, possibility, a point of departure, and a point of return, and they are not all the same.

DAN

Timing is essential to whatever it is we withhold— labor, or payment on debt—for whatever reason it's withheld. The acts of withholding must be coordinated to come at the same time or more or less at the same time, and so the date on which it happens, or the point around which it is coordinated, matters. And so, to that, there are specific moments in time which seem to loom and maybe provide some more organization around the themes that have come up so far.

In our conversation around drug cartels, I was reminded of oil cartels. Depending on what kind of news you follow, the oil price was actually negative this week, and it's in some ways kind of a technical trinket that you can be fascinated by. But, it does seem consequential in terms of the organization of the global flow of capital that, this week, people were paid to take oil off the hands of oil producers, rather than the other way around. The ripples of that are definitely not done playing yet. This is bound to trigger a fairly major compensation and adjustment. We'll see where it goes.

At the same moment, we have fascists being organized to start to use increasingly violent measures to try to get the labor market operating again. So, maybe, without knowing exactly what the way to coordinate is, one can actually see increasing desperation from the other side. Maybe it's not right to guide a strategy based on that, or launch a countermovement on those terms, but they are signs of desperation. So, May 1st is upon us. There's talk of a rent strike —it might be a first ripple. And, at the same time, the first states are making the obviously wrong decision to "reopen" their "economies." It is fairly predictable that, within three weeks, they're going to have to shut back down. One can see something going into the summer, and the timeline of the election in the United States looms at the other end of that. There's quite a degree of predictability and visibility along some of these lines that should have some consequence if we're trying to arrive at a strategy.

ASMA

Yes, and it certainly speaks to the nature of rejoinders that Ciarán brought up in relation to assessing the politics of the wildcat strike. In order to extend political terrain and education, what can be pulled off in response to what? Especially as a corrective to the way unions organize themselves in this country, which is very different from other places. What Gramscian role have unions have had in this society beyond a certain point? What was the right place in society for those raised inside unions before they became corporatized? What were the natural limits of that education, and qualification, and for which kind of leadership in society? I think that has to be contended with also.

GABE

Right, just on that point, a few thoughts on the role of unions and I guess the University of California (UC) union question, because, you know, at Penn, we don't have a formally recognized union. We have scattered remnants of a previous official drive to build a union as a legally-recognized institution, and what we've been talking about in the last week is how we can pressure the university to respond, and what kind of actions we can take.

Withholding the submitting grades is the clearest example of an action that has been taken by students recently somewhere else, and also seems to be clearly beyond what we're able to do—not necessarily because we don't have the union itself, but because we don't have everything that is built up around a union as premise or occasion. To me, it is an interesting fact about the UC union that it didn't authorize that strike originally. Many unions, because of the way that they're enmeshed with the institutions of the state, and because of the way they try to manage discontent, build highly restrictive strike clauses in the first round of organizing or trying to form a union as well. It's interesting to think about both the necessary conditions the union created for what happened at the UCs, and where it was exceeded.

COLIN

I feel like, at the beginning of that—and this goes to what Ciarán said as well—the interplay between the wildcat strike and the union seemed good, in the sense that, yeah, obviously, the union had its hands tied. It couldn't authorize it, so, with a wink and a nudge, the UC Santa Cruz campus kicked it off. Then the other campuses supported, and then they pressured the union, insisting that the union should call a vote regardless of legal standing. But, then everything fell apart when the vote kept dying by committee, basically, right? And then coronavirus happened, and everyone was fired, and now it's too late. Or, that was my understanding of how that worked. So, I don't know, I felt like the initial dance of the union was okay, but then it never ever really showed up.

GABE

Yeah, I completely agree with the sense of that initial dance. I was also alluding to how many unions unnecessarily—to me at least it seems unnecessary—push to have very restrictive strike clauses in the formation of new locals. While having a high threshold is important, it seems like at least the AFT as a union is very heavily invested in limiting access to that tool—even where it doesn't seem necessary for the union to do that, such as in its internal negotiations with different locals, or such. That's what was less productive than that initial dance.

COLIN

To my mind, these questions and observations recall parts of the *Cosmonaut* interview between Marisa Miale, Kali Akuno, and Adam Ryan—labor organizers in the American South—who seem to open up similar questions in their shifting visions of communities continuously organizing themselves, while also explicitly reminding us of something that Spivak says about the efficacy of the general strike as a tactic. She says, like Rosa Luxemburg, we can perhaps claim that the citizen strike is no longer a step back towards the bourgeois revolution:

If, at the inauguration of the International, Marx had felt that workers should keep abreast of international politics and diplomacy enough to intervene, then at this moment of capitalism's sublation the citizen, the agent of the general strike redefined, must keep abreast of the laws regulating capital. It can, I think, be suggested that strikes have worked better against imperialism than they have specifically in the economic or political spheres.[4]

She goes on to use examples from Gandhi and others, basically saying that within the Marxist tradition, the definition of the general strike and what its aims are have undergone a number of reterritorializations. She makes the point that a general strike or some sort of international organizing can only be aimed at these larger systems, rather than any incrementalisms that prematurely limit themselves to the ersatz domains of politics or economics. This is interesting because a lot of the organizing I'm seeing in California—and even in the US in general around the rent strike—is a re-emergence of this thinking. Some people are really saying, "Go for it all; cancel it all; this is where you need to start even if we're not quite there yet."

The *Cosmonaut* interview with Southern organizers says exactly that: we're not ready for a general strike yet, but that's why we're saying on May Day we need to aim towards a general strike or to aspirationally move in that direction.[5] It seems to me that this is an example of having a feel for institutions, a feel for organizing and strategy that places its emphasis on explicitly trying to tackle a system more generally, rather than trying to secure momentary advantages like pushing Gavin Newsom to do something specific about putting a moratorium on rent until the shutdown stops. Because we're already seeing how that is a moving marker: states are already opening up, so as to kick people off unemployment, so that the evictions can happen.

ASMA

Our conversation has been gesturing toward questions of alignment in particular forms of organizing and action—and there are folks with whom we've been in discussion with who speak to the forms that labor power and its organizing takes in different spaces, and what the work can (or does) summon differently therein. I think we have really interesting examples of what converges around the notion of the "worker" or, on the other hand, what it cannot contain. These considerations also seem to return us to the issue of essence. And, from there on, to ask us to think of other political subjects of this crisis, and the summoning of new actors and agents.

DAN

It's partly just an amusing etymology, I suppose, but maybe there is something worth parsing here. In thinking about this word "essential," which has become such a pivot for discussions of labor during the pandemic, especially in terms of what work is "essential." What is essential is what is of the essence—essence referring to the question of being. So what work is of the being or of the existence itself of life or health? With the possibilities and enactments that we are seeing today across the world, utilizing that characterization is oddly ambiguous; the range of kinds of work or kinds of activity that can be enclosed within the idea of the "essential" makes plain that there's another question that is, "essential to whom?" This is inescapable, because it's also obvious that, in many cases the answer is just this: "essential to capital."

There's something to be made of "essential," and part of it is that our work is not meant for the sustenance of capital. Not only are we not doing it because it's essential to capital, but we're demanding what is essential to us. Maybe "essential," as characterizing a need, or what is necessary, or what cannot be done without, is a usage of the word that is so ingrained that we forget that where it comes from is about being itself. I'd like to hold in our minds that it goes with the word "essence," which is a silly word that calls attention to itself, and can remind us not to give up on the "essential" too easily.

As with housework, we believe that we must organize to demand not abstract claims to the means of production—commodified as symbols within capital's financial legal regime—but control of the means of production themselves.

Spivak's calls for organizing from sites of production, where symbolic abstractions can be overwritten by facts from the ground, seem right. We must, at the same time, create and occupy our own sufficiently abstract symbolic sites to cohere across the globe, across diverse materialities of production and across the breadth of memories and experiences bequeathed to us by the old order.

ASMA

Could we speak to the questions of debt and eviction even as we invoke the "striker" who is in debt, or who is a "resident" without a home? How could debt not be the lynchpin of this crisis (the role of credit in the presumptuous zombie immortality of capital is not new to those who read Marx)? Is the worker the only subject through which to invoke the relation between capital and labor? Or, the form in which the political actor or agent will be contained? If, in neoliberalism, the transition from industrial to finance capital signals an absencing of the worker, should the worker not at least be accompanied by the debtor in this fight? If only because one carries the erasure of the other?

How does the system understand and narrate itself as a supersession of something that went before? Even capital has, in its own head, transmogrified from a particular relationship to labor to this relationship to finance, and so I am thinking in terms of organizing principles and invocations. I do not trust that the question of finance and the question of labor will unify themselves and resuture themselves to each other politically (beyond simply relying on the fact that they exist together in history) without being compelled to. That has to be done in our conceptualization and action.

Dan, might I ask you to guide us through that terrain on which something like this might unfold? That of global debt maps, I mean.

DAN

Thinking back to previous acts, which make a clear case for how the conditions for the emergence of a virus like SARS-CoV-2 are the substance of a globalized capitalism that depends on precarity and pushes its most essential work to its most extreme margins: socially distanced but logistically integrated.

As we consider the question of strategy, we have an obligation to deconstruct Capital's tactics to reveal its most basic strategy and the ways that strategy is encoded into crisis intervention, most of which are yet to come. Two tactics I want to call attention to are the stimulus funds, which are structured as loans, and central bank money creation whose purpose is to deprive those same loans of economic substance.

When the continuity of debt payments is no longer a sure thing, when there is threat not to any particular contract but to debt in general, capital has a way of responding at a symbolic level. Stimulus-lending to prop up business was offered in the guise of loans, though already it was clear that many could not be paid back. But the guise matters: it means that though many debts in fact would not be honored, capital would not be asked to concede the legitimacy of debt in general, of the principle of profiting for the use of money, but only the payability of this or that specific contract.

Leftists are quick to critique the unprecedented mobilization of financial resources for bailouts at a time when neoliberal governments struggle to provide basic care. To be sure, the spectacle of banks paying dividends to shareholders at a time when they're benefiting from the easy issuance of central banks exposes the mechanistic, algorithmic dismemberment on which it has always been premised.

This tension can be recognized under the heading "wages for housework," which makes the response plain. We don't want wages for housework, we want to overturn the system of wages altogether. So far, economic relief has been offered as loans to "small businesses" and one-off cash payments to households. Next will be school vouchers, contact-tracing by Mike Bloomberg, and an educational system owned and operated by Zoom. Continuity, income or connection, each of these crisis concessions by capital asking us to confirm the overriding validity of money relations themselves: it asks us to confirm that we agree to pay.

Turning to organizing strategy, Universal Basic Income or Universal Health Care would be major reformist wins, to be sure, and if we can, we should take them and celebrate the victory. But neither one overturns the debt relationship: we would still be in a world where money, where debt and the ability to pay determines who can access what. The whole premise of a debt hinges on the less-than-humanity of the borrower and the more-than-humanity of the lender. All of capitalism's legal and financial systems are built to reify and sustain the form of that relationship, especially when it's called into question. When there's a possibility that a debt won't be paid—as many debts during this pandemic will not be paid—what's clear to capital is that what has to be defended is the principle that debts must be paid. Not the fact of any particular debts being paid, just the idea that that's what our debts are for, because to lose that would be an even harsher defeat for capital.

Some of the biggest numbers that you see, if you measure things by the scale of dollars involved, are central banks' allocations of the largest sums in a single move: they can lend one and a half trillion dollars in a couple weeks. I think we should remember the importance of that very technocratic institution with a misleading appearance of neutrality, while not failing to grab onto whatever material concessions might be offered along the way.

To link this reflection on organizing to the category of the worker, I think we should remain attentive to what we hear from the dispatches that people will be sharing today from various struggles that are underway, because my sense is that we're seeing a broadening of the idea that "we don't have to be in the category of the worker." There are lots of categories which are comparable, and understanding that the centrality of the money relationship can tie them together doesn't lend itself obviously or immediately to an organizing strategy, which maybe is a puzzle. One could see a form of organic resilience, an international struggle not organized around only one form of relation. But then the work of organizing is harder.

COLIN

Looking forward to the dispatches: one thing that might be interesting to look at would be the explicit international dimensions of collaboration and of organizing ways of being together. Even nine months ago, this involved thinking with and against supply chains in the global market. This strategy spawned promising achievements for international collaboration: strikes that happened in the ports of Oakland against companies that are supporting terrible policies in the West Bank really strike at capital in a way that it can comprehend.

Organizing together internationally has relinquished this emphasis on the supply chain (or that kind of technical strategic orientation) in favor of other things—and often this means centering conditions of empire that are continually present in the diverse experiences of global subjects at this moment. What those precise strategies might be, and how the question of relation takes shape against particular issues, as amplified by the pandemic, might be something that we have to hear for in the May Day Dispatches ahead.

Notes

1. Sabrina Orah Mark, "Fuck the Bread. The Bread Is Over.," The Paris Review, May 7, 2020, https://www.theparisreview.org/blog/2020/05/07/fuck-the-bread-the-bread-is-over/.

2. Mark, "Fuck the Bread."

3. Mark, "Fuck the Bread."

4. Gayatri Chakravorty Spivak, "General Strike," *Rethinking Marxism: A Journal of Economics Culture & Society*, 26:1 (2014): 9–14.

5. Marisa Miale, "Toward the Mass Strike: An Interview with Two Southern Organizers," Cosmonaut, April 29, 2020, accessed April 30, 2020, https://cosmonaut.blog/2020/04/29/toward-the-mass-strike-interview-with-two-southern-organizers/.

sixth interlude
WINDOWS
/
BREATH

DISPATCHES FROM WITHIN THE KNOT OF PANDEMIC FASCISM

Questions of relation, subject, essence, and the struggle to imagine a world unfettered by the scripts of strategy we have inherited from compromised institutions cannot be made any easier to negotiate prior to engagements with those that we hear ourselves thinking with, around, and amidst. It is impossible to work on any difficult question without inhabiting it. In this spirit, we invited our friends to share from within the specific sites of struggle they inhabit, immediately or as invested comrades, in the midst of the global pandemic and right-wing resurgence. Every dispatch identifies the sites being brought into contact in this reporting and witnessing. — Colin and Dan

Lebanon | Hudson Valley

Nathaniel Madison

This year in Lebanon, May Day was marked by the hunger of the country's poorest, who failed to receive crucial aid promised by the government. Even those with savings have been unable to access them recently, as the banks no longer allow them to withdraw foreign currency and limit the withdrawal of domestic currency to the equivalent of $200 USD, which is roughly three hundred thousand Lebanese pounds. Alongside this, little to nothing has been done to address the massive increase in food prices during the pandemic.

The prime minister Hassan Diab's response on May Day was to formally ask the IMF for aid, a move that provoked massive demonstrations outside of Central Bank branches across the country with cries of "Molotov instead of a candle" and "we will not pay the price."

Turkey | Little Rock

Safi Alsebai

May Day in Turkey is not only a commemoration of International Workers Day but the remembrance of the 1977 massacre of thirty-four labor demonstrators at Taksim Square. The past few years, however, have seen a ban on May Day demonstrations with the government citing "security concerns." No less this year, total lockdowns are being posted this week in Istanbul and thirty-one Turkish provinces as the government attempts to reign in outbreaks of COVID-19.

Nevertheless, the reign over labor and production is not on lockdown as factory and care workers in many sectors are still required to go to work with minimal or no protections and ever-dropping wages. This year, against this double ban, members of the Confederation of Progressive Trade Unions, who have organized May Day demonstrations since 1976, attempted to lay wreaths at Taksim, leading to clashes with the police and the arrest of fifteen union members, including trade union leaders.

This comes on the heels of an attempted strike in February of 140,000 metalworkers, members of various metalworkers' unions, in a country where the government readily employs strike bans. This would have been one of many strikes by metal and auto workers since 2015, following the 2018 failed negotiations and rallies throughout the major sites of metal production throughout the country. The call of these rallies was "This is just the beginning, continue the struggle!" The 2019 strike, however, ended before it began, with leaders of two major unions signing agreements with bosses eschewing workers' demands and international calls of solidarity. Labor in Turkey may find new forms struggle from such beginnings: Elgin Kullu from the United Steel-Workers' Union notes that, while unions have been able to fight successful fights for their own members in the past, non-union and informal workers (including the growing number of Syrian refugees in the country) are, "trying to survive this under the fist of their bosses and the government."[1] Such heterogeneous landscapes of labor and political subjectivity in the country, alongside new stakes in the wake of the virus, will raise new questions of the unions to be fleshed out by next May Day.

Note

1. Filiz Gazi, "Turkish unions criticize gov't for neglecting workers' rights on May Day overshadowed by COVID-19," *Duvar English*, May 1, 2020, accessed on December 28, 2020.

Hong Kong | New Jersey

Ezra Lee

In Hong Kong, May Day demonstrations were limited after severe government censure. There were numerous small actions, but they were violently addressed by many riot police preemptively deployed across the city. In one such instance, nearly one hundred protesters were attacked for singing pro-democracy songs in a shopping mall. In another, labor leaders were fined for violating social distancing.

This is no surprise as the past few months saw a decrease in street demonstrations. Mass mobilizations in Hong Kong before the spread of COVID-19 have been funneled into intense labor organizing in the past few months, with the city seeing nearly fifty new unions formed in previously unorganized sectors. Many are optimistic about the expanding role of labor as a political force in Hong Kong as political calls in the electoral and regulatory spheres have greatly expanded since the movement slowed in January to contend with COVID-19, framing the pro-democracy protests as not only a struggle for independence but also against austerity.

San Diego | San Diego

Isabella Lee

An update from California: I went yesterday to a rent strike action. On April 1st, there was a notice to Governor Newsom that May 1st would commence a rent strike, and that the demands are the cancellation of rent and mortgages until the end of the crisis. It was really quite an experience to participate in an action from within your car. The action was about rent, and we were traveling through these different neighborhoods with our signs and honking, and families were coming out on their porches and raising their fists in solidarity. But we also saw differences in reactions based on the different socioeconomic positions of the neighborhoods.

So in a middle-class neighborhood, we had this one guy come out and pound on our car telling us to shut up because he was napping. I thought that was really interesting compared to pedestrian actions where you're on foot. In San Diego, you'd be downtown in front of the government buildings, but here you're traveling through neighborhoods and people are coming out of their houses as families and seeing this. The other crazy thing that happened was that we actually intersected with the "Re-open" protest. So coming up one street we were the rent strike demonstrators, and perpendicular came the reopen protesters who were waving their American flags and yelling at us. There wasn't really a confrontation other than a symbolic opposition happening.

Brazil | Oaxaca

Colin Eubank

Brazil spent most of the day celebrating a May Day coalition event. They called for the ousting of Jair Bolsonaro by way of an early special election. However, the most interesting development about May Day actions in Brazil was the decision by union leaders to invite neoliberal politicians to the May Day coalition-building event: politicos that have announced their opposition to Bolsonaro and look a lot like some of the establishment Democrats in the US. It seems that they're gearing up for a power grab—folks like the governor of Rio de Janeiro, the governor of the state of São Paulo, and the conservative president of the Chamber of Deputies. What ensued was that half of the event broke off the intended platform (ousting Bolsonaro) and basically started having conversations about why it's important to build a united labor front or a coalition that puts the interests of workers at the front of its movement rather than simply opposing Bolsonaro.

Mexico | Oaxaca

Colin Eubank

Here in Mexico, the Communist Party had a day-long conference of international solidarity on the themes of health, bread, and labor. The most interesting developments in the country yesterday were the continuation of wildcat strikes in maquiladora factories that are happening close to the northern border. These US factories located in Mexico have continued to produce, despite the national order to cease non-essential production.

We see an interesting tension or dynamic about different definitions of essential labor: on the one hand, the US says that military production in these factories is essential and the Mexican workers need to show up. The Mexican government, on the other hand, says it's not essential, but at the same time austerity policies won't actually stop the US because they want the business, they want the money. The US military factories in Mexico also sometimes produce components for medical supplies, so the question about the nature of essential production shifts and contradicts itself within its own rhetorics. Are these factories essential because weaponry is essential, because of the components that could contribute to the creation of medical equipment which comes out of certain sectors of these factories, or does it really matter at all?

The day before May Day itself, there was a report released by the Maquila Solidarity Network about the maquiladora factory workers in order to publicize the conditions faced in these spaces, and to provide a kind of chain of information to see what factory workers are doing—who's striking, what approaches have been effective, how they've been able to secure health supplies in the workplace (and if that is even remotely a viable option for adding to worker safety). Right now, only about 30% of maquiladoras are shut down.

In Southern Mexico, folks have been focusing more on small May Day actions. There was a call in Oaxaca to do things under quarantine that would be supporting the cause of labor, such as organizing something in your community, teaching your friends and family that you share quarantine with about the history of the labor movement in Mexico and internationally, as well as studying what can be done in your little town and community during a time of increased surveillance and militarized control that could be helpful for other people.

Karachi | Karachi

Zahabia Khuzema

There are more than 19,000 Corona cases in Pakistan and there are more than 400 deaths thus far. The working-class makes up 80% of Pakistan's population, approximately 65.2 million workers form the labor force here and so far 21 million workers have lost their jobs on a permanent or arbitrary basis, out of which 9.3 million are women. The ones who haven't been laid off are facing severe pay cuts. The government has launched a program which will be providing monetary relief of 3,000 rupees (approximately $18.8 USD) to working class families for 4 months, which is terribly insufficient. In fact, instead of providing relief to the working class, the government is providing relief to businessmen and industrialists. The government has failed to provide equipment to doctors and nurses treating coronavirus patients. There's a huge shortage of Personal Protection Equipment (PPE) for healthcare workers, ventilators, and other equipment required in the hospitals. But, instead of fulfilling this need, the government is harassing the doctors and nurses that are protesting and demanding this equipment. Strikes have coalesced in several cities, be it YDA in Quetta, or young doctors and nurses who are protesting in Lahore and have even gone on a hunger strike. With 65% of female workers being laid off, there are many reports of increased domestic violence.

The strategy we—by "we" I mean some leftist organizations here—are working with is forming a united front which will bring different leftist organizations, trade unions, and associations together and organize a joint action. We are working on giving a call to committees that will be formed at workplaces and in different areas. We believe that we cannot have a reformist approach become a tripartite approach.

We are working on workers' health and safety because a lot of the janitorial staff at hospitals and at different health facilities are not given PPEs or other protective gear. That is one of our demands. Another demand is that the government must open its health accounts. The government is working toward the privatization of hospitals, so they're not doing this directly but they've introduced this MIT act according to which there will be a Board of Governors in hospitals who will work as an autonomous body, and they will make whatever decisions they like. Another demand is enforcement of existing labor laws. Housing remains a big problem and unsolved question in Karachi. Recently, the areas of these informal settlements were being evicted, and I was also involved in organizing the residents of those areas. That has stopped for now because of the lockdown. We are moving towards demanding electricity, water, and gas for all, three basic requirements to live. We are trying to introduce laws on patriarchal and domestic violence. Agricultural reforms focused on the nationalization of land have taken the form of a demand that

50 acres or more land should be distributed among small farmers and landless agricultural labor and peasants. We are also demanding the abolition of that contract-based employment, which squeezes many workers, in favor of permanent employment. We seek legal insurance for basic income. People were saying that these workers should get at least 30,000 rupees per month as relief, but then if that doesn't happen there should be legal insurance for them. There should also be a ration system; they should be provided food by the government. So yes, these are some of our basic demands.

Italy | Italy

Renata Summo-O'Connell

I'm Renata Summo-O'Connell. I'm responsible for the Artegiro Contemporary Art, which is a project of a small organization called AILAE that works in a cultural context, and I'm based in Italy. In the European context, I would say that Italy has gotten rather interesting treatment lately as a country, particularly by the Netherlands. And although it has been quite difficult to even discuss these matters in the current lockdown atmosphere, we all anticipate that there will be big repercussions of the current crisis on cultural life and organizations.

I am talking very much from the point of view of contemporary art, and what many people feel is that this enormous beast which has become the art market is collapsing. As a project, Artegiro Contemporary Art has never been in the art market of course. We've been against the art market, and we've tried to question and redefine it. Today it certainly is collapsing, but it's doing so with a lot of creaks and bangs, and it's quite painful to watch and difficult to predict what's going to happen. I don't want to present an apocalyptic vision, but it is quite interesting to observe that before any discussion or analysis, there's constantly money being offered or promised.

For example, the first thing offered to businesses were bank loans endorsed by the government. Businesses had to present an enormous array of paperwork, making it practically impossible for anyone to actually apply for these loans or any other sort of help that has been put forward to citizens. I'm sure in the United States you are in a very difficult situation at the moment, so you can relate to what's happening here, where anything that has been promised seems to be unattainable. It's a very filtered discussion, and people are really quite lost. Today, I heard that a historic business in Venice will simply close after over a century. And despite the gravity of the situation, symbolised by this example, there is a cloud that filters everything.

From an art point of view, we couldn't be happier that the whole disastrous system falls through in a disgraceful way ultimately, because it's never had anything to do with art. Frankly, nobody's shedding any tears about that. However, at the same time, we do have musicians, performers, painters, photographers who can't move about, and they won't be able to move about for a very long time. As much as we don't want to endorse the big art markets, at the same time any other avenue seems to be very restricted, as this particular government has marked culture as the very last of their priorities. It is indeed a dramatic situation.

I really think that people who work in the arts or within the art world—at least some of us—are experiencing at present an intense and new degree of connection to one another that is relevant. This is a viral time, a moment in which we are connected, beyond the previous rhetorics: in this time we are connected for real, encompassing multiple levels of survival, co-existence, co-thinking—an unprecedented reciprocity.

I think that, in the past, the intellectual, ethical flirting has taken place between artists and the so-called art world, with double and at times triple standards. That has really been very difficult to navigate for the actual players as well as for the by-standers. The fact that many of us, and Artegiro in particular, had taken distance from all that, was considered either an unwillingness to have a say, or simply a convenient way to cut us out of the main game. So, over the years, we had to wait for somebody to give us some form of agency. We had to wait for somebody to give us an arena where we could be heard. When this happened some time ago, we started to gain some sort of ability to say something. The dynamics of it are questionable and should be discussed further, but it should be highlighted that coherence does pay off and a lack of compromise may eventually clear the path for more effective action.

As far as the art world notion is concerned, I really would like both that world as well as the notion of the "art world" to disappear, to implode somehow, because I think that over time it has written an incredibly upsetting and difficult story. First of all it has hijacked art, and that's highly upsetting to me. It has possessed it. It has enveloped it in a fabricated bubble that should be pulled apart. By creating the world we see today—what is commonly considered the art world of big art fairs, big art markets, biennials, and faraonic events—a mechanism of monopolium has been applied and its promises have been fulfilled.

Listening to voices from struggles we are situated amidst and alongside, we continue thinking about how the routes we use to navigate our questions of relation, subject, knowledge, sociality, institutionality, themselves reflect the needs we as subjects have that keep us from imagining different answers to the questions we pose. Stories and dispatches skipping and hopping between global north and south, metropole and colony, the colonies of the not-yet-self-determined and the always-already-overly-determined post-colonies, cohabit with each other in different and complicated ways that are rich with tools that might be shared, but only if we know what to ask for and what we're hoping for it to address. — Colin

South Asian Peninsula | Karachi

Sami Chohan

I belong to a community of inexplicably optimistic individuals who knowingly interact with the spatial, and unknowingly interact with the mutually-dependent social, economic, and environmental conditions with which the spatial, too, shares a symbiotic relationship, and in which both human and non-human life struggles to occur. I am an architect—and I am based in Karachi, one of the many uneven cities of the South Asian peninsula. What follows is just another call for change.

Since the COVID-19 outbreak, architecture communities around the world have suddenly experienced a moment of great revelation. This epiphany has already inspired a string of webinars and articles centered on the role of the built and the open in response to both under-pandemic and post-pandemic scenarios, not to mention the many international design competitions, one of them titled Pandemic Architecture.1 The focus is entirely on cities, because the urban is where the majority of the global population now resides, and perhaps also because architects have traditionally seen little or no value in non-urban development. Discussions are underway on how we should now look to design and construct our buildings—from residential to educational, institutional to assembly, business to mercantile. Spatial domains between and around buildings have been of much interest as well with discussions suddenly shifting from fostering social interactions in urban open spaces for public use to maintaining social distancing in them.

The South Asian architecture community is also participating in this global discourse, or at least trying very hard to. With design and construction activities momentarily coming to a halt in the major cities of India, Pakistan, and Bangladesh during city-wide lockdowns, architects here seem to have discovered some room to think about their responsibilities in times of crises, almost as if this pandemic is the first and only catastrophe to have ever struck cities like Delhi, Mumbai, Dhaka, Karachi, Calcutta, Lahore, Bangalore and Chennai, all of which now qualify as mega-cities with populations of more than 10 million people.2 Delhi, Mumbai, and Dhaka, in fact, qualify as meta-cities with populations exceeding 20 million. In the last two decades, the populations of these cities have been growing at an alarming pace with millions migrating from rural areas to urban centers in search of employment and livelihood.

Much of this transition can be attributed to neoliberal policies which since adoption in the 1980s have considerably weakened the public sector which in turn has reduced agricultural protection and infrastructure building in the region's massive rural sphere, leaving its massive agricultural community with no option but to migrate to urban centers.3 But, a weakened public sector also meant that urban centers themselves were in no position whatsoever to meet the most essential needs of this rapid influx: housing and employment. It is, therefore, in these cities that we now find millions with no access to formal affordable housing and formal employment opportunities. It is here that we find the majority living in highly dense and overcrowded informal settlements with substandard constructions and little or no access to proper sanitation and clean water. It is here that we find the majority working in informal economies, mainly engaged in informal retail, service, manufacturing, transportation and construction sectors.

In Karachi, Pakistan's largest city with almost 16 million inhabitants, for instance, around 60 percent of the population lives in informal settlements and around 70 percent of the city's urban workforce is involved in informal economic activities.4 Be it Karachi in Pakistan, Dhaka in Bangladesh, or Mumbai in India, these settlements and economies remain largely unprotected, unrepresented and unrecognized, for which reason they remain in constant fear of eviction and harassment by "public" administrators operating under direct influence of the elite or that small group of people with disproportionate amount of wealth, privilege and political clout. These residents and workers are visible on the one hand and invisible on the other. These are the marginalized, the disenfranchised, and the poor. These are the urban subaltern. But these are also real people who live and work in real social, economic, environmental, and hence spatial crises.

Wait, did we as architects not know that? How can we not? These are the same real people who power the construction industry and at the same time remain exploited by it. Are we for real? How lost must we be in our activities and accomplishments on that end of the spectrum of spatial perspectives produced by the neoliberal agenda? The end that places the imagined over the actual, the pedagogic over the performative. The end that considers urban informality an eye sore and remains hell-bent on turning our cities into global urban spectacles by constantly displacing and veiling our subaltern populations. The same populations that support the formal sector and make significant contributions to both local and national economies.

Needless to say, the pandemic is not the first and only crisis where we are. But perhaps it is an unprecedented crisis for architects since it has come in the way of those commissions we seek and dream of, like the Antilia, a 27-storey private home owned by billionaire Mukesh Ambani, which Gyan Prakash refers to as a gated community in the sky and a reflection of how the rich are turning their faces away from the city.5 This 173 meter-high, single-family residence towers above the urban fabric of Mumbai and looks down on the many informal settlements of the city. One of these settlements is the Dharavi, which first came into existence under British colonization of the Indian Subcontinent.6 It was during the Bombay Plague of 1896 when the self-righteous invaders began to expel polluting industries and undesirable residents from the city center to a sparsely populated neighboring island. This island soon became home for every distressed rural migrant heading towards Mumbai. Today, 73 years since independence, it sits in the heart of Mumbai as one of the largest slums in the world with a tightly packed population of about 1 million residents.7 It has experienced a long history of fatal epidemics, fires and floods, over and over again, before reporting its first case of COVID-19 in April this year.8 Enough said.

It makes complete sense for architecture communities that demonstrate strong notions of spatial justice and the right to the city to engage in discussions on the role of architecture and the responsibilities of architects in times of such a global health and socio-economic crisis. But, if there is anything to be discussed here by architecture communities such as ours which for decades have knowingly and unknowingly remained complicit in our growing urban crises, it should be our priorities, values and ethics. If it is indeed the spatial that we deal with, then our first and foremost responsibility should be to address the widespread spatial injustice that plagues our cities today. Where we do find formidable challenges, we may also find insurmountable opportunities—and it is precisely at this juncture that we can come together to initiate alternative forms of spatial practices and spatial productions that exist on the opposing end of that same spectrum of spatial perspectives—the end where architects understand limitations, discover prospects, and collaborate with public administrators, policy-makers, civil societies and organizations, and most importantly local communities to arrive at spatial solutions that foster social equity, economic empowerment and environmental protection—the end that keeps cooperation over competition, people over profit.

Notes

1.   Archisearch.Gr, "Open Call—Pandemic Architecture International Ideas Competition," Press Release, March 16, 2020, https://www.archisearch.gr/architecture/open-call-pandemic-architecture-international-ideas-competition/.

2.   United Nations, Department of Economic and Social Affairs, Popular Division, *The World's Cities in 2018: Data Booklet*, United Nations, 2018, https://doi.org/10.18356/c93f4dc6-en.

3.   ESRI. (n.d.), *21st Century Urbanism: Capitalism and Urban Form*, ArcGIS StoryMaps, https://www.arcgis.com/apps/MapJournal/index.html?appid=9def17048f214e2089c65f0d4c449889.

4.   Arif Hasan, "Emerging urbanisation trends: The case of Karachi," International Growth Centre, May 16, 2016. https://www.theigc.org/wp-content/uploads/2016/12/Hasan-2016-Academic-Paper.pdf

5.   Jim Yardley, "Soaring Above India's Poverty, a 27-Story Home," *The New York Times*, October 29, 2010. https://www.nytimes.com/2010/10/29/world/asia/29mumbai.html.

6.   Aparna Bhat, "Dharavi, India is more than Asia's largest slum," *Culture Trip*, November 13, 2017. https://theculturetrip.com/asia/india/articles/dharavi-more-than-asias-largest-slum/.

7.   Habitat for Humanity GB, "The World's Largest Slums: Dharavi, Kibera, Khayelitsha & Neza," *Habitat for Humanity*, September 7, 2018, https://www.habitatforhumanity.org.uk/blog/2017/12/the-worlds-largest-slums-dharavi-kibera-khayelitsha-neza/.

8.   Sahil Joshi, "First coronavirus case reported from Mumbai's Dharavi slum," *India Today*, April 1, 2020, https://www.indiatoday.in/india/story/first-coronavirus-positive-case-reported-from-dharavi-in-mumbai-1662265-2020-04-01.

Karachi | Karachi
Tracing Feeling
Yashfeen Talpur

The strangest, most novel historical moment to have been experienced yet by those living through it, one markedly defined by separation and distance, was actually commemorated in Pakistan by thousands of marchers coming together to, one could say, defend the right to life. With the Aurat March being organised for just the third consecutive year in a row, it's difficult to say which moment commemorated the other, or whether commemoration was the only way the two events addressed each other. It was perhaps just the slightest degree of novelty then, however naïve, that somehow put the outbreak one step ahead of the March. Despite the two coming together seemingly at odds with each other, both events carried with themselves lingering histories of discontent into the present. Some having been brought painstakingly to the surface as recently as three years ago, marked by at least some repetition and familiarity; others entirely newer in the sense of how they registered on one's psyche—while still being constructed underneath the surface by feelings of unrest that looked all too familiar, too repetitious. The registration of this newness made for the strangest response, unable to fit into previously given categories of lamenting, anger, and outcry.

I remember easing into isolation, which is only to say that it was gradual and turned up quietly. The (dis)allowances that make such an introduction possible are not lost on me; it takes a degree of proximity to habitual slowing down, and even locking down, that makes room for these periods of adjustment. As the second week of February came to a close, a toxic gas leak in the Kemari Port area in Karachi, a little ways away from my university, led to a scattered shutting down of schools. This halt was not meant to last too long. Downstairs at the canteen, we sat on a bench under a tree, some of us scrolling down and further down, placing all possible narratives and ruminations about the virus on the table, others choosing to be recipients who could pick and choose until definitive mandated action made it a little more real. There is an uncanniness here waiting to be pointed out, shared by the absence of visual aid that marks sickness, death, and the bodies that are (un)marked by this contamination. While 7 people died of the gas leak, we all covered our noses trying to ascertain whether the headache was a regularache or a specialache.

Timing and fate were clearly not the only things that organized these two events together in the space of each other. When a spectacle or occasion is imagined as one of the gateways to altering the material realities of the oppressed—with the hopes that an enactment and demonstration will jolt one out of a spell of apathy, and as a ripple effect destabilize state-maintained sentiments about the status quo~ one becomes skeptical about certain allowances by the state. This year, organizers for the Aurat March were able to, for the first time since its initiation in 2018, officially enlist the help of the Sindh Police unit to provide security for the demonstrators. In extension, securing the right to defend.

This same force that was called in to protect demonstrators in March, whether they were able to show up or not, was the one acting as state apparatus just a month later, to punish and publicly humiliate those they saw trespassing the rules of the lockdown as a display of law enforcement; to warn, scare and make an example of. The bodies on the receiving end of such public humiliation were not marked by the virus itself, owing to the asymptomatic condition of its make-up, but were rather marked by material conditions indicative of a daily wage laborer, markers and conditions that place certain bodies in closer proximity to the virus than others, bodies eventually made to carry the burden of contagion. The question this asks is not what kind of failures are embedded within the expectation that a mirroring of feeling will produce solidarity, but questions rather the ways in which the same feeling of unrest is managed by the state to produce different results at different levels of the hierarchical ladder. It's a question of what kind of acknowledgement or registration of feeling threatened goes amiss, and why, that barely allows for demonstrations such as Aurat March to proceed, but does not stop the state from placing the burden of contagion, over and over again on those it renders expendable.

My younger sister was meant to join me at the march. In the days leading up to it, we largely kept hidden our desire to show up, at the very least. In the outburst of confrontation that followed at the last moment, however, just as we were ready to leave, I was asked over and over again about the "use" or "purpose" of participating in such a demonstration. Receipts. The exchange ended with a clear enactment of harm and violence on my person; heaving and panting through harder questions of why so many pairs of eyes scan me up and down when I step outside, why the most casual reports of femicide show up on t.v. every day, and all other kinds of harsh violences stored not in the mind but alive on the body, and easier to access, no matter how harmful the enactment in the way it does not guarantee being heard.

Later, when it's month five into immobility and disintegrating structures of feeling surround us like smoke in the air, my sister and I develop a codeword for being able to withdraw from enacting grief in order to prove its presence. We periodically say the words "not looking" and continue sharing silence.

Guyana | Baltimore

Christopher Carrico

I have been thinking about my discomfort, uncomfortable with how universalized the narrative, of neoliberalism as the throughline for the international left's discussion of the world economy, has become. What drops out of the picture because it doesn't fit the narrative? And how does the real difficulty of questions of internationalism and solidarity get obscured when we accept the universalized narrative as "good enough" at connecting the Global North and South?

James Ferguson brings up a few of these in his book *Give a Man a Fish* (Duke University Press, 2015). There are a number of ways in which his analysis is problematic, but he is correct to note that there are many places which have expanded certain kinds of social spending. Whether or not we could call these "welfarist" is debatable, but there has been a proliferation of experiments with programs like conditional cash transfers and basic income schemes, for instance in parts of Latin America, or the region of Ferguson's fieldwork, Southern Africa. These kinds of programs are now discussed, and pilot programs have been implemented in Europe and North America. Their appeal seems to have only increased during the economic crises in the wake of Coronavirus.

Debate about conditional cash transfers, in particular, has entered into the conversation in Guyana, where I did fieldwork and lived for about 7 years. During the last 5 years, ExxonMobil workers discovered a number of offshore oil deposits, and began production last year. Guyana now has around 6 billion barrels of known oil reserves, and the estimates suggest that this could bring something like $170 billion in royalties to the country. The implications are huge for a country that has only around 780,000 people and currently has one of the lower per capita incomes in the Western Hemisphere. Understandably, before even a single barrel of oil was extracted, there were elaborate proposals about what the government of Guyana should do with the royalties.

Meanwhile, the Oil Curse wasted no time in coming to Guyana. Around a year before any oil drilling even began, there was a vote of no-confidence in Guyanese parliament, which meant new elections were required by law. The ruling party delayed this with legal challenges and other stalling tactics for over a year, but March 2 of this year new elections were finally held. Once the votes were counted and showed a ruling party victory, the opposition accused the ruling party of rigging the elections. The courts ordered a recount, and the recount showed the opposition party winning. Only now the ruling party accused the opposition party of stuffing the ballot boxes. With several months of back-and-forth in the courts, including the regional Caribbean Court of Justice, it remains unclear what will happen when all of the legal challenges have been exhausted. Neither party seems like it will be willing to concede. Meanwhile, Western powers are pressuring the ruling government to step down, threatening sanctions if the government refuses to comply.

I won't get into the entire long and complicated history of UK and US interference in Guyana's elections, but it seems important to note that the US always ends up being opposed to whomever is in power. While we can clearly understand US involvement in today's dispute as being motivated by Exxon (a U.S. corporation) having billions of dollars of oil revenue on the line, the US position on Guyana's internal affairs is also shaped by Guyana's relationship with Cuba and Venezuela. Both major parties have had good relationships with Cuba when they have been in power. And while there is an age-old border dispute with Venezuela, neither party has wanted to take an aggressive stance against its neighbor. One of the reasons that Guyana has historically had a good relationship with Cuba is that both major parties have common roots in the socialist tradition. The opposition People's Progressive Party still declares itself Marxist-Leninist in its party constitution, though there isn't much that is visibly socialist about its policy positions today.

Where should an internationalist leftist stand in solidarity with the people of Guyana in a situation like this? International sanctions would be a tragedy for everyone involved, yet the leader of the People's Progressive Party has called for sanctions if the ruling party doesn't step down. Guyanese workers are organized into trade unions that break down neatly along party lines. They do not stand in solidarity with one another along class lines, but rather in solidarity with parties whose support is largely divided along racial/ethnic lines. And, the parties today might be socialist in name but really have no ideology other than themselves in power.

In the West Indies, there's this phrase "crabs in a barrel." Everybody is just trying to climb on top of everybody else, and tearing each other apart, fighting to get out of the pot, not recognizing that everyone is dying in there. It's cut-throat politics and, in the end, there are no winners.

In spite of the promise of oil money, it seems to me that the current moment is potentially even bleaker than it was at the height of the People's National Congress' authoritarian socialism of the 1970s. I say this because even in those days of rigged elections, and party paramountcy, and a cult of personality around Forbes Burnham (who was first Prime Minister, then President), Guyana's government still had an internationalist vision, was committed to the Non-Aligned Movement, and the people in power had a vision of a co-operative republic. The state and co-operative sector would control the commanding heights of the economy, there would be a universal program of national service. The country would be committed to meeting basic needs. Education emphasized solidarity, there was a conscious effort to build a General Will. People addressed each other as "comrade."

In contrast, the values that dominate today are the individualist egoism of the market and civil society. There is no conscious effort on the part of any of the mainstream politicians to be about anything other than their own self-aggrandizement. Any leader who actively calls for sanctions to be brought against his own country clearly does not care at all for the welfare of its ordinary citizens. They actively seek to undermine anything like real solidarity, of the working class or of the nation. And, while they may still have memberships in international institutions that once meant something, this internationalism is today a hollow and empty formalism.

Chile | Oaxaca

Colin Eubank

Last October, in Chile, the neoliberal order was shaken by a popular revolt and organizing that has continued amidst the pandemic. The ongoing uprising in Chile started in October 2019, which was sparked by a student protest of 3% Metro fare increase, and which quickly grew to a mass revolt against the entire market model of the neoliberal enterprise that has dominated Chile since its introduction under the Pinochet regime. While the main participants are young students and the chronically underemployed working class, the continuous force behind "the explosion" has grown through the intensification of diverse movements that share power and maintain pressure against governmental forces, which have sprouted up in virtually every neighborhood in the country and are even expanding internationally amongst Chilean expats. Although differing in approach and emphasis, these councils highlight continuity between the Pinochet era and neoliberal dictatorship of the 1970s; virtually every policy which reinforces the mass inequality, sweeping privatization, economic austerity policies, and hyper-militarization of the state.

Chile has been the epicenter of the international feminist movement in Latin America, wherein millions took to the streets of major cities on the March 8 and 9. For May Day, for instance, the internationalist committee of the March 8 Feminist Collective announced a call for the creation of a feminist organization of workers, intended as a space for women and gender non-conforming workers—whether unionized or non-unionized, waged, unwaged, formal or currently unemployed—to be able to collaborate in solidarity and unified action. It comes as a response to the feeling of dissatisfaction with the traditional roles unions have played amid organizing the left during the popular revolt and especially their incapacity to effectively agitate for the transformation of all aspects of society in combating misogynist violence and patriarchy.

The significance of the intervening years, according to the narrative of the ongoing protests, is that the center, the left, unionists and former Allende era socialists have actively contributed to (or at least remain terribly complicit in) the maintenance of Chile as a playground for these free-market fantasies. A broad initiative known as Unidad Sociales, comprised of the feminist March 8 collective, ecological movements, the NO+AFP anti-austerity group, and a segment of labor represented by the C.U.T., had been vital in pressuring governmental forces to back down during the state of emergency. Embracing a feminist platform in the worker's movement, for instance, is something that the Chileans see as absolutely essential for any kind of internationalism. To celebrate this on May Day, the feminist organization of labor held a 12-hour digital conference, where folks discussed feminist imperatives for labor and organizing as well as publicizing and sharing strategies for what they call an international feminist emergency plan to combat misogynist violence and contribute to the development of an international feminist general strike during the pandemic.

It's interesting to note that left political parties and trade unions seem to have played no major part in the intensification of "the explosion." Many have even heavily procrastinated when they did eventually decide to execute solidarity strikes. They, importantly, thwarted a call for a general strike attempted by the mass protests, and have tried to moderate the "vulgar" calls for the President's immediate resignation, instead suggesting that the route of impeachment is the more politically efficacious street to walk down.

Many cabildos and street protests have used the authoritarian posture of the state's response to the popular explosion—in the form of the state's murder and maiming of protesters, increased militarization of public space, and the states' continued adherence to Pinochet's constitution—as evidence to support their demand that the current Chilean president Pinera evacuate office immediately. It's vital to note that the government has taken it upon itself to announce the decision to hold a referendum to undergo a constitutional convention. (Just a brief note here that the referendum was originally scheduled for April 26, but with COVID-19 it's been rescheduled for October.)

While some protesters believe that it could be a good thing to revise the Constitution if the communities are involved in the process, all are adamant that the referendum and subsequent constitutional convention has never been an objective for the "explosion." Similar mass revolts in opposition to neoliberal governments are currently unfolding in Iraq, Iran, and Lebanon. The knee-jerk decisions by those governments and Chile's, to opt for constitutional conventions or submit unsolicited confessions, are maneuvers worthy of study, especially as protesters now strain their voices to insist that this isn't, and never was, the goal of their mobilizations. The Chilean explosion's insistence on inhabiting a moment within a longer narrative of struggle might help warn us against the trap the Constitutional Convention represents as we try to turn away from the market and attempt to map politics differently.

Thank you, everyone. For now, just want to tie some ends together to bring forward to next week. From institutionality to historicity to politics has been our journey today—but we leave confronting an enormous task of having to extract unifying propositions, and shared legends for navigating through politics and building institutions fitting the subjects responding to these crises. From the elements highlighted in these accounts, the irreducibility of the difficulty even of comparativist work around what categories function and in what way is clear. An enormous normative task lies ahead, which requires more intricate maps and blueprints, but also cutting and folding land differently, new attempts at structuring sociality and institutionality as part of our falsework. — Asma

Who Cares About Care If Care Is The Alibi:
A Lamentation in 3 Fragments and 7 Songs (Part Three)

Bonaventure Soh Bejeng Ndikung

FRAGMENT 3

Letta Mbulu

To fight back is to be hopeful, and to hope is to be able to fight back. In 1978, while shit was going down in Apartheid South Africa, as Black South Africans were still recovering from the torture and murder of Steve Biko during police detention and interrogation the previous year, and as, in 1978, the Eastern Cape Attorney-General refused to prosecute the policemen responsible for his murder, South African artist Letta Mbulu released an album with the title "Letta." In 1978, the Apartheid regime ravaged and killed as the years before, with support from the South African Defence Force that was often mobilised to "neutralise" riots in the country, but also involved in foreign attacks like on Cassinga in Angola for Operation Reindeer. In the middle of these turmoils, Letta Mbulu released an incredibly moving and hope filled song titled "Buza (There is a light at the end of the tunnel)." The question is not really whether there was really light at the end of the tunnel, but the possibility of imagining light at the end of the tunnel. The impossibility of imagining that light is what leads to inertia. It is that possibility that makes people rise, despite all odds, despising all dangers, to go out and protest and fight for what is right and for justice.

A few days ago, on the way with my children to the protests against police violence, against racism, and for justice, after the brutal killing of Mr. George Floyd, we boarded an Uber. The driver, a Turkish immigrant in Berlin, immediate brought up the topic of the murder as we got into the car. He was so furious that he had foam around his mouth as he spoke. He said enough is enough and he was willing to fight. He went on to say that rich black people needed to create an army to fight back, and when I said I wasn't sure if more violence was the solution, he replied that if violence is the only language your opponent understands then you must speak that language. In the past days, I have seen so much indignation as I have never seen in my lifetime. Indignation and solidarity. People that would normally stay under the comforts of their duvet are suddenly coming out and expressing their deep resentment towards the deep racist situation of the world today. To say the least, and I sure might be wrong, I have a feeling of seeing light at the end of the tunnel. But it can't be wrong to be hopeful, as to be unhopeful is to rot in apathy, in oscitancy. I have often written about a conversation I once watched between Noam Chomsky and Harry Belafonte, with whom Letta Mbulu and her husband the great musician and composer Caiphus Semenya worked with while on exile from South Africa in the USA.

Anyways, in that conversation, which was about the dilapidated state of the world, Chomsky, rightly so, lamented, as we say "till thy kingdom come." He sounded pessimistic and seemed to be giving up on the world. At the end of the conversation, Belafonte, who at the time was already in his 90s, said something like he can't afford to give up, and he was willing, in his 90s, to pick up a weapon and fight. I think you can say that if you can imagine that there must be light at the end of the tunnel. That sounded to me like Letta Mbulu's "Buza (There is a light at the end of the tunnel)."

Song 4[1]

The next song I would like to introduce on this album is "I need you." It is easily one of the most beautiful love declarations.

Song 5[2]

Mbulu's voice is full of majesty and still twists towards melancholia as she sings "I need you, I love you!" One hears the brilliance of Semenya's musical writing and arrangement, and exquisitely brought to life by Mbulu's singing and Paulinho Da Costa's percussions. In this day, this song seems to mean much more. There has been much talk about solidarity in the past months... be it towards our state of refugeeness, the COVID-19 crisis or the racist regimes that reign. "I need you" could easily go down as the anthem for this moment in which we need each other. Gone are the days where one could say I am fighting just against sexism, or just for the rights of the Anglophone people in Cameroon or the rights of the people in Western Sahara. It is the time to come together and fight for and with the oppressed peoples of the world. To declare that it is in the "I need you" that we find and exercise solidarity. To paraphrase Audre Lorde, there cannot be hierarchy in that space of the oppressed. And those who fall in the pool of the oppressors do also need to declare "I need you" to free themselves from their myths of superiority and exceptionalism and free themselves from their racist crosses they have been carrying for 500 years. It must be a heavy and shameful burden to carry for so long, especially knowing fully well that that cross is so heavy because it is a lie. And with every lie and every black and brown person killed, that cross becomes even heavier and crushing.

The story of one of South Africa's most important artists, Letta Mbulu, is a fascinating one that cannot be told in such a short writeup. But suffice it to say that since the age of 13 she has been in the music business, playing with a local band as much as touring around the world with the musical "King Kong," before leaving for the US on exile and working there with Makeba, Masekela, Gwangwa, Semenya, as well as touring with Cannonball Adderley and others. After Apartheid,

Mbulu and Semenya moved back to South Africa and continued their music careers. I recently heard that they have or are setting up a school for performing arts and music.

At any rate, there are two more songs on this "Letta" album that have blown my mind. They come from a very deep space and I thought it was worth writing something about them. Because of the language barrier, I reached out to my brother Tumi Mogorosi for a brief translation and context. We give thanks for the help @ tumimogorosi. The song is called "Hareje," a Southern Sesotho word that can be freely translated as "we will not eat." To go on hunger strike as a form of protest, in my opinion, is one of the most heartbreaking ways of expressing one's dissatisfaction towards a situation. I think this comes only when everything else has failed. I am of course thinking of the Istanbul band Grup Yorum, known for their protest songs against capitalism and imperialism, and for the Kurdish cause. In 2019 some of Grup Yorum's members went on hunger strike to protest the unfair treatments of the Turkish Government. In January 2020 two band members Bölek and Gökçek moved from hunger strike into a death fast, and in April and May 2020, Böle and Gökçek died after more than 288 days on hunger strike. The refusal to eat as a form of protest. This form of deprivation that Mbulu was singing about in the line "we will not eat until we are free," as the last way out for some individuals to raise pressure on the government that in 1978 was not only under pressure from the ANC and PAC from within but also from without as countries like South Korea ended diplomatic relations in protest of apartheid and the General Assembly of the UNO proclaimed 1978 as the International Anti-Apartheid Year. In "Hareje (Ha-Ree-Gee)," Mbulu does these long breath-searching howls and yodels. At some points it is a fight with herself before she is accompanied by a chorus. The base and the drums give the tone and frame for Mbulu's haunting singing. The exigencies are not taken away by the groove of the music:

Song 6[3]

"Mamani" is a beautiful soulful piece of music. Gentle. The guitar and whistling and the rattles and magnificent interventions of percussions. Mbulu's incredibly lamentations voice sings a praise for the young auntie. As @tumimogorosi puts it "in most cases (the younger sister of the mother) is close to the children and less strict than the mother which is mamani's elder sister. This word is interchangeable in various languages in S.A. and in this case it takes a TshiVenda language group. up while collecting lobster earlier in the afternoon.

Thinking of the nation-state set up by the Apartheid Government when Letta sings in a language of a rival nation-state or what colloquially was called Bantu Stand. She evokes a conceptual framework of struggle that the Black Consciousness foregrounds the unity of these different Bantu stands. Meaning all black people unite irrespective of ethnic divide or identity in the struggle against the Apartheid government. Letta sounds as if pleading with her favorite aunt." What else to say, especially now?! Listen for yourselves...

Song 7[4]

Notes

1. Letta Mbulu, "Buza (There's A Light At The End Of A Tunnel)," 1978, track 2 on Letta, A&M Records, vinyl LP, https://www.youtube.com/watch?v=Hjg0Els927Q&list=OLAK5uy_mJMOx_Szux-FKfoW_mhhMI74ydeFKdeYKI.

2. Letta Mbulu, "I Need You," 1978, track 3 on Letta, A&M Records, vinyl LP, https://www.youtube.com/watch?v=HanU4y_2aJM&list=OLAK5uy_mJMOx_SzuxFKfoW_mhhMI74ydeFKdeYKI&index=3.

3. Letta Mbulu, "Hareje (Ha-Ree-Gee)," 1978, track 6 on Letta, A&M Records, vinyl LP, https://www.youtube.com/watch?v=a0jlkrF81Ps&list=OLAK5uy_mJMOx_SzuxFKfoW_mhhMI74ydeFKdeY-KI&index=6.

4. Letta Mbulu, "Mamani," 1978, track 7 on Letta, A&M Records, vinyl LP, https://www.youtube.com/watch?v=n6tADx_lrdo&list=OLAK5uy_mJMOx_SzuxFKfoW_mhhMI74ydeFKdeYKI&index=7.

"what would the world be without accomplices?"

Vianny Ruiz

Cazuela
an adaptation of the "stone soup" fable
Sean Brannock

Once upon a time, a pair of poor travelers were journeying far from home. While navigating a small boat along the coastline, a storm sweeps the boat far across the horizon and sets the travelers adrift for several days. At last the travelers make landfall on the small, arid island of Santa Catalina.

Having lost all their supplies to the stormy sea except a large clay cazuela cooking pot, the travelers decide to search for other forms of life on the island. Soon they encounter a small island village! Hungry and fatigued, the travelers hope for a bit of hospitality from these strangers. However, the villagers are unwilling to share food with the travelers. Suspicious of foreigners and worried about maintaining their own supplies during a particularly difficult season, the village greets the travelers coldly.

The travelers go to a stream and fill their clay cazuela with water, drop a large stone in it, and place it over a small fire they build near the shoreline. One of the villagers becomes curious and ventures down the beach and asks the travelers what they are doing. The travelers answer that they are making "stone soup," which tastes wonderful and which they would be delighted to share with the villager, although it is missing a bit of garnish, which would improve its flavor. The villager, excited to enjoy a share of the soup, remembers a brazilian pepper tree located near the village which could provide some flavor for the soup. Another villager walks by and inquires about the soup. The travelers again mention their stone soup which has yet to reach its full potential. Curious about this soup, the villager tells the travelers that she has some extra miners lettuce and bladderpod peas that she would gladly contribute to the soup. Soon a local fisherman makes his way over to the cazuela, explaining to the travelers that he heard a rumor about a delicious stew that was being cooked. The travelers tell the fisherman about their stone soup, and mention that its flavor goes really well with a bit of freshly caught fish. The fisherman offers an abalone he picked up while collecting lobster earlier in the afternoon.

Little by little, more villagers walk by to add ingredients they can spare. A few carrots, a couple extra potatoes, some nopales, a handful of beans and lentils, a whole onion, and a couple chilies are added to the cazuela as it simmers. Finally, the travelers announce that their cazuela is ready. Their announcement travels quickly and the village gathers for dinner on the beach. The stone, being inedible, is removed from the cazuela, and the villagers and travelers enjoy a delicious and nourishing cazuela filled with an array of flavorful ingredients.

As the sun passes over the horizon, together the travelers and the village folk talk and laugh late into the night. Although the travelers tricked the villagers into sharing their food, the villagers are thankful for such a flavorful meal which leaves everyone with full bellies, a smile on their face, and a new recipe to write in their cookbooks.

Reflection: This simple fable carries with it huge lessons. In creating a common goal, believing in the kindness of others, and being brave enough to share oneself, we can create beyond our simple means. Together we achieve more, with each contribution providing new lessons and flavors for our shared product. — Sean Brannock

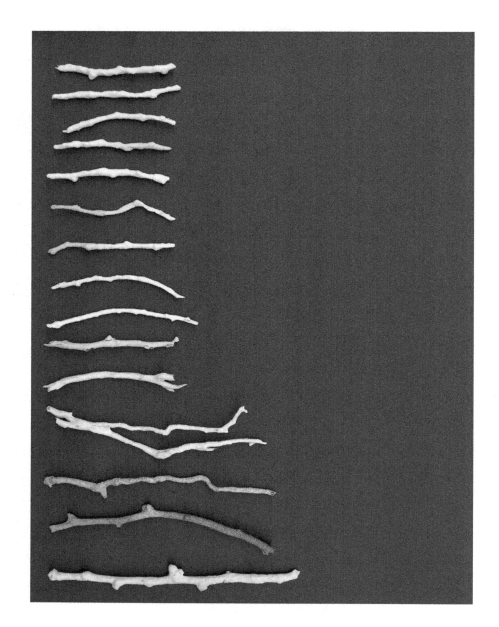

Sadia Salim, *A Roaming Aesthetic VII*

seventh dialogue

FALSEWORK
FUTURES

16 May 2020

Companion Texts for Studio Session

Duhalde, David. "Our Revolution Failed to Live Up to Its Potential. But the Bernie Movement Needs a Mass Organization Now." *Jacobin*, April 28, 2020. https://www.jacobinmag.com/2020/04/our-revolution-bernie-sanders

Frank, Thomas. "The Pessimistic Style in American Politics." *Harper's Magazine*, May 2020. https://harpers.org/archive/2020/05/how-the-anti-populists-stopped-bernie-sanders/

Fontaine, Joëlle. "How Churchill Crushed Greece's Anti-Fascist Resistance." *Tribune.* May 8, 2020. https://tribunemag.co.uk/2020/05/how-churchill-crushed-greeces-anti-fascist-resistance

Loach, Ken, dir. *Land and Freedom.* 1995; United Kingdom: Gramercy Pictures. DVD.

Morris, William. "The Day Is Coming." In *Poems by the Way & Love Is Enough.* New York: Longmans, Green, and Co., 1896.

Subcomandante Marcos. "Teachers Are a Mirror and Window: Closing Session of the 'Democratic Teachers and Zapatista Dream' Encuentro." *Zapatista Army of National Liberation,* August 1, 1999. http://www.struggle.ws/mexico/ezln/1999/marcos_teachers_close_aug.html.

Subcomandante Marcos. "Who Should Ask for Pardon and Who Can Grant It?." In *Our Word Is Our Weapon.* New York: Seven Stories Press, 2002.

Zapatista Army of National Liberation. "Sixth Declaration of the Selva Lacandona." *Mexico: Clandestine Revolutionary Indigenous Committee – General Command of the Zapatista Army of National Liberation,* June, 2005. https://enlacezapatista.ezln.org.mx/sdsl-en/.

Hosts | Asma Abbas, Colin Eubank, Nathaniel Madison

Speakers | Asma Abbas, Colin Eubank, Marvin González, Ezra Lee, Gabriel Salgado, Nathaniel Madison, Philip Zorba, Sara Mugridge

Scribes & Annotators | Asma Abbas, Safi Alsebai, Ari Fogelson, Sanya Hussain, Ezra Lee, Nathaniel Madison

ASMA

Welcome, all of you, for the last session in our Saturday Studio conversations. We began nine weeks ago, thinking of a lot of things that would get really bad as we went through these days, thinking that maybe they would also end. But it seems like they're not done with us. At this point, there are multiple candidates for what we would like to end sooner than the other. It's a really strange position to be in.

We had started this journey, talking about assembling a future, in some way, spurred by both Bernie's defeat and our defeat embedded in that, and the pandemic unfolding as it has, as it promised to, even when we weren't eager to believe it—a rare fulfilled promise, that should have been spared fulfilment. And, really, there's no surprise at all when we reflect on the consistently unequal value of different lives and the unabated abandonment of life to death.

It has been a really difficult time to be reading and engaging with things across the world, and to be then caught within the weird desire to make someone say something differently, to have them blame someone other than those they're blaming. Hoping that perhaps thinking that a small change in how somebody says something will have an effect on who is deemed worthy of life or death—because we also know it can get much worse and on many, many levels, whether in terms of ongoing racism, annihilation of populations, and the ways of being that were destroyed in giving life to those that didn't deserve to be preserved.

Thankful for those who have continued, given the fact that one of the existential fears and worries I have had is who will continue to talk to us, and who will stop talking? There's a way that certain voices allow each of us to be where we are with some comfort of being heard and of being able to hear them. And, also, establishing common points of departure requires getting over the naiveté and delusion of always already being in the same place. This stuckness in a moment of time that we are currently experiencing, maybe allows certain things to get buried deeper, certain things to be revealed, certain attachments to get severed, certain connections yet to be built.

Even as a Collective, we have struggled a lot with what unites us outside of the small rooms history gave us to be in, and the things we generally hope for—so, we have also had to defend against an expectation of consensus or univocality in our work together. How, one might ask, are we to invite and be with others in spaces where it's not completely clear if we agree with each other or not? It requires a particular kind of hospitality fed by an ethos of wanting to just speak to each other, hear differently, and be engaged by each other. I hope and believe that this doesn't mean that there aren't things to fight over and fight for (and those things are not the same!). I hope that as we have expanded our conversation, and welcomed people into this space, that it can be owned by all of us and all the new friends we have also made. I really want to acknowledge how important that is.

Anyway, without delaying today's conversation further, it's important to thank each other and remember why we started doing this and also what has changed in nine weeks. We have to keep holding space for the new correspondents and voices that came along, the going-beyond existing attachments to thinkers to engage someone new, the voices that would otherwise not be part of programmatic left conversations. Otherwise, what's the point of already knowing what has to be said? How do we keep space for that when everything seems so urgent and so critical? Which conversations will we prioritize, and which will we refuse to have altogether? Those questions are still here with us, as they were nine weeks ago.

The question we've been continuing to entertain for the last couple of weeks is that of internationalism, as articulated within the US's dual post-colonial and contemporary colonial context, also marked by its own history of left trauma which ultimately translates into some fairly boring and unimaginative articulations of internationalism. These need to be expanded and improved upon.

Another ongoing question for me through these weeks, which I want to connect to these imaginations, pertains to how we feel invited to rethink and remake, and to hold our own rethinkings and remakings, when we are invited to participate in movements and institutions. What to make of the constant feeling that they properly belong to someone else, that we are merely guest workers? Can we speak of community and authority as we try to unpack, disarticulate, and then rearticulate institutions which we want? Are we allowed to run together questions of subject, knowledge, and institutions? Today, I hope that we will add another layer to that conversation by speaking of outcomes of movements, and of taking power outside of a market context of ideas and battles.

While many of us thought that the pandemic might have taken a few decrepit institutions with it, there are remarkable resiliencies that remind us of the fact that capital feeds on crisis, and always recovers stronger, by precisely colonising more spaces and more times. Might we probe further into the relations that are holding together the institutionalities in crisis—a long crisis, far predating the pandemic that is interpretable as the inability to validate the actual actions of actors, an inability to hold and contain their historicity? Given this moment and what is it exposing for us, what could we build—what are we in a position to build—that might return us to the potentiality of our labor and action to produce new mutualities and validations, and maybe even new desires? What do we want ourselves to be able to accomplish? What mutualities that already contain us must we recover from this rubble? What and how might we assemble ourselves into mutualities and institutionalities anew?

Our May Day dispatches provided us with the materials for certain maps—maps drawn by those, like us, trying to find their way, observing what others are doing, not those who are trying to guide others from a space of expertise or overconfidence. As in study, so in struggle.

Confronting these urgencies also crystallises the pressures some of us feel to conduct analyses or build movements and connections across spaces in prescribed ways. Certain sources of knowledge start to feel privileged, with a partiality to a kind of "usefulness" without a real sense of the history of the capacities of subjects and how they mediate that, an oversight that is entirely sponsored by an understanding of the constantly expending (and expendable) body. The consensus on this body is quite disturbing, because it brings with it modalities of relations to others, and ways of occupying space and time. Dare I say that the critical discourse on neoliberalism, in bemoaning a particular unfolding of the subject, also loves to look past production as a problem that we cannot really tackle right now. Thus my refrain that we have to connect what has happened to work with what has happened to the worker; before we place the worker at the centre of our stories of redemption, might we not redeem labor itself from what has happened to it?

Most of our maps for politics are provided by the market today. The "market," a term that basically signifies the spatiality and mobility of capital's production, reproduction, and distribution—one might even say its mobility as spatiality—cannot provide the epistemological foundations for this attempt. Its narrative of being transparent to itself, and to us, leads us to believe that all relations across bodies and spaces work in that self-evident, homogenising, and transparent way, normalising the modes in which they exist now, erasing their histories and hence other possibilities.

If historicity and politics predate the "market" as supra-institution, then are there capacities and understandings that exceed the imagination of liberal capitalist modernity? What if we were to earnestly unsettle these "settler" and reductive maps, these maps that sought to settle us? How might we falsework new institutions or new maps of political possibility when we are in no position to presume that crises land on the bodies of different people in the same way and use the same words. The pandemic insists that we ask this question very honestly, given how boundaries are being deepened and institutions are being given another life when they should be destroyed.

The Limits of Some Present Maps

GABE

In thinking about the maps that will replace the ones economics provides for our politics today, and taking up the invitation to take note of other historical moments for insights into relating to each other across political topographies, something comes to mind from research that I've been working on on the Spanish colonization of the Americas and the school of Salamanca.

There used to be debates about why the laws that are passed in the mid-sixteenth century exempt indigenous people from slavery while continuing the perpetuation and incredible growth of the African slave trade. One of the things that a lot of the literature points to is that these theorists take the question of African slavery into account as a question of economics, whereas the question of indigenous slavery is taken up as a question of sovereignty. It follows that the Americas become a space for the considerations over sovereignty, whereas Africa becomes a space for mapping the concerns over economics.

While this is interesting, it doesn't necessarily tell us much without further questioning and study. At this exact time, the very same theorists in the school of Salamanca are actually rethinking what economics means. And they're doing this specifically in terms of the setting of just prices. Their entire enterprise is not only saying, "Oh, these are economic concerns versus concerns of sovereignty," and making that kind of division; it goes ahead to make that division a part of the operation which defines what an economic interest is, or what the realm of economics is as distinct from questions of justice that belong to religion or sovereignty. So, while it's not the King's duty to investigate the justness of wars in Africa, it is the King's responsibility to do that in the Americas. With the school of Salamanca, the market is beginning to be seen as having certain capacities based on an idea of people as economic actors.

I've become fascinated by that one moment that brings all of these things together, especially because it has forced me to question the narrowness of what an economic interest is, and how—or whether—that gets projected onto other things, and gets construed with such precision (and distinct from an interest of the crown or an interest in justice).

ASMA

Is part of the trap that the topographic distortions inherent to capitalism allow us to fabricate proximities and a form of flatness that are present not only in neoliberalism but in liberalism itself—a landscape and timescape lacking valleys and hills and trenches? If you really think about it, political imagination, even colonial imagination, really can't be so delusional, right? Colonial imagination was almost more interesting than liberalism.

It had to do a lot of conquering of things that were very hard. We are talking about invaders having to go through the Khyber Pass. People dying. Workers on slave ships who would be no more valuable than the slaves thrown overboard for an insurance claim. We're talking about all the failed wars between empires. So what sort of trauma response is the turn to economics as an independent variable, and what kind of trauma does the market hide but also, in a way, deny?

So, I'm wondering whether the maps of our politics that we seek to draw around ourselves have to contend with the fact that this thing called the local, to which we are local (even if it is not local to us), is never simple or selfsame. The distance, if any, is not one that produces complexity or difference. This way of thinking creates a ranking of what we are accountable to, and that is its only aim. So how do claims to, for example, local farming actually manifest in thinking about local problems? Clearly, we know we are affected by people working near us, but, in that very concrete way, how the local imagines itself is a big part of this as well. That local problems have local solutions is possibly the biggest and most harmful lie, but oh-so-normal in the US, a nation of Christian, racist, and settler-colonial exceptionalism that is not done being built.

Have you ever worked for a local small business in the pandemic? — Nathaniel

EZRA

I think that, in a lot of ways, to imagine the local as simple or to imagine the production of the local as simple (even and especially as some answer or counter to a marketplace, which often is the expressed aim) often falls into the same type of trick that we see the market do: it makes itself out to be a logic, in order to clarify things or to eliminate the very hardships or difficult/complicated parts that make production possible.

In a lot of ways, the market often seeks to make it seem as though production is natural and production will always be there; so why waste time thinking about it further? There is a danger in making the argument that a local market, or a conception of the local as a form of trade (or a return to that), will eliminate or help us solve some of these problems of the market. It denies us the possibility that these are complex problems—and that that's why they become marred by violent actions.

COLIN

It's a challenge: re-thinking or breaking with some given concept of the local, alongside these revolts and movements that are happening…. The declared returns to the local are not at all like national liberation movements or agitations for self-determination, but they are being scripted as such and easily cast into such a role.

It seems to me that this scripting and casting is easily done if we allow ourselves not to examine the onsets of commodified locality that are being absolutely and continually pulverized in the forms of revolt that are quite cognizant of relations of proximity and distance that are being negotiated differently in their stead.

This point came up for me in thinking about the councils in Chile, the language they are using, and how the Explosion unfolding is trying to do that work. It seems to me that the hyper-locality, or the neo-liberal locale, is Chile par excellence. Chile is the case study incarnate, the representative example that is ever-the-glocal. It's just like every other third world economy and it also is not; it represents difference in its capacity for neoliberal success. It's the Latin American Jaguar, not the South Asian Tiger.

But, what are these racialized emerging markets and their mythologies of character, but the active production and mythologisation of native to a free-market moment? It's that codified locale that gets produced, recreated, maintained, and it has to be negotiated before, in, and on the ground with, any of these revolts against the market. A couple of days ago, it was the 101st day of the Chilean Explosion. When they tell time now, they say it's the hundredth day of October—like it's always October temporally and spatially. How to break with that glocalism, the international aberration we're seeing today?

Just to back up a bit, I find Chile especially appropriate for the challenge of mapping politics beyond the market because as we might recall, it's the colonial site where the neoliberal experiment is first birthed. This is where Friedman & the Chicago Boys were given free rein to create "Latin America's Tiger" (or the Jaguar), which demonstrated the ferocious growth free market principles could bring to the Third World, and which in turn heavily influenced the lending strategies of the IMF and World Bank dating all the way back to the 1970s.

The current neoliberal order, and the ruptural possibility of the Explosion, seem narratively to follow on the compressed history of a smothered socialist uprising (Allende), and then an internationally sponsored fascist right-wing coup (Pinochet). This allows us to understand the domination by the market to be closely related to the wave of state births that came to be dubiously known as the era of "decolonization" or "self-determination" which swept over the incipient revolts of nearly self-liberated colonies in the '50s, '60s, and '70s. Historically, self-determination during the Cold War might have always meant the opportunity for colonies to choose their own neo-colonialism, to create their own state with their own administrators to oppress, abuse, and extort their own people for the gains of others. So, maybe we understand this repetition of the consecration of the pure political space, or its restoration in the form of the unsolicited constitutional convention, as precisely the function of the political realm's social-contract liberalism, wherein the state facilitates transitions from one form of colonialism to another.

If this is the case, then, while the neoliberal order comes under attack in these movements, the state positions itself also as a victim to the crimes of dictators and runaway economies, confessing its incapabilities to the public and suggesting a constitutional convention as a moment for society and the polis to again be decolonized of aggressive market forces.

We might pause, briefly, to note here that Milo has long reminded us of the strong overlap between conservative political operations of government and the virtually synonymous theoretical commitments of those academics that see themselves as defenders of political tradition understood broadly, or at least the tradition of "political" thought. This is expressed especially by the left and liberal thinkers. Wendy Brown, for example, mourns the takeover of the polis by market forces, and calls for its restoration through the defense and strengthening of liberal democratic institutions as the only hope or the only option we have for politics to continue in these times.[1] That's the only "return" to the polis that we get. If anything, the conscious historical narrative of the Chilean Explosion provides an explicit context which can adamantly remind us that salvations of political possibility beyond the market won't be found by returning to the old model of mapping politics, as it was always already only the staging ground for coloniality to redouble its efforts.

This path might not stay this way forever. It's true. Even now, there are deep fights in the cabildos where the fervor of the movement right now is ruining the chances for the people to seize control of the state and finally receive their Allende-style government. So, too, have the powerful feminist chants and dances that repudiate all rapists, and thus all states—because all states are rapists—already filtered over to other mass movements and revolt now having been translated for protests in places like Iraq and Iran.

The normative task ahead of us is animated by an anti-colonial sentiment which, in refusing the market and the polis, necessarily experiences itself internationally. This is so despite the overtures of states that attempt to nationalize these struggles. We might both agree and disagree with Spivak by insisting on this point. With critical distance between us and the Occupy movements, we can see that their performative internationalism dealt in the weak multiplicity of the logic that "anyone can protest anything because the neoliberal market has infiltrated everything." This is is categorically different from the ambiguity of today's Chilean multiplicities that ask to be understood as international—in the sense that their local activities have a deep historical anti-colonial muscle formed in the posture of their rejection of the institutional dance between liberalism, fascism, coloniality, and the nation-state.

As we have, the past few sessions, struggled to locate the "revolutionary subject of history"—and have tried on the figures of the citizen, the worker, the debtor, the renter, the striker, the party, the union—it might be helpful to learn what's going on also in the context of Chile. Slogans have centered around dignidad, dignity, understood not as the respect given to something vis-à-vis human rights conferred by the liberal humanitarian order, but dignity as understood through the notion of responsibility. Those with dignity are those who see themselves as responsible in the labor of world-building—the people themselves: those responsible for allowing the world to continue on the trajectory it has for the past forty years in Chile, as well as those that might at the same time be responsible for fashioning it differently. In this respect, I see the mass movements and autonomous actions of the councils working without unions and left parties as affording these very same institutions (the unions, and the parties) dignity as well. Dignity as fascist and neoliberal collaborators, scabs, who are responsible for their actions in every moment, even responsible now for their capacity to continue to drag their feet as weakened appendages of colonial administration, or as newly inspired co-conspirators with the anti-coloniality afoot in the Chilean Explosion.

I bring up dignity, not because I'm advocating that we break it by attempting to universalize it. Rather, I want to point to it as a localized expression of anti-coloniality, which our mapping might use as a point in a constellation of anti-colonial internationalist world-building, and which grows to embrace more diverse manifestations of collective agitation between the difficult failed discourses of national liberation, human rights, and decolonization.

Our attempts at mapping the new old institutional connections of anti-colonial internationalism must continually strive to learn with movements as they unfold, generous in our interpretations of particularities that are always difficult and promising to negotiate because of their ambiguities, not in spite of them. We don't have any easily universalizable tools here, but we are at the very least granted access to the archives of the previous cartographic permutations, like the carvings up of colonies into countries and the wave of decolonization, which might be momentary ciphers for us to communicate in the sign language of anti-colonial aspirations that persist today, when the global ubiquity of capital also signals the ever presence of colony.

That's my riff on the provocation to think about the impetus to falsework thinking through locations and maps of political possibility.

ASMA

The situation in the US is so, so far from this, isn't it? It occurs to me that quite often even the claim to an international*ish* politics that comes from parties here, or from a Bernie supporter, always only sees the empire as subject, and themselves by (guilt, white man's burden-style) association. If you're voting for a "good" person in America, you have to think about yourself and what the country does elsewhere. So it's just a particular way to frame the world and other people in it, right? Even if it's through an anti-war sentiment, the optics, the frame, centres on and radiates outwards from "us." There's a strain of non-interventionism, always fed more by the right, that doesn't shift the framing of those relationships or enable us to see the other in any real way. It's fun to ask "look who's deciding to not intervene today!" For example, right libertarians, like Rand Paul or Ron Paul, won't call their non-interventionism "anti-imperialist" and they'll be more honest! It's interesting to examine the persistent narcissism even in moments of culpability, not to mention the relations between subjects that are normalized when Americans go internationalist in their thinking. It all seems a bit creepy.

COLIN

Creepy in what way? Creepy because internationalist thinking seems so difficult on the left in America and, yet, so feasible for the right?

ASMA

Yes—in one way, it does the same thing as a right-workerism that infiltrates the left. I think that confessional anti-imperialism does the same because the world likes thinking about Nigeria or Pakistan or Bangladesh or Iraq or Iran or Syria in a way that sees them as extensions of imperial desire or fantasy. So, just holding it back becomes a way to care! A kind of expanded orientalist tolerance, or bad arguments for the hijab. So theological in its own way!

A couple of things come up for me. Returning to the question of responsibility in relation to dignity you brought up—a kind of claiming of equality en route to justice—what are we setting up the subject that moves through these maps to be? I ask in terms of capacity for political imagination or forms of empathy, but also the way subjectivity has been imagined in relationship to class and, and why. Are there subjective qualities and expectations that "class struggle" invokes historically in a subject that are not, and were never meant to be, merely economic? I've been thinking a lot about Marx in relation to the political and its difference from the social that we have been trying to play with through Marxist texts earlier on, which was especially the reason why I was interested in the 1840s and the Brumaire when we started our conversations on crisis.

The question we've been working on around mapping politics beyond the market, specifically with respect to internationalism, really necessitates that we take a look at how we organize our relations with each other, and how they can be maintained institutionally and by whom, and in whose interest. Particularly, we know that internationalism, as articulated with the US post-colonial context, or in contemporary imperial context (with its own history of left trauma), ultimately translates into some fairly boring and unimaginative articulations of internationalism, that need to be expanded and improved upon. So, when we talk about the outcomes of movements and how a poor or ineffective political campaign can lead itself to becoming a movement without abandoning the lessons and all that other good stuff we've gathered, we are really putting front and center the question of taking power.

This is where I want to welcome Marvin González, a beloved and old fellow student of politics, and whom I personally look toward to show me ways of studying as a thoughtful political organizer on the ground suspicious of the right things. I'm very, very fortunate to have learned so much from both Marvin and Gabe throughout the last few months. Marvin, welcome, and please tell us a little bit about where you are, what you're thinking, and then take those moments to leap into other things. The floor is yours.

Our Future with Political Institutions and the Internationalist Imagination

MARVIN

Hello, everyone. I am a member of NYC-DSA. I joined DSA a little after Bernie lost the first run in 2016, but before Trump had been elected, so I've seen the DSA go from 5,000 people nationwide to 66,000 now—allegedly. I'm really interested in the question Asma raised about the relationships that class struggles bring to us which are not merely economic, because for me this involves us in asking about ideology and the limit of ideology. I think that the way that ideology functions in DSA is to sort of mask certain institutional limits which is, I think, a very necessary conversation to have. DSA is a very weird space because it's really a confederation of locals with somewhat of a national bureaucracy attached to it, but you can be fairly active in the organization without ever having to interact with anything like a national.

I'm in a communist caucus called Emerge. We've been trying to intervene in New York specifically, but also grow relationships with other communists in DSA. It's a little bit difficult, for reasons that we can talk about more. But DSA is an interesting place because in order to be a communist you have to furnish that with a certain type of concreteness that isn't really needed for people who call themselves socialists or democratic socialists.

COLIN

This conversation about ideology and its limits, with respect to mapping and internationalism, reminded me of a scene from *Land and Freedom*,[2] which was the Ken Loach film about the Spanish Civil War that many of us saw together. It focused on a debate in a community that has just expelled their fascists. The community members are trying to decide whether they're going to abolish private property entirely, or redistribute some land but maintain the institution of private property. The thing that was really interesting to me, or that provoked a question ancillary to the conversation we have been having about internationalism and organizing, was the moment when the community members invited the internationalist militia—or, really, a crew that could resemble the political figures on the left of all different stripes, some more moderate than others—to share their thoughts. The question I had was in response something that comes up halfway through the conversation when the local community understands that their actions, or what they decide as a group, as a collectivity, can in many ways influence the aspirations and the possibilities that folks from other parts of the world understand as politically possible, or more relevant.

So, the American brings up the need to moderate one's slogans to appeal to the Western institutions and their financial capacities in order to save or help sustain the revolution. Then a lad from Germany says something along the lines of, "Well, in the German context, we waited for revolution and we got Hitler. If you act decisively now and do what you need to do, which is full revolution, you might be inspiring for folks in Germany and folks in France and Italy who might be able to understand with your actions that something else is possible." What intrigues me about that scene is how ideology and the institutionalizing of politics function in relation to this example. There's this consciousness that their actions are relevant as exemplary, and that folks that have their eyes turned towards the Spanish situation.... I'm interested in how, with respect to what Marvin said, the capacity or habit of turning concrete situations into examples that are instructive or useful for others at a distance might actually inflect the trouble or the "problem" that Asma had mentioned in earlier in our conversation about the American getting involved in international politics or attempting to think internationally, which is an outgrowth of a bad relation to the function of examples.

Do we see this turn to examples as a product of a leftist need to prove that what they're proposing can work, or that it's worthy of being tried by others? And, in what way do examples kind of fail by reducing life to an object which is entrusted to a skeptical audience? How does an inaccurate understanding of the actual conditions that are inhabited by these kinds of historical case studies often lead them to be used as just the opposite justifications instead of toward radical possibility? Recall the familiar, endless, invocation of something as a failure or a bad example of socialism or why it doesn't work.

So we often talk about the need for concrete examples, as Marvin just mentioned. I'm interested in us interrogating who they're for and what ends they serve. If they're to be used as justifications, might we finally understand that those who we want to be instructive toward— on whose behalf we look for these examples—are already predisposed to read all our examples in the wrong way? So, I wonder if consigning a struggle to the realm of example evacuates the lives of those it affects, ever reliant, from here on out, on benevolent narrators or instructors to handle them with care?

If this is the case, it seems like our internationalism is always doomed to fail or fall into this unsatisfactory trap. It's worth asking, in trying to transition to some of the Zapatista stuff that was posted for the readings, if there is a way to understand struggles which intentionally function both as exemplary and as narrators? Might these show us how to maintain that agency (even dignity!), and how to interact with potential collaborators while also understanding their histories or broken subjectivities?

This, at a level of institutional questions, broaches the question of what kind of space opens up for others as collaborators in a movement/moment of struggle. Ultimately, in the film, the international militia is invited to give their thoughts, but they also function as witnesses, those that can speak and lend their two cents without being implicated in the decision that that locality makes. It seems to me that Subcommandante Marcos or Rousseau are examples here, showing us the possibility for fashioning oneself or one's own struggle as both exemplary and something that doesn't cede the agency entirely. It's a narrative that the person still is able to maintain in their own telling of the events and an ongoing narration of what is occurring.

NATHANIEL

Land and Freedom provides a really good example of how moments of internationalism get pressed into defeats that are said to be inevitable and begin looking like a script for nationalism. As you were talking, Colin, I was thinking of all of the historical moments or examples that might be said to have had a great deal of possibility but are narrated as inevitable. Narration obviously very easily becomes revision and makes us think about how we are relating to a struggle. Maybe instead of asking what is to be done, we might think about what's going on, or what do we need?

You also made me think about judgment, and this double bind of being asked to pass a particular kind of judgment on struggles in history that makes them look utopian or farcical, and the complete unwillingness to contend with the present moment. At least even the Stalinists in Land in Freedom, who are portrayed as traitors, can give an account of what they want. There is a political goal there even if they do come away looking like cops. A quote from Julia Cámara from today's reading, "Anticapitalist Strategy and the Question of Organization," might be useful here:

> Seen in these terms, the future is not simply the inevitable result of a chain of causes. Rather, the future is itself a cause that makes us choose one or the other decision in the present, it is the regulatory horizon of our political practice. And in turn, our ability to imagine the present is conditioned (not determined) by our understanding of the past. Escaping teleological politics—where everything happens inevitably and nothing could have been otherwise, escaping the mechanical rigidity that mistakes conditioning with determination and eliminates the subjective factor of history—is a necessary precondition for strategic thinking. Bensaïd expressed this sense with a phrase that I have always liked: "the past is full of presents that never came to fruition."
>
> In opposition to those who write History as an inevitability after it has already come to pass, we should follow Bensaïd's suggestion that there is always (and always has been) a range of real possibilities. Whether or not one of them finally ends up being realized depends, fundamentally,

on the correlation of forces and the level of class struggle. Typical accounts of the Spanish transition to democracy after the end of the Franco fascist regime and the often-praised Pactos de la Moncloa present a good example of how the discourse of what happened happened because it was the only thing that could possibly have happened to obscure political decisions and actions that contributed to the short-circuiting other outcomes which, at a specific moment, were also possible.[3]

MARVIN

I like a lot of what Colin said, especially about the pathology of the instructive example. I think it does rely on something that I've been thinking about the question of ideology becoming concrete when we ask what is the experience of ideology for me, concretely as a phenomenon? To me, in DSA, ideology is always that the world is already given, that the answers are already given, that the questions are already given. That means that when people talk about being a socialist, they don't need to frame it, or give any of their politics any sort of concreteness, because again, it's already given. But, when you take certain other politics, be it communist or anarchist, it's that the concreteness itself requires imagination. It's a challenge for this world because the politics are not already given for everyone: it's not already present and therefore has to actually be thought.

I think that this situation allows for a short circuit where everyone references something that's already given, but never actually thought. And, so that has been my experience in DSA. You know, it was always already given that Bernie was the best thing that we should do; it was already given how he would change the world by capturing state power; it was already given that his failure to do so was actually not a failure, just a different type of success. These answers are already given. The questions are already given.

ASMA

That's really horrifying and wonderful at the same time. That's your narration of being in that space—but how have you managed to move and what was DSA Emerge trying to do to counter or to press its concreteness via contradictions forward? And did it do it by creating its own space, or did it actually have access to these other spaces where things went along as uninterrupted?

MARVIN

I think that the experience that Emerge has had is of doing both: creating a separate space, while also showing up to meetings and being disciplined about not telling everyone that they're being stupid, or not trying come off as paternalistic or sectarian. So, showing up and being present but also having a different space to work in, and then using that space and trying to find ways to bring it back to DSA.

For instance, we recently published something like, "What do we think about Bernie?" Which got a little bit of traction and, interestingly enough, one of the big things that people didn't like was that we made a very small claim that rather than thinking of Bernie as creating class consciousness, we can think about Bernie as perhaps riding the wave of a long series of events of rising class politics. That, surprisingly, got a lot of people angry. There's so much investment in the idea that Bernie is a ruptural break and that there really wasn't any politics beforehand. And, it just really surprises me that fucking Marxists don't get that what they're going against is the idea that class struggle exists in the world.

ASMA

When you mentioned the world, I couldn't help but think about how that internal confidence is a masking of some other kind of insecurity, the denial of another starting point, the denial of a context, the denial of a reinterpretation that might shift somebody's own position or a complicity, or their understanding of their complicity in something. How does that map on to a relationship to other people in the world beyond the US?

I think we've talked about how, even for many of us, just Bernie's presence became an instance wherein we can just do the things we want to do and we can bring certain things back to the table, even if we are not sitting at it. And at the same time, I used to always wonder, like, is he going to be somebody who just says, "Oh, that's too complicated," you know? So a number of times I've asked so many of you, "Is it okay for me to like Bernie?" But again, of course, when you and I first talked about Bernie—last summer, right, Marvin?—you asked me the question at that talk. And I said, well, it's really just who enables you to ask what questions, you know? And that's really the most we can do. But, where is the world figuring in these conversations, from your perspective? Like, DSA's idea of left politics that's more worldly and not just their own?

MARVIN

I don't think that the DSA has very good left international politics. And, I don't know why that is other than maybe it is a sort of American exceptionalism. I think, again, that people want to have better internationalist politics. But, the question is always, how do you furnish that internationalist politics with concreteness? Because that's not something that's already given.

I think that the DSA also exists in the context of a weird institutional history. One of those is that before it became sort of this embryonic mass institution, or proto mass institution, it was composed of the remnants of the International Socialists. As a result, a lot of the big national committees are filled with people who've just been in the organization for five, six years, and can really take these positions. As a result, there's a really strong public third campist position that DSA often takes that can be in contradiction with things that get passed from the general membership at convention. For instance, we had a resolution that was like, "we should probably be trying to build solidarity with Cuba" that got passed at the convention. But, then, an immediate rollback was attempted by these other people. So there are organizational problems in DSA that make internationalism as a project difficult because the people who would have the resources to begin materially constructing this as a project appear to be at odds with it.

On "what does one do if failures of politics cannot be translated into any other kind of victory?"

In *The Queer Art of Failure*, Jack Halberstam writes, "The queer art of failure turns on the impossible, the improbable, the unlikely, and the unremarkable. It quietly loses, and in losing it imagines other goals for life, for love, for art, and for being" (2011, 88.) When we ask what to do if failures of politics cannot be translated into any other kind of victory, I want to move toward an embrace of failure and its arts. I want to perpetually be reconsidering and revising what our measures for success are, against the binary of success and failure, offering a nod to what transformative work happens through time and space that do not result in the mandated, expected, anticipated, or hoped-for end. I don't know that this justifies admission to defeat as a kind of victory (the grip of fascism, whether spectacular or mundane, is unacceptable), so much as rearranges the conditions under which we face defeat, which is to say, how we respond to our undoing and ruination. We learn from queerness and its deviations as political practice which makes good on the promise of failure by taking a "detour around the usual markers of accomplishment and satisfaction"[4] — Heidi

On an imagination that doesn't cede the entire world to the monster of neoliberalism

A preliminary step would require thinking about the market as an institutionality itself, rather than the institutionality in order to more thoughtfully interrogate those spaces that we try to create or envision as kindred in their relative autonomy from the market.

A variety of voices in these sessions echo this sentiment: dispatches from places like the academy and the art studio, which often imagine themselves as contrary to work or labor. Instead of writing off these spaces as blind to their own marketization, we might see this opportunity to learn from these histories of particular subjects that have "always been posited as the other of the worker" to learn how these subjects will get parlayed into new movements and new institutions, rather than falling back upon the presumptive general equivalence between all spaces and subjects. — Colin

Bringing Forth:
An Education in Politics, or a Political Education?

ASMA

I was reading Sandy Grande, an indigenous scholar of education, and I was teaching her alongside Gabriel Baramki's book about building Birzeit University in Palestine. There is a really interesting way in which both Grande and Baramki raise the question of a relationship to land that has absolutely nothing to do with ownership in property, but actually a relationship to land as a particular mode of decolonizing. She talks about "love as land," as a kind of ground that is not foundational. Here, I found the quote:

> If furthering the aims of insurgence and resurgence (and not individual recognition) is what we hold paramount, then perhaps one of the most radical refusals we can authorize is to work together as one; to enact a kind of Zapatismo scholarship and a balaclava politics where the work of the collectivity is intentionally structured to obscure and transcend the single voice, body, and life. Together we could write in refusal of liberal, essentialist forms of identity politics, of individualist inducements, of capitalist imperatives, and other productivist logics of accumulation. This is what love as refusal looks like. It is the un-demand, the un-desire to be either of or in the university. It is the radical assertion to be on: land. Decolonial love is land.[5]

There's just something really beautiful there. Part of it has to do with countering the individual that became established as the subject of the University, both in terms of students and also in terms of the producers of knowledge. And, she makes that distinction in a way that mimics what Renata has pointed to as the art word's sense of itself. Pretty much that "there are no workers here." This has to do a lot with a distinction of the artist from the worker, and the academic from the worker—or graduate workers or adjunct faculty — which allows people to think of these markets as somewhat inelastic. Not only do I think the academy and the art world have something in common, but because they imagine themselves as contrary to work, to labor in a certain way, and have always posited their subject as the other of the "worker." So how do we frame that positively, and toward making new political agents, new historicities, and new institutions?

I'm wondering if there's a way to connect this history of institutionalized self-understandings and the potential to exploit them in a positive way, with what Marvin and Colin have been speaking of—the role of examples, and also the phenomenology of ideology, with a particular economy to support both. Both questions of method, I think, rather than ideology.

COLIN

Yes. During the same scene in *Land and Freedom*, we see a protracted tension between the lives of people in this militia who have joined up and understood the Civil War as a moment for revolution, and what comes to be kind of understood or framed as the larger decisions made by the Stalinists. Our struggle as viewers, even comrades, is to maintain our relationship with these people in what they're experiencing and what they've come to know and eventually feel betrayed by because they experienced possibility for a moment. We could choose to opt for a larger narrative or logic that can be thrust upon the historical moment: the alliance with the Soviet Union as a way to continue the fight against fascism under certain more stringent organizational imperatives. But what then happens is that the brilliant, really diverse, messy expression of internationalism that we might see in the anarchist formations or the Spanish Workers Party gets smoothed over in order to understand internationalism as just this one thing.

What Marvin described as the tension within DSA about holding certain committee positions and what ends up just being the things that are easiest to accomplish at the moment, brings up this question: When or where does the moment for political education occur, or is understood to occur, in an organization? Where, Marvin, do you see that site for education occurring within the membership (or where maybe others might presume to locate it)? Or, does it not take place at all because everything is self-evident, or because the only actionable items are things that everyone can fully agree on without doing the difficult work of thinking?

I have always had a lot of organizational questions about the Zapatistas, and I think it is helpful to put their political educational question alongside Marvin and the DSA, because it is a movement that does not see itself as a party but one very involved in political education. So, while there are other instructive organizations that will tell you what to do, and offer critique and advice on where you should be going, it seems to be that support for the Zapatistas is on a substantially anti-ideological basis, and in turn the organization commits in its entirety to political education.

The whole thing they learned is "learning to learn" and that's what they can share. I think that proceeding from that point allows them to be both an example and a narrator of not only their struggles but also those with which they see themselves aligned. Some of the different readings assigned for today show a general drift in their mapping, tracing a transformation of their own political outlook of explaining their struggle in Chiapas—what got them to explaining what they're doing in conversation with others as a way to embed themselves in the struggles of others. They say, for instance, in their appeal to Democratic Teachers of Mexico, that they were involved in what the teachers are doing and the teachers might be inclined to see themselves as involved in what the Zapatistas are doing. And, they manage to ask provocative questions—like how the teachers are connected to their corporate union bosses, and such—that still allow them to hold onto narration and exemplarity in a balanced way.

MARVIN

From a local perspective, DSA is not very good at doing political education. In the first few years that I was a member, two different political education committees were formed, and both dissolved because they couldn't agree on what to read. I think that that speaks to the question of what we need to set out to interpret—which a lot of different forces within the DSA recognize as an important question.

As a result, DSA has not done much political education as an organization. Instead, DSA caucuses have become sites of political education, each inflecting something different. And I think that puts us in a very weird and interesting place—not necessarily a good or bad one.

I think that speaks to the orientation of DSA—that it's too big to be categorized in any neat way, even if it's oriented towards the capture of state power. Maybe that's why it's not a very good international organization, since it's fairly difficult to be internationalist when your focus is capturing power within the nation-state, especially one like the US. Then again, the reason it's oriented to the nation-state is because the problems DSA sets out to "solve" are already given, and those problems are not about exploitation or about global economies. The problems of politics in DSA are, for example, "fairness." That's the intuitive, already-given, world within any political imagination, including that of the "international," happens.

GABE

I want to return to that question, Marvin, that an orientation towards the capture of state power presents itself as a barrier to internationalism, specifically in the US context. There's a lot of scholarship and conversations around decolonization—and post-WWII decolonization in particular—that are not as invested in nationalism necessarily, but in an anti-nationalist decolonial turn.[6] I agree, Marvin: in the US context, the capture of state power ultimately has to be the unmaking of state power, more so than in other places probably, to be confronted as what it is, as a barrier to internationalism.

Regarding the lack of political education happening on a broad level in DSA, or being mostly relegated to the different caucuses: maybe that highlights what a certain pedagogical secularism can lead to. At that same time, it's hard for me to imagine DSA continuing to be a "big tent" organization, and to consolidate a political education plan around that. The question of what a "big tent" reading list would look like is a contentious one. I think one of the reasons that Philly DSA has had a robust program of political education is because it has been pretty much captured by one tendency—unlike chapters with a "healthier" balance of powers and room for expressions of other tendencies.

PHILIP

In one of the pieces we read this week, Joelle Fontaine attempts to connect a past reality to a current one—the reality of Churchill to the reality of Merkel. She traces the turns from fighting those who helped you fight the fascist, to setting up a fascist government and claiming that the people of Europe can set up any kind of government they please, into the present-day presentation of austerity as the only way out for countries like Greece that have piling debt. The "reality" has entailed making sure Germany's debt is repaid as pensions are lost. And you have Dimitris Christoulas killing himself in Syntagma Square because he can't survive without the pension he paid into for 35 years. In his suicide note he compares the current government to that post nazi government of Greece. We cannot change this "creditor makes the reality" system without refusing to negotiate on neoliberalism's terms.

ASMA

That reminded me of Benjamin, of unfulfilled hopes and promises. Only certain things become realized in history and in order to make what we call "history." The Merkel reality is also, unfortunately, related to the post-WWII "American Century," and of a particular kind of state formation, the postcolonial mimicries of the exploiters rather than the masses, and the unfulfilled promises of decolonization.

If we look at the formation of the U.S. imperial state, the first founding the founding, and the second founding the Civil War. Then a particular relation to the international that develops: WWII as the moment of a pact towards a particular international order within which the US will be specifically something, a third founding—extractive, opportunistic, and expertly projectionist, making Germany in its own image. Maybe that's one way to think about the triangulation between, in this example, Churchill and Merkel and the role of the US, some configuration of the national and the international that ultimately sabotages left politics in the US.

COLIN

Going back to what Philip was saying: an "international" that does not capitulate entails an internationality that can only be built or maintained without any serious reliance on the US or Europe. Obviously, the efficacy of that international is bolstered by the involvement by Western academics, personalities, filmmakers such as Oliver Stone, or folks like that, who bring the movement to light. But it knows better than to interpellate the US as a singular imperial entity high up on some pecking order, or one that is fractured and in turn preys on others' flailing subjectivities that are looking for validation or inspiration.

I think internationalism understands the danger posed by both of these modes of Euro-

American centrality. In stark contrast is the distant internationalism of a non-party entity such as the Zapatistas. It is difficult to maintain a conversation when you're right next to somebody, rather than when there is distance in between. The space in between is space for conversation, to actually learn about something, and to proceed from a lack of presumed mastery or of total knowledge of what needs to be done.

Maybe that's a more charitable or capacious way to think about the term "distance learning." We all meet in a classroom, and we have time to move about, to percolate and think about the things that are bothering us—things that keep us up at night. Then, we are able to come back and continue a conversation. That playing with space seems so essential for the symbolic and also the very concrete internationalism, something like the intuition of the Zapatista is trying to inspire.

There's more. A commitment to not critique other movements which, at least in good faith, are trying to learn and to have conversation. The imperative to critique or the "corrective tendency" that is part of the modality of the party mode, is replaced by a tradition of raising questions and making sympathetic requests. There is one "ask" that is a demand; for instance, if democratic teachers in Palestine and the Zapatistas are connected, they might ask that you consider doing X, Y, and Z in your movement, or changing A, B, and C, or getting rid of your bad union bosses. The second "ask" is that of asking questions. It riffs on the Socratic method: teaching without critiquing, allowing you to reform yourself without having change thrusted upon you from the outside. That proceeds from an internationalism built on generosity, trial and error, attempt in the true sense.

It seems like a lot of this is the opposite of what we have come to associate with the relationship between ideology and party. It seems like the party harnesses or enjoys the benefits of ideology, and functions in a way that allows one simple or predictable mode of communication. It gets people together, but it also offers a shared terminology. For instance, there isn't going to be a lot of confusion if the party is doing the right thing, nor is there going to be a lot of confusion about what the party slogans are supposed to invoke.

The question of futurity seems to be shut down—at least comfortably displaced—as the present is consolidated. This tendency isn't just something present in DSA. We see it in a lot of leftist attempts in the US: we are just happy that people showed up, and we want to presume that we are all there for the right reasons or at least the same reason. I wonder to what extent we see people attracted to parties for their didactic instruction rather than learning that is messy and complicated.

GABE

This made me think a lot about something Marvin and I had talked about last year. One of the things the party makes easier—I don't know what the benefits or the detriments of it are—is that it becomes a site or a node for internationalism to peer into. And, Marvin, I was thinking about what you mentioned earlier today about the third camp as well as conversations the two of us were having about the coup in Bolivia. Those third campist responses were very critical of Evo Morales—invoking solidarity with the people of Bolivia. That seemed like a moment in which the party and ideology functioning together were helpful to the extent that it allowed some on the left to say about the party-line that this is not a moment to critique Evo, but to very clearly stand against the coup, to even call it a coup, etc.

At the same time I am wondering what the limits of that are. When we imagine an internationalism, it doesn't seem entirely satisfactory to me to justify a situation where you have whatever party you can find, that becomes the only node of internationalist interface.

Something like the Tricontinental Institute is instructive and clear. Part of the base of their internationalism in the ability to find sites for the work they do. That's often premised on a party as well, on already-existing movements with a certain amount of traction under their feet—which is why, for example, they have yet to do their work in the US. That seems like a valid line to draw when one is approaching it as an institution like the Tricontinental Institute.

What other forms of either institutions or movements—or just the elements of a robust internationalism—need to exist without this stipulation in order to engage in political education and political action?

ASMA

As Vijay Prashad told us at the MAD Studio in Brno, Tricontinental works with, is energized by, and is accountable to local movements that have some form, and are institutionalized. He posed the Tricontinental's work as ideological intervention—not just research, but research that aids in the furtherance of the movement, and provides resources for the battle of ideas. That can be a way to think about the concrete versus the abstract, although I struggle with that distinction as you all know.

My sense is that the political education bit separates itself from the research that pushes forth these specific concrete demands and that also brings validity to the movement itself. The idea would be that this work allows them to broaden the terrain and resources in an internationalist battle of ideas. Their weekly publications, their memos, their publishing arm (Leftword Books)—there's a whole structure of cultural intervention and cultural production beyond political economic research.

Maybe there's a way to glean a particular politics out of it that offsets American limitation.

Do we have a good model and what are its potentialities?

So, there's the instruction we take from Tricontinental—the idea that there needs to be assertive work happening at the national level. And from DSA: we need to focus on state power. Then, the Tricontinental Institute might agree with DSA, and say: "You have to do that to a certain extent in order to be a real contributor internationally or to benefit things that are outside of you."

So, I want to ask Marvin: knowing that the DSA is wholly focused on a struggle for state power, how have you thought about this over time? Where do you sit with it now?

Falsework on Halfway Homes: Communing at the Party Contra Party

MARVIN

I guess I don't think that the DSA is completely interested in state power, just that it's an orientation that predominates. I guess my answer to your larger question is that, standing in the eye of the DSA, the party question gets confused, becaused everything gets mixed up in notions, for example, of third parties and electoralism. But if the party is the kind of place where leftists raise their banners, then for better or worse, DSA is the party and it's a very problematic one, one that needs a lot of intervention but it is what we have.

It seems to me that the party isn't something you can really intentionally build. It is emergent from the conditions of the conjuncture. I think that all of us, if we could build a better party, would not choose DSA as the vehicle. And I think this speaks to causality and necessity in politics that have to be further interrogated.

COLIN

So, what does the party look like in relation to ideology? Does it, for example, take on the task of ideological disarmament clearing away more of the givens and the self-evident circumstances, in order to more fully be able to inhabit the party-form as this space of communing? Or, is the ideological work of parties to better seize what it is that the party can do as a vehicle for power for us?

MARVIN

I'm pretty agnostic on the party question. I think, again, the party is an outcome of all of class struggle, not something that happens to facilitate the Revolution. That's, in my opinion, a pretty orthodox Marxist stance: that the party is not prefigurative of the revolution. It articulates it but it doesn't create it. So I'm agnostic about the party question, and sometimes even antagonistic to it. I sometimes feel that the "party" is supposed to do something similar to "making" dead labor: supposed to take social movements and make them into things. A different Marxist analysis that I like is that the working class creates and destroys—as it goes along—whatever forms it needs to do whatever it needs to do. As much as I used to think about the party as an outcome—and maybe something that would be produced in the course of our struggle—I think more about what we need to build in order to continue expanding the field of struggle. I think we live in a world characterized by de-politicization, so to me the question is not about the party.

And, how do we counter de-politicization? To me, this requires creating working-class ecosystems that can articulate class struggle better and amplify class struggle.

SARA

Yes, I've just been thinking about parties and building parties and what parts of building are also breaking. But, then, I'm rethinking based on what Marvin has been saying: that this is a more initiative coalition rather than the party, challenging us to think a little bit more broadly.

ASMA

Yes, that was really helpful. Thanks, Sara. Thank you, Marvin. Thinking of form: what is given form? And what is form-giving? Of course, they're connected questions, right?!

Would others like to say a few things before we leave? And, also, can we strategize a little?

Notes

1. Wendy Brown, *Undoing the Demos: Neoliberalism's Stealth Revolution* (Princeton: Zone Books, 2015). Also Brown, *In the Ruins of Neoliberalism: The Rise of Antidemocratic Politics in the West* (New York: Columbia University Press, 2019).

2. *Land and Freedom*, dir. Ken Loach. 1995 (London, UK: Parallax Pictures). DVD.

3. Julia Camára, "Anticapitalist Strategy and the Question of Organization (Part 1)," *No Borders*, No Borders Media, published May 6, 2020, accessed on December 28, 2020.

4. Jack Halberstam, *The Queer Art of Failure* (Durham: Duke University Press, 2011), 186.

5. Sandy Grande, "Refusing the University," *in Describing Diverse Dreams of Justice in Education*, eds. Eve Tuck and K. Wayne Yang (Abingdon: Routledge, 2018), 61-62. 6. A recent example is Adom Getachew's *Worldmaking after Empire: The Rise and Fall of Self-Determination* (Princeton: Princeton University Press, 2019).

Zohaib Zuby, *Garden Sketch*

About the Contributors

Asma Abbas is a political theorist and educator. She is Professor of Politics and Philosophy and Director of Transdisciplinary and Experimental Studies at Bard College at Simon's Rock. She is associate faculty at the Brooklyn Institute for Social Research, former Fulbright-Masaryk Distinguished Chair in Social Studies in Brno, Czech Republic, and former Dean of Academics at the Indus Valley School of Art and Architecture in Karachi, Pakistan. Asma is founding organizer & director of Hic Rosa (and its Studio in Materialist and Anticolonial Politics and Aesthetics), the Falsework School for alternative community political education, and the ACCREW cultural workers caucus of the Democratic Socialists of America. She is the author of *Liberalism and Human Suffering: Materialist Reflections on Politics, Ethics, & Aesthetics* (2010), and *Another Love: Overtures to a Politics of the Unrequited* (2018). She is working on an experimental political ethnography titled A*nti-Odysseus: Fugues of the Non-Homeric* and essays on the "hatred of education" (in the key of Rancière's *Hatred of Democracy*). Anchor and producer of the "Assembling the Future/Tense" Studio, she co-edited & co-designed this volume.

Ethan Ackelsberg is a mathematician and socialist activist in Columbus, Ohio, USA, currently pursuing a PhD in mathematics at Ohio State University. He has written about anti-fascist, anti-imperialist, and anti-austerity struggles in higher education and is a founding member of the Graduate Student Labor Coalition, a rank-and-file organization of graduate student workers at OSU. Ethan participated in the Studio session that led to the Second Dialogue.

Eric Aldieri is a graduate student in Philosophy at DePaul University in Chicago, IL. Tentatively titled *Deleuze's Soteriology*, his dissertation tracks the ethical, theological, and political implications of Deleuze's reception of Spinoza. While his academic research focuses on early modern & twentieth-century French philosophy, he remains more broadly interested in the relation between/among ethics, political life, and the divine. Such themes tend to spill over into other realms. His contribution to this collective work was written in the midst of this COVID summer when (as today) dream life seemed to both anticipate and warp one's encounter with the waking day.

Ashna Ali is a queer, non-binary, Bangladeshi-American poet, researcher, and educator raised in Italy and based in New York City. Their poetry has appeared or is forthcoming in several independent poetry journals, and their chapbook, *The Relativity Of Being Well,* from which "Trump Threatens to Defund Education If Schools Refuse To Open Amidst Global Pandemic" is taken, will be published by The Operating System in 2021. The chapbook reflects on and documents the experience of being a queer, brown New York City public high school teacher inflected with COVID-19 in the first five months of the crisis.

Safi Alsebai is a healthcare worker currently based in Upstate New York. His concerns lie in materialist inquiries into biomedical knowledge and history, literary forms, and Islamic thought and aesthetics across various temporalities. He graduated from Bard College at Simon's Rock with a BA in Politics, Ethics, & Aesthetics and Biology. He is an occasional translator of Arabic.

Zara Anwarzai is a philosophy and cognitive science PhD student in the midwest. Previously, she taught at the Indiana Women's Prison through the Bard Prison Initiative Women's College Partnership. Her piece in this project stems from her interest in language and its capacities for collective action. Her other work explores the relationship between technology and the structure of thought.

Sean Brannock, also lovingly known as Mr. Sean, is the owner and creative director of Kids at Play, a children's theater company located on beautiful Catalina Island. Over the past 30 years he has encouraged Catalina's youth to embrace their inner talents and individuality, while fostering their imaginations and self-esteem. Amongst other things, he sees his vocation as a way to build life-skills under the guise of theater and other creative outlets, such as the publication project *Cazuela* which he co-created with Colin Eubank. Mr. Sean's contribution for this manuscript, entitled "Cazuela," is a Catalina-style adaptation of the beloved children's fable "Stone Soup" which transmits messages of hospitality, sense-making, and creativity in a manner accessible to children of all ages.

Isaac Brosilow is a writer and independent researcher from Chicago. He is currently based in New York City and is a contributing writer at *Jewish Currents*.

Silvana Carotenuto is an Associate Professor of "Literatures in English" at l'Università di Napoli "L'Orientale" where she directs the Centre for Postcolonial and Gender Studies (CSPG). She writes on Deconstruction, *écriture feminine*, and cultural, postcolonial and visuals studies. Her publications include: "The 'Vegetarian' Writing of Han Kang," In L. Curti (ed), *Femminismi futuri* (Rome, Iacobelli, 2019); with F. M. Gabrielli, R. JambrešićKirin (eds.), *Disrupting Historicity/Reclaiming the future* (Naples, UniorPress, 2019); "Translating Africa Elsewhere: The 'Task' of Shailja Patel," in J-B. Ouedraogo, M. Diawara and E. S. Madamo (eds.), *Translation Revisited. Contesting the Sense of African Social Realities* (Cambridge Scholars Publishing, 2018); "Writing Time: The (Late) *Oeuvres* of Jacques Derrida and William Kentridge," *English Academy Review*, vol. 35 (1) (2018); "The Return of the 'Great Stranger': Interrogation, Writing and Sharing of Literature," in *Ritorni Critici* (Roma, Meltemi, 2017); "'Go Wonder': Plasticity, Dissemination and (the Mirage of) Revolution," in B. Bhandar and J. Goldeberg-Hiller (eds.), *Plastic Materialities: Politics, Legality, and Metamorphosis in the Work of Catherine Malabou* (Duke University Press, USA, 2015); "Passages d'innocence: la différence photographique dans l'oeuvre de Jacques Derrida," *Etudes Francaises*, Toucher *des yeux. Nouvelles poétiques de l'ekphrasis*, vol. 51, 2, 2015. She is responsible for the research group M.A.M. and the digital archive "Matriarchivio del Mediterraneo" (www.matriarchiviomediterraneo.org). Her book *La pupilla di Demetra. La decostruzione e le arti* is coming out in 2021. She has been stuck in Naples since the beginning of March 2020.

Christopher Carrico is a cultural anthropologist whose main fieldwork is in Guyana, South America. His research has focused on ecology, political economy, indigenous rights, and sexuality. He was a participant in the "Assembling the Future/Tense" Studio, and contributed the essay "Quarantine Meditations." He is an adjunct at Towson University, where he teaches Anthropology and Philosophy. He lives in Bel Air, Maryland with his wife and two teenage daughters. They are all trying not to drive each other mad during COVID lockdown.

Starling Carter grew up in Knoxville, Tennessee, and now makes her home in Amman, Jordan. She received a Bachelor's degree in Political Studies from Bard College at Simon's rock, and a master's degree in Middle East Studies from George Washington University. Her most recent research focused on political contestations over the rampant privatization of public space in Beirut. In her daily work she assists programs that seek to develop community-centered cultural heritage management and tourism in Jordan. Feeling physically distant from growing mass political mobilizations in the US and elsewhere in spring and summer 2020, she sought out the Falsework School as a form of engagement and togetherness with friends and comrades in timely, critical, and imaginative discussions.

Sami Chohan completed his undergraduate and graduate studies in architecture and interior-architectural design from Pakistan, Germany, and Turkey between 2003 and 2011. He currently serves as Assistant Professor in the Department of Architecture at the Indus Valley School of Art and Architecture where he teaches both studio and seminar courses. His pedagogical and research interests explore emerging (alternative) spatial perspectives, practices and productions that resist and counter the hegemonic spatial developments promoted by neoliberal policies and agendas, particularly in the global South. In 2018, he also served as curator of *The Fold*, Pakistan's first national exhibition project in the Venice Biennale of Architecture.

Miri Davidson is a PhD student in London. Her thesis investigates the intersections between anthropology and Marxism in postwar France. Her writing has appeared in *The New Inquiry*, *Radical Philosophy*, and *Social Text Online*. She participated in the Hic Rosa Studio in Materialist and Decolonial Politics and Aesthetics in May 2018.

Ejeris Dixon is an organizer and political strategist with over 20 years of experience working in racial justice, LGBTQ, anti-violence, and economic justice movements. She is the Founding Director of Vision Change Win Consulting (www.visionchangewin.com), partnering with organizations to build their capacity and deepen the impact of their organizing strategies. She also serves as a consultant with Roadmap Consulting (www.roadmapconsulting.org), a national social justice consulting team. From 2010 to '13 Ejeris served as the Deputy Director in charge of the Community Organizing Department at the NYC Anti-Violence Project where she directed national, statewide, and local organizing and advocacy initiatives on hate violence, domestic violence, police violence, and sexual violence. From 2005 to 2010, Ejeris worked as the Founding Program Coordinator of the Safe OUTside the System Collective at the Audre Lorde Project where she worked on creating transformative justice strategies to address hate and police violence. She is the co-editor of *Beyond Survival: Strategies and Stories from the Transformative Justice Movement*, which was released by AK Press. Her essay, "Building Community Safety: Practical Steps Toward Liberatory Transformation," is featured in the anthology *Who Do You Serve, Who Do You Protect? Police Violence and Resistance in the United States*.

Colin Eubank is a teacher, editor, and organizer splitting time between Oaxaca and Catalina Island. He is passionately involved in community projects around migration and displacement, immigrant rights, and cultural education. He is a member of Hic Rosa and the Falsework School, as well as a co-founder of the experimental publication project *Cazuela*. Colin's written contributions for this volume take up moments in film, literature, and daily conversation as companions in the practice of thinking politically. He is also co-editor of this project.

Valerie Fanarjian is an artist, educator, and member of Hic Rosa, and is based in Great Barrington, Massachusetts. Published in *Fiberarts Design Book Six*, her work can be found in homes and collections across the US and abroad. Words from faceless voices bracket and inform the space and pages before her. Uncomfortable speaking in what she felt was a hallowed space, she instead spent moments in the "Assembling the Future/Tense" Studio as a witness: layering ink over tissue, wrapping thread around sticks, roads colliding with the roses of Hic Rosa and becoming red ink. In solidarity, untangling and mending, the dialogue of old companions and new friends became her soundtrack to this odd exile of the pandemic. She wishes that, when we all are ghosts and her pictures are ash, the echoes of these days may bring a similar comfort to fellow travelers and crusaders.

Ciarán Finlayson is the Managing Editor of Blank Forms Edition. He is a member of Hic Rosa and serves on the political education committee of the New York City Democratic Socialists of America's Central Brooklyn branch.

Avonlea Fisher has worked in public education, policy advocacy, and community engagement around grassroots movements. She received her master's in Political Science from Central European University, where her research explored feminist critiques of emerging reproductive technologies. She contributed to the transcription stage of this project.

Ari Fogelson is based in London, where he is currently a student at the London School of Hygiene and Tropical Medicine. He has been active in research and advocacy related to counterterror policing and Palestine solidarity. He is also a Yiddishist, involved in various projects probing the history and present of the Jewish left. He holds a master's degree from Trinity College Dublin's Irish School of Ecumenics and has an abiding interest in the critical study of Christianity and various colonial and postcolonial intersections of politics, religion, and theology. He is a graduate of Bard College at Simon's Rock with a BA in Politics, Ethics, & Aesthetics. He is a recent and enthusiastic member of the Islington North Labour Party. A member of Hic Rosa, he participated in the "Assembling the Future/Tense" Studio.

Elizabeth Glass is completing her MFA in Actor/Performer training in London. Zibby has worked as assistant and transcriber to Judith Malina of the Living Theatre, the Berliner Ensemble as assistant dramaturg. Her first play was workshopped & published at Le Théâtre du Soleil in 2015. She has worked as performer with the Odin Teatret in Denmark & Studio Matejka of the Grotowski Institute in Poland. She participated in, edited, and annotated the Second Dialogue.

Lillian Goldberg is a teacher and writer from Philadelphia. She currently teaches English in a Philadelphia public high school and will soon have an M.S.Ed. from the University of Pennsylvania. She also has a BA in Political Studies from Simon's Rock and an MA in Comparative Literature from the University of California, Irvine. These days, with her students, she's learning about change, contemporary poetry, world literature, dystopia, and how to write.

Marvin González is a political organizer and member of the Democratic Socialists of America (DSA) as well as Red Bloom Communist Collective. He was a founding member of DSA's Emerge Communist Caucus in NYC and serves on the International Committee Secretariat, the national DSA body that oversees diplomatic relationships. In Red Bloom, he is part of the Transit Rider's Union Coordinating Committee, which is building an independent, democratic, member-run union of MTA riders. He is a rank-and-file member of Campaign Workers Guild (CWG).

Lewis Gordon is an American philosopher at the University of Connecticut who works in the areas of Africana philosophy, existentialism, phenomenology, social and political theory, postcolonial thought, theories of race and racism, philosophies of liberation, aesthetics, philosophy of education, and philosophy of religion. He is Honorary President of the Global Centre for Advanced Studies. He has written particularly extensively on Africana and black existentialism, postcolonial phenomenology, race and racism, and on the works and thought of W. E. B. Du Bois and Frantz Fanon.

Stephen Hager a musician in the Berkshires. He oversaw audio production for the "Assembling the Studio" sessions.

Sanya Hussain is a Karachi-based visual artist. Since receiving her BFA from the Indus Valley School of Art and Architecture in 2017, Hussain has participated in multiple group shows as well as the Karachi Biennale 2019. Her artistic practice seeks to explore the curious nature of spaces and memory and post-memory with an interest in ideas of home, belonging, and identity.

Hajra Haider Karrar is invested in articulating questions that recognize and reconfigure the colonial and capital episteme that lays at the foundations of contemporary art production and representation. Highlighting the aspects of responsibility and accountability within art production she attempts to create a space for artistic practices that portray alternative narratives.

She was a core member of the Tentative Collective (2014–2018). Her curatorial and collaborative works have been shown in Europe, South Asia, Central Asia, and Russia. She was the recipient of the research fellowship and ISAP DAAD Scholarship at the Women, Gender, & Sexuality Studies Program at Yale University (2019-2020).

Sy Klipsch-Abudu incorporates found imagery and text to weave together narratives of the Black American experience, and finds beauty and power in the ordinary. *great/grand/golden* is a passion project of theirs. Their work has been featured in *The Harvard Advocate*, at the Overture Center for the Arts, *Marie Claire*, and *Society6*.

Zahabia Khuzema is a graduate in Fine Art from the Indus Valley School of Art and Architecture, with a focus on New Media. She is involved in various leftist and progressive organizing in Karachi. During the "Assembling the Future/Tense" Studio sessions, she reported on the ground realities for students & marginalized populations in Pakistan during the pandemic.

Ezra Lee is a farmer based out of the Northeast United States. A simultaneous interest in land use and food production while studying politics as an undergraduate has led to several years of work on various farms in the region, most recently on a 2.5-acre urban education oriented farm. Given the seasonal nature of agriculture, they spend Winters with family on both coasts of the United States, reading and writing. These seasons of work center questions of food distribution versus production technique, agricultural practices, land access, commodities and class structure, and the farmer as a cultural worker. Throughout this project they have participated in sessions and helped to transcribe, edit, and annotate as themes and chapters took form.

Isabella Lee is a law clerk working in plaintiff's civil rights and employment law litigation. With the onset of the pandemic and eviction crisis she began organizing in the housing justice movement and utilizing her legal experience to provide rights education and counseling for tenants with the Hudson/Catskill Housing Coalition and San Diego DSA's Tenant Solidarity Network. She will begin law school at UCLA in the fall of 2021, where she intends to embark on a career as a peoples' lawyer. Isabella is a member of the Hic Rosa Collective and was a participant in the "Assembling the Future/Tense" Studio. She transcribed, edited, and annotated the Second Dialogue.

Jody Leonard is a programmer based in the United States. He particapated in the "Assembling the Future/Tense" Studio, and also transcribed, annotated, and edited for this project.

Kenji C. Liu is author of *Monsters I Have Been* (Alice James Books, 2019), finalist for the 2020 California and Maine Book Awards for poetry, and *Map of an Onion*, national winner of the 2015 Hillary Gravendyk Poetry Prize (Inlandia Institute). His poetry is in numerous journals, anthologies, magazines, and two chapbooks, *Craters: A Field Guide* (2017) and *You Left Without Your Shoes* (2009). An alumnus of Kundiman, the Djerassi Resident Artist Program, and the Community of Writers, he lives in Los Ángeles.

Nathaniel Madison graduated with a BA in Political Studies from Bard College at Simon's Rock. He is a Hic Rosa member, participated in the "Assembling The Future/Tense" Studio, and worked on the editorial team of *Falsework, Smalltalk*. He has an interest in internationalism, revisionism, and the politics of memory. He manages a food pantry in Troy, New York.

Coco Marcil is a translator and writer based out of Los Angeles, California. She holds a BA in Literary Studies and Political Studies from Bard College at Simon's Rock. She contributed to this project by transcribing the studio sessions.

Bindu Menon Mannil is faculty at the School of Arts and Sciences, Azim Premji University, Bangalore, India. Her scholarship and research is positioned at the intersection of Cinema and Cultural Studies, Cultural History, and Cultural Anthropology. Her research, spanning a history of cinema publics, audio histories, cinema and the nonhuman animal, and oceanic Humanities, has appeared in peer-reviewed journals such as *Biography*, *Migration, Mobility & Displacement*, *Bioscope*, *Journal of Creative Communication*, *Seminar-India,* and other edited volumes. She is currently working on her manuscript titled *Cine-Assemblages in the Princely State: Senses, Publics and Materialities* (1900-1950). She serves on the editorial board of *Studies in South Asian Film and Media* (Intellect Journals, UK).

Dresda Emma Méndez de la Brena is a PhD Candidate in Women's Studies at the University of Granada, Spain. Her research work lies at the intersection of political, cultural, and visual Studies. Her work focuses on issues of disability, debility, necropolitics in relation to chronic illness and social death conditions. Her essays in these areas have appeared in peer-reviewed journals and other edited volumes. She has also been awarded with Honorary Mentions such as the prestigious "Enma Tirado" Award (Spain). She is at work on her manuscript titled *Morbid States*, a cultural approach to chronic pain in contemporary societies" and a Photobook titled "Arts of Flourishing" (some visual materials already displayed in international exhibitions, https://capturing-chronic-illness.com/2020/11/12/dresda-emma-mendez-de-la-brena-granada-spain-6-photos/). She is also a member of TuTela Learning Network (https://tutela.network), and an International Fellows Program Alumna at the Center on Philanthropy and Civil Society at the Graduate Center, City University of New York.

Sara Mugridge is in clinical social work training at Smith College School of Social Work. She received her master's in Comparative Literature from the CUNY Graduate Center, and has taught and worked in educational spaces for the past decade, including the Falsework School, a site of political education convened by Hic Rosa, of which she is a member. Sara is based in the Berkshires in Western Massachusetts, where she is also a volunteer with the grassroots social and racial justice organization BRIDGE.

Hasan Mujtaba writes poetry in Urdu, Punjabi, and his native Sindhi. Two collections of his Urdu and Punjabi poetry have been published in recent years: *Koel Shehar ki Katha* (*A Tale of the Cuckoo's City*) in 2015, and *Tum Dhanak Orrhe Lena* (*Keep Wearing the Rainbow*) in 2020. He is also a writer, an award-winning journalist, and human rights defender, who has worked for BBC Urdu as their New York correspondent. His first book of Sindhi poetry is forthcoming. Hasan had to flee his native country Pakistan, because of his journalism and human rights activism, into self-exile in New York, USA where he now lives. Currently he is working on a novel.

Bonaventure Soh Bejeng Ndikung is a contemporary art curator and writer. He holds a doctorate in medical biotechnology from the Heinrich-Heine-Universität Düsseldorf /TU Berlin, and a post-doctorate in biophysics from the University of Montpellier. Ndikung is the founding director of SAVVY Contemporary, an independent project space in Berlin, which situates itself on the threshold between concepts of the West and non-West in order to understand and deconstruct them. He has been co-curator at Galerie Wedding, and of the year long Danish art project *Images 2016—An Age of Our Own Making*, as well as the Performeum at the Wiener Festwochen in 2017. Ndikung is Curator-at-large for *documenta 14*, and guest curator for the 13th Dakar Biennale in Senegal. As part of the Miracle Workers Collective, he curated the Finnish Pavilion at the 58th Venice Biennale. He was artistic director of the *12th Bamako Encounters* in Mali, and is artistic director for *Sonsbeek 2020-2024* in Arnhem the Netherlands. Ndikung was a guest professor in curatorial studies and sound art at the Städelschule in Frankfurt (2017-19), and a professor in the Spatial Strategies MA program at Weissensee Academy of Art, Berlin. In October 2020, he was awarded the Order of Merit of Berlin, in "recognition of the work Savvy Contemporary has been doing over the past decade."

Daniel H. Neilson is a writer and teacher based in western Massachusetts. He is faculty in Social Studies at Simon's Rock and holds a PhD in economics from Columbia University. Dan is the author of *Minsky* (Polity 2019), a reading of the works of the theorist of financial crisis. His recent writing is on questions of disciplinarity and meaning in economic theory and practice; an ongoing interest is in the role of monetary institutions and technologies in social reproduction. Dan teaches economics classes that touch on money and banking, debt, international finance, China's financial system, economic transition and the construction of authority. He is a user of Arch Linux, an opponent of closed platforms, and, in general, a minimalist.

Edgar Flores Noriega is a language teacher and veteran of Oaxaca's music scene. As drummer and lyricist for punk and metal bands such as "Mortal Mutilation" and "Rekto de Cerdo," his contributions to the manuscript are the lyrics to the song "CRANEOS ROTOS," which had been translated with students amidst the pandemic as part of a series of virtual Spanish lessons focusing on protest music from different parts of Mexico.

Lucy Peterson is a PhD student in the Department of Political Science at the University of Michigan, Ann Arbor. In addition to her academic research focusing on feminism and political theory, she is also an activist dedicated to mutual aid project, anti-fascist and anti-austerity organizing, and racial justice. Lucy participated in the session of the "Assembling the Future/ Tense" Studio that led to the Second Dialogue.

Brianna Pope is the Three Point Strategies Operations Manager. She is the chief air traffic controller for Three Point and has been vital to the expansion and growth of major events, campaigns, and the financial operation. Brianna has coordinated the Movement for Black Lives Fellowship program, the major volunteer volunteer effort for the She the People Presidential Forum, and even served as the Interim Campaign Manager for Lesley McSpadden for Ferguson City Council Campaign. Brianna is a playwright, fiction writer, and avid reader. She is a graduate of Bard College in Upstate New York and was born and raised in San Diego, California. She is made up of California sunshine, sarcasm, abundance, naps, text love letters with her sister, and cooking the perfect steak.

Anna Poplawski is a writer currently based in Chicago. Her written contribution to this project follows from her other work on questions of value, patriarchy, race, and subjectivity.

Shahana Rajani is an artist based in Karachi. Her work and research traces the emerging visualities and infrastructures of development and militarisation using interdisciplinary methods and media. She is a co-founder of *Karachi LaJamia*, an experimental project seeking to politicize art education and explore new radical pedagogies and art practices. She is an Assistant Professor in the Liberal Arts Programme, at the Indus Valley School of Art and Architecture.

heidi andrea restrepo rhodes is a queer, Colombian/Latinx, disabled, poet, scholar, and cultural worker. Her poetry collection, *The Inheritance of Haunting* (University of Notre Dame Press, 2019) is a meditation on themes of inter-generational and collective inheritances of historical memory and post-colonial trauma, the responses they elicit, the forms of refusal, life, and love, that emerge in their wake. A 2021 Radar Productions Fellow, a 2019 CantoMundo Fellow, and 2018 VONA alum, her poetry has been published in *Poetry*, *Academy of American Poets Poem-a-Day*, *Split This Rock's Quarry*, *Nat.Brut*, and *Foglifter*, among other places. With a background in creative and performing arts, and anthropology, she is a doctoral fellow in political theory. Her dissertation is titled, "Afterlives of Discovery: Speculative Geographies in the Colombian Political Landscape." Largely informed by decolonial, feminist, queer, and black critical theories, as well as her research on human rights and social justice, heidi's contributions to this volume are as author of the pieces titled, "Defense Strategies" and "Choreography of the Body's Collapse: The Anti-Capitalist Politics of Rest"; as a speaker in the Second Dialogue's studio session; and as a contributor of annotations and editorial remarks in the Fourth Dialogue. Born in Arizona, and raised in California, she currently lives in Cleveland.

Sumana Roy is the author of *How I became a Tree*, a work of nonfiction, *Missing: A Novel*, *Out of Syllabus: Poems* and *My Mother's Lover and Other Stories*, a collection of short stories. Her poems & essays have appeared in *Granta*, *Guernica*, *LARB*, *Drunken Boat*, *Prairie Schooner*, *Berfrois*, *The Common*, and other journals. She lives in Siliguri and Sonipat, and teaches at Ashoka University.

Vianny Ruiz is a Oaxacan artist who works on a number of traditional and digital mediums. As a student, she attended Centro De Educacion Artistica "Miguel Cabrera" (CEDART), Centro Fotografico Manuel Alvarez Bravo (CFMAB), and Centro de Las Artes de San Agustin (CASA), where she developed her interest and techniques in mixing Oaxacan culture and arts. Her contribution, a collage entitled "what would the world be without accomplices?," juxtaposes ongoing social movements across Latin America and the tactics and principles that inform their respective notions of feminism, cultural combat/preservation, and political performance.

Gabriel Salgado is a PhD Candidate in the Department of Political Science at the University of Pennsylvania. His research focuses on issues of race, colonialism, & temporality in Latin America. He is a member of Hic Rosa, and participated in the "Assembling the Future/Tense" Studio.

Sadia Salim's multidisciplinary art practice is informed by the narratives of geographical spaces, lived experiences and everyday objects. She has investigated multiple mediums but ceramics remains her forte and her practice has evolved into an intensive study of materials and techniques associated with the medium. The study and research have evolved into a focus in themselves, for the benefit of pedagogy and for the promotion of crafts, specially *kashikari*, practiced in Sindh and Southern Punjab. Salim is a recipient of numerous grants and has participated in and presented at local and international conferences, residencies and exhibitions. She received a BDes in Ceramics from Indus Valley School of Art and Architecture, Karachi, and an EdM in Art and Art Education from Teachers College, Columbia University, New York.

Renata Summo-O'Connell is a curator and responsible for the Artegiro Contemporary Art project, a nomadic and transnational curatorial project in contemporary art based in Italy. Artegiro is a program that operates within AILAE, an organization Summo-O'Connell co-founded in 2007. Having worked for a long time in the fields of research and teaching in Sociolinguistics and Gender Studies in Australia, she has continued to write and conduct critical research independently after returning to Europe, focusing mainly on topics related to the roles of the artist and the curator in society, the artistic practice in new forms of captivity by migration, through new transnational research models that, beyond institutional boundaries, can decisively advance the international debate on art, creative, and cultural planning in relation to political and social life. She has launched various collaborative projects amongst which is *Imagined Australia*, a reflection on the mutual construction of identity between Australia and Europe, published by Peter Lang in 2009 and by Decolonize! in 2018. In particular, especially with the creation of COCOAA, a collaboration established between AILAE and the Municipality of Conzano in Monferrato, where Summo O'Connell curates the Artegiro art residencies taking place annually since 2010, she proceeds in a dimension of reciprocity and attempts to redefine art production as well as reflection around art. Within this reflection, for this collective work, she shared her perceptions of the current crisis specifically in the "artworlds," due not only to the pandemic but to the post-anthropocenic world we have lived in for sometime, unaware of the fruitful potential its challenges can provide.

Yashfeen Talpur holds a bachelor's degree in Architecture from the Indus Valley School of Art and Architecture. In her thesis project, *Urban Subjects*, she focused on the production of urban space to re-center the everyday user as primary subject and author, as opposed to capital which aids the production of abstracted space. She participated in, and helped transcribe, edit, and annotate the Fourth Dialogue of "Assembling the Future/Tense" Studio. Her contribution stemmed from a desire for sharing and building space that can hold personal inquiries undeniably tied into and with the collective; her essay, "Tracing Feeling" (appearing in the Sixth Interlude: Windows/Breath), explores personal positionality within the larger political moment that marked the year with themes of isolation and alternate ways of coming together, restructured relations, and the constantly shifting lines of exchange between the two. In addition to writing, Yashfeen practices thinking, making, and feeling in the mediums of visual art & poetry. She is currently based in Karachi, Pakistan.

Rei Terada is a professor of Comparative Literature at UC Irvine. She is a faculty member in the Culture & Theory Ph.D. program and director of Critical Theory at UCI. She is the author of *Feeling in Theory: Emotion after the "Death of the Subject"* (2001) and *Looking Away: Phenomenality and Dissatisfaction, Kant to Adorno* (2009). She is writing about enlightenment philosophy and the antiblackness of anti-racism, and lives in Los Angeles.

Hannah Walker is a cultural worker, aspiring butcher, and sometimes farmworker in Massachusetts, USA. She received her BA in German Translation & Literature and Political Theory from Bard College at Simon's Rock, and more recently has spent pandemic-hours exploring different visual art mediums. She attended most of the "Assembling the Future/ Tense" Studio, and participated in the transcription, editing, and written contribution stages of this project.

Milo Ward is a PhD candidate in political theory at the CUNY Graduate Center. He is currently working on James Q. Wilson's political theory of the police. He is a member of Hic Rosa and was a participant in the "Assembling the Future/Tense" Studio.

Omer Wasim is an intermedial artist whose practice queers space, subverting the frames of development and progress that shape human relationships to the city and nature. His work bears witness to the relentless erasure, violence, and destruction of our times by staying with queer bodies as they hold space and enact desire. He teaches at the Indus Valley School of Art and Architecture, served on the Editorial Board of *Hybrid* (2017-19), editing its third issue. He graduated with a BFA in Interdisciplinary Sculpture with a concentration in Video & Film Arts, and an MA in Critical Studies from the Maryland Institute College of Art, Maryland, USA.

Charlie Yates is an undergraduate student at Bard College at Simon's Rock concentrating in Politics, Ethics, Aesthetics, and Music. He is the producer and lead backup vocalist for a band called drab ave. He is currently trying to write a proposal for his senior thesis and decide, once and for all, what his favorite font is.

Philip Zorba is a photographer from South Florida. He is the founder and editor of the online art magazine, *honeysweat*, and serves as a tutor for the Refugee Assistance Alliance. His contributions to this project come in the way of participation in the "Assembling the Future/ Tense" Studio sessions, transcribing, and editing.

Zohaib Zuby has always had varied interests and time has made him an interdisciplinary professional with a practice in teaching Philosophy as Therapy, Philosophy for Children, and Islamic Reformism; and a practice in architectural design with a keen interest in Affordable Housing and Sacred places. Since 2012, he has been most interested in thinking of how Philosophy, in its Form, has more to offer than what is present as the work of professional philosophers. As a subject from a post-colonized context, he endeavors to raise questions about how philosophical ways of thinking may find an authentic voice in the here and now. His contributions in this timely corpus are mementoes of his own journey in searching for an answer for these questions. It entails an edited compilation of personal diary entries, and two sketches.

Bibliography

Abbas, Asma. *Liberalism and Human Suffering*. Palgrave Macmillan, 2010.

———. "Promises Past the Sovereign: The Fanatic and the Case for an Inefficient Politics." Unpublished manuscript, May 2018 version, electronic.

Acampora, Ralph. *Corporal Compassion: Animal Ethics and Philosophy of Body*. Pittsburgh: University of Pittsburgh Press, 2006.

Acosta, niv. Quoted in Michael Love Michael, "If You're Black, Rest is Power." *Paper Magazine*. http://www.papermag.com/black-power-naps-2626998633.html. Accessed on January 1, 2019.

Acosta, niv, and Fanny Sosa, "Black Power Naps," https://blackpowernaps.black/. Accessed on January 1, 2019.

Adami, Camilla, and Jacques Derrida. *Primati. Corpi che ti guardano*. La casa Usher, 2011.

Adorno, Theodor W. *Minima Moralia: Reflections from Damaged Life*. Translated by E.F.N. Jephcott. New York: Verso, 2005.

———. *Negative Dialectics*. Translated by E. B. Ashton. London: Routledge, 1990. 5.

———. "Marginalia to Theory and Praxis." in *Critical Models*. Translated by Henry W. Pickford. Columbia University, [1969]2005.

———. *Can One Live After Auschwitz?: A Philosophical Reader*. United Kingdom: Stanford University Press, 2003. 19-33.

Agamben, Giorgio. *The Open: Man and Animal*. Translated by Kevin Attell. Stanford: Stanford University Press, 2003.

———. "The State of Exception Provoked by an Unmotivated Emergency." *Positions, 26* February 26, 2020. http://positionswebsite.org/giorgio-agamben-the-state-of-exception-provoked-by-an-unmotivated-emergency/. Accessed on December 28, 2020.

Alexander, Michelle. *The New Jim Crow: Mass Incarceration in the Age of Colorblindness*. New York: The New Press, 2010.

Anwer, Megha. "Three Photographs, Six Bodies: The Politics of Lynching in Twos." *Kafila Online*. Published on June 5, 2016. https://kafila.online/2016/06/05/three-photographs-six-bodies-the-politics-of-lynching-in-twos-megha-anwer/. Accessed on December 28, 2020.

Archisearch.Gr. "Open Call: Pandemic Architecture International Ideas Competition," Press Release, March 16, 2020. https://www.archisearch.gr/architecture/open-call-pandemic-architecture-international-ideas-competition/.

Arendt, Hannah. *The Promise of Politics*. New York: Schocken, 2007. First published 1993.

Attridge, Derek. "The Humanities without Condition: Derrida and the Singular *Oeuvre.*" *Arts and Humanities in Higher Education*, vol.13 (2014): 54–61.

Badiou, Alain. *The Communist Hypothesis*. United Kingdom: Verso Books, 2015.

Beauvoir, Simone de. *The Ethics of Ambiguity*. United States: Citadel Press, 1970.

Benanev, Aaron, and John Clegg. "Crisis and Immiseration: Critical Theory Today." *in The SAGE Handbook of Frankfurt School Critical Theory*. SAGE Publications Ltd., June 2018.

Berger, John. *Why Look at Animals?* London: Penguin, 2009.

Bergson, Henri. *Matter and Memory*. Translated by N.M. Paul and W.S. Palmer. Cambridge, MA: Zone Books, 1991. First published 1908.

Berlant, Lauren. "Slow Death (Sovereignty, Obesity, Lateral Agency)." In *Critical Inquiry*, vol. 33 no. 4 (2007): 754–80.

———. "Thinking about Feeling Historical." In *Political Emotions: New Agendas in Communication*, edited by Janet Staiger, Ann Cvetkovich, and Ann Reynolds. London: Routledge, 2010.

Bernstein, Eduard. *Evolutionary Socialism: A Criticism and Affirmation*. Translated by Edith C. Harvey. New York: B. W. Huebsch, [1899]1911. 202.

Bhat, Aparna. "Dharavi, India is more than Asia's largest slum." *Culture Trip*, November 13, 2017. https://theculturetrip.com/asia/india/articles/dharavi-more-than-asias-largest-slum/.

Bhattacharya, Tithi, and Sarah Jaffe. "Social Reproduction and the Pandemic, with Tithi Bhattacharya," https://www.dissentmagazine.org/online_articles/social-reproduction-and-the-pandemic-with-tithi-bhattacharya. Accessed on December 23, 2020.

Bingyi. *Apocalypse*. Ink Studio. 2015. See also: "Apocalypse: An Interview with Bingyi," 2015. http://www.inkstudio.com.cn/video/8/; "Bingyi: Apocalypse." Translated by Alan Yeung. http://www.inkstudio.com.cn/press/27/; "Bingyi 冰逸 –Overview." http://www.inkstudio. com.cn/artists/75-bingyi/overview/; http://www.inkstudio.com.cn/press/27/; Accessed on December 28, 2020.

———. *Till It's Gone.* http://www.istanbulmodern.org/en/exhibitions/past-exhibitions/till-its-gone_1743.html; https://www.artforum.com/uploads/guide.003/id18941/press_release. pdf. Accessed on December 28, 2020.

———. "Painting is a Flood and a Wild Beast." *INK Studio,* 2017. https://www.inkstudio. com.cn/press/17-painting-is-a-flood-and-a-wild-beast/.

Blanc, Eric, and Jane McAlevey. "A Strategy to Win: A Conversation with Eric Blanc and Jane McAlevey." *Jacobin,* Apr. 18, 2018. https://www.jacobinmag.com/2018/04/teachers-strikes-rank-and-file-union-socialists

Bogues, Anthony, ed. *After Man: The Critical Thought of Sylvia Wynter.* Ian Randle Press, 2006.

Brossat, Alain, and Sylvia Klingberg. *Revolutionary Yiddishland: A History of Jewish Radicalism.* Translated by David Fernbach. New York: Verso, 2016.

Brown, Wendy. *In the Ruins of Neoliberalism: The Rise of Antidemocratic Politics in the West.* New York: Columbia University Press, 2019.

———. Undoing the Demos: Neoliberalism's Stealth Revolution. Princeton: Zone Books, 2015.

Cai Jin, on.. http://www.artnet.com/artists/cai-jin/biography; C. Archer, "Womanly Blooms: Cai Jin's Beauty Banana Plant Paintings", *n.paradoxa. International Journal of Feminist Art,* vol.30, n.48, 2012; Chambers, "Beijing: Cai Jin" (exhibition review), *Art in America.* October 2013. http://www.chambersfineart.com/attachment/en/584f165387aa2cda4ccff03e/ News/5877f280c4c138f01d8b4567;Goodman, J. "Cai Jin: Return to the Source." Chambers Fine Art. 2013. Accessed on December 28, 2020.

Calado, Manuel. "Standing stones and natural outcrops: the role of ritual monuments in the Neolithic transition of the Central Alentejo." *Monuments and Landscape in Atlantic Europe: Perception and Society during the Neolithic and Early Bronze Age,* edited by Chris Scarre, 17-35. London: Routledge, 2002.

Cámara, Julia. "Julia Cámara: Anticapitalist Strategy and the Question of Organization (Part

1 and 2)." *No Borders Media*, May 6 and 7, 2020. https://nobordersnews.org/2020/05/06/julia-camara-anticapitalist-strategy-and-the-question-of-organization-part-1/

Carotenuto, Silvana. "A 'Treatise on Ruins:' The Loving Work of Lida Abdul." In *Re-enacting the Past: Museography for Conflict Heritage*. Siracusa, Italy: Lettera Ventidue, 2013.

———. "Derridean Cinders/Sacred Holocauses," in *Darkmatter in the Ruins of the Empire* (special issue) "Impossible Derrida," ed. By S. Carotenuto, May 2012. http://www.darkmatter101.org/site/2012/05/18/deriddean-cinderssacred-holocausts/.

Césaire, Aimé. *Discourse on Colonialism*. New York: New York University Press, 2000. First published 1950 by Éditions Réclame.

Chatterjee, Piya, and Sunaina Maira. *The Imperial University: Academic Repression and Scholarly Dissent* University of Minnesota Press, 2014.

Chauthi Koot (Fourth Direction). 2015. India. DVD. Directed by Gurvinder Singh.

Chilean Orchestra, A. "El pueblo unido, jamás será vencido!" ("The people united will never be defeated"). *Redfish*. October 28, 2019. https://www.facebook.com/watch/?v=47426586677719.

Chuang. "Social Contagion: Macrobiological Class War in China." http://chuangcn.org. Published in February 2020. http://chuangcn.org/2020/02/social-contagion/.

Cixous, Héléne, and Jacques Derrida. *Veils*. Stanford: Stanford University Press, 2001.

Costello, Anthony. "Despite what Matt Hancock says, the government's policy is still herd immunity." *The Guardian*, 3 April 2020. https://www.theguardian.com/commentisfree/2020/apr/03/matt-hancock-government-policy-herd-immunity-community-surveillance-covid-19.

Cradle Will Rock. 1999. DVD. Touchstone Pictures, USA. Directed by Tim Robbins.

Cummings, Vicki. "All Cultural Things: Actual and Conceptual Monuments in the Neolithic of Western Britain." In Scarre, *Monuments and Landscape in Atlantic Europe*, 107-121, Figure 7.10, p. 118.

Deleuze, Gilles. "A New Cartographer (Discipline and Punish)." *In Foucault*, Translated and edited by Seán Hand, 21. New York: Continuum, 1999.

De Mendieta, Gerónimo. *Historia Eclesiástica Indiana: A Franciscan's View of the Spanish Conquest of Mexico.* Edwin Mellen Press, 1997.

Derrida, Jacques, and Michaela Heinich. *Mille e tre, cinq: Lignées.* William Blake & Co, 1996.

———. *Acts of Religion.* London: Routledge, 2002.

———. *Glas* Lincoln: University of Nebraska Press, 1986. First published 1974.

———. *Memoirs of the Blind.* Chicago: Chicago University Press, 1993.

———. *Prégnances: Lavi de Colette Deblè. Paintures.* Mont-de-Marsan: Atelier des brisants, 2004.

———. "At This Very Moment in This Work Here I Am." *Psyche: Inventions of the Other*, vol. 1 (2007): 165. Stanford, Stanford University Press, 2007.

———. "The Animal That Therefore I Am (More To Follow)." Translated by David Wills. *Critical Inquiry*, vol. 28, no. 2 (2002): 369-418.

———. "The University without Condition." In *Without Alibi,* edited by Peggy Kamuf. Stanford: Stanford University Press, 2002.

———. "White Mythology." In *Margins of Philosophy.* Chicago: University of Chicago Press, [1971]1982.

———. *Cinders.* Minneapolis: University of Minnesota Press, [1987]2014.

———. *Memoirs of the Blind: The Self-Portrait and Other Ruins.* Chicago: The University of Chicago Press, [1991]1993.

———. "The Spatial Arts: An Interview with Jacques Derrida." In P. Brunette and D. Will (eds.), *Deconstruction and the Visual Arts*, Cambridge, Cambridge U.P., 1994.

Derrida, Jacques, and John P. Leavey, "Of an Apocalyptic Tone Adopted in Philosophy," *Oxford Literary Review*, vol. 6, no. 2 (1984): 20-21.

Dixon, Ejeris. "Fascists Are Using COVID-19 to Advance Their Agenda. It's Up to Us to Stop Them." *Truthout.* May 6, 2020. https://truthout.org/articles/fascists-are-using-covid-19-to-advance-their-agenda-its-up-to-us-to-stop-them/.

Dols, Michael. "The Comparative Communal Responses to the Black Death in Muslim and Christian Societies." In *Viator Volume 5*. Brepols Publishers, 1974. 269-287.

Du Bois, W. E. B.. *Black Reconstruction in America 1860-1880.* United Kingdom: Free Press,

1999.

Endicott, Katie. On a panel of striking teachers in West Virginia, WeAreManyMedia, 2018. 21:54–26:13.

Engels, Frederick. *Socialism: Utopian and Scientific*. Translated by Edward Aveling. Progress Publishers, [1880]1970. https://www.marxists.org/archive/marx/works/1880/soc-utop/index.htm

ESRI. *21st Century Urbanism: Capitalism and Urban Form*. ArcGIS StoryMaps. https://www.arcgis.com/apps/MapJournal/index.html?appid=9def17048f214e2089c65f0d4c449889.

Faiz, Faiz Ahmad. *Nuskha-Hai-Wafa*. Delhi: Educational, 1980.

Fandry. 2014. India. DVD. Directed by Nagraj Manjule.

Fanon, Frantz. *A Dying Colonialism*. Translated by Haakon Chevalier. Grove/Atlantic, Inc., 1994.

———. *The Wretched of the Earth*. Contributions by Jean-Paul Sartre. Translated by Constance Farrington. New York: Grove Press, 1963.

Federici, Silvia. *Caliban and the Witch: Women, the Body and Primitive Accumulation*. New York: Autonomedia; London: Pluto Press, 2004.

Ferguson, James. *Give a Man a Fish*. Durham: Duke University Press, 2015.

Finney, Nikky. "Breath > Body > Voice: Humanities Futures Capstone Conference." Performance keynote. Durham, NC: September 14, 2017.

Fisher, Mark. *Capitalist Realism: is there no alternative?*. Winchester, UK; Washington [D.C.]: Zero Books, 2009. 17.

Foucualt, Michel. *"Society Must Be Defended": Lectures at the Collège de France*, 1975–1976. London: Picador Press. 2003.

Fowler, Chris. "Pattern and diversity in the early Neolithic mortuary practices of Britain and Ireland: contextualizing the treatment of the dead," *Documenta Praehistorica* 37 (2010), pp. 1–22.

Gandhi, Leela. *The Common Cause: Postcolonial Ethics and the Practice of Democracy, 1900-1955*. Chicago: University of Chicago Press, 2014.

García Márquez, Gabriel. One Hundred Years of Solitude. New York: Harper Collins, [1967]2006.

Gates, Theaster, and Elize Myrie. Black Artists Retreat [B.A.R.]. Chicago, 2013.

Gazi, Filiz. "Turkish unions criticize government for neglecting workers' rights on May Day overshadowed by COVID-19." Duvar English. May 1, 2020. https://www.duvarenglish.com/human-rights/2020/05/01/turkish-unions-criticize-govt-for-neglecting-workers-rights-on-may-day-overshadowed-by-covid-19/.

Getachew, Adom. Worldmaking After Empire: The Rise and Fall of Self-Determination. Princeton: Princeton University Press, 2019.

Ghalian, Sonia. "In Search of the Elusive Bird: Childhood from the Margins in Fandry." In The Palgrave Handbook of Children's Film and Television, edited by Casie Hermansson and Janet Zepernick, 315-328. Cham: Palgrave Macmillan, 2019.

Glissant, Édouard. Poetics of Relation. Translated by Betsy Wing. Ann Arbor: The University of Michigan Press, 1997.

Gornick, Vivian. The Romance of American Communism. Basic Books, 1977.

Govindarajan, Radhika. Animal Intimacies: Beastly Love in the Himalayas. New Delhi: Penguin Random House India Private Limited, 2019.

Gramsci 44. 2016. Ram Film, Italy. DVD. Directed by Emiliano Barbucci.

Grande, Sandy. "Refusing the University." In Describing Diverse Dreams of Justice in Education, eds. Eve Tuck and K. Wayne Yang. Abingdon: Routledge, 2018. 61-62.

Habitat for Humanity, GB. "The World's Largest Slums: Dharavi, Kibera, Khayelitsha & Neza." Habitat for Humanity. September 7, 2018. https://www.habitatforhumanity.org.uk/blog/2017/12/the-worlds-largest-slums-dharavi-kibera-khayelitsha-neza/.

Halberstam, Jack. The Queer Art of Failure. Durham: Duke University Press, 2011.

Hamilton. Omar Robert. "Irreversible Shift," n+1. 2019. https://nplusonemag.com/online-only/online-only/irreversible-shift/. Accessed on December 28, 2020.

Harney, Stefano and Fred Moten. The Undercommons: Fugitive Planning and Black Study. Wivenhoe: Minor Compositions, 2013.

Hasan, Arif. "Emerging urbanisation trends: The case of Karachi." International Growth

Centre, May 16, 2016. https://www.theigc.org/wp-content/uploads/2016/12/Hasan-2016-Academic-Paper.pdf

Hedva, Johanna. *Get Well Soon!*. Co-commissioned by Chronus Art Center (Shanghai), Art Center Nabi (Seoul) and Rhizome of the New Museum (New York). https://getwellsoon.labr.io/.

Hersey, Tricia. "The Nap Ministry." https://thenapministry.wordpress.com/about/. Accessed on December 23, 2020.

Hoffman, Amy. "Love One Another or Die." Boston Review, April 2, 2020, http://bostonreview.net/gender-sexuality/amy-hoffman-love-one-another-or-die.

Holloway, John. *Change The World Without Taking Power: The Meaning of Revolution Today.* London: Pluto Press, 2002.

Holloway, John. "Why Adorno?." July 3, 2011. http://www.johnholloway.com.mx/2011/07/30/why-adorno.

Ingle, Hrishikesh. "Fandry and Sairat: Marginal narratives and subjectivities in the new Marathi cinema." *New Cinemas: Journal of Contemporary Film,* vol. 15 no. 2 (2017): 175-190.

Inouye, Mie. "Frances Fox Piven on Why Protesters Must Defend Their Ability to Exercise Disruptive Power." *Jacobin.* June 17, 2020. https://jacobinmag.com/2020/06/frances-fox-piven-protests-movement-racial-justice.

Jaaware, Aniket. *Practicing Caste: On Touching and Not Touching.* New York: Fordham University Press, 2018.

Joshi, Sahil. "First coronavirus case reported from Mumbai's Dharavi slum," *India Today*, April 1, 2020. https://www.indiatoday.in/india/story/first-coronavirus-positive-case-reported-from-dharavi-in-mumbai-1662265-2020-04-01.

Kanafani, Ghassan, interview by Carleton, Richard. Beirut, 1970. 2:21-4:07. https://www.youtube.com/watch?v=3h_drCmG2iM&feature=youtu.be&t=141

Kapoor, Shivani. "'Your Mother, You Bury Her': Caste, Carcass, and Politics in Contemporary India," *Pakistan Journal of Historical Studies*, 3(1), 2018. 5-30.

Karetzki, Patricia Eichenbaum. "Time and Love: Cai Jin's New Work." *Yishu. Journal of Contemporary Chinese Art*, vol. 12, no. 6 (2013): 47. http://yishu-online.com/wp-content/uploads/mm-products/uploads/2013_v12_06_karetzky_p_p045.pdf

Keller, Catherine. *Cloud of the Impossible: Negative Theology and Planetary Entanglement.* New York: Columbia University Press, 2014.

Khaldun, Ibn. *Muqaddimat Ibn Khaldun.* Beirut: Al-Matbaa' Al-Adabiyyah, 1900. First published 1377.

————. *The Muqaddimah: An Introduction to History.* Abridged Edition. Translated by Franz Rosenthal, edited by N.J. Dawood. Princeton: Princeton University Press, 2020.

Khalili, Laleh. *Time in the Shadows: Confinement in Counterinsurgencies.* Stanford: Stanford University Press, 2012.

Khanmalek, Tala, and Heidi Andrea Restrepo Rhodes. "A Decolonial Feminist Epistemology of the Bed: A Compendium Incomplete of Sick and Disabled Queer Brown Femme Bodies of Knowledge." *Frontiers: A Journal of Women Studies* 41, no. 1 (2020): 35-58. https://www.muse.jhu.edu/article/755339.

Kollontai, Alexandra. "Make Way for Winged Eros: A Letter to Working Youth" Translated by Alix Holt. Molodoya Gvardiya, 1923. https://www.marxists.org/archive/kollonta/1923/winged-eros.htm

Kracauer, Siegfried. "Boredom." *The Mass Ornament: Weimar Essays.* Translated by Thomas Y. Levin. United Kingdom: Harvard University Press, 1995. 333.

Kwon, Juhee. "We Are Not Machines." In *Rest for Resistance* Zine, edited by Dom Chatterjee, Kofi Opam, and OAO. QTPOC Mental Health, 2017.

La Estrategia del Caracol, 1993. Directed by Sergio Cabrera. 1993. Colombia. Vimeo.

Lepore, Jill. "What Our Contagion Fables are Really About." *New Yorker.* March 2020.

López Petit, Santiago. *Los hijos de la noche.* Barcelona: Bellaterra, 2014.

————. "El coronavirus como declaración de guerra.'" *El Cuaderno*, 30. March, par. 3. 2020. https://elcuadernodigital.com/2020/03/31/el-coronavirus-como-declaracion-de-guerra/. Accessed on August 1, 2020

Lorde, Audre. "Poetry is Not A Luxury." In *Sister Outsider: Essays and Speeches.* Freedom: The Crossing Press, 1984. 37-39.

Lowell, James Russell. "The Present Crisis." 1844. https://poets.org/poem/present-crisis. Accessed December 26, 2020.

Lucas, Rob, and Andy Blunden. "Introduction." In *Marx Myths and Legends*. Marxists.org, April, 2005. https://www.marxists.org/subject/marxmyths/index.htm.

Luxemburg, Rosa. *Reform or Revolution*. Translated by Integer. Three Arrows Press, [1899] 1937.

Majid, Amjad. "Seeing the Unseen World: The Art of Bingyi." In *Yishu Journal of Contemporary Chinese Art* (14:6). Nov/Dec 2015.

Mark, Sabrina Orah. "Fuck the Bread. The Bread Is Over." *Paris Review*. May 7, 2020. https://www.theparisreview.org/blog/2020/05/07/fuck-the-bread-the-bread-is-over/.

Marx, Karl. *The Civil War in France*. London, 1871.

———. *The Eighteenth Brumaire of Louis Bonaparte*, 1852. Translated by Saul K. Padover CreateSpace Independent Publishing Platform 2015. First Published in 1852. Accessed on December 27. 2020.

———. "Critique of the Gotha Program." Moscow: Progress Publishers, 1970. First published in 1875. https://www.marxists.org/archive/marx/works/1875/gotha/. Accessed on December 27, 2020.

Marx, Karl, and Frederick Engels, "Part III: The Tendency of the Rate of Profit to Fall." in *Capital,* Volume III. New York: International Publishers, 1894.

———. *The Manifesto of the Communist Party*. Penguin, [1848]1985.

———. *The German Ideology*. New York: International Publishers, [1932]2004.

Mbulu, Letta. "Buza (There's A Light At The End Of A Tunnel)." 1978. Track 2 on Letta. A&M Records. Vinyl LP. https://www.youtube.com/watch?v=Hjg0Els927Q&list=OLAK5uy_mJMOx_SzuxFKfoW_mhhMI74ydeFKdeYKI.

———. "Carry On," YouTube. 6:12. https://www.youtube.com/watch?v=EyHT9PQIg3w. Accessed December 26, 2020.

———. "Carry On." 1998. Track 6 on Not Yet Uhuru. Columbia Records. Compact disc.

———. "Hareje (Ha-Ree-Gee)." 1978. Track 6 on Letta. A&M Records. Vinyl LP. https://www.youtube.com/watch?v=a0jlkrF81Ps&list=OLAK5uy_mJMOx_SzuxFKfoW_mhhMI74ydeFKdeYKI&index=6.

———. "I Need You." 1978. Track 3 on Letta. A&M Records. Vinyl LP. https://www.

youtube.com/watch?v=HanU4y_2aJM&list=OLAK5uy_mJMOx_SzuxFKfoW_
mhhMI74ydeFKdeYKI&index=3.

———. "Mamani." 1978. Track 7 on Letta. A&M Records. Vinyl LP. https://www.
youtube.com/watch?v=n6tADx_lrdo&list=OLAK5uy_mJMOx_SzuxFKfoW_
mhhMI74ydeFKdeYKI&index=7.

Melamed, Jodi. "Proceduralism, Predisposing, Poesis: Forms of Institutionality, In the Making". *Lateral*, vol. 5, no. 1 (Spring 2016). https://doi.org/10.25158/L5.1.10.

Miale, Marisa. "Toward the Mass Strike: An Interview with Two Southern Organizers," *Cosmonaut*. April 29, 2020. https://cosmonaut.blog/2020/04/29/toward-the-mass-strike-interview-with-two-southern-organizers/.

Mill, John Stuart. "Considerations on Representative Government." In *On Liberty, Utilitarianism and Other Essays*, ed. Mark Philp and Frederick Rosen, Second ed. Oxford: Oxford University Press, 2015).

Mishra, Sudhir, dir. *Hazaaron Khwaishein Aisi.* 2003; PNC Film. Netflix.

Moore, Hilary, and James Tracy. *No Fascist USA!.* San Francisco: City Lights Publishers, 2020.

New Edition of the Babylonian Talmud. Translated by Michael L. Rodkinson. Boston: New Talmund Publishing Company, 1903.

Nicholas of Cusa. *On the Vision of God.*

Nietzsche, Friedrich Wilhelm. *On the Genealogy of Morals.* Translated by Walter Kaufmann, and R J Hollingdale. New York : Vintage Books, 1989. First published 1887.

Odell, Jenny. *How to Do Nothing: Resisting the Attention Economy.* New York: Melville House, 2019.

Osborne, Peter. "A Sudden Topicality Marx, Nietzsche and the Politics of Crisis." *Radical Philosophy*, 160. Published in March/April 2010. 19-26. https://www.radicalphilosophy.com/article/a-sudden-topicality

Pariyerum Perumal. 2018. Neelam Productions, India. DVD. Directed by Mari Selvaraj.

Philip, M. Nourbese. *The Ga(s)p.* https://nourbese.com/wp-content/uploads/2020/03/Gasp.pdf.

Possenti, Ilaria. "Is the Social Antipolitical?." *Soft Power*, vol. 4 no. 2 (2017): 329. http://www.softpowerjournal.com/web/wp-content/uploads/2019/10/21-possenti.pdf

Puar, Jasbir K.. *The Right to Maim: Debility, Capacity, Disability.* Durham: Duke University Press, 2017.

———. "Coda: The Cost of Getting Better: Suicide, Sensation, Switchpoints." *GLQ: A Journal of Lesbian and Gay Studies*, vol. 18, no. 1 (2012): 149-158. doi: https://doi.org/10.1215/10642684-1422179.

Quint, The. "Lynchistan: Mob Lynching Cases Across India." https://www.thequint.com/quintlab/lynching-in-india/. Accessed on December 28, 2020.

Ray, Tarence. "A Way Out." *Popula*, November 18, 2018. https://popula.com.

Rest for Resistance, QTPOC Mental Health, https://restforresistance.com/. Accessed on January 1, 2019.

Richards, Michael P., et al. "The Mesolithic and Neolithic Subsistence in Denmark: New Stable Isotope Data." *Current Anthropology* 44 (2003), pp. 288–295

Robinson, Cedric J. *Black Marxism: The Making of the Black Radical Tradition.* University of North Carolina Press, 2005.

Rousseau, Jean-Jacques. *Correspondance Générale.* Vol. II Paris: A. Colin, 1957.

———. *Essay on the Origin of Languages and Writings Related to Music.* Dartmouth, 2000.

Klausen, Jimmy Casas. *Fugitive Rousseau: Slavery, Primitivism, and Political Freedom.* New York: Fordham University Press, 2016.

Roy, Arundhati. "The Pandemic is a Portal." *Financial Times,* Apr. 3, 2020. https://www.ft.com/content/10d8f5e8-74eb-11ea-95fe-fcd274e920ca,

Russell, Karen. "How the Coronavirus Has Infected Our Vocabulary." *New Yorker.* April 6, 2020. https://www.newyorker.com/magazine/2020/04/13/a-temporary-moment-in-time.

Sauveur, Sony. "Antoine Rossini Jean Baptiste "Ti Manno" was born in 1953 in Gonaïves a province in Haïti." 2016. https://www.snsfm.com/copy-of-info-13. Accessed on December 28, 2020.

Sharpe, Christina. *In the Wake: On Blackness and Being.* Durham: Duke University Press, 2016.

———. "The Weather." *The New Inquiry*, January 19, 2017. https://thenewinquiry.com/the-weather/.

Shelley, Mary. *The Last Man.* London: Colburn, 1826.

Smith, Jacob. *Vocal Tracks: Performance and Sound Media.* Berkeley: Univ of California Press, 2008.

Smith, Rogers M.. "A Discussion of Jessica Blatt's Race and the Making of American Political Science." *Perspectives on Politics* 17, no. 3, 2019: 801–2. doi:10.1017/S1537592719002445.

Spivak, Gayatri Chakravorty. *Death of a Discipline.* New York: Columbia University Press, 2003.

———. *Aesthetic Education in the Era of Globalization.* Cambridge: Harvard University Press, 2012.

———. "General Strike." *Rethinking Marxism: A Journal of Economics Culture & Society.* Vol. 26, iss. 1 (2014): 9-14.

Strong, Tracy B. *The Idea of Political Theory: Reflections on the Self in Political Time & Space.* South Bend, IN: University of Notre Dame Press, 1990.

Tentative Collective and their Projects, on. http://tentativecollective.com/; https://whogetstotalkaboutwhom.com/.

The Greatest Story Ever Told. 1965. UK. Directed by David Lean, George Stevens, and Jean Negulesco. DVD.

The Pakhtun Memory. Directed by Tentative Collective. http://tentativecollective.com/pakhtunmemory.html. Accessed on December 27, 2020.

Tianmiao, Lin. "An Interview: Bound Unbound," Asia Society Museum, https://www.youtube.com/watch?v=9JyiY9J6bHY.

Tianmiao's Oeuvre, on. http://asiasociety.org/new-york/exhibitions/bound-unbound-lin-tianmiao-0; ."Weekly Highlight: Chinese Female Artist @ MOMA - Lin Tian Miao" 專題： 紐約現代藝術館的中國女畫家林天苗,October-2010 http://carrieartdesignjournal.blogspot.it/2010/10/weekly-highlight-chinese-female-artist.html; "Against the Tide," The Bronx Museum of the Arts, 1997. Accessed on December 28, 2020

Ti Manno. "Neg Kont Neg," on Gemini All Stars De Ti Manno, A2, Chancy Records, 1982.

———. "Sort Tiers Monde," on Gemini All Stars De Ti Manno, A1, Chancy Records, 1982 .https://www.youtube.com/watch?v=7KiySdhL0Io. Accessed Dec 26, 2020.

—————. "Nan Danje," on Gemini All Stars De Ti Manno, Chancy Records, 1982. https://www.youtube.com/watch?v=DmeJRwrGDkg. Accessed Dec 26, 2020.

United Front Against Fascism. *Communists on Campus.* https://www.c-span.org/video/?463374-1/communists-campus.conference in 1969. Accessed on December 28, 2020.

United Nations, Department of Economic and Social Affairs, Popular Division, *The World's Cities in 2018: Data Booklet.* United Nations, 2018. https://doi.org/10.18356/c93f4dc6-en.

United States Department of Defense. *Summary of the National Defense Strategy of the United States of America: Sharpening the American Military's Competitive Edge.* 2018. https://dod.defense.gov/Portals/1/Documents/pubs/2018-National-Defense-Strategy-Summary.pdf

Valencia, Sayak. "Economía: Cuerpos en Negocio." Universidad Internacional de Andalucía 2010. http://ayp.unia.es/index.php?option=com_content&task=view&id=649. Accessed on August 1, 2020.

Wallace, Rob. "Notes on a Novel Coronavirus." *Monthly Review Online.* Published on January 29, 2020. https://mronline.org/2020/01/29/notes-on-a-novel-coronavirus/

Weber, Max. *Politics as a Vocation.* Translated by Hans-Heinrich Gerth and Charles Wright Mills. Fortress Press, 1965.

—————. "Politics as a Vocation." In *The Vocation Lectures: Science As a Vocation, Politics as a Vocation.* Edited by David S. Owen, Tracy B. Strong, Rodney Livingston, 80–85. Cambridge: Hackett Publishing, 2004.

Wolfe, Cary. *Animal Rites.* Chicago: University of Chicago Press, 2003.

Yardley, Jim. "Soaring Above India's Poverty, a 27-Story Home." *New York Times.* October 29, 2010. https://www.nytimes.com/2010/10/29/world/asia/29mumbai.html.

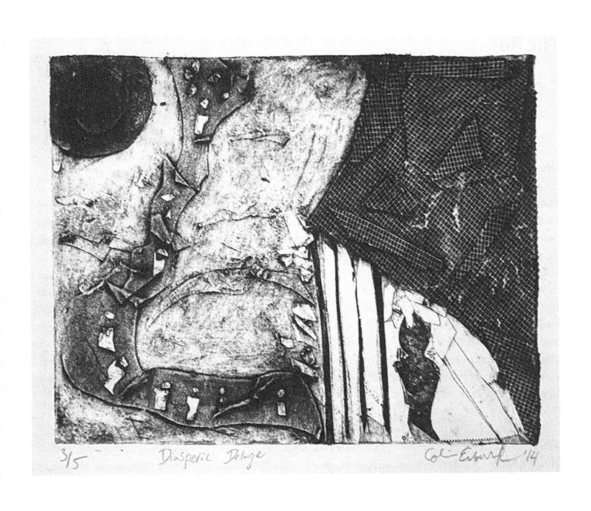

3/5   Diasporic Deluge   Colin Eubank '14

Colin Eubank, *Diasporic Deluge*, 2014

Hic Rosa

Hic Rosa came together in 2015. It curates educational and aesthetic experiences crossing boundaries of genre and place, in the service of philosophical and intellectual provocations that dismantle the walls between teacher and student, artist and audience, participant and observer, to produce radically intimate collectivities of thought and practice. It supports collaborative publication, broadcast, and dissemination of commentary, critique, and work that strengthens links between thought and expression towards transformative action. Our enrichment takes on a personal yet global scope by mentoring and encouraging participants to access networks of artists and thinkers with shared vocations across the world, and collaborating with other organizations. Our initiatives seek to provide time and space for intellectual engagement and developing conversations under conditions of rampant crises, when they all too often get sacrificed in urgencies and exhaustion of fixing broken worlds in the face of economic, political, and social inequalities and injustices. By linking artistic, cultural, political, and intellectual struggles, and projects around the world to each other, Hic Rosa necessitates a study of what connects us and, also, what keeps us apart in projects of similar intellectual and aesthetic inflection. It is our hope that incorporating critical and humanistic thought and action into our lives will educate toward overall sensibilities that are more just, fair, and hospitable in this troubled world.

Who are the Hic Rosa Collective?

We come together to convoke a platform for thought, action, provocation, production, respite, and recovery in the realms of aesthetics, poetics, and politics and their common material bases. What unites us is attentiveness to the methods and processes that irrevocably link everyday life with knowledge and cultural production, and we are interested in ventilating and revivifying the politics suffocated by moralistic or order-conserving foreclosures of thought, inquiry, critique, form, expression, and action. From the manner in which we organize ourselves in this collective, to the form and content of what we put out in the world, we seek to manifest a mode of solidarity and practices of counter-productions in art, education, and politics that are accountable to histories of exclusion and marginality, histories that are by turns a benign or insidious mockery of humanity, but more often maddening and murderous. Some of this work requires going "off the grid" in the manner of traversing planes of collaboration and coexistence, in the face of many arguments to the contrary, that link up the poetics and aesthetics of survival and reclamation: via the proliferation of productive and liberatory proximities between unsuspected partners across the world whose struggles call to be connected to and embraced by each other. To this end, our work is attentive to its actual, intersecting, and intended geographies.

We are all fortunate to have emerged from educational backgrounds that made us think about education and institutions, as well as from particular political contexts that compel the bringing about of a new possibility, certainly beyond what is scripted by dominant institutions whose legitimation we cannot help having sought, but also beyond what many of our particular affiliations and homes to which we are often told to return have scripted for us. So, some of our faith in taking time, conspiring meaningfully and even joyfully, and resisting the sabotage of the loudest threat is owed to these spaces, as flawed and complicit as they may be, and it is a privilege we choose not to unlearn. However, this is not a naïve or flamboyant act, even if it is one of abundance in the face of austerities: it is an act that accepts, in the words of Langston Hughes, that there is "no such home," and also as Aziz tells Fielding at the end of A Passage to India that we cannot be friends, not here, not yet. And then there are always the women who disappear into walls at the end of stories or are killed before the "real" story begins, or the refugees who make the border their home, who remind us that only the outsider ever has a real stake in making something fit enough to be home, and often the homes may not claim them back. So, in these impossibilities of time and space, we hope to invite, convoke, and conjure, scenes of possibility.

Valerie Fanarjian, *Eid Card*, 2016

Made in United States
North Haven, CT
30 April 2022

18745988R00239